The Transformation of Family Law

The Transformation of Family Law

State, Law, and Family in the United States and Western Europe

Mary Ann Glendon

The University of Chicago Press
Chicago and London

Mary Ann Glendon is a professor at Harvard Law School. Among her previous books are *State, Law, and Family: Family Law in Transition in the United States and Western Europe* (1977), to which the present volume is the successor; and *Abortion and Divorce in Western Law* (1987).

The University of Chicago Press, Chicago 60637
The University of Chicago Press, Ltd., London
© 1989 by The University of Chicago
All rights reserved. Published 1989
Printed in the United States of America

98 97 96 95 94 93 92 91 90 89   5 4 3 2 1

Library of Congress Cataloging-in-Publication Data

Glendon, Mary Ann, 1938–
    The transformation of family law : state, law, and family in the
United States and western Europe / Mary Ann Glendon.
        p.   cm.
    Bibliography: p.
    Includes index.
    ISBN 0-226-29969-4
    1. Domestic relations—United States.   2. Domestic relations—
Europe.   I. Title.
    K670.G443   1989
    346.7301'5—dc19
    [347.30615]   88-31842
                                                                CIP

In Memory of
MAX RHEINSTEIN

Contents

Acknowledgments

This book had its genesis in my long collaboration with the late Max Rheinstein, first on a book dealing with the law of succession, and later on a book-length chapter of the *International Encyclopedia of Comparative Law* concerning the personal and property relationships of spouses. For several years, beginning in the late 1960s, we were immersed in the minutiae of those changes that were to completely unsettle traditional family law all over the world. The process of change was at its most intense while we were working on the encyclopedia chapter, which required us to examine and compare the legal effects of marriage in a large number of countries in North and South America, in Eastern and Western Europe, and in the Middle East. As the project proceeded, we found that we were having to do a great deal of rewriting. No sooner was the ink dry on one section than we had to revise another, as major law reforms took place in country after country. Even worse, the legal categories we had used to structure the entire enterprise were breaking down. Gradually, however, we began to notice certain patterns and directions in the changes that were taking place. It became apparent, too, that the entire field of family law was affected, not merely the property-related areas in which we were concentrating our efforts. In the mid-1970s, I decided to undertake a study of this general transformation of family law, limiting the field of comparison to four countries where early and influential law reforms had taken place or were in progress. The result was *State, Law and Family: Family Law in Transition in the United States and Western Europe*, published in 1977.

The contributions of Max Rheinstein to that book were substantial. I would have to say they began long ago when, as his student at the University of Chicago, I was first exposed to his contagious fascination with the complex interaction of law and society and to the remarkable example set by his habits of work and thought. Later, as his coauthor, I had the extraordinary privilege of being able to observe closely a master at work on the technical intricacies as well as the grand design of an enterprise. While I was writing *State, Law and Family*, Max in his characteristically generous way found time to read and comment on every chapter. Although he died in the summer of 1977, shortly before the book appeared, he was the first and most attentive reader of the manuscript. In the course of preparing this successor volume, I have been conscious of continuing, in some way, our happy collaboration. Thus, it has seemed fitting to me to dedicate this book to the memory of my beloved friend and teacher.

When I began work on the present book, my plan was simply to update the previous volume by taking account of the many legal developments, large and small, that have occurred since 1977 in the areas of family law with which the book deals. I discovered, however, that significant changes had taken place over the years, not only in the law, but also in my own point of view. Thus, in the end, hardly a single page was left unrevised. The difference between the two books is best described as one of emphasis. My earlier preoccupation with the relationships between law and behavior has shifted to an increased interest in the influence of ideas on both. Where formerly it was the broad similarities among legal systems that attracted my attention, of late I have been more intrigued by the nuanced differences among them. My earlier surprise at discovering how widespread the deregulation of marriage had become has given way to curiosity about new forms of state intervention in family life. The fact that family law has become less marriage-centered now seems less significant than the fact that it has become increasingly focused on individuals. Finally, as Eric Clive predicted in reviewing *State, Law and Family*, I have come to see the theory of human groups as highly important to the understanding of family law.

Exchanges of ideas with many friends and colleagues over the years have given me new insights into the subject matter. I am especially indebted to Joseph F. Flanagan, the Chairman of the Boston College Philosophy Department, and my fellow participants in his Perspectives program, where I had the good fortune to participate in developing and coteaching an interdisciplinary course on the foundations and horizons of the modern social sciences. Special thanks are due, too, to the distinguished civil law scholar Marie-Thérèse Meulders-Klein, who has deepened my understanding of the Romano-Germanic legal systems.

A few hardy souls read large parts of the manuscript, made helpful suggestions, and supplied me with hard-to-obtain material. For such acts of collegial generosity, I am extremely grateful to Anders Agell of Uppsala University; Dagmar Coester-Waltjen of the University of Munich; Michael Coester of the University of Göttingen; John Eekelaar of Pembroke College, Oxford; Harry D. Krause of the University of Illinois; Catherine Labrusse-Riou of the

University of Paris-I; Martha Minow of Harvard University; and Aviam Soifer of Boston University. I benefited, too, from the able research assistance of Margarita Sweeney and Eva Wolfisberg, members of the 1987 LL.M. program at Harvard Law School. My greatest debt is to my husband, Edward R. Lev, for his valuable contributions to the form and substance of the work, and above all for his unfailing friendship and encouragement.

Mary Ann Glendon

Cambridge, Massachusetts

Abbreviations

Frequently Cited Works

Note: The short forms given in bold face in the following listings appear in italics in the footnotes.

Beitzke   Günther Beitzke, *Familienrecht*, 24th ed. (Munich: Beck, 1985).

Bénabent   Alain Bénabent, *Droit civil: La famille*, (Paris: Librairies Techniques, 1982).

Brissaud   Jean Brissaud, *A History of French Private Law*, trans. Rapelje Howell (South Hackensack, N.J.: Rothman Reprints, 1968).

Bromley   P. M. Bromley, *Family Law*, 4th ed. (London: Butterworths, 1971).

I Carbonnier   Jean Carbonnier, *Droit civil*, vol. 1, 15th ed. (Paris: Presses Universitaires de France, 1984).

II Carbonnier   Jean Carbonnier, *Droit civil*, vol. 2, 11th ed. (Paris: Presses Universitaires de France, 1979).

Carbonnier, Flexible droit   Jean Carbonnier, *Flexible droit*, 2d ed. (Paris: Librairie Générale de Droit et de Jurisprudence, 1983).

Clark   Homer H. Clark, Jr., *The Law of Domestic Relations in the United States* (St. Paul, Minn.: West, 1988).

Commaille   Jacques Commaille, Patrick Festy, Pierre Guibentif, Jean Kellerhals, Jean-François Perrin, and Louis Roussel, *Le Divorce en Europe Occidentale: La Loi et le Nombre* (Paris: Institut Nationale d'Études Démographiques, 1983).

Corbett   Percy E. Corbett, *The Roman Law of Marriage* (Oxford: Clarendon Press, 1930).

Cornu   Gérard Cornu, *Droit civil*, vol. 1, 2d ed. (Paris: Montchrestien, 1985).

Cretney   Stephen M. Cretney, *Principles of Family Law*, 4th ed., (London: Sweet & Maxwell, 1984).

Eekelaar   John Eekelaar, *Family Law and Social Policy*, 2d ed. (London: Weidenfeld & Nicolson, 1984).

I Esmein   Adhémar Esmein, *Le mariage en droit canonique*, vol. 1, 2d ed., ed. Robert Génestal (Paris: Recueil Sirey, 1929).

II Esmein   Adhémar Esmein, *Le mariage en droit canonique*, vol. 2, 2d ed., ed. Robert Génestal and Jean Dauvillier, (Paris: Recueil Sirey, 1935).

Field of Choice   The Law Commission, *Reform of the Grounds of Divorce: The Field of Choice* (London: Her Majesty's Stationery Office, 1966).

Gaudemet   Jean Gaudemet, *Le mariage en Occident* (Paris: Éditions du Cerf, 1987).
Gernhuber   Joachim Gernhuber, *Lehrbuch des Familienrechts*, 3d ed. (Munich: Beck, 1980).
Goode   William J. Goode, *The Family* (Englewood Cliffs, N.J.: Prentice-Hall, 1964).
Helmholz   Richard H. Helmholz, *Marriage Litigation in Medieval England* (Cambridge: Cambridge University Press, 1974).
Hübner   Rudolph Hübner, *A History of Germanic Private Law*, trans. Francis Philbrick (South Hackensack, N.J.: Rothman Reprints, 1968).
Hunt   David Hunt, *Parents and Children in History: The Psychology of Family Life in Early Modern France* (New York: Basic Books, 1970).
Jolowicz   H. F. Jolowicz, *Historical Introduction to the Study of Roman Law*, 2d ed. (Cambridge: Cambridge University Press, 1967).
König   René König, "Sociological Introduction," in *International Encyclopedia of Comparative Law*, vol. 4, ed. Aleck Chloros (Tübingen: J. C. B. Mohr, 1974).
Krause   Harry D. Krause, *Illegitimacy and Social Policy* (Indianapolis: Bobbs-Merrill, 1971).
Labrusse-Riou   Catherine Labrusse-Riou, *Droit de la famille. Les personnes.*, vol. 1 (Paris: Masson, 1984).
Müller-Freienfels   Wolfram Müller-Freienfels, *Ehe und Recht* (Tübingen: J. C. B. Mohr, 1962).
Pollock and Maitland   Frederick Pollock and F. W. Maitland, *The History of English Law*, vol. 2, 2d ed. (Cambridge: Cambridge University Press, 1968).
Putting Asunder   Archbishop's Group, *Putting Asunder: A Divorce Law for Contemporary Society: The Report of a Group Appointed by the Archbishop of Canterbury* (London: Society for the Propagation of Christian Knowledge, 1966).
Rheinstein   Max Rheinstein, *Marriage Stability, Divorce, and the Law*, (Chicago: University of Chicago Press, 1971).
Stone   Lawrence Stone, *The Family, Sex and Marriage in England 1500–1800* (New York: Harper & Row, 1977).
Weber   *Max Weber on Law in Economy and Society*, ed. Max Rheinstein, trans. Edward Shils and Max Rheinstein (Cambridge: Harvard University Press, 1954).

Codes, Statutes, and Collections of Judicial Decisions

Note: The short forms given in bold face in the following listings appear in roman type in the footnotes.

A.2d   *Atlantic Reporter*, 2d series (West Publishing Co.).
A.C.   *The Law Reports, Appeal Cases*, (London).
BGBl.   *Bundesgesetzblatt* (Statute Book of the West German Federal Republic).
Cal. Rptr.   *California Reporter* (West Publishing Co.).
Ch.   *The Law Reports, Chancery Division* (London).
D.   *Recueil Dalloz Sirey de doctrine, de jurisprudence, et de législation* (unofficial collection of French cases, statutes, and legal articles). *D.Jur.* refers to the section where court decisions are reported; *D.Chr.*, articles; and *D.Leg.*, legislation.

EheG   Ehegesetz (West German Marriage Law).

EheRG   Erstes Gesetz zur Reform des Ehe- und Familienrechts (West German Marriage and Family Reform Law).

Fam.   *The Law Reports, Family Division* (London).

F.2d   *Federal Reporter*, 2d series (West Publishing Co.).

F.Supp.   *Federal Supplement* (West Publishing Co.).

GleichberG   Gesetz über die Gleichberechtigung von Mann und Frau auf dem Gebiet des bürgerlichen Rechts, 18 June 1957 (West German Sex Equality Law).

J.C.P.   *Juris-Classeur Périodique (La Semaine Juridique)* (unofficial collection of French cases, statutes, and legal articles).

J.O.   *Journal Officiel de la République Française. Lois et Décrets.* (Statutes and Decrees of the French Republic).

KRABl.   *Amstblatt des Kontrollrats in Deutschland* (Ordinance Book of the Allied Control Council in Germany).

N.E.2d   *North Eastern Reporter*, 2d series (West Publishing Co.).

N.W.2d   *North Western Reporter*, 2d series (West Publishing Co.).

N.Y.S.2d   *New York Supplement*, 2d series (West Publishing Co.).

P.   *The Law Reports, Probate Division* (London).

P.2d   *Pacific Reporter*, 2d series (West Publishing Co.).

PStG   Personenstandgesetz, 8 August 1957 (West German Civil Status Law).

Q.B.   *The Law Reports, Queen's Bench Division* (London).

RGBl.   *Reichsgesetzblatt* (Statute Book of the German Reich until 1945).

So.2d   *Southern Reporter*, 2d series (West Publishing Co.).

S.W.2d   *South Western Reporter*, 2d series (West Publishing Co.).

StGB   *Strafgesetzbuch* (West German Penal Code).

UMDA   National Conference of Commissioners on Uniform State Laws, Uniform Marriage and Divorce Act of 1970 (with 1971 and 1973 amendments), 9A *Uniform Laws Annotated* 147 (1987).

UMPA   National Conference of Commissioners on Uniform State Laws, Uniform Marital Property Act of 1983, 9A *Uniform Laws Annotated* 97 (1987).

UPAA   National Conference of Commissioners on Uniform State Laws, Uniform Premarital Agreement Act of 1983, 9B *Uniform Laws Annotated* 369 (1987).

U.S.   *United States Supreme Court Reports* (U.S. Government Printing Office).

W.L.R.   *Weekly Law Reports* (London).

1
Law, Ideas, and Behavior

Introduction

Beginning in the 1960s, there was an unparalleled upheaval in the family law systems of Western industrial societies. Legal norms which had remained relatively undisturbed for centuries were discarded or radically altered in the areas of marriage, divorce, family support obligations, inheritance, the relationship of parent and child, and the status of children born outside marriage. At the same time, in other branches of law not ordinarily thought of as family law, such as public assistance, employment, social security, and taxation, official regulation has increasingly touched everyday family life. The new bodies of family law that emerged from this process in the United States and Western Europe employ a variety of legal techniques, and have been influenced by somewhat different constellations of political interests. In several countries, their appearance was preceded by long and careful study; in others, law reforms often took place with little deliberation. The process was accompanied in some places with little fanfare; in others, it was attended by a high level of public debate and controversy. But despite contrasts in the legal and political contexts of law reform, the national differences among Western family law systems have diminished steadily over the past two decades. Indeed, in countries that are culturally quite diverse, there has been a remarkable coincidence of similar legal developments produced at about the same time, in apparent independence from one another.

When the predecessor to this book, *State, Law and Family: Family Law in Transition in the United States and Western Europe* (Amsterdam: North-Holland), appeared in 1977, most of these new legal arrangements had been in force for less than a decade. Some were just beginning to appear. Major demographic indicators such as marriage, divorce, and women's labor force participation rates had not yet stabilized as they did in the 1980s. With the benefit of ten more years of experience with the legal innovations that transformed traditional family law, the time seems propitious to step back once again to try to discern what has been going forward in the process.

As we shall see, the principal converging tendencies had set in long before the law on the books started to change. In many ways, the intense legislative activity of recent years merely formalized and systematized transforming trends that had long been diffuse and partially realized in each country's law. These trends have not reached the same stage everywhere, and they have assumed distinctive forms in many of the countries affected, but the overall movement shows remarkable consistency. It is characterized, in varying degrees, by a progressive withdrawal of official regulation of marriage formation, dissolution, and the conduct of family life on the one hand, and by increased regulation of the economic and child-related consequences of formal or informal cohabitation on the other. At the same time, the rise of modern administrative states has brought about a marked increase in the degree and types of bureaucratic control to which families and their members are subject.

Contemporary family law reflects new ways of thinking, not only about marriage and family life, but also about law and government. New and strikingly similar legal images of family roles and relationships have appeared. Many traditional family law norms have been found inconsistent with the values contained in constitutions or international conventions. A historic shift in the relationship of the state to the family has taken place. Regulation has been withdrawn where it once was taken for granted, and intensified where until recently it had been unknown.

For the most part, these developments do not appear to have taken place in conscious furtherance of any coherent set of objectives. There are few signs that the countries involved were either attempting to emulate each other or to implement a specific internal family policy. Rather, each country seems to have been pursuing a number of different (and often conflicting) aims in its laws and its programs affecting families. Thus, viewed alone, developments in each country often have a rather haphazard character. In some countries, this air of disarray owes something to the fact that the field of family law has become an arena for a variety of political, religious, and ethnic struggles.[1] In addition, family law everywhere has become a major testing ground for new ways of imagining the relationships between the sexes and the generations.

Yet behind the disorderly appearance, underneath the rhetoric and slogans, and transcending local and regional particularity, a similar story is being told about the roles and relationships that are central in most people's lives. To set forth that story, to explore significant variations in the narrative, and to raise

1. This is especially so in the heterogeneous society of the United States. See Martha Minow, "We, the Family: Constitutional Rights and American Families," 74 *Journal of American History* 959 (1987).

questions about the complex relationship of the tale told by the law to family behavior and ideas about family life is the purpose of this book.

It is not possible, obviously, to present an exhaustive survey of all legal changes affecting family life in the past twenty-five years in one country, let alone several. Some selection has to be made, both as to subject matter and geographical coverage. So far as the former is concerned, I have chosen several legal developments that seem to me to be among the most striking and suggestive and are well enough advanced to have given rise to clearly discernible patterns. Many of them are the standard stuff of family law treatises, but I have also made reference to trends in related bodies of law that importantly affect family life, as well as to what civil law scholars call the *lex ferenda*: the law which may or may not be in the making. In this latter category I include not only official law reform proposals, but also the major currents emerging from the scholarly writing. In addition, I have tried not to lose sight of the fact that, while highly publicized processes of divorce law-reform and implementation of equal rights for women were occupying the center of the stage, hundreds of smaller, less well-known changes, involving every aspect of the way each legal system interacts with families, have also been occurring. Since these molecular movements often produce structural changes with far-reaching consequences, I have sought to give due attention to those seemingly minor but potentially transformative legal events.

As in the previous book, I concentrate here primarily on the law of England, France, the United States, and West Germany, making occasional references to important developments in other nations, especially Sweden. Comparisons among these countries continue to seem fruitful, not only because of the great influence their legal systems exert in the civil and common law worlds, but also because each has generated a rich assortment of legal and social science materials on the subjects here considered. Most importantly, developments in the family law of these countries are illustrative of the transforming trends that are also at work, with varying degrees of strength, in the law of places as diverse as Ireland, the Nordic group, and the nations of Southern Europe.[2]

Naturally, as an American comparatist with an interest in family life, I entertain the hope that the survey presented here will not only illuminate the

---

2. It is revealing of the extent and profundity of the current process of change in family life and law that, beginning in the mid-1970s, Italy, Portugal, and Spain all revised their civil code provisions on marriage in the light of the principle of equality between the sexes, made divorce available (or, in the case of Portugal, extended it to Roman Catholics), and legalized abortion under certain conditions. Such changes in these countries where the political influence of Roman Catholicism has been strong are in some ways more striking than those in the countries studied

significance of the current period of legal change generally, but will also contribute to law reform in the United States. We can only benefit from a heightened awareness of the ways in which other nations have approached problems
with which our own legal system is currently struggling. Even though legal
devices developed in other countries are rarely suitable for direct transplant,
they often serve the cause of law revision and reform by showing that our
range of choice may be wider than we had imagined, and by alerting us to the
potential drawbacks as well as the possible advantages of alternative methods
of proceeding. The study of foreign experiences can also be a fertile source
of inspiration and ideas. And even when it does not immediately move us into
a new stage of thinking, it nearly always affords us a deeper understanding
of, and a more balanced perspective on, our own law.

Legal and Social Institutions

The legal developments treated in this book, striking as they are, are of course
but an aspect of the fact that society itself is in flux. Geographic mobility,
changes in the relative importance of various forms of wealth, the apparently
declining influence of formal religion, transformations of the economic and
social roles of women, greater longevity, and increased control over the reproductive process are just some of the factors that have had an effect on the
seemingly eternal yet slowly changing institution of the family and its frequent concomitant, the more polymorphous and mutable institution of marriage. Over the centuries, family behavior and ideas about marriage and
family life have undergone constant fluctuations. But what seems to cause the
events of the present period to stand out in high relief against the tableau of
history is the rapidity with which the roles of the sexes, the relations of the
age groups, the marriage relation, and the structure of the family are being
transformed.

Although we deal here primarily with the bodies of legislative and judge-
made norms that constitute the family law of four countries, it is essential to
keep in sight the obvious fact that in these nations, as in every society, family
behavior never exactly corresponds to the set of official norms. The ways in
which family life is conducted may bear more resemblance to the patterns
enshrined in the law at some times and places than they do at others. Thus,

---

here, in view of the greater ideological distance between the new laws and those they replaced.
See, generally, Mary Ann Glendon, *Abortion and Divorce in Western Law* (Cambridge: Harvard
University Press, 1987). For Ireland, see William Duncan, "The Divorce Referendum in the
Republic of Ireland: Resisting the Tide," 2 *International Journal of Law and the Family* 62
(1988), and Mary Ann Glendon, *Irish Family Law in Comparative Perspective*, The Frances E.
Moran Memorial Lecture (Dublin: Trinity College, 1987).

in addition to taking stock of the intense ferment that has occurred in family law and behavior separately, we must endeavor to keep track of the changing relationship between two moving systems: the set of laws affecting families and the patterns of behavior that constitute the social institution of the family. Closely related to these changes in law and behavior are still other movements that we must try to keep in view. These are developments in the realm of ideas: the ideas that are widely held concerning the legal and social institutions of marriage and the family, and ideas about law itself.

Throughout the chapters that follow it will be useful to distinguish for analytical purposes between what a particular legal system may classify as "families" or "marriages" and the conduct which an anthropologist or sociologist is likely to describe as family or marriage behavior. Lawmakers dealing with social phenomena act through linguistic and imaginative characterization of behavior which is to a large extent unconscious. This process produces legal norms which are at times expressions of someone's values or ideals; at times merely "ideal types" (in the sense of theoretical abstractions from, or attempts at systematic summary of, social data); and at times (more often than not) mixtures of both. To achieve precision in the legal terminology relating to families and marriage is, of course, by no means easy, since within a single legal system, these terms are often variously employed for different purposes. The task is even more complicated when it comes to identifying what constitutes family or marriage behavior in society.

One can, however, make certain general observations. Families and marriage are pre-legal institutions. Although, intuitively, based on our individual observations and experiences, we modern women and men may tend to think of marriage as preceding the family, it is the family which is the primary institution.[3] Some form of the family, as a discrete group within the horde, can be found in all human, and many animal, societies. Marriage, however, in the sense of a highly individualized heterosexual relation, is said to be barely visible in some of the simplest human societies, and in others it is viewed as irrelevant to family formation.[4] It is helpful, especially in contemporary cultures where marriage and procreation are increasingly separate, to distinguish between the family as a social group that includes more persons than the marriage partners (if any), and marriage, which may or may not

3. *E.g.*, "The beginning of family formation may be either marriage or parenthood. It should not be concluded from the fact that sexual intercourse is a prerequisite for pregnancy that all peoples regard marriage or the establishing of a man-woman relationship as the first step in family formation. . . . [I]n the extreme case marriage is viewed as irrelevant to family formation." Robert F. Winch, "Marriage," in *International Encyclopedia of the Social Sciences* (New York: Macmillan, 1968), 10:1.

4. *Id.* ; *König* 38, 40, 58–59.

coincide with the existence of a family.[5] To say that "the family" is the primary institution, however, can be misleading unless we specify that families exist in a variety of forms. Indeed, it seems that no known society has had only one family type. On the other hand, the range of family types and, for that matter, of the forms of marriage has not been very wide.[6] Yet the limited extent of the ranges has not precluded a constant process of change which results in the continued development and emergence of family forms, new at least to the societies in which they appear. This process of change is slow, however, and slower in the case of family forms than it is for patterns of marriage.[7]

In order to make meaningful comparisons among the family law systems of four countries, it is essential to be alert to these differences between legal and social phenomena—between the institutions imagined, described, and elaborated in the law, and marriage and family behavior as imagined and lived in a given society. Thus, it seems worthwhile to pause at the outset for some brief reflections on these matters.

The Tinker's Wedding

In John Synge's play, *The Tinker's Wedding*,[8] the principal characters, Michael Byrne and Sarah Casey, are tinkers—traveling menders of metal household utensils. Their association began one day at Rathvanna, when Michael hit Sarah "a great clout in the lug," after which she came along with him "quiet and easy . . . from that hour to this present day." By the time we meet them, Sarah has been "going beside [him] a great while, and rearing a lot of them." The action of the play is set in motion by Sarah's sudden demand, backed up by a threat of leaving, that she and Michael be married. We can infer from their spirited and affectionate banter that Sarah's demand is not a symptom of any serious trouble that has arisen between Michael and herself. Except for this one point, she seems generally happy, "thriving, and getting [her] good health by the grace of the Almighty God." As the play opens, Michael has already agreed to go along with Sarah's desire for a wedding, although he does not understand it, and he is putting the finishing touches on her home-made wedding ring. All that remains to be done is to find a priest to do the job.

---

5. *König* at 38.

6. *Id.* at 21, 33, 37.

7. *Id.* at 39: "[M]an's ideas concerning the topic of love-and-marriage are much more diverse and flexible than the structure of the family. While notions concerning love and marriage often change with fashion, the family, as a universal human institution, is not so easily changed."

8. *The Complete Plays of John M. Synge* (New York: Random House, 1960) (first published in 1907), 180–209.

But things are not so easily arranged. The local priest comes walking along the road by the tinkers' camp, but he rejects as preposterous Sarah's request that he perform a wedding ceremony for them for no fee and give them a bit of silver into the bargain "to pay for the ring." After some discussion, he says he could see his way clear to offer the tinkers a special reduced price of one pound. But Michael and Sarah do not have a pound. Finally, after prolonged bargaining, the priest agrees to marry the couple for ten shillings and a gallon can which Michael has almost finished making—such a little sum "as wouldn't marry a child." The priest is not moved by Sarah's claim of poverty, unkindly pointing out that the tinkers are well known to steal "east and west in Wicklow and Wexford and the County Meath."

After the deal is struck, the wedding is set for the next day. But alas, during the night, Michael's old mother, Mary, is overcome by the temptation to take the newly made can and to sell it at the local pub in order to get a "pint for her sleep." To put off the moment of reckoning with Sarah, she sneaks a couple of empty bottles into the sack which had contained the can. Naturally, when the priest opens the sack the next day and finds only the bottles, he thinks that Michael and Sarah have tried to deceive him. He indignantly refuses to marry them for ten shillings without the can. After increasingly harsh words are exchanged, Sarah's disappointment turns to anger and the play ends with the priest trussed and thrown into a ditch. As the tinkers leave him, Sarah places her wedding ring on his finger to remind him of the promise he has made—under duress—not to tell the police he has been roughed up.

This little tale poses a number of interesting questions. It is Sarah's desire to get "married" that precipitates the action. But are not Michael and Sarah already married? A sociologist would probably consider that Michael and Sarah had been married for some time according to the long-standing customs of the subculture of the traveling people of Ireland. In the play, all indications are that Michael and Sarah intended that their union would be of some duration, and it is clear from the text that they held themselves out to the community of tinkers as belonging together. Furthermore, Michael's account of how he "got" Sarah at Rathvanna is reminiscent of descriptions by anthropologists of "marriage by capture," which is not really a kind of marriage, but rather a form of *wedding*.[9] Thus, from a sociologist's or anthropologist's point of view, the "tinker's wedding" may well have taken place when Michael hit Sarah in the lug and carried her off.[10]

9. *König* 40–41.
10. The formation of marriage, in simple societies, is often better understood as a process rather than an event, with the "wedding" of relatively minor importance. Customary marriages may be initiated by negotiation between families or by a ceremony of some sort, but often they merely involve living together, having a child, and gradually becoming accepted as a couple by

If the union of Michael and Sarah constituted behavior which a sociologist would call "marriage," is that the only sense in which they are married? In Ireland at the turn of the century, when Synge's play takes place, a couple validly married under the law of the Church was also married under the law of the state. Now, there is little doubt that Michael and Sarah would have been considered married under canon law as it stood until the Council of Trent made the presence of a priest at weddings mandatory in 1563. Prior to that time, Christians, like other people, could form marriages simply by exchanging consents and cohabiting.[11] But it is far from clear that the Tridentine requirement applied to Michael and Sarah, because its coverage was expressly limited to marriages of baptized persons. The priest in Synge's play repeatedly alludes to the "heathen" state of the tinkers. This does not seem to be a mere epithet. At one point the priest speculates, "I'm thinking you were never christened, Sarah Casey," and remarks, "It would be a queer job to go dealing Christian sacraments unto the like of you."

If, in fact, Michael and Sarah were unbaptized persons, their marital status under canon law is unaffected by the marriage legislation of Trent. Under canon law, marriages between unbaptized persons are presumptively valid, provided the crucial element of consent exists.[12] Furthermore, even if Michael and Sarah were baptized persons, and the Tridentine formalities were in principle required, the Church does not always insist on the priest's presence if compliance with this requirement would present "grave inconvenience."[13] Grave inconvenience, it has been said, can arise from poverty.[14]

Why then, if Michael and Sarah are already married in one or more senses of the word, should it be important to the state, to the Church, or to the parties, that a "wedding" should take place or that they should be "married" in another sense? If we ask this question from the point of view of the state and the Church, we fall upon a point of great significance for our inquiry into the changing relationship of family law to family life. In the case of Michael

---

relatives and neighbors. This is the case today, for example, for most New Guineans. See Owen Jessep and John Luluaki, *Principles of Family Law in Papua New Guinea* (Waigani: University of Papua New Guinea Press, 1985), 17–28. The marriages of as many as a fifth of the English population as late as the eighteenth century could also be characterized as having come into being in this way. See Stephen Parker, "The Marriage Act 1753: A Case Study in Family Law-Making," 1 *International Journal of Law and the Family* 133, 139 (1987).

11. See text below at note 57.

12. See James A. Coriden, Thomas J. Green, and Donald E. Hentschel, eds., *The Code of Canon Law: A Text and Commentary* (New York: Paulist Press, 1985), Canons 1055–1060, and commentary thereto.

13. *Id.*, Canon 1116.

14. John de Reeper, "The History and Application of Canon 1098," 14 *Jurist* 148, 169 (1954).

and Sarah, poor itinerants in Ireland at the turn of the century, it is fairly clear that neither the state nor the Church had much interest in their marital status. They belonged to what Max Rheinstein called the "neglected groups" of society and the law.[15] By that he meant that, historically, family law paid little attention to the concerns of the poor, or of such ethnic minority groups as the Indians of North and South America or the Afro-Americans of the United States. Prior to the twentieth century, propertyless individuals came to the attention of the legal system chiefly as subjects of the criminal law. As Rheinstein observed, one of the great trends presently transforming the law of the family is precisely that of paying increasing attention to the needs and demands of hitherto neglected groups.

But we are running ahead of our story. Suffice it to say that Synge's priest repeatedly makes it plain that he considers tinkers to be outside the normal scope of his sphere of action and interest. He regards Michael and Sarah as different from "my own pairs living here in the place." He is, in fact, as puzzled about why Sarah wants to get married as are Michael and Michael's mother. When, during their haggling over the price of the wedding, Sarah begins to cry at the thought that she may never get married, the priest exclaims in surprise, "It's a queer woman you are to be crying at the like of that, and you your whole life walking the roads."

When we turn to the question of why Sarah, a member of a neglected group, with its own customary way of marrying, seeks nevertheless to be married in another way, we have a number of theories from which to choose. Yet those apt to come to mind first today can be ruled out. The playwright gives us no reason to believe that Sarah is motivated by any thought of improving her economic position or "legitimizing"[16] her children through bringing herself within the framework of legal rights and duties attaching to marriage. Nor does Synge give us the slightest hint that Sarah thought marriage by a priest was somehow related to the salvation of her immortal soul. Rather, it seems that she is concerned about the social approval of groups other than tinkers. After she is married, she thinks, "there will be no one have a right to call me a dirty name and I selling cans in Wicklow or Wexford or the city of Dublin itself."

15. Max Rheinstein, "The Family and the Law," in *International Encyclopedia of Comparative Law*, vol. 4, *Persons and the Family*, ed. Aleck Chloros (Tübingen: J.C.B. Mohr, 1974), 12–13.

16. Note that the legal classification of children born outside legal marriage as "illegitimate" may or may not correspond to social concepts of legitimacy. The legal definition of legitimacy is a function of the definition of legal marriage, whereas a sociologist's definition of legitimacy has to take into consideration other cultural norms besides legal ones. Note, too, that the legal category of "illegitimacy" may include children who are living in families with both of their parents, while the set of "legitimate" children includes many who are living with only one parent.

But why should a hastily performed ritual make such a difference? For the purposes of our inquiry, this question opens up the subject of how imaginative representations in the law can sometimes affect the way people perceive and experience the reality of something as central to our lives as marriage. We are accustomed to viewing law as importantly shaped by beliefs and behavior, but we frequently overlook the reflexive and continuous nature of the interaction among laws, ideas, feelings, and conduct. Often mesmerized by the coercive power of law, we tend to minimize its persuasive and constitutive aspects.

In Synge's play, it is Mary Byrne who has the last word (inspired no doubt by the necessity of putting the best possible light on the situation which her own great thirst has brought about). To Michael, still fearful about Sarah's earlier threat to leave him if he doesn't marry her, she says: "And you're thinking it's paying gold to his reverence would make a woman stop when she's a mind to go?" With Sarah, whose hopes of marriage have been dashed, the rough, boozy old woman for the first time adopts a gentle tone: "It's as good a right you have surely, Sarah Casey, but what good will it do? Is it putting that ring on your finger will keep you from getting an aged woman and losing the fine face you have, or be easing your pain?" Feeling a little guilty about what has happened—but not too guilty—Mary affirms the folkways of the traveling people: "[I]t's a long time we are going our own ways—father and son and his son after him, or mother and daughter and her own daughter again—and it's little need we ever had of going up into a church and swearing."

And so, in the end, Sarah's notion of getting married is left in the ditch with the priest and the wedding ring. Why would a poor tinker, married and wedded in custom and the eyes of God, want in addition to be married by an official? It may, suggests Mary, have been the "changing of the moon." But, at the turn of the century, Ireland was changing too. And as part of that change, people like Sarah all over the world were beginning to associate legitimacy with legality.

What is Marriage?

The title of this section does not really await an answer; rather it invites further reflection on, and refinement of, the question. Let there be a set of men and women married to each other according to the rules of the legal system to which they are subject. Call this Set A. Now let there be a set of men and women cohabiting with each other in unions that are entered with some idea of duration and are openly manifested to and approved (or at least not disapproved) by the relevant community. Call this Set B (see fig. 1).

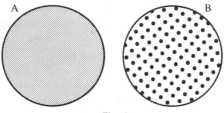

Fig. 1

In Set A, as we have defined it, marriage is whatever the legal system says it is.[17] The contents of Set B call for more lengthy comment. In constructing Set B as the set of heterosexual unions undertaken with some idea of duration and in which the partners attest to the relevant social environment (relatives, neighborhood, clan, community) that they regard themselves as belonging together, and are accepted as such, I have included behavior that a sociologist or anthropologist would be apt to describe as "marriage behavior." The element of intended duration does not mean that the unions in Set B are necessarily permanent or even enduring, nor, as this set is constructed, need the unions it contains be sexually exclusive or even monogamous. Nor is the element of legitimacy (in the sense of social approval) isomorphic with the concept of legality. I am here following the family sociologist René König in using the factors of intended duration, attestation, and legitimacy to help move past the difficulty of defining what turns a sexual relation into "marriage."[18] Nevertheless, the imprecision of these terms leaves a number of cases that will be hard to classify. In particular, the distinctions between sexual conduct which is approved and that which is disapproved are everywhere in flux. Set B is therefore a leaky set that includes a wide variety of formal and informal unions, some of which are recognized by the legal system and some not.

Notice that while it will be useful, and indeed essential, for us to distin-

17. It should not be assumed, however, that it will always be easy to determine the content of this set. The legal system may define marriage by referring to the rules of some other system, as is described in the text at note 22. Or the legal system itself may recognize more than one type of marriage, for example, "full" marriage, and marriages which have fewer legal effects than full marriage, such as the morganatic marriages of royal and aristocratic European families, or the union of male and female slaves known in Roman law as *contubernium*.

18. *König* 39. American courts have struggled heroically with this problem in trying to determine whether and when a legally recognized common law marriage has taken place. For example, a common law marriage has been held to exist after a couple had spent a few nights together in a hotel, *Madewell v. United States*, 84 F.Supp. 329 (E.D. Tenn. 1949), but not where the man suddenly died shortly after the couple checked into a hotel, *Estate of Kieg*, 140 P.2d 163 (Cal. App. 1939).

guish in theory between the set of *de jure* marriages on the one hand, and the set of *de facto* marriages or marriage-like behavior on the other, in the countries that are the principal objects of our study, the two sets overlap (see fig. 2).

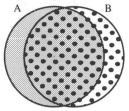

Fig. 2

The intersection of Sets A and B is the set of *de facto* unions that are stamped as legal marriages by the state, which, in the countries that concern us here, is the social control organization with a juridical monopoly over marriage and divorce. The part of Set A which does not intersect with Set B contains those men and women between whom a legal marriage bond exists, but who are not in a *de facto* union with each other. In everyday experience, then, this would include separated but undivorced couples and those couples between whom the *de facto* union but not the legal bond has been terminated by what is sometimes called a *poor man's divorce*: the departure of one of the spouses with no intent to return.

The part of Set B which does not intersect with Set A includes all those *de facto* unions as defined above which are not recognized as marriages by the legal system. In everyday experience in the countries under consideration, this would include cohabitation without compliance with the procedures established by the state for formation of a legal marriage. Here we would commonly find, for example, those cohabitants who have chosen not to marry legally, as well as those who are prevented from forming a legal marriage because of the existence of a prior undissolved legal marriage of one or both of them.[19] Set B would also include persons cohabiting in religious marriages

19. The American institution of common law marriage belongs in the domain of Set A because it is a form of legal marriage, deemed by some fourteen states to come into being when a man and a woman, legally eligible to be married, agree to be husband and wife and "hold themselves out to the world" as such. Common law marriage is, in legal theory, binding until terminated by a formal legal divorce. The same is true of marriage "by habit and repute" in Scotland (see below, chapter 6, text at note 3). In Set A, too, belong those unions converted into legal marriages by legislation of a type common in Central and South American countries, providing that stable cohabitation for a certain number of years is the equivalent of formal marriage. In Latin America, where application of the formal marriage requirement of the Council of Trent was long suspended because of the scarcity of priests, informal marriage is still very common. See José Arraros, "Concubinage in Latin America," 3 *Journal of Family Law* 330 (1963).

not recognized as legally valid by the state. This can occasionally happen, for example, in countries like France and West Germany where civil marriage is compulsory, or in divorceless Ireland, where the religious marriage of a person whose previous marriage has been dissolved by ecclesiastical annulment is not recognized as valid under secular law.

In practice, in the four countries whose law is examined in this book, the overlap between Sets A and B is considerable, as figure 2 in rough fashion suggests. Most marriage behavior in these countries still takes place within a legal framework. Ease of divorce helps keep that part of Set A which does not intersect with Set B small. But that part of Set B which does not intersect with Set A, *de facto* but nonlegal unions, has increased considerably in recent years, accompanied, as we will see in chapter 6, by the development of a new body of cohabitation law. The decreasing orientation of marriage behavior to legal norms in Western societies is so readily observable that it is perhaps unnecessary to stress that the contents of Sets A and B and their relation to each other have varied greatly from time to time and from place to place.

How wide these variations can be is plain when we stand back from our immediate historical and cultural context. In Western Europe prior to the Reformation, for example, there was *no* Set A of legal bonds created in compliance with secular norms of the state.[20] Rather, we would have to speak of those marriages recognized as such by the norms established by other social control organizations, chiefly those of canon law. Even today, many men and women in England, France, the United States, or West Germany consider themselves subject to the systems of law of the Church of England or the Roman Catholic Church, or to Islamic or Jewish law. These religious legal systems are now independent of the state, and their marriage law is not recognized by the states with which we are here concerned, except to a limited degree in England. For such persons, we must construct a Set C, the set of marriage bonds established according to the law of the religious group of one or both parties. This set may overlap but does not necessarily coincide with the sets of either legal or *de facto* marriages (see fig. 3).

In countries where religious family law is still important, such as Israel, India, and many Islamic nations, it is not normally the case that legal regulation of marriage coincides only accidentally with religious regulation. Though we are accustomed in the United States and Western Europe to systems of direct marriage regulation by the state, this is by no means the universal mode of regulation in the world today. In many pluralistic societies, where the legal system must accommodate diverse marriage practices and cultural ideals, it is

20. In the medieval world, "law" was not equivalent to the norm system sanctioned by the state, because the "state" was only one of several political organizations vying with each other for jurisdiction over various aspects of social life as well as for political power.

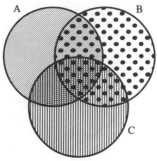

Fig. 3

useful to distinguish, as Max Rheinstein did, between the *Occidental* and *Oriental* patterns of regulation of family matters.[21] He used these terms, not in any strict geographical sense, but rather to distinguish, respectively, between those countries which treat family law questions as in principle subject to the laws of the secular state, and those which treat them as governed in principle by the customary or religious law of the groups to which the individuals involved belong.

Within the Occidental pattern, one can distinguish two major variants. The first attempts to devise legal rules that correspond to patterns of belief or behavior that are widely shared among the groups and subgroups of which the society is composed. This is the approach taken in England, France, and several other European countries. Needless to say, secular family law of this type can never fully correspond to *all* the patterns of life that actually exist in society. Thus, some countries, like the United States and Sweden, have adopted an alternative approach based on what Rheinstein called the *ideology of tolerance*. Secular family law in such countries substantially refrains from trying to articulate a common morality. It confines itself merely to defining the current outer limits of permissible diversity in family matters, (e.g., no simultaneous polygamy), while leaving maximum room for choice and avoiding value judgments other than those favoring individual liberty.

The Oriental approach to pluralism is followed in many countries where a number of well-defined religious and ethnic communities with their own settled marriage rules coexist, such as India, Indonesia, Israel, Lebanon, and most, but not all, Islamic countries.[22] One variant of this approach is exem-

21. *Rheinstein*, above, note 15 at 8–10.

22. It is characteristic of these systems, where jurisdiction over family matters depends on the group affiliation of one or both parties, that complex conflict of laws and jurisdictional problems can arise when persons of different religions, groups, or nationalities are involved in the same case, or when the status of persons married or divorced in one country must be determined by the courts of another country.

plified by India, where Hindu, Muslim, Parsi, Christian, and Jewish religious laws concerning such matters as marriage and divorce are applied by state judges in the secular courts. The predominant model, used in Israel and in several of the Islamic countries, leaves matters of personal status to be decided by the religious or customary tribunals of the group involved. In the Oriental systems then, Set A *includes* Set C.

The countries whose law is examined in this book long ago opted for family law enacted and applied by governmental organs and have for the most part forgotten that marriage and family matters were once left mainly to regulation by manners, custom, ethics, or religious norms. Yet legal regulation of these matters in the modern sense did not exist in pre-Reformation Europe, and they were largely ignored by the law in Roman times. One of the questions raised by the recent developments discussed in this book is whether the direction of the current period of change in the family law of all or some of the countries examined here is toward the emptying of the set of legal marriage relationships. Is it true, as a Swedish writer has claimed, that legal developments in his country have been marked by the disappearance of official interest in marriage as an institution?[23] If so, has Sweden, as has often been the case in family law, marked out the course which other Western countries sooner or later will follow?

Three further observations are in order at this point. First, the same kinds of distinctions just drawn among legal marriage, *de facto* marriage, and unions recognized as "marriages" under religious or customary laws, can also be perceived in other institutions which are both legal and social. Thus, for example, later on we will wish to distinguish among legal divorce, *de facto* termination of "marriage," and dissolution of marriage bonds under religious or customary law. Second, as we examine the effect of rapidly changing mores upon older legal norms, we will notice that as the discrepancy widens between legal rules and actual marriage behavior in society, the outline of a shadow institution of marriage within the set of *de facto* unions often becomes increasingly discernible. As the shadow of the formal institution of marriage grows in extent and importance to the point where the legal system one way or another must take it into account, the relationships among law, behavior, and ideas shift again. Finally, besides the distinction between marriage as a legal institution and marriage as a social institution, it will be useful in reading the chapters that follow to keep in mind another distinction, one

23. Jacob Sundberg, "Nordic Laws," in *Das Erbrecht von Familienangehörigen in positivrechtlicher und rechtspolitischer Sicht* (Frankfurt: Alfred Metzner, 1971), 40, commenting on the fact that directives for the reform of family law issued in 1969 by the Swedish Minister of Justice specified that future legislation should be drafted so as not to favor in any way the institution of marriage as compared with other forms of cohabitation.

lying entirely within the realm of legal regulation: the distinction in legal effect between the status of being married and the status of being unmarried. Here, too, we will see that far-reaching changes are taking place, and that a once important distinction is becoming blurred.

The Road from Rome

A book about family law, perhaps even more than books in other domains of law, has to grapple with the problem of the complex relationship of events in the world of law to widespread social practices and to what French historians call *mentalités*. As Otto Kahn-Freund once said about family law, "Here, if anywhere, the law must be seen as the outcome of social forces and as a force which in turn impinges on people in society, on their habits and their convictions."[24] Yet this is easier said than done. It is often possible to trace the emergence of legal norms and rituals to the ideas or practices of influential groups, but it is extremely difficult to determine what effect legal constructs themselves may have on attitudes or behavior. Max Rheinstein's research on divorce law and marriage behavior in a number of countries established that there is no clear and simple relationship between strict divorce law and marriage stability in a given society, nor between lenient divorce law and marriage instability.[25] His findings, which challenged widely held beliefs at the time he began his work, have been supported by later studies.[26] Such studies do not, however, shed much light on the possible long-term, indirect effects of legal norms or of abrupt changes in long-standing legal traditions.

History and legend, as well as the world around us, furnish abundant examples of the resistance of certain types of conduct to regulation by edict. Ahasuerus, who, according to the Book of Esther, laid down the unalterable law of the Medes and the Persians that the husband is the head of the household, is also said to have sent out his soldiers with whips to beat the stormy sea into submission. Legal norms, to be sure, often may have some effect on the way people think, feel, and act, but it is striking how stubbornly the forms of behavior involved in family life seem to follow their own patterns independently of the legal system.

A thousand years of marriage regulation in what is now Italy provide a case in point. At the time of the late Roman Republic and in Imperial Rome, we

24. Otto Kahn-Freund, quoted by Aidan R. Gough in "Book Review," 37 *Modern Law Review* 118 (1974).

25. *Rheinstein.*

26. Jacques Commaille, Patrick Festy, Pierre Guibentif, Jean Kellerhals, Jean-François Perrin, and Louis Roussel, *Le Divorce en Europe Occidentale: La Loi et le Nombre* (Paris: I.N.E.D., 1983).

have it on good authority that "[M]arriage was to the Romans, as to the other peoples of antiquity, a *de facto* rather than a *de jure* matter, in the sense that two people were held to be married, not because they had gone through any particular ceremony, but because they in fact lived together as man and wife." [27] It was usual, it seems, for marriages to begin with a ceremony of some sort: in Rome, instead of getting a clout in the lug, the bride might be lifted over the threshold of the bridegroom's house and presented with gifts of fire and water. Just as marriage began with the setting up of life in common, so it ended when the community of life was terminated by either spouse. Divorce was available to either party and, by the end of the late republic, we are told that it had become common, at least among the upper social classes (the only sectors of Roman society of which we have much knowledge). [28] The formation of a Roman marriage was not a legal transaction. It was a factual event which, of course, had legal consequences.

Even after the conversion of Constantine, matters did not change quickly. As Rheinstein wrote, "Full freedom to terminate a marriage was a rule so firmly rooted in the mores that it took centuries of Christian effort to replace it by the new principle of indissolubility." [29] For one thing, it took some time for this novel doctrine to be settled in the teaching of the Church itself. At first, the post-Constantine Roman legislation did no more than threaten to punish a husband who repudiated his wife without cause. The effort by the Byzantine emperor Justinian in A.D. 542 to extend penalties to divorce by mutual consent was so unpopular that it was promptly repealed by his successor.

Marriage became indissoluble only when, after centuries of striving, the Church gained jurisdiction for its own courts over matrimonial causes. [30] Once such jurisdiction was established in the various states and kingdoms which covered the territory of present-day Italy, the principle of the indissolubility of marriage became the legal norm (except for the brief period of Napoleonic rule) until a controversial national referendum introduced divorce in December 1970. To a great extent, over time, marriage behavior became oriented to canon law norms. On the other hand, all through the long period of legal indissolubility, many Italians followed the age-old custom of dissolving their unions by departure, not even bothering to take advantage of the possibility of divorce briefly introduced by French laws imposed in the course of Napo-

---

27. H. F. Jolowicz, *Historical Introduction to the Study of Roman law*, 2d ed. (Cambridge: Cambridge University Press, 1967), 113.

28. *Id.* at 245.

29. *Rheinstein* 16.

30. See, generally, *Rheinstein* 7–28, and below, text at note 64.

leon's conquest.[31] In 1958, estimates prepared in connection with proposals for the introduction of divorce indicated that there were about six hundred thousand married couples in Italy whose life together had in fact ended, and that about a million Italian men and women were living in irregular unions, in which one or both were legally married to someone other than the person with whom they were cohabiting. In 1969, a report to the Italian Chamber of Deputies stated there were then 1.16 million separated couples in Italy. Many of these involved so-called white widows and their husbands, who were working in other European countries. The number of persons involved in informal cohabitation arrangements (not counting unions formed by Italian guest-workers abroad) was believed to be around 4 million, if children were included. Thus, over a long period of time, it seems that the practices of informal marriage and separation were as rooted in Italian culture as was the ideal of indissolubility of marriage. The strict Italian divorce law of 1970 by no means represents a return to the legal state of affairs that prevailed in Roman times. Rather, it seems to have been an effort to conform the law somewhat more closely to behavior and to bring *de facto* households within the law.

The course of marriage regulation in Italy suggests a number of questions. How and why did the ideas of indissolubility and ceremonial marriage become established in the law in the first place? How did canon law and, later, secular law succeed in securing, to the extent that they did, general acceptance, if not general practice, of these ideas? If the ideal of indissolubility enshrined in religious and, eventually, in secular law was out of correspondence with a good deal of actual Italian marriage behavior, why was it so difficult to secure the acceptance of the new legal principle of limited dissolubility? Is there any reason why the ideals embodied in the law should reflect whatever form or forms of behavior are widespread in society? Or, to the contrary, does the state or society have an interest in maintaining legal symbolism which does *not* precisely correspond to behavior patterns? Do individuals have an interest in the maintenance of such symbolism? What are the relationships of politics and ideas to family law and behavior, and vice versa?

Considerable light can be shed on these matters by tracing the main stages in the process through which marriage became a legal institution in the West and the principal ways in which official interest in the family was manifested prior to the twentieth century. In addition, a brief account of that process helps explain how Western family law assumed the forms that were in place when the events to which this book is devoted began.

31. For a description of Italian marriage law up to the 1970 reform, see Walther Fleig, *Die Ehescheidung im italienischen Recht* (Bielefeld: Gieseking 1975), 19–38.

From Custom to Law

What did you want meddling with the like of us, when it's a long time we
are going our own ways . . . ?

J.M. Synge, *The Tinker's Wedding*[32]

Regulation through enacted legal norms is but one mode of social control.
Moreover, it is one which has appeared on a large scale only rather late in
history, as a characteristic component of those processes of rationalization
and consociation that have gradually penetrated all aspects of social life.[33]
Thus, it might occur to an inquisitive person, contemplating the elaborate
modern systems of family law that now surround us, to wonder how marriage
and family matters once governed only by custom, ethics, manners, or religion came to be regulated so extensively by law. We know that, let us say,
Cro-Magnon men and women did not present themselves before an official to
be joined together, nor did they need to ask a judge for permission to separate.
How is it then that, in the West, the innovations of law became, to a great
extent, our marriage customs?

No one knows when the shift from biological to cultural patterns of mating
occurred. Nor, for that matter, does anyone yet know much about what is
innate and what is cultural in man. With the help of ethologists, anthropologists, and sociologists, we have gained some understanding of how different
mating customs and rituals may have evolved in simple societies. But the
origins of regularity and usage in human conduct are still shrouded in
darkness.

With respect to the Germanic and Roman antecedents of modern Western
marriage systems, historians are able to tell us something about how community or kinship-group interest in mating manifested itself, and about the
early forms of rank and status derived from marriage and birth. Marriage was
a definite social status, but the wedding, or marriage rite, seems to have been
important only under special circumstances, in particular where property was
exchanged. The two earliest forms of Roman marriage rituals are said to have
been a religious rite used by the patrician class, and a symbolic purchase.
Although there are traces of marriage initiated by capture in the earliest Germanic laws, the usual form was a purchase marriage whose principal function
seems to have been to enable the bride's kinfolk to bargain for her honorable
treatment as a wife and widow.[34] Among the early Germans, marriage differed from other sexual unions in that the wife and children of the marriage

32. See above, note 8 at 207.
33. *Weber* 35.
34. *Hübner* 593; *Pollock and Maitland* 364.

enjoyed a more secure position in relation to the husband and his kinship group than other women with whom he may have cohabited and their off-spring.[35] The distinction between legitimate marriage and other unions which, though not disapproved, are of lower status appears not only in primitive systems but also in Roman law and in the civil law of many continental countries until early modern times.

From a sociological point of view, the significance of the legitimate marriage is that it enables the family to function as a status-conferring institution. Only the legitimate wife and children share the social rank of their husband and father. In the widespread custom of high-ranking families to give away their daughters only on assurances of preferred status for the daughter and her children, Max Weber saw the origin of the earliest *legal* characteristics of marriage: dowry, the agreement to support the wife and pay her compensation upon abandonment, and the successoral position of her children.[36]

In cultures or social groups where marriage is simply the decision of the partners to live together and to raise common children, and where marriage involves no exchange of property, the couple relationship tends to be dissolved simply by desertion or separation.[37] But as marriage formation becomes more complex, the procedure for dissolving it typically does too. The emphasis on procedures for both seems to vary with the roles of rank and property. Where these are important, rules appear to distinguish clearly which sexual relationships will give rise to rights. The need arises to justify the dissolution of marriage and to furnish reasons to neutralize the objections of relatives.[38]

This was already beginning to be the case in the earliest periods of Roman and Germanic customary law. It is said that the early Germanic folk were relatively monogamous, although plurality of wives was permissible among them, and that Rome, for its first five hundred years, had a tradition of marital stability, despite the fact that marriages were dissoluble there. In the morally strict society of early republican Rome, a man would incur disapproval if he repudiated his wife without some cause, such as barrenness or infidelity.[39] Old Germanic law recognized marriage dissolution by agreement between the husband and the wife's relatives and permitted the husband, and eventually the wife, to end the marriage unilaterally for certain serious reasons.[40]

35. *Hübner* 588.

36. *Weber* 134.

37. *König* 58–60. See, for contemporary illustrations, Owen Jessep and John Luluaki, *Principles of Family Law in Papua New Guinea*, (Waigani: University of Papua New Guinea Press, 1985), 53–57.

38. *König* 59.   39. *Jolowicz* 117–18.

40. *Brissaud* 142; *Hübner* 613.

Thus, in Roman times and among the Germanic peoples by whom the Roman empire was eventually overrun, lack of legal regulation did not mean that marriage was completely beyond social control. Nor, in Rome, did the fact that marriage was not regulated by law mean that the law was indifferent to marriage. The existence or nonexistence of a marriage was indirectly significant for Roman law when it had to deal with problems involving membership of the "houses" of which the body politic was composed, with succession on death, or with allocation of responsibility for civil wrongs.[41] But in dealing with such matters, Roman law accepted as a marriage whatever was customarily recognized as such. As has been mentioned, however, Roman law did not recognize marriages between free persons and slaves or, at one time, between senators, or other upper-class men, and women of lower rank.

Over the long period of Roman history, marriage customs varied considerably. In early times, marriage among the leading class of patricians was initiated by a religious ceremony, *confarreatio*. There were two other ways of confirming marital status: *coemptio*, involving a formality which is thought to have been a symbolic purchase; and *usus*, which entailed no particular formality but came into existence when a couple had lived as husband and wife for a year. The forms available for initiating marriage were, according to Corbett, "in great part legally indifferent" (except to a limited degree in *confarreatio*), in the sense that the validity of the marriage did not depend on their observance.[42] Originally, it seems, marriage, however formed, always brought the wife under the legal control (*manus*) of her husband.

By late Republican times, these three methods of marrying had become obsolete. They gave way to the so-called *free consensual marriage*, marriage without *manus*, in which the man and woman married simply by starting life in common, provided they had *affectio maritalis*, that is, that they regarded each other as husband and wife. Free marriage was known at the time of the earliest Roman code of laws, the Twelve Tables (451–450 B.C.). It was common in the third and second centuries B.C. and became the usual mode of marriage in the late Republic. There was nothing but *affectio maritalis* to distinguish free marriage from any other type of sexual union. If this state of mind ceased on either side, the marriage, in principle, was at an end. Legally, the free marriage was treated as dissolved when the parties separated by agreement, or when one spouse departed and notified the other of his or her intention to terminate the relationship. At one time, it may have been the case that only the husband could unilaterally terminate the marriage. But the parties were on an equal footing in this respect at least by the end of the third

41. *Rheinstein* 15.
42. *Corbett* 68–105; 218–48.

century B.C., and perhaps from the beginning. The use by both husband and wife of the power to terminate a marriage is said to have been common in the first century B.C.; almost the only deterrent was the existence of rules governing the return of the dowry. Thus, one can say that, in Rome, marriage had become a formless transaction dissoluble at the will of either party, and remained so at the time of the first Christian emperor, Constantine (c. A.D. 285–337).

The Christian emperors made little effort to regulate family behavior. From Constantine until Justinian (c. A.D. 482–565), Roman marriage legislation had no ambitions beyond punishing unjustified repudiations. If one spouse repudiated the other without some good reason, he or she might have to give back the marriage portion or lose other property rights. Eventually, the offending spouse could even be deported, confined within a monastery, or subjected to restrictions on remarriage. But even these more restrictive laws permitted repudiation for cause, and they did not affect divorce by mutual agreement. John Noonan's research led him to the conclusions that the legislation of the Christian emperors presumed that marriages were dissoluble and regarded remarriage as the normal sequel to dissolution.[43] According to Noonan, it was "a good question . . . whether the prohibitions of divorce from Constantine to Anastasius had any teeth to them," so long as someone was able to pay the price or work out a settlement.[44] Naturally, so long as the sanctions were only property-related, any effects would have been limited to the wealthier classes.[45]

Even the strongly religious Byzantine Emperor Justinian at first did not interfere with marital dissolution by mutual agreement, declaring at one point that "of those things that occur among men, whatever is bound is soluble."[46] Later, however, Justinian broke with Roman tradition and established penalties for mutual consent divorce as well as for unjustified repudiation.[47] Significantly, however, he did not assert that marriages were in principle indissoluble. His restrictions on consensual divorce were neither well-received nor well-observed. They were also short-lived, being repealed by Justinian's successor in one of his first acts after ascension to the throne.[48]

At the close of the Roman period, then, it can be said that the law had little direct involvement with the social institution of marriage. The idea of legal regulation of marriage formation or the conduct of married life was unknown,

---

43. John T. Noonan, Jr., "Novel 22," in *The Bond of Marriage: An Ecumenical and Interdisciplinary Study*, ed. William W. Bassett (Notre Dame, Ind.: University of Notre Dame Press, 1968), 44–46.

44. *Id.* at 53.   45. *Id.* at 44–46.

46. *Id.* at 57.   47. *Id.* at 65–68; *Gaudemet* 84.

48. *Rheinstein* 16.

and legal control of marriage dissolution had been attempted only to a very limited degree by the legislation of the Christian emperors, which implicitly accepted the premise that marriage was dissoluble. In Rome and among the Germanic peoples, marriage was thus not a legal institution. To discover how it became formal, indissoluble, and subject to far-reaching official regulation, we must turn to another source of social control which, at the time of the Christian Roman legislation, was not a legal system at all but only an evolving body of doctrine: Roman Catholic canon law.

Ecclesiastical Jurisdiction

The Struggle for Control

After the Roman empire in the West broke down in the course of the fifth century A.D., the Christian Church not only remained intact but grew stronger than ever. The new kingdoms of the West had not yet developed those political organizations on the Roman pattern that were to develop subsequently into various forms of feudalism and still later into what we now call the state. The Church was able to exercise great influence over, and was closely associated with, the secular power of the early Visigothic kings and the later Merovingian and Carolingian dynasties.[49] Even so, the establishment of the doctrine of the indissolubility of marriage and the acquisition of ecclesiastical jurisdiction over matrimonial matters took centuries.

The Church's claim to exclusive jurisdiction over marital causes and the novel idea that marriage was indissoluble were both closely connected to the Christian idea that marriage was not only a natural institution and a contract between the spouses, but also a sacrament, that is, a channel of divine grace. But the sacramental nature of marriage and the ideal of indissolubility were not settled all at once as matters of firm church doctrine. Both ideas had powerful proponents: St. Ambrose (c. 339–397) for indissolubility and his convert, St. Augustine (354–430), for the sacrament. St. Augustine went on record for indissolubility too, by opposing "adulterous marriages" (remarriage by one who has put aside a spouse, even for a grave reason such as adultery). But near the end of his life, he returned to this matter dissatisfied with his treatment of the problem of whether a spouse who puts aside his partner for adultery commits adultery himself if he marries again. In his *Retractations*, he wrote, "I think that I did not reach a perfect solution of this question." [50] He calls it a "very difficult question" and speaks of its "obscurities." What was difficult and obscure for one of the learned doctors of the

---

49. *I Esmein* 14.

50. St. Augustine, *The Retractations*, in *The Fathers of the Church* (Washington, D.C.: Catholic University Press, 1968), 60:247. See also *Gaudemet* 71–74.

Church was apparently less so for ordinary Christian men and women. Noonan tells us that all during Roman history under the Christian emperors, "Christians in good faith could believe that marriage was dissoluble or indissoluble. . . ."[51]

The greatest obstacle to the direct enforcement by the Church of the new Christian ideas about sex and marriage was that marriage was regarded everywhere in Europe in the first half of the Middle Ages as a personal and purely secular matter. Conversion to Christianity in the Roman empire and in the lands inhabited by the Germanic tribes did not automatically result in immediate acceptance of the Christian notions that marriage had to be strictly monogamous and that all sexual relations outside marriage were prohibited.[52] Nor did the Church insist on this. Marriage continued to be regulated by social rules about marriage age, choice of partners, and legitimate descent. Sometimes these rules were grounded in custom and convention, sometimes in ancient pagan religion. Ecclesiastical jurisdiction over marriage was acquired only very gradually, and in large part, through a process of compromise with, adaptation to, and even incorporation of indigenous practices. At first, the Church barely tried to exercise jurisdiction in its own name, keeping its intervention in family affairs primarily within the confines of the relationship between priest and penitent.[53] Its involvement in the formation of marriage, for example, developed only slowly, with the priestly blessing of marriages which began as a custom and centuries later became a requirement.

The idea of the indissolubility of marriage did not easily gain a foothold in the ancient world. Within the early Church, some had held the opinion that the passages in the Apostolic writings, upon which Church fathers based the principle of indissolubility, did not absolutely prohibit divorce, at least in the case of adultery.[54] Eventually, the point was more or less settled in ecclesiastical doctrine, but the Church still had to contend with deeply rooted secular customs. The Anglo-Saxons, the Franks, the other Germanic tribes, and the Romans all had permitted divorce. Marriages were dissoluble (without intervention of any judge) by mutual consent or by unilateral repudiation, sometimes with payment of a penalty.[55] For centuries, when all that the Church had

51. Noonan, above, note 43 at 87.
52. *Rheinstein* 13–14; *Gaudemet* 123–29.
53. William W. Bassett, "The Marriage of Christians—Valid Contract, Valid Sacrament?" in *The Bond of Marriage: An Ecumenical and Interdisciplinary Study*, ed. William W. Bassett (Notre Dame, Ind.: University of Notre Dame Press, 1968), 129.
54. *Id.* 50–51; *Gaudemet* 45–46.
55. *II Esmein* 49; *Gaudemet* 106.

to back up its norms was its disciplinary power over Christians, it was compelled to exercise a great deal of tolerance. To some extent, it even accepted divorce and remarriage.[56]

As for the rule that a couple must exchange consents in the presence of a priest in order to be validly married, that did not appear until the sixteenth century. The variety of marriage customs among the Christian nations was great, and the Church from the beginning had adapted its own rituals to them. Christians began to seek a priestly blessing for their marriages as early as the second century, but the Church's consistent position (with some diversity of opinion) was that consent of the parties alone sufficed to constitute a valid marriage, and no particular form was required for the exchange.[57] During the Middle Ages, the custom of exchanging marriage vows at the church door developed. Then the Church began to prescribe this public religious ceremony, but the sanctions for noncompliance did not include nullity.[58] Thus, until the Council of Trent, private and informal marriages were as valid as public, formal ones. Thereafter, even though informal marriages were no longer valid, it remained the case that consent was the essential factor and that the parties, not the priest, were the ministers of the sacrament. Though the priest's presence was made obligatory, he attends only as a witness. Furthermore, the Council did not impose this requirement on all Christians in the world for the very good reason that priests were not everywhere available to officiate at weddings.

The Church's long tolerance of and adjustment to secular and pagan customs, even when they were at variance with its own evolving doctrine, was thought by Pollock and Maitland to be due to its concern not to "multiply sins."[59] But it was strategic as well. When the Pope told the first Irish missionaries to England not to be too severe with their new converts so far as incest and marriage prohibitions were concerned, he was no doubt trying to help assure the success of their missions.[60] It is hard to separate the Church's policy of accommodation to local practices from its gradual and eventually successful assertion of control over regulation of marriage.

56. *II Esmein* 49–50; *Brissaud* 143–44; *Hübner* 614; *Pollock and Maitland* 392–93.

57. Richard Helmholz has pointed out that even on this point there was a divergence between law and custom, with most people holding to an older tradition in which consummation was required to make a marriage complete. "Comment: Recurrent Patterns of Family Law," 8 *Harvard Journal of Law and Public Policy* 175 (1985).

58. John de Reeper, "The History and Application of Canon 1098," 14 *Jurist* 148, 152 (1954).

59. *Pollock and Maitland* 370.

60. *Id.* at 366.

Canon Law Prior to the Council of Trent

Ecclesiastical jurisdiction over matrimonial causes and the rudiments of a canon law system were established in what is now France and the Germanies by the end of the tenth century,[61] and in England by the middle of the twelfth century.[62] In its long competition with secular powers for temporal authority, the Church had tried to gain control over other legal areas, such as succession on death, matters pertaining to Church land, and civil and criminal cases involving the clergy.[63] But it was only with respect to marital causes that its path was clear and its success was eventually complete. The development of the doctrine of sacramental marriage furnished the theoretical basis for the assertion of ecclesiastical authority over an area of life which previously had not been subject to any kind of systematic official control. The idea that regulation of marriage or adjudication of disputes concerning marriage could or should be conducted by the secular political community was not seriously considered before the sixteenth century and the Protestant Reformation.

The acquisition of jurisdiction over marriage by ecclesiastical courts and the application by these courts of the various church doctrines which eventually coalesced into a body of canon law[64] was something new in human history. Weber has given us the classic description of how the Church, having assumed a bureaucratic and hierarchical structure, went on to develop a system of courts and procedures and a body of legal rules of the type he called "formally rational," radically different from the law of other religious legal systems.[65] The norm system of the canon law, formulated and systematically organized after the manner of the law of the late Roman empire, did not gain immediate acceptance in social life, but over time it had far-reaching and long-lasting effects on all Western marriage law, effects which have lasted down to the present day.

We now begin to discern the answers to some of our questions: how marriage came under any official regulation at all, how it was interpretively constructed by legal norms, and how it came to be legally indissoluble. But we are only beginning, for there is abundant evidence that marriage was widely considered as basically a private matter even after ecclesiastical jurisdiction was established and the norm of indissolubility was fixed in canon law. In

---

61. Bassett, above, note 53 at 129–30; *Brissaud* 88–89; *Hübner* 614.

62. *Pollock and Maitland* 367.

63. *Rheinstein* 18.

64. Gratian is credited with beginning the application of scholastic methodology to the study of the sources of canon law. His Decretum of 1140, together with the Decretals of Pope Gregory IX of 1234, formed the core of the *Corpus Juris Canonici*, which was for centuries the official source of the positive law of the church. Bassett, above, note 53 at 130.

65. *Weber* 250–55.

other words, even when the Church's authority was securely established *vis-à-vis* political powers (which had never regulated marriage as such anyway), its norms had not yet fully penetrated the mores. The Church bided its time, winning social acceptance of its doctrines in much the same way as it had acquired jurisdiction, through a long patient process of action and interaction with everyday life. Meanwhile, the canon law of marriage assumed the form that was to be of such crucial importance for the future, even where and when, much later, the authority of the Church had been eroded.

Once the rule of indissolubility was established, an important consequence followed. It had to be spelled out in minute detail exactly which unions were of the type that now could not be dissolved, and outside of which all sexual intercourse was unlawful. *Marriage* had to be defined with more precision than ever before. Out of this need came the whole complex canon law system of marriage impediments and prohibitions. The multiplication of these causes of nullity in turn led to the need to investigate in advance of marriage whether impediments in fact existed and thus to the origin of the publication of the banns and the Church's increasing insistence on public marriage,[66] as well as to the elaboration of procedures for declaring marriages invalid. Since marriage between persons not under any impediment was based uniquely on consent, it became relevant to determine whether their consent had been real and free. The result was that the apparent rigidity of the principle of indissolubility was considerably mitigated in practice by the rules on consent and by the existence of a variety of potential grounds for annulment based on blood or in-law relationships, spiritual affinity (as between godparents and godchildren), impotence, insanity, and nonage. The proliferation of bases for annulment has been variously viewed as logically compelled by the theory of marriage; related to money and power in the sense that annulments gave the Church a source of revenue and a certain amount of control over families; a humane response to the desires of some individuals to escape from intolerable situations and to remarry; and a "safety valve," substituting for the necessary but missing institution of divorce. No doubt all these factors played a role.

The Church's own records show that the habit of contracting marriages informally continued, and reveal the stubborn persistence of older notions of marriage as a private matter. Richard Helmholz found, after studying records of thirteenth- and fifteenth-century marriage litigation in church courts in England, that it took a long time for the idea that people could regulate marriage

---

66. Prior to making public marriage a requirement, the canon law had developed a distinction between fully licit marriage and those informal marriages which were valid, but whose "illicit" character could subject the parties to public penance. Helmholz, above, note 57 at 178.

for themselves to disappear.[67] At the same time, however, he was able to trace a process, equally gradual, of social assimilation of the Church's standards and to document how much room for variety and growth there was within the canon law itself.

The Church alleviated the severity of its indissolubility rule by establishing a procedure for judicial separation as well as by providing many causes for annulment. Separation could be decreed in situations where one spouse had committed adultery, apostasy, or heresy, or had deserted or seriously mistreated the other. But unlike annulment, judicial separation did not permit the parties to remarry and does not seem to have been used on a large scale. Ecclesiastical separation from bed and board was, however, of immense significance for the shape that divorce law would one day take in Western societies. Foreshadowed itself by the grounds of justifiable repudiation in the imperial Roman decrees, the canon law of judicial separation prefigures that doctrine of divorce as a sanction for marital misconduct which reappeared in the ideas of the Protestant reformers and which dominated Western divorce law until the recent events described in chapter 4.

Tridentine Marriage Law

So far we have not discovered how the formation of marriage came to require, in nearly all Western legal systems, the presence of an official. Up to the time of the Council of Trent, the Church had only gone so far as to make a public blessing in church a religious duty, sanctioned by penance or censure. To find out why a public formal ceremony was made a condition for the *validity* of marriage (by the Decree *Tametsi* in 1563), we must look, not to ecclesiastical doctrine, but to pressures and events in the secular world.

In continental Reformation Europe, the stress under which the Church found itself, combined with social and economic changes that increasingly caused families in certain levels of society to seek control over the shifts of wealth and power that marriages could produce, prepared the way for a modification of the time-honored doctrine that Christian marriages could be formed by consent alone. This traditional doctrine, it should be noted, had the effect of liberating individuals from the constraints which parents, kinship groups, or political authorities might try to impose on their choice of spouses. But it was this very liberating effect which began to be perceived as troublesome in sixteenth-century Europe, in those circles where large amounts of money could change hands upon the right sort of marriage.

It had undoubtedly always been the case that so long as informal marriages

---

67. *Helmholz* 5. See also, Charles Donahue, "The Canon Law on the Formation of Marriage and Social Practice in the Later Middle Ages," 8 *Journal of Family History* 144 (1983).

were permitted, the difficulty of either proving or disproving them would allow some persons to slip out of the bonds of valid marriages, and others to profit through inheritance or in other ways by falsely alleging the existence of a secret marriage. This longstanding potential for abuse became an increasingly serious issue with the rise of the new economy and the appearance of the merchant class. Such secular concerns may explain in part why the same bishops who were the chief proponents of compulsory ceremonial marriage at the Council of Trent also endeavored to have the Council make parental consent an ecclesiastical marriage requirement.[68] The parental consent proposal conflicted too sharply with the Christian idea of marriage as a voluntary union to win approval, but after long and vigorous debate, the compulsory ceremony was accepted. The validity of informal marriage had been defended by theological purists, who maintained that one's spiritual liberty to marry or not should be protected from interference by others, particularly parents.[69] But this is just what troubled more pragmatic souls. The advocates of change claimed that informal marriages threatened property rights, and endangered social peace and private morality.[70]

The requirement of a public ceremony was eventually adopted by a close vote and embodied in the Decree *Tametsi* which provided that henceforth no marriage was valid which had not been celebrated in the presence of a priest and other witnesses. The Decree also mandated the publication of banns of marriage and the keeping of official records of marriages. Thus, the Church helped families at least to keep up with the marriage plans of their children, but it did not go so far as some delegates to the Council would have liked in reinforcing family control.

Those seeking legal support for parental control over marriage found a warmer response from the secular authorities in many places. A French royal edict of 1556 empowered parents to disinherit children who married without their consent and provided punishments for anyone assisting such a marriage.[71] After Martin Luther condemned clandestine marriages for enabling strangers to marry into wealthy families without prior parental approval and to obtain a share of estates, a minister's presence at weddings was made mandatory in the Reformation ordinances of the Protestant principality of Württemberg (1553) and the Palatinate of the Rhine (1563).[72] A similar ordinance was promulgated in Geneva in 1561.[73] In addition, all these ordinances re-

---

68. *Brissaud* 115.

69. Beatrice Gottlieb, "Getting Married in Pre-Reformation Europe: The Doctrine of Clandestine Marriage and Court Cases in Fifteenth-Century Champagne," (Ph.D. dissertation, Columbia University, 1974) 59–60, 62–63.

70. *Id.* 38–39.   72. Gottlieb, above, note 69 at 124–35.

71. *Hunt* 60.   73. *Id.*

quired couples to obtain the consents of their parents before they could marry. The validity of marriage was made dependent on parental consent in France by the Ordinance of Blois of 1579, and throughout the seventeenth century, French law continued in various other ways to try to discourage secret marriages.[74] England, however, long remained a case apart. The Church of England, which had deprived the Roman Catholic Church of jurisdiction over matrimonial causes in 1534, continued to recognize informal marriages as valid until 1753.

It seems likely that the Decree *Tametsi* and all its secular counterparts had little effect on the marriage practices of persons other than the well-to-do. And even in the circles of the affluent, the social historian David Hunt found a persistent

> conflict between public legislation on the one hand and generally accepted popular custom and usage on the other. The edicts and ordinances clearly show that legists recognized the strength of the tradition they were trying to uproot: the continuing belief that cohabitation, simple mutual consent, made a marriage.[75]

The Church, as we have noted, did not even try to impose its new ceremonial marriage requirement on all the peoples in all the territories subject to its influence. *Tametsi*, by its terms, was not effective where it was not promulgated, and the Church made no effort to enforce it in places like the New World, where priests were scarce. Thus informal marriages continued to be valid under canon law in many parts of the world until a decree of Leo XIII in 1892, followed by the decree *Ne Temere*, which went into effect in 1907. Even today, canon law still recognizes the validity of informal marriages under certain circumstances.[76]

Reformation and Secularization

The history of canon law up to the Council of Trent discloses how marriage was gradually brought under a kind of official and legal regulation, namely, that of the Church courts applying canon law. We find the beginnings of legal indissolubility in the establishment of the sacramental character of marriage, and we see the origin of compulsory ceremonial marriage in the movement from blessing at the church door to the banning of clandestine marriage. But how did these matters become concerns of the secular authorities who previously had been largely indifferent to them? From the sixteenth to the eigh-

---

74. *Hunt* 62.
75. *Id.* 63. See also *Gaudemet* 235–36, 364.
76. See above, Coriden et al., eds., at notes 12 and 13.

teenth century, in great parts of Western Europe, the Catholic Church lost its jurisdiction over marriage. In Protestant regions this occurred as a consequence of the Reformation, and in France it took place in connection with Gallicanism and the progress of the monarchy. When the Church lost its monopoly over matrimonial causes, the newly emerging states acquired jurisdiction more or less by default. Rather than develop an entirely new body of law · to apply in such cases, secular governments simply took over much of the ready-made set of rules of the canon law, modeling their new divorce law on the ecclesiastical rules governing separation from bed and board.[77] Thus, many rules which had been developed in the canon law continued to govern marriage, although they received new interpretations on certain points.

This is not surprising when we recall that, although Luther and others had claimed that marriage was properly subjected to the control of civil, rather than church, courts, they never dreamed that it would be regulated according to other than Christian principles.[78] The reformers rejected the notion that marriage was a sacrament, but they took for granted that secular marriage regulations should conform to Christian teaching.[79] Christian teaching was, of course, reinterpreted by them to permit divorce as a punishment for grave violation of marital duties—for adultery in particular, but gradually for other causes as well. Even the significance of this well-known instance of departure from Catholic doctrine should not be exaggerated, however, for it was accompanied by a tightening up of nullity, which the Church had at times offered rather freely.[80] Protestantism did not return divorce to the private order by any means: no divorce by mutual consent was recognized, and divorce for cause had to be granted by the state. Only with the Enlightenment did a true antithesis to traditional Christian attitudes toward marriage begin to appear.

Awareness of how the Reformation brought matrimonial affairs under the jurisdiction of the secular state in many places helps us to understand how much of the law described in chapters 2 and 4 of this book (marriage formation and dissolution) acquired its original shape. However, we have yet to learn how the state came to devise its own secular norms of law, rather than merely retaining ecclesiastical norms. In addition, we still have no answer to the question of how secular law came to regulate, or at least to purport to regulate, a matter from which both canon and Roman law had abstained,

77. *I Esmein* 34.

78. See for a detailed and well-documented discussion of the relationship between the Lutheran reformers' law of marriage and the preexisting canon law, John Witte, Jr., "The Reformation of Marriage Law in Martin Luther's Germany: Its Significance Then and Now," 4 *Journal of Law and Religion* 1 (1986).

79. *Rheinstein* 22.

80. Witte, above, note 78 at 38–44.

namely, the organization and conduct of family life, the subject considered in chapter 3. That body of law has its origin in two developments for which the Protestant reformers cannot be held responsible, although in a sense they helped pave the way. These are the appearance of the humanistic and individualistic thought of the Enlightenment and the rise of the absolutist state. The developments occurred in different fashion in France and the various regions of Germany, but led in both places to unprecedented attempts at legal regulation of ongoing family relationships. England, once again, remained in this respect a special case, and so, in consequence, did the United States.

On the continent, Frederick II of Prussia, Joseph II of Austria, Napoleon, and their legal scholars and bureaucratic administrators felt the need for a clear and complete codification of all private law.[81] Further, these rulers were in a position to impose their own ideas (or those of their advisors) as rules of positive law in their codes. To be sure, the new secular law of the Enlightenment-era codes borrowed extensively from pre-existing law, just as the reformed Protestant church had drawn heavily on canon law. But marriage law, cut loose from its religious moorings in the established medieval order, increasingly began to be affected by the trends of the times, by humanism and individualism, as well as by the practical concerns and interests of the secular state and the influential groups within it.[82]

With Reformation and Enlightenment, the idea of marriage as a contract took a new turn. As we have seen, consent was the essence of marriage in ecclesiastical law. But thinkers as diverse as Martin Luther and John Locke began to emphasize the aspect of marriage as a civil contract. This was a point of view that appealed especially to the French revolutionaries who were eager to eliminate the last vestiges of ecclesiastical jurisdiction. Several consequences followed from accentuation of the contractual aspect of marriage, the most important of which were laying the groundwork for divorce by mutual consent and for state regulation not only of the formation and dissolution of the marriage contract, but of its very content. The great continental codifications enclosed the spouses in a network of legal rights and duties that gave each spouse a full set of claims against the other that could be made the basis of legal action before a judge.[83] Indeed, some of these codes purported to regulate the smallest details of the most intimate relationships in a way unknown to Roman and canon law. Sometimes these extremes of juridification were in furtherance of some interest of the state (such as increasing population); sometimes they served the interests of dominant groups in society (as by reinforcing family control over marriages). Often they seem to have been

81. *Rheinstein* at 25–26.   82. *Müller-Freienfels*, 18–25.
83. *Id.* at 20–21.

merely the result of that urge for completeness so evident in other aspects of, say, the Prussian General Code of 1794.[84] In the endeavor not to leave any gaps whatever in the law, the Prussian Code pronounced on such matters as when marital intercourse may be declined, when the absence of a spouse from home is excused, and until what age a baby can be nursed in the parents' bed. Jean Carbonnier coined the word *panjurism* to describe this legal ethos pervaded by the idea that everything is law, or "at least that law has a vocation to be everywhere, to envelop everything, and, like a god, to hold up the entire inhabited world."[85]

In France, the penchant for legislative regulation during this period gave rise to the development of two important modern institutions affecting the family: the compulsory civil marriage ceremony and the system of comprehensive public registration of civil status. The civil marriage ceremony had been available as an option in the Calvinist Netherlands and in New England, but it was made mandatory by a French revolutionary decree of 20 September 1792. From France, the civil ceremony spread all over the world, as at least an optional method of marrying. France also furnished the model for the systems of secular registration of civil status which are now in worldwide use.[86] Unlike many other innovations of French revolutionary law, the compulsory civil marriage was carried forward by the Napoleonic Code of 1804. Early in the nineteenth century, civil marriage was made compulsory in various regions of Germany, becoming part of the law of the unified German empire by the Personal Status Law of 6 February 1875, and taking its present form in the German Civil Code of 1896.

As mentioned, England followed a somewhat different course. The ecclesiastical jurisdiction of the Church of England over marriage continued without significant interference until the middle of the nineteenth century. Briefly under Cromwell, it seems, civil marriage was available, and divorce may have been permitted. But with that brief exception, civil marriage did not appear in England until 1836—in connection with the passage of a spate of bureaucratic legislation concerning registration of vital statistics. Informal marriages remained valid in England until Lord Hardwicke's Act in 1753. This statute, a secular version of the Decree *Tametsi*, made an ecclesiastical marriage ceremony compulsory and required publication of the banns. Divorce became available after 1660, but could be obtained only by special parliamentary act,

84. *Id.* at 22–23.
85. *Carbonnier, Flexible Droit* 24.
86. The forerunner of state registration of civil status, in France and elsewhere, was ecclesiastical record-keeping (baptismal records, marriage records, etc.), followed in many places by a stage of governmental regulation of church registers, *Rheinstein* 198; see also below, chapter 2, text at note 167.

and then only for adultery. It was expensive, complicated, and rarely used. Judicial divorce was not introduced until 1857.

In the United States, those areas settled by Protestants had divorce laws from early times, while those with a strong Anglican influence initially had no divorce at all. Legislative divorce survived in many colonies and states into the nineteenth century. The Western frontier states took a more liberal approach, with the result that by 1860 migratory divorce was already part of the American scene. Because of the English legal background (and in the Southwest with the indulgence of the Church),[87] informal marriage became an established legal institution in some places, and still survives as "common law marriage" in several states.

The processes of secularization of marriage jurisdiction and eventually of the content of marriage law coincided with certain tendencies in legal thought which were to reach their high point in the nineteenth century. In both the common law and civil law worlds of the late nineteenth century, legal norms and concepts tended to be formalized and expressed in the conceptualistic way that had been typical of revived Roman law and the canon law. Legal rules, which often were but the temporary resolution of conflicting interests, acquired a life of their own, producing "logical" and "necessary" consequences. At the same time, the notion of *legitimacy* was increasingly coming to be identified with *legality*, understood as the quality of enactments which are formally correct and issued according to established procedures.[88]

The idea that legitimacy can be conferred by law, however, is by no means self-evident. Family behavior in pre-modern societies was long oriented to ideas of legitimacy that were embodied in custom, convention, and religion. For centuries after legal norms appeared on the scene, they expressed ideas about family life that were customary and religious in origin. Yet, just as custom can in time become law, so law to some extent can acquire the force of tradition. As Daniel Lev has pointed out, "In the nature of legal systems, concepts and structures developed in one age carry over as myth thereafter, transforming what once were straightforward matters of interest and power into principles and habits."[89] But as the bureaucratic, secular state has increasingly injected its own content and pursued its own aims in family law, the relationship between legality and legitimacy has become ever more problematic.

87. See, generally, Hans Baade, "The Form of Marriage in Spanish North America," 61 *Cornell Law Review* 1 (1975).

88. *Weber* 9.

89. Daniel S. Lev, "Colonial Law and the Genesis of the Indonesian State," 40 *Indonesia* 57, 69 (October 1985).

2

Formation of Legal Marriage

> Much of what I . . . shall have to relate, may perhaps, I am aware, seem
> petty trifles to record. . . . Still it will not be useless to study those at first
> sight trifling events out of which the movements of vast changes often take
> their rise.
>
> Tacitus, *Annals* 4.32.

In none of the four countries whose law is examined in this book has there
been any recent change in the rules of positive law governing the formation
of marriage that deserves to be singled out as of overriding importance. There
has been no wave of thoroughgoing revision, as happened with divorce law
in the 1960s and 1970s, and no sudden reversal of principle such as occurred
with the legal position of children born outside legal marriage. For the most
part, the law concerning an individual's eligibility to enter the married state,
the permissible range of choice of spouses, and the preliminaries and procedures required to conclude a legally valid marriage, has remained relatively
stable. What change there has been has mainly involved adjustment of age
and parental consent requirements, or waiting periods, or administrative matters. The picture is one of many small changes, unremarkable in themselves,
but together signaling a major transition in the way modern legal systems
intersect with marriage behavior. One aspect of this shift, a significant deregulation of the formation of marriage, might be seen as an indication of the
declining importance of marriage as a determinant of social standing and economic security in modern societies. Another aspect is that, somewhat paradoxically, the same developments that represent a withdrawal of state interest
in the formation of marriage have prefigured and culminated in the legal recognition of marriage as a basic human right.

Viewed in their historical context, the apparently trifling changes described
in this chapter are the culmination of a long series of events that, beginning
around 1800, gradually freed individuals from most constraints on their
ability to marry or on their choice of marriage partner.[1] Strict parental and
family consent requirements designed to give families control over the admis-

---

1. The development of French and German family law from the time of the Prussian General
Code of 1794 and the French Civil Code of 1804 through the Industrial Revolution is traced in
the valuable book by Heinrich Dörner, *Industrialisierung und Familienrecht* (Berlin: Duncker &
Humblot, 1974). For the larger context of the modernization of private law generally in this
period, see Franz Wieacker, *Privatrechtsgeschichte der Neuzeit*, 2d ed. (Göttingen: Vandenhoeck
& Ruprecht, 1967), 348–586.

sion of new members began to be established in European laws in the mid-sixteenth century and were the subject of elaborate regulation in the codes of the Enlightenment period, such as the Prussian General Code of 1794 and the French Civil Code of 1804. Over the course of the nineteenth century, these consent requirements began to be relaxed. Certain other constraints on marriage which had been established less in response to concerns of propertied families than according to various conceptions of the public interest began to disappear too. The latter type of restriction had sometimes taken the form of legislation directed against marriages of paupers.[2] Other such laws had sought to protect the financial independence and social respectability of army officers and high civil servants by requiring that they obtain permission to marry from their superiors. Still another type of official interest appeared in the early twentieth century, particularly in the United States, where many states adopted laws directed against the marriages of persons with epilepsy, tuberculosis, alcoholism, or venereal disease.[3] Today, most of these health-related statutes have disappeared, or their prohibitions have been replaced by the simple requirement of a premarital examination for venereal disease. The eugenic marriage legislation of National Socialist Germany, which tried to weed out those deemed racially, physically, or mentally unfit for marriage,[4] has vanished without a trace.

In all respects, the transformation of marriage law has taken place through small steps. But in recent years the difference between the extensive regulation of marriage formation, which was once taken as self-evident, and the minimal controls which now exist has become so great that the idea of a basic individual right to marry has emerged. If one looks to contemporary constitutional pronouncements, to the scholarly writing, and to the law reform proposals put forth in France, the United States, and West Germany, it is clear that a banner has been raised over the slowly shifting minutiae of marriage law. The banner is one of the gaily-colored pennants of the pursuit of happiness, and the words inscribed on it are "Freedom to Marry" and "Marriage—A Basic Human Right." Thus, the changes, though small and gradual, have been given a certain direction and impetus in those countries. In England, the law seems to be subject to the same influences as elsewhere, but these influences so far have not been sloganized.

2. These laws are described in Klaus-Jürgen Matz, *Pauperismus und Bevölkerung* (Stuttgart: Klett-Cotta, 1981).

3. Chester G. Vernier, *American Family Laws* (Stanford: Stanford University Press, 1931), vol. 1, §43.

4. See, generally, Magdalene Schoch, "Divorce Law and Practice under National Socialism in Germany," 28 *Iowa Law Review* 225 (1943); see also Karl Loewenstein, "Law in the Third Reich," 45 *Yale Law Journal* 779, 797 (1936).

   This chapter examines the current evolution of American, English, French, and West German law concerning the formation of marriage. Since the object is to explore the nature of the interest of modern states in marriage formation, the selection and organization of material here does not follow the conventional pattern of legal treatises, in which the law of marriage formation is usually presented either in conjunction with, or with a view toward resolving, questions regarding the validity of a marriage. Here, in order to see more clearly what recent changes in the law reveal about the relationship of the state to the family, we will examine first those aspects of marriage formation law which pertain to one's ability to enter legal marriage (who may get married); second, the law relating to the choice and number of spouses (who may marry whom); third, compulsory premarital procedures; fourth, compulsory formalities for the solemnization of marriage; and finally, the emergence of legal expressions of the ideology of freedom to marry.

   Reference will be made here to the sanctions for nonobservance of legal norms only where they give some clue as to the weight of the policy which a particular norm represents. Thus, the following discussion of "state-imposed limitations" and "compulsory procedures" will focus on which marriage prohibitions, preconditions, and rites have been cast as legal rules and how some of these rules or their sanctions have recently changed. The violation of a given norm may prevent a legal marriage from coming into existence at all (as seems so far to be the case with same-sex marriages in all four countries). It may make the marriage voidable upon the application of one of the parties or even occasionally upon the application of certain other persons (as is sometimes the case with the marriage of underage persons). It may entail criminal sanctions as well as the voidability of the marriage (as is often the case with bigamy or incest). Without affecting the validity of the marriage, it may entail penal sanctions for those who knowingly violate the norm (as is sometimes the case when an unauthorized official celebrates the marriage). Finally, it may entail no legal sanctions for the parties at all (as when a couple marries before expiration of a statutory waiting period between the termination of a prior marriage and entry into a new one). Where the sanction for nonobservance of a norm is the voidability of the marriage, the nullity of the marriage may be absolute or relative. That is, certain marriages in violation of legal norms may be declared null simply upon proof that the norm was violated, and the decree of nullity will operate retroactively. Others are valid until voided, and will usually be declared null only if certain conditions other than violation of the norm are present: the suit must be brought by the proper party, within a specified period of time, and no events curing the defect must have intervened.

Who May Marry

Legal Eligibility in General

All of the legal systems here examined carefully avoid imposing conditions concerning personal characteristics which would tend to rule out completely the possibility of marriage for certain people. Those provisions which do limit a person's legal eligibility to marry tend not to do so definitively. Rather, they prescribe that a certain age must be reached, a preliminary consent must be obtained, a waiting period observed, or the condition which has prevented the person from marrying must be cured.

Thus, various mental conditions which are or can be permanent do not in principle prevent a person so afflicted from marrying. All four systems of marriage law are based on the premise that marriage is a consensual union. Consequently, a consent which is defective because of mental disease or deficiency affects the validity of the marriage.[5] But the provisions governing the matter are everywhere characterized by their leniency and their tendency to promote the validity of the marriage. In the first place, the mental capacity required for marriage is minimal, often described as less than that required for the transaction of business.[6] Second, if a marriage is to be invalidated for want of consent, it must be proved that the ability to consent was lacking at the precise moment the marriage was celebrated.[7] Proof of the mental condition at an earlier or later time will not in itself suffice. Finally, even if defective consent at the time of marriage can be proved, the parties who are permitted to avoid the marriage and the time within which they must act are limited.[8] In the United States, restrictions on marriage based on physical[9] or mental capacity have been called into question as possible infringements of the right to marry recognized by the United States Supreme Court in 1967.[10]

5. **England**: *Cretney* 72; **France**: French Civil Code art. 146 ("There is no marriage where there is no consent."); **United States**: *Clark* 102; **West Germany**: *EheG* §2.

6. *Cretney* 73; *Labrusse-Riou* 45. But the consent of a conservator or guardian may be required for certain individuals: *Labrusse-Riou* 45; EheG §3.

7. *Cretney* 73; *Labrusse-Riou* 39; *Beitzke* 44.

8. *Cretney* 72–81; *Labrusse-Riou* 73–79; *Gernhuber* 131–46; *Clark* 92–95; UMDA §208 (1).

9. Only a few American states still have marriage impediments based on physical conditions such as venereal disease. *E.g.*, Michigan Comp. Laws Ann. §551.6 (West 1967); Nebraska Rev. Stat. §42–102 (1984). In England at one time incapacity to consummate the marriage was treated as an impediment. See *Cretney* 63–67. The trend now is to treat conditions such as impotence or communicable venereal disease as grounds for voiding the marriage if they were unknown to the other party at the time of marriage and if they are raised within a reasonable time after the marriage.

10. Henry H. Foster, "Marriage: A 'Basic Civil Right of Man,'" 37 *Fordham L. Rev.* 51,64 (1968).

The draftsmen of the Uniform Marriage and Divorce Act of 1970 (UMDA) concluded that even the purely informational premarital medical examination required in many states served no useful purpose, although they did make it the subject of an optional subsection.[11] The spread of the AIDS virus in the 1980s, however, made this sort of requirement once again the subject of debate. In France, a premarital medical examination, including blood testing for sexually transmitted diseases, is compulsory, but its results are shown only to the person examined, not to the other party to the marriage, nor to any public official.[12] The purpose of the French requirement is simply to ensure that each prospective spouse is well informed about his or her state of health and receives certain information bearing on the transmission of genetic defects.[13] There is no requirement of a premarital medical examination in England or West Germany.

Only a few laws and administrative regulations remain which require certain categories of persons to obtain official permission to marry.[14] Most regulation of remarriage is also dying out. However, in France and West Germany a woman is still prohibited from marrying within a time, roughly corresponding in length to the gestation period, dating from legal separation or dissolution of her previous marriage, unless she has meanwhile given birth or can produce a doctor's certificate stating that she is not pregnant.[15] This rule,

11. UMDA §203 and Comment thereto. The Uniform Marriage and Divorce Act (UMDA) was recommended in 1970 by the National Conference of Commissioners on Uniform State Laws as a model for adoption in all states. It was approved (after amendments in 1971 and 1973) by the American Bar Association in 1974. The provisions of UMDA are the focal point of the discussion of American law in this chapter because they are typical of the type of change which had already taken place in the various states as they modernized their marriage law and because they have been the principal model available for states that have since revised their law of marriage formation.

12. French Civil Code art. 63. *Labrusse-Riou* 64.

13. *Labrusse-Riou* 64–65.

14. In the **United States**, a regulation prohibiting prisoners from marrying unless the prison superintendent grants them permission after finding that there are compelling reasons for doing so has been held to be an unconstitutional burden on the prisoners' right to marry. *Turner v. Safely*, 107 S. Ct. 2254 (1987). In so holding, the Court indicated that some restrictions on inmates' marriages might be appropriate if reasonably related to security and rehabilitation concerns. In **England**, under the Royal Marriages Act 1772, the consent of the Sovereign is required for the marriage of the descendants of George II. But as the Act exempts the issue of princesses who have married into foreign families, it seems that there are few if any members of the royal family to whom it still applies. *Cretney* 15, n. 30. In **France**, all military personnel on active duty, and members of the diplomatic corps had to obtain administrative authorization to marry until 1972 and 1980, respectively. Military personnel must still obtain permission to marry if their prospective spouse is not a French national or if they are serving abroad. *Labrusse-Riou* 47.

15. French Civil Code arts. 228, 296; West German *EheG* §8. This prohibition does not apply in France in cases where the divorce was granted on the ground that the marriage has been

carried forward from the Prussian General Code of 1794 and the French Civil Code of 1804, was supposed to prevent "confusion of paternity" arising from the interplay of legal presumptions. In both France and West Germany, the prohibitions are now deprived of most of their force by liberal policies of dispensation and by the fact that marriages contracted in violation of them are valid.[16] But, curiously, when the divorce law was completely overhauled in both France and West Germany in the 1970s, the remarriage restrictions were retained, despite their anachronistic character and their uneasy fit with the principle of sexual equality.

In the United States, the Uniform Marriage and Divorce Act contains no restrictions on remarriage such as those sometimes found in older state laws imposing a delay before a "guilty" party could remarry or a waiting period before the divorce decree became final. But another, more modern, type of state interest in remarriage surfaced briefly in a Wisconsin statute requiring persons subject to child-support orders to obtain judicial permission to marry or remarry. Even if it had not been held unconstitutional,[17] the statute would probably have had little practical effect, since it could not prevent such persons from marrying in another state or acquiring new dependents without benefit of marriage.

An exception to the general trend of reduced official involvement in the question of who may marry still exists regarding the age at which one may marry. State regulation of this subject remains extensive, but the basis of regulation has shifted from the reinforcement of family participation in (and sometimes control of) the marriage decision to societal concern about the risks supposedly involved in youthful marriages. Age restrictions are typically justified by reference to the welfare of the young persons themselves and any offspring they may have, in view of the high divorce rates generally reported for early marriages.[18] But even here a minimalist approach prevails. In the late 1960s and early 1970s, England, France, West Germany, and most American states, set eighteen years as the age of marriage without parental consent for both men and women. For the most part this represented a *lowering* of the age, although in some places it has meant raising the age for women.

Current regulation of the age of marriage is more an expression of what the legislature and possibly society at large deem an appropriate minimum age

---

"disrupted" for at least six years by separation or by the mental illness of one spouse. French Civil Code art. 228.

16. *Beitzke* 54; *Labrusse-Riou* 70.

17. *Zablocki v. Redhail*, 434 U.S. 374 (1978).

18. *Beitzke* 43; *Cretney* 58.

than an actual impediment to early marriage. Most age requirements are subject to broad exceptions, and the sanctions for their violation are limited. Meanwhile, in practice, the median age at which a first marriage takes place has been gradually drifting upward in recent years. It is well above the legal minimum in the countries with which we are here concerned.[19] At the same time, especially in the United States, mounting concern with teenage pregnancy has virtually eclipsed worry about the fragility of teenage marriages.

Age of Marriage

France

In the original scheme of the French Civil Code of 1804 the parents' consent to a marriage had to be obtained, on pain of nullity, by women up to age twenty-one and by men up to age twenty-five.[20] Even after the parties had passed the ages at which consent was required, they were legally obliged to solicit the consent of their parents through formal requests known as *actes respectueux*.[21] Three such requests had to be made by men under thirty and women under twenty-five, and men and women above these ages—no matter how old—still had to make one such request so long as a parent was living to hear it. After each request, a month had to pass to await an answer. So, in cases where three requests were required, the wedding could be held up for three months—time for the "child" to think it over, to be subjected to family pressure, and perhaps to abandon his or her plans. The Civil Code draftsmen brought forward these consent rules from the prerevolutionary law because they seemed a necessary feature of a system in which marriage created responsibilities on the part of the family of origin of each spouse and potentially involved the dispersal of family wealth. The degree to which the extended family could be implicated in any given marriage decision can still be seen in the complicated provisions governing consent where a parent or close relative is not available.[22]

In the early part of the twentieth century, much of this legal reinforcement of family control was dropped. The age at which a person could marry with-

19. In the United States, for example, the median age of persons marrying for the first time in 1986 was 23.1 for women and 25.7 for men. U.S. Dept. of Commerce, Bureau of the Census, *Marital Status and Living Arrangements: March 1986*, CPR Series P-20, No. 418 (December 1987).

20. Alain Bénabent, "La Liberté individuelle et le mariage," 1973 *Revue trimestrielle de droit civil* 440, 449.

21. *II Carbonnier* 60–61.

22. French Civil Code arts. 149–60 spell out in detail the formalities and procedures to follow if parents or other relatives are dead, or incapable of consenting, or cannot be found, or where the child is adopted or illegitimate.

out consent was lowered to twenty-one for both spouses in 1907. The *actes respectueux* became simple notice requirements in the same year (but were not abolished entirely until 1933). For persons under twenty-one, consents became much easier to obtain in 1927 when the Civil Code was amended to provide that in case of disagreement between mother and father, the division of opinion would be equivalent to consent. Previously, the father's refusal would block the marriage even if the mother had consented. In 1974, the age of majority (and thus the age at which one can marry without first obtaining parental consent) was reduced from twenty-one to eighteen.[23] The ages of legal capacity to marry *with* the requisite consents are fifteen for the female partner, and eighteen for the male.[24] Even these minimum age requirements of fifteen and eighteen can be dispensed with "for serious reasons."[25] Pregnancy is usually deemed to be a sufficient reason.[26] The procedure for seeking such dispensations (once available only from the head of state) was simplified in 1968, when the fee was lowered, and again in 1970, when the power to dispense was transferred from the president of the republic to local authorities.[27]

Although there has been a steady liberalization of its parental consent requirements, French law on this point remains the most strict of the four countries here examined. At present, if both parents refuse permission for the marriage, minors have no option to seek permission from a court, as they can do in England, West Germany, and in most of the United States. Although French courts have no power to grant dispensations in such cases, they have shown their disapproval of certain instances of parental withholding or revoking of consent (at least when the marriage age was twenty-one) by awarding damages against an obstinate parent for "abuse of right."[28]

An interesting survival from the scheme of 1804 is the system of formal objections (*oppositions*) to marriage.[29] The opposition is a procedure for formal notification to the appropriate officials that a legal obstacle exists to a projected marriage. Once an objection has been filed by a person legally permitted to do so, the marriage cannot proceed until the opposition has been lifted by a court order. Thus, even a poorly founded claim can be a tactic of

23. Law No. 74–631 of 5 July 1974 (J.O. 7 July 1974, p. 7099). French Civil Code arts. 148, 388, 488.

24. French Civil Code art. 144.

25. French Civil Code art. 145.

26. *Bénabent* 51.

27. Art. 145 of the Civil Code as modified by Law no. 70–1266 of 23 Dec. 1970. See Bénabent, above, note 20 at 451.

28. *Id.* at 451.

29. French Civil Code arts. 172–79.

last resort for parents who feel that time is on their side. The system has largely fallen into disuse, and the Commission for the Reform of the Civil Code has proposed that the right to file objections should be limited to the *ministère public*, who would be informed by interested persons of the legal barrier to the marriage.[30]

Elaborate as all these rules concerning age of marriage are, the sanctions for violating them are not severe. A marriage of a girl under fifteen or a youth under eighteen is valid until declared null by a court. The defect in such a marriage can be cured by the attainment of majority by the underage party or by the pregnancy of the female partner.[31] A marriage in violation of the consent provisions can be nullified only upon the suit of the parties or the person whose consent was required within one year from the attainment of the age of majority by the underage party or parties, or within one year of the discovery of the marriage by the person whose consent was required.[32]

West Germany

The pattern of evolution of German law on marriage age is most clearly seen if we begin, not with the German Civil Code of 1896, but with that one of its antecedents which has been termed the first modern code, the Prussian General Code of 1794.[33] Like the nearly contemporaneous Code Napoleon, it broke with the idea that parents should be permitted to impose the family's choice of spouse upon their child. Instead, like the French code, the Prussian Code contained an elaborate system of rules obliging a child to get parental or family permission to marry the person of his or her *own* choice.

Nearly a century later, work began on a civil code for a unified Germany. By this time, social and economic changes had already diminished the influence which most parents could in fact exert on their children's choice of spouse as well as the interest of the older generation in maintaining legal structures more appropriate to an earlier mode of social organization. This was already evident in an 1875 law which eliminated the requirement of parental consents to marriage in the case of a daughter over twenty-four and a son over twenty-five.[34]

---

30. *Labrusse-Riou* 73. Recently, however, the ancient system was pressed into service by a father who wished to prevent his daughter from marrying a transsexual. Paris Court of Appeal Decision of 17 February 1984, D. 1984. Jur. 350, note by M.-L. Rassat.

31. French Civil Code art. 185.

32. French Civil Code art. 182, 183.

33. The *Allgemeines Landrecht für die Preussischen Staaten* (ALR) was a project especially favored by Emperor Frederick II of Prussia. It became law in 1794, eight years after his death. *Rheinstein* 25.

34. Dörner, above, note 1 at 94, 95.

Nevertheless, the second draft of the German Civil Code of 1896 required parental consent for both sons and daughters up to age twenty-five, even though the age of majority for other purposes was set at twenty-one. The draftsmen attempted to justify the consent requirement, not by reference to the duty of the parents as custodians to protect the interests of their children, but on the basis of the children's duty to observe filial respect and piety.[35] After debate on this draft, however, the Reichstag decided to make the age of capacity to marry without consent the same as the age of legal majority. The arguments that carried the day were not based on the theoretical inconsistency of having different ages of majority for different purposes, but on social and economic considerations. It was pointed out that the pattern of economic relationships of a great part of the population was not one of dependence of young adults on their parents. Many persons aged twenty-one and even younger were in fact self-supporting, often contributing to the subsistence of their families of origin and in a position to found a family themselves.[36] The notion surfaced, too, that legal reinforcement of parental authority in this area was irreconcilable with the modern ideal of marriage for love, irrespective of the wealth and social position of the partners.[37]

What had happened between the second draft and the Code provisions as eventually adopted was the acceptance of a new conception of marriage. The draft had been more responsive to the views of those to whom a child's marriage had significance for property and other interests of the family of origin, while the Code made the interests of the couple central. At the same time that the Civil Code marked another stage in the decline of parental control generally, it represented the beginning of legal attention in Germany to the interests of wide groups of the population in which economic dependence on parents ended early and substantial property did not pass from generation to generation.

The family law of the National Socialist period briefly brought about a lowering of the age of majority for men to eighteen for marriage purposes.[38] But after World War II it was changed back to twenty-one by the Marriage Law of the Allied Control Council of 1946. The age of legal majority was changed again in West Germany in 1974 (the same year it was changed in France) to make both men and women legally free to marry without parental consent at eighteen.[39] Under the 1974 law, a minor requires the consent of his

35. *Id.* at 96.
36. *Id.*
37. *Id.*
38. *Marriage Law of Greater Germany* of 6 July 1938, RGBl. 1.807 §1.
39. Law of 31 July 1974, effective 1 January 1975, BGBl. I 1713, amending *inter alia* the West German Ehegesetz (EheG) §1. See generally, *Gernhuber* 89–91.

legal representative in order to marry below the age of eighteen.[40] West Germany differs from France, in that the consent of both parents is in principle required, but if the consent of the parents or legal representative is withheld without substantial reason, the minor may request a dispensation from the guardianship court.[41] But dispensation of one party from the basic requirement of having reached majority is available only if the other party to the prospective marriage has reached majority and the party seeking dispensation has reached the age of sixteen.[42] This, too, represents a change from the prior law, under which a man could marry with dispensation from the age requirements only if he had reached eighteen, while dispensation was available to the female partner even if she was under sixteen.[43]

With respect to the raising of both the age of marriage and consent for the female partner, the 1974 reform was in part motivated by concern that young women should not impair their life prospects through premature marriage.[44] As in France, dispensation from the age requirements has been given commonly for the reason that a child is expected, but not without uneasiness about treating marriage as the automatic solution to this problem.[45] In view of the facts that early marriages in West Germany, as elsewhere, are especially prone to end in divorce; that the children of divorced parents can be as disadvantaged as nonmarital children; and that the personal development and education of the minor spouse may be impaired by the marriage, the courts try to determine in each case whether the marriage is desirable, taking into account both the interests of the prospective parents and the welfare of the expected child.[46]

England

The characteristic of English law concerning age of marriage which has consistently differentiated it from the French and German patterns of regulation is its restraint in dealing with the whole question. In the past, there was no such elaborate system of legally reinforced family control of or participation in the marriage decision in England as there had been in the Prussian General Code or the French Civil Code. Currently, English family law specialists seem inclined to doubt that law is an effective means for discouraging youthful marriages, which are, in any event, increasingly atypical in England as elsewhere in the developed world.

The seeming indifference of English law to matters which were once

---

40. Where the legal representative does not have the care of the person of the minor, or where there is another custodian besides him, the consent of the custodian is also required by EheG §3.

41. EheG §3.   42. EheG §1.

43. *Beitzke* 43.   44. *Id.*

45. *Id.*   46. *Gernhuber* 90–91.

viewed as crucial in continental law is of long standing. In *The Spirit of the Laws*, Montesquieu noted the divergence of the English customs from those which prevailed in eighteenth-century France:

> In England the law is frequently abused by the daughters marrying according to their own fancy without consulting their parents. This custom is, I am apt to imagine, more tolerated there than anywhere else from a consideration that as the laws have not established a monastic celibacy, the daughters have no other state to choose but that of marriage, and this they cannot refuse. In France, on the other hand, young women have always the resource of celibacy.[47]

The main difference between England and France in this respect, however, was that England had left the regulation of marriage primarily to other agents of social control, notably the Church of England, which had its own ecclesiastical rules and regulations for matrimonial matters. It is true that until the middle of the eighteenth century, a valid marriage could still be contracted in England by an informal present exchange of consents. But by then it had long been customary for marriages to be celebrated in church and for the Church authorities to require the consent of parents of parties under twenty-one.[48] These practices became legal requirements in 1753 when Lord Hardwicke's Act was passed, partly in response to the concerns of well-to-do parents of daughters and partly in pursuit of the more modern objectives of bringing the family behavior of the poor under more control and regulating the marriage mills in the Fleet district of London.[49]

Lord Hardwicke's Act was not completely effective in putting a stop to marriages without parental consent. Many couples evaded it simply by marrying in Scotland.[50] However, as Friedrich Engels observed, commenting on the relative leniency of English marriage law, there is more than one way to influence a child's marriage decision: in England, although children could marry without consent, their parents were legally free to disinherit them; in France and Germany on the other hand, where parental consent was required, children could not, in principle, be disinherited.[51] So long as English property

47. Montesquieu, *The Spirit of the Laws*, Book 23. Ch. 9, trans. Thomas Nugent (New York: Hafner Press, 1949). (First published 1748.)

48. *Bromley* 27.

49. For a highly informative discussion of marriage practices in eighteenth-century England and an analysis of Lord Hardwicke's Act as marking the beginning of state intervention in the family in England, see Stephen Parker, "The Marriage Act 1753: A Case Study of Family Law-Making," 1 *International Journal of Law and the Family* 133 (1987).

50. *Bromley* 28.

51. Friedrich Engels, *The Origin of the Family, Private Property and the State*, ed. E. B. Leacock (New York: International Publishers, 1972), 136. (First published 1882.)

law permitted and even facilitated indirect control of the marriage decision by such devices as the strict family settlement, well-to-do families had less need for direct control through marriage law.

In present-day England, the age of capacity to marry is sixteen for both sexes. Consent of both parents is required for persons between sixteen and eighteen.[52] Persons over eighteen can marry without consent. With respect to the age of capacity, it was only in 1929 that one had to have reached age sixteen. Until then, the ages of capacity had long been fixed at fourteen for a boy and twelve for a girl. The reason for the change in 1929 seems to have had little to do either with issues of parental authority or with concern about marriages among the twelve- and fourteen-year-old population. It must have seemed to be a prudent step at the time since Great Britain was then actively engaged in a League of Nations effort to outlaw child marriage in what were considered to be less civilized parts of the world.[53] Occasional suggestions to raise the age still higher in view of the increased chance that an early marriage would end in divorce have not met with much enthusiasm.[54] There is at present no dispensation available from the minimum age requirement.

As to the age at which one may marry without consent, it was lowered from twenty-one to eighteen in 1969, when the age of majority generally was set at eighteen.[55] But the consent provision in English law is not backed up by provisions making the marriage contracted without parental consent voidable. If a couple succeeds in having a marriage ceremony performed without it, their marriage is valid.[56] If consent of the parents is sought and one or both parents refuse to give it, the refusal can be reviewed by a court which will dispense with the requirement of consent if the denial is found to have been unreasonable.[57]

There is some sentiment in the learned writing to the effect that the case for even this relatively limited retention of a requirement for parental consent is weak.[58] In neighboring Scotland, the absence of a consent requirement

52. Marriage Act 1949, as amended. If the parents are not alive or are unavailable for other reasons, detailed statutory provisions govern the steps to be taken to obtain authorization to marry. Marriage Act 1949, s. 3(1), 2d Sched., as amended by Children Act 1975.

53. *Cretney* 56.

54. *Id.* at 59.

55. Marriage Act 1949 s. 2(1), as amended by the Family Law Reform Act 1969. Interestingly, Eekelaar points out, there was a brief but sharp upturn in marriages of those aged eighteen to twenty immediately after the passage of the legislation. But the rates sank throughout the 1970s to levels well below those of the years preceding the reform. *Eekelaar* 33.

56. Marriage Act 1949 s. 48.

57. Marriage Act 1949 s. 3(1), provisos (a) and (b).

58. *Cretney* 17–19.

seems to have produced no ill effects.[59] It has been urged that positive harm may in fact result from the requirement of consent, in that parental opposition may actually strengthen a young couple's determination to enter an ill-advised marriage or may encourage pregnancy as a means of extracting consent.[60] But the Latey Committee on the Age of Majority recommended that the parental consent requirement be retained, pointing out that there seemed to be little public desire for change, and surmising that the law was perhaps at least one factor in keeping the rate of youthful marriages low.[61]

United States

As in England, there is no elaborate legal framework in the United States for direct family participation in, or control of, the marriage decision. But in recent years the laws of the various states have not been characterized by quite the same degree of *laissez-faire* as has the law of England. Concern about the high incidence of failure of marriages involving youthful partners has been a major factor influencing the setting and retention of parental and judicial consent requirements and of the age thresholds in the various states. A few states have even gone so far as to require premarital counseling before any couple, one of whom is under eighteen, will be allowed to marry, even where parental consent has been obtained.[62] But in practice it seems that counseling is often perfunctory and that judges seldom refuse permission to marry. The predominant pattern is that followed by the Uniform Marriage and Divorce Act, which established the age of marital capacity for both parties at sixteen and the age of marriage without parental consent at eighteen.[63]

The path chosen by the authors of the Uniform Act seems to reflect agreement with the English judgment that any attempt to make marriage more difficult for young people would be ineffective and perhaps even counterproductive. That the concern of the Uniform Act in its age provisions is almost exclusively for the young partners themselves appears from the fact that a

59. *Cretney* 17.

60. *Id.*

61. Report of the Committee on the Age of Majority (Latey Report) par. 106 (1967), quoted in *Cretney* 18.

62. See Ohio Rev. Code Ann. §3101.05 (Supp. 1986); Utah Code Ann. §§30-1-30, 30-1-33 (Supp. 1984). California requires that a judge decide whether premarital counseling is necessary in each such case. California Civil Code §4101(c) (Deering Supp. 1987).

63. UMDA §203 (1). An optional subsection permits marriage of persons below the age of sixteen with both parental and judicial consent. State statutes setting a higher age of majority for males than females were rendered unconstitutional by the Supreme Court's decision in *Stanton v. Stanton*, 421 U.S. 7 (1975), holding that a statute which made such a distinction for purposes of determining when the duty of child support terminates violated the guarantee of equal protection.

marriage contracted in violation of the age provisions is valid until decreed null, and that the conditions under which nullity can be decreed are strictly limited.[64]

Who May Marry Whom

The freedom to choose one's spouse is complementary to the right of an individual to enter the married state. But long before either of these ideas was cast as involving a basic right, legal restrictions on the field of possible spouses available to any given person were diminishing.[65] Presently in England, France, West Germany, and the United States, the only such restrictions that are framed as absolute prohibitions are those based on kinship and currently existing marriage.[66] (Same-sex marriage is not usually conceptualized as the subject of a marriage prohibition, but rather as outside the scope of marriage altogether.)[67] Even the prohibitions related to polygamy and incest have become in fact less absolute than is generally believed. With respect to kinship restrictions, the circle of prohibited degrees of relationship is everywhere being drawn more narrowly, and restrictions based on affinity, that is, on the relationships which come into being through marriage (such as step- and in-law relationships) are disappearing. While simultaneous marriage to more than one person remains formally forbidden, such marriages in fact produce legal consequences ever more closely resembling those of any other marriage.

In all four countries, prohibitions other than those on simultaneous marriages, homosexual marriage, and marriage between close relatives either are only directory (that is, they do not affect the validity of the marriage concluded in spite of them), or a dispensation from their application is possible. Of this latter type, for example, was the former prohibition in the German Marriage Law against marriage between a spouse divorced for adultery and

64. UMDA §208 and Comment thereto.

65. In practice, of course, the choice of spouse is probably much less free than generally supposed. See *König* 39, 49–51, (dealing with mate selection and marriage markets).

66. UMDA §207 Comment ("The Act eliminates most of the traditional marriage prohibitions and, consistent with the national trend, eliminates all affinity prohibitions. Only bigamous and incestuous marriages are prohibited"); *Beitzke* 57 ("The existing law follows a modern tendency to diminish marriage prohibitions where feasible. . . . According to the Marriage Law, only the prohibitions based on relationship or currently existing marriage are absolute prohibitions.") See also *Bénabent*, above, note 20 at 462.

67. The point is important, since if the union of two persons of the same sex were considered a "void" marriage, a court, in declaring it void, would have power to make orders for support and property division.

the named co-respondent.[68] A marriage entered in violation of this provision was invalid, but the prohibition was long of little practical consequence because dispensations were so freely granted.[69] In 1976 it was repealed as a logical consequence of the elimination of the fault principle from the divorce law.[70] A similar prohibition in France had been repealed in 1904.[71] Modern marriage law everywhere has become as solicitous of people's ability to freely choose a spouse, as it is of their ability to marry, even sheltering it from many kinds of private pressure exerted through conditions in gifts and wills.[72]

Male and Female

Marriage between persons of the same sex is expressly excluded in England[73] and is generally considered to be invalid by implication in France, West Germany, and the United States.[74] In the United States, the constitutionality of denying the right to marry to same-sex couples has been challenged from time to time. But so far, the courts have upheld the state's power to reserve the marital status to heterosexual couples,[75] and the Supreme Court's 1986 decision that state laws making homosexual sodomy criminal are constitutional reinforces these decisions.[76] Even in the state of Washington, where the marriage statute uses the term *persons* instead of *man* and *woman* in defining the marriage relation and where the state constitution provides that equal rights may not be denied on account of sex, it has been held that homosexuals do not have the right to marry.[77]

Decisions that same-sex couples may not marry seem to follow logically from express or implied statutory definitions of marriage as the legal union of a man and a woman. But recent cases involving persons who have undergone

68. EheG, former §6.

69. *Beitzke* 53.

70. EheRG 1976 art. 3.

71. *Bénabent*, above, note 20 at 463.

72. In all four countries such private restrictions are upheld to a limited extent if the court deems them "reasonable," and if they do not absolutely preclude or require marriage. But they are not favored, and the tendency everywhere is to construe them strictly. French law on this subject is critically examined in Nicole Coiret, "La Liberté du mariage au risque des pressions matérielles," 1985 *Revue trimestrielle de droit civil* 63.

73. Matrimonial Causes Act 1973, §11(c).

74. *Beitzke* 31 (Marriage between persons of the same sex is *Nichtehe*, that is, no marriage comes into existence); *II Carbonnier* 46; UMDA §201 and Comment thereto. In Louisiana, "same sex" was made an impediment to marriage in 1988. Louisiana Civil Code art. 88.

75. *Baker v. Nelson*, 191 N.W.2d 185 (Minn. 1971), *appeal dismissed* 409 U.S. 810 (1972); *Jones v. Hallahan*, 501 S.W.2d 588 (Ky. App. 1973).

76. *Bowers v. Hardwick*, 106 S.Ct. 2841 (1986).

77. *Singer v. Hara*, 522 P.2d 1187 (Wash. App. 1974).

sex-change operations present the interpretive problem of what aspects of sexuality are to be regarded as controlling for purposes of determining whether a given individual is male or female, especially when surgery has merely resolved an existing anatomical ambiguity in favor of one or the other sex. The fact that a person's psychological sense of gender identity, anatomical characteristics, and chromosomal makeup may not coincide renders the statutory terms *man* and *woman* somewhat ambiguous. The English Court of Appeal has taken the position that for purposes of marriage a "sex-change" procedure cannot change a person's gender.[78] French and West German courts initially also adopted the view that such surgery would not justify a change of sex designation on an individual's official records, a necessary prerequisite to marriage. The French Court of Cassation has adhered to this position too, while not entirely excluding the possibility of a different result under certain circumstances.[79] In West Germany, however, the Constitutional Court held in 1978 that a postoperative transsexual had the right to have the gender designation changed on official records, and that such a person would be free thereafter to marry a person of the former sex.[80] In the United States, one state court has recognized, or at least has refused to invalidate, a marriage entered into by a transsexual in a suit for separate maintenance brought when the transsexual partner was abandoned two years after the marriage ceremony took place.[81] Elements of estoppel in the case, however, make it of doubtful authority on the issue of whether a marriage license must be issued to such a couple.[82]

The fact that legal marriage seems to be ruled out for same-sex couples has led some to attempt to secure a formal legal status for their relationship through the adoption laws. So far, however, the courts have not proved receptive to this strategy, generally holding that the adoption statutes were not

---

78. *Corbett v. Corbett*, [1971] P. 83. The European Court of Human Rights has held that the refusal to issue an amended birth certificate to a postoperative transsexual does not violate Article 8 of the European Convention of Human Rights (guaranteeing respect for private life) or Article 12 (the right to marry). *Rees v. United Kingdom*, 9 European Human Rights Reporter 56 (1986).

79. Court of Cassation decisions of 3 and 31 March 1987, D. 1987. Jur. 445. Note, Patrice Jourdain.

80. Decision of the Bundesverfassungsgericht of 11 October 1978, reported in 1979 *Neue Juristische Wochenschrift* 595. The matter is now regulated by statute: Gesetz über die Änderung der Vornamen und die Feststellung der Geschlechtszugehörigkeit in besonderen Fällen (Transsexuellengesetz) of 10 Sept. 1980, BGBl. 1980, 1654. The statute provides that an existing marriage of the transsexual must be dissolved before name and gender designations on official records can be changed (§16).

81. *M. T. v. J. T.*, 355 A. 2d 204 (N.J. Super. 1976).

82. Walter O. Weyrauch and Sanford N. Katz, *American Family Law in Transition* (Washington, D.C.: BNA, 1983), 431.

intended to be used for this purpose.[83] Meanwhile, in Denmark and Sweden, the legislatures have simply awarded certain rights directly to same-sex cohabitants.[84]

What is at stake here is not merely the question of who is to enjoy the rights and privileges accruing to the status of being married, nor the desire expressed by the parties to some of these unions for an outward and visible symbol of their bond. The main issue, hotly contested both by those in favor and those opposed to legal recognition of "family" relationships between persons of the same sex, is legitimation—which in modern societies (for better or worse) is closely bound up with legality.

Polygamy

At first sight it seems too obvious for words that in England, France, the United States, and West Germany one may not be married to more than one person at the same time. In each country, statutes provide that no one may enter a marriage prior to the dissolution of a previous marriage and that the act of entering such a marriage is criminal.[85] No dispensations are allowed.

Let us note, however, that this one-marriage-at-a-time rule behind which the legal systems of the West have seemingly thrown so much weight is not what a sociologist would call a general prohibition of polygamy. Polygamy can be simultaneous (if more than one spouse is simultaneously present) or successive (if spouses are married one after the other).[86] Only simultaneous polygamy is prohibited by the laws with which we are here concerned. These statutes reserve the use of the word *polygamy* for that kind which is not very common among us. They do not at all affect the serial form, which is so popular in the United States and Western Europe that, as we shall see, the law is fast changing to adapt to it.

The difference between viewing polygamy as a legal phenomenon and as a social phenomenon is well illustrated by the contrast between the majority

---

83. See *In re Robert Paul P.*, 63 N.Y.2d 233 (N.Y.C.A. 1984). The French decisions are discussed in Pierre Raynaud, *Un abus de l'adoption simple: les couples adoptifs*, D. 1983. Chr. 39.

84. See below, chapter 6, n. 93.

85. French Civil Code art. 147; **England**, Matrimonial Causes Act 1973, s. 11(b); **West Germany**, EheG §5; **United States** UMDA §207. The relevant criminal statutes are: French Penal Code art. 340; **England**, Offenses Against the Person Act 1861, s. 57; **West Germany**, StGB §171. The bigamy laws of the American states are in the appendix to Ralph Slovenko, "The De Facto Decriminalization of Bigamy," 17 *Journal of Family Law* 297, 307–08 (1978–79). Alaska appears to be the only state where bigamy laws have been repealed.

86. *König* 41–42.

and dissenting opinions in *United States* v. *Cleveland*.[87] That case involved the question of whether members of a sect of polygynous heretical Mormons traveling with their wives had violated a federal statute making it a crime to transport a woman across state lines "for the purpose of prostitution or debauchery, or for any other immoral purpose." Mr. Justice Douglas, writing for the majority, upheld the convictions of the Mormons saying, "The establishment or maintenance of polygamous households is a notorious example of promiscuity. . . . These polygamous practices have long been branded as immoral in the law. . . . [T]hey are in the same genus as the other immoral practices covered by the Act."[88] Mr. Justice Murphy, in dissent, did not agree that the Mormons' conduct was comparable to prostitution and commercialized vice. Pointing out (rather pedantically) that the practice involved in the case was, properly speaking, not polygamy but polygyny, he said "[W]e are dealing here with . . . one of the basic forms of marriage. . . . [It] is basically a cultural institution. . . ." The fact that it is condemned by the dominant culture "does not alter the fact that polygyny is a form of marriage built upon a set of social and moral principles."[89]

The passage of time has not caused the Supreme Court to soften its view. It was quite content in 1978 to give its approval to the right to enter as many marriages one after the other as one wishes, regardless of one's financial ability to provide for dependents,[90] but gave short shrift in 1985 to a Utah police officer who claimed constitutional protection for his practice of simultaneous polygamy, even though it was undisputed in the policeman's case that his two wives and five children "receive love and adequate care and attention and do not want for any necessity of life."[91]

In the capillaries of the legal system, however, there have been many signs that the degree of our disapproval of the type of polygamy we do not commonly practice has diminished, even as our practice of the kind we tolerate has increased. It is true that the prohibition still stands, but the sanctions for simultaneous polygamy have begun to be softened in three ways. In the first place, the legal effects of a marriage entered in violation of the prohibition

87. 329 U.S. 14 (1946). The Church of Jesus Christ of Latter Day Saints (Mormons) officially abolished simultaneous polygyny in 1890. The practice was continued however by certain Mormons who doubted the authenticity of the direct revelation from God on which its abolition was based.

88. 329 U.S. 14 at 19.

89. *Id.* at 26.

90. *Zablocki v. Redhail*, 434 U.S. 374 (1978).

91. *Potter v. Murray City*, 760 F.2d 1065, 1069 (10th Cir. 1985), *cert. denied*, 106 S.Ct. 145 (1985).

are beginning to resemble the legal consequences of any other marriage. For example, the children of such a union can be legitimate.[92] If proceedings are brought to invalidate the marriage, support and property division may in certain cases be ordered as after a divorce.[93] Second, the attitude of the state toward such marriages as expressed through the criminal law seems to be growing less harsh. The criminal law is very seldom enforced against bigamists in the United States, and in at least one American state, Alaska, bigamy has ceased to be a crime altogether.[94] In West Germany it may be punishable merely by a fine.[95] Finally, in conflict of laws cases, foreign simultaneously polygamous marriages are increasingly recognized, at least for some purposes, perhaps indicating a diminution of the strength of local public policy against them.[96] Despite these indications of limited acceptance, the prohibition of simultaneous marriages seems likely to stand. It is hardly ever challenged, and its most common form—simultaneous polygyny—affronts the principle of sexual equality.

As for the proliferation of successive polygamy among us, the ways in which the law has changed to accommodate it will be described in the discussion of divorce in chapters 4 and 5. Here it may merely be pointed out that the experience of other parts of the world with simultaneous polygyny (by far more common than polyandry) may be instructive as to the limits of our practices as well as theirs. Simultaneous polygyny has always been self-limiting owing to the necessity to keep within control the tensions in society that a

92. In France, West Germany, and several of the United States, a child of a void or voidable marriage is deemed legitimate regardless of the good or bad faith of one or both of the spouses in contracting the marriage. In England and in some American states, children of void marriages are deemed legitimate if at least one of the parties to the marriage reasonably believed the marriage was valid.

93. **England**, *Cretney* 88–92; *Bromley* 49; **West Germany**, *Gernhuber* 128, 144; **United States**: *UMDA*, Prefatory Note p. 4 and §207, 209; **France**, *Labrusse-Riou* 80–81.

94. See the statutes listed in Ralph Slovenko, "The De Facto Decriminalization of Bigamy," above, note 85 at 307–8.

95. **West Germany**: StGB §171 (confinement up to three years or a fine). Under the French Penal Code art. 340, the penalty for bigamy is six months to three years confinement and a fine.

96. **West Germany**: *Gesetz zur Neuregelung des internationalen Privatrechts* of 25 July 1986, §13 EGBGB, excerpted in 1986 Das Standesamt 262. **France**: *Labrusse-Riou* 71. **United States**: *UMDA* §210 codifies the principle that marriages valid by the laws of the state where contracted are valid everywhere and intentionally omits the traditional exception for those marriages which contravene some strong public policy of the jurisdiction. In **England**, the Matrimonial Proceedings (Polygamous Marriages) Act 1972, c. 38, made polygamous marriages justiciable in English courts for the first time. Reenacted as s. 47 of the Matrimonial Causes Act 1973, c. 18, it nullified the long-standing rule of English law denying either party to a polygamous marriage the right to seek the adjudication of disputes or remedies offered by English courts in matrimonial cases.

shortage of women can create and to the economic limits on the number of wives one man can support.[97] We in the modern industrial states have not yet come to grips with this second point. All Western legal systems are currently wrestling with the question whether responsibility for successive spouses belongs to their one-time marriage partners or to society at large and with how to provide support for children produced in the course of successive unions. Montesquieu, noting in his pragmatic way that "a plurality of wives greatly depends on the means of supporting them," observed that this does not necessarily mean that a man with multiple wives has to be wealthy, provided that he lives in a clime where it costs little to maintain wife and children.[98] Interestingly enough, the countries which Montesquieu thought favored by nature in this respect have been moving in modern times toward the abolition of simultaneous polygamy, while serial polygamy seems to flourish under the conditions of the relatively affluent welfare states in the industrialized part of the world.

Incest

As with polygamy, when discussing incest it is useful to distinguish between legal and social conceptions. In addition, it is important not to confuse *marriage* prohibitions based on kinship or affinity from what has been called the *incest taboo*, which pertains to *mating*. The four legal systems examined here have in common that their lists of marriage prohibitions were once quite extensive,[99] but have gradually been reduced. Of the remaining prohibitions, some are absolute, and others are within a zone of tolerance, in the sense that they can be officially dispensed or that marriages entered in violation of them are not invalid. Remaining absolutely prohibited in all four countries are marriages between parents or grandparents and their descendants and between brothers and sisters, whether of full or half blood. Beyond this, there are minor variations among the countries.

In France, in addition to the core relationships listed above, marriage is absolutely prohibited between ascendants and descendants related by adoption or by affinity, if the person through whom the affinity was created is living.[100] Thus, for example, the father of a divorced son cannot marry his former

---

97. *König* 41–42.

98. Montesquieu, *The Spirit of the Laws*, Book 16, Ch. 3, trans. Thomas Nugent (New York: Hafner Press, 1949).

99. The extensive lists came from the canon law prohibitions, which once reached to the eighth degree of kinship by civil law computation. "Marriage," in *Encyclopaedia Britannica*, 11th ed. (New York: Encyclopaedia Britannica, 1911), 753, 755.

100. French Civil Code arts. 161–64.

daughter-in-law so long as the son is alive. Over the years, the possibility of dispensation has been made available in the following cases: marriage between adoptive brother and sister; marriage between aunt and nephew or uncle and niece; marriage between persons related by affinity in the direct line if the person creating the link is deceased; and marriage between brother- and sister-in-law if the marriage creating the alliance is dissolved by divorce. In this last case, if the marriage creating the alliance has been terminated by death, no dispensation has been necessary since 1938.[101] In all these cases, dispensations are said to be freely given.[102]

In West Germany, there are no absolute prohibitions apart from those mentioned above as being common to the four systems.[103] Dispensations are available, and are generally granted, in the case of marriages between persons related by affinity in the direct line. Marriages between adoptive parents and children are valid even if entered into in violation of the laws purporting to forbid them, the adoptive relationship ceasing to exist upon the marriage. Affinity among collaterals is no longer an impediment of any kind. A prohibition of marriage between persons when one of them has had a sexual relationship with a relative of the other was declared unconstitutional in 1973.[104]

In the United States, the Uniform Marriage and Divorce Act adds the following to the prohibitions listed above as common to all four countries: marriages between ascendants, descendants, or siblings related by adoption; and marriages between aunt and nephew or uncle and niece with a special exception as to these if they are permitted by "the established customs of aboriginal cultures."[105] The Act does not forbid first-cousin marriages, but they are prohibited under the laws of some American states.[106] Prohibitions based on affinity and remote consanguinity have been gradually dropping out of state law, do not appear in the Uniform Act, and seem to be of doubtful constitutionality.[107]

Absolute prohibitions which exist in England, in addition to the core prohibitions mentioned above, forbid marriages between adoptive parents and

101. *Bénabent*, above, note 20 at 462.

102. *Id.*

103. EheG § 4; *Beitzke* 51–53.

104. Bundesverfassungsgericht decision of 14 November 1973, reported in 1974 *Neue Juristische Wochenschrift* 545.

105. UMDA §207. The exception for aboriginal cultures has the curious effect of permitting uncle-niece marriages among American Indians but not among Jews, although such marriages are accepted in Jewish religious law.

106. *Clark* 84.

107. See the tables of state statutes in Carolyn S. Bratt, "Incest Statutes and the Fundamental Right of Marriage," 18 *Family Law Quarterly* 257, 298–309 (1984–85).

their children; aunt and nephew or uncle and niece; or between stepparents and stepchildren where the stepchild has been "treated as a child of the family." [108] No dispensations from any of these prohibitions are available, and the prohibitions continue even after the death of the person creating the prohibited relationship. [109] Extensive affinity prohibitions pertaining to in-laws existed until a series of reforms beginning with the Deceased Wife's Sister's Marriage Act of 1907. A ban on all marriages between allies in the direct line except stepparents and children was dropped in 1986.

There is no simple explanation of the basis for current legal regulation of marriages between persons related in various ways. Though the French legal sociologist Carbonnier has referred to the core of absolute prohibitions common to all four countries as the "zone of horror," [110] this small circle of prohibitions does not constitute an irreducible minimum for Western countries. Sweden, in reaction to a case which had aroused wide public sympathy, changed its law in the 1970s to provide that the marriage prohibition between half-brother and sister could be dispensed. [111]

A genetic explanation for the prohibitions is popular, but too facile. Many of the prohibitions involve persons who are not blood relatives. Furthermore, no country forbids marriages between unrelated persons (such as hemophiliacs) whose mating is also problematic from a genetic point of view. The theory that certain relationships have been socially and legally discouraged because of their potentially disruptive effects on family life within a single household affords a plausible explanation of why most affinity prohibitions have been dropped as households have become smaller. It may also shed some light on why the prohibition against marriage of half-siblings has lost much of its force in countries where it is common for half-brothers and sisters to be raised in different households. Still, the family discord theory does not explain why marriages between persons related by adoption are forbidden in some American states, while marriages between stepparent and stepchild are permitted under the same statutes. [112] The area is one where the law seems to be characterized more by vague and somewhat inconsistent notions about legitimacy than by systematic consideration of the purposes of regulation.

108. Marriage Act 1949, sched. 1, as amended. The English prohibitions apply to illegitimate and half-blood relationships.

109. *Bromley* 26.

110. *II Carbonnier* 71.

111. Note, "Family Law—Sweden," 22 *International and Comparative Law Quarterly* 182 (1973); Note, "Family Law—Sweden (follow-up)," 22 *International and Comparative Law Quarterly* 766 (1973).

112. *E.g.*, UMDA §207(a)(2).

In all four countries, the sexual relationships which are the subject of absolute marriage prohibitions are also typically prohibited by the criminal law. On the one hand, this would seem to indicate the strength of the policy against certain types of sexual relationships. On the other hand, there are signs of a movement to decriminalize some of this behavior, or at least to drastically reduce the penalties applied to it, and to reconceptualize the criminal law of incest, directing it primarily toward the protection of minors.[113] In England[114] and most American states, sexual relations between members of the core family are still classified as criminal. West Germany revised its treatment of the problem in the 1970s. The title of the offense was changed from Incest (*Blutschande*: literally, "shaming of the blood") to Sexual Relations between Relatives. Offenses under this heading may now be punished with a fine rather than with imprisonment, and brothers and sisters under age eighteen have been exempted from the application of the section.[115] Expert opinion in all three countries, however, supports an approach similar to that of France, which has eliminated the crime of incest as such and now penalizes only those sexual relations between relatives that involve a minor and a person who, by virtue of his position with respect to the minor, is in a position to abuse his or her authority.[116] Since nonrelatives too are punishable under this classification, the French law should be regarded not as primarily an incest prohibition but as a law for the prevention of sexual exploitation of minors. To complete the legal picture, it must be pointed out that incestuous marriages, like polygamous marriages, even where void, can produce many of the same legal effects as any other marriage.[117]

The fact that the content of the marriage prohibitions and other regulation of sexual relationships between related persons in Western societies seems to be gradually changing should not be too surprising. While the incest taboo has often been said to be universal, this must be understood as meaning that some sort of prohibition on mating is universal, not that a particular set of relationships is universally tabooed.[118] The content of the taboo and the range of prohibited marriages has altered with the changing structure of societies and changing patterns of family relationships.

113. Reduction of penalties has been the approach of the Model Penal Code in the United States: American Law Institute, *Model Penal Code* §230.2 (Proposed Official Draft 1962); as well as that of West Germany, StGB §173.

114. Sexual Offences Act 1956, ss. 10 and 11.

115. StGB §173.

116. French Penal Code art. 331. See also D. J. West, "Thoughts on Sex Law Reform," in *Crime, Criminology and Public Policy*, ed. Roger Hood; (London: Heineman, 1974), 481.

117. *Beitzke* 57–60; *Cretney* 87–92; UMDA §207, 209; *Labrusse-Riou* 80–81.

118. *König* 21, 32–33.

Premarital Procedures

In the infancy of official marriage regulation, nullity was the only sanction available as a practical matter for marriages which political or ecclesiastical authorities desired for one reason or another to prevent. So long as valid marriages could still be concluded informally, there was only the crude technique of avoiding the marriage so entered or the still cruder technique of punishment to back up whatever marriage policies were sought to be implemented. But as the machinery of public administration became more efficient in England, France, and Germany, it became possible to require a public ceremony preceded by publicity and eventually to require a license. These methods of enforcing official marriage policies are less effective, however, in the United States because of the lack of a nationwide system of registration of civil status there and because it is still possible to conclude a valid marriage informally in several American states.

The preliminaries required by modern legal systems before a marriage can take place are revealing indications of the degree to which the state is actively interested in regulating marriage formation, as opposed to contenting itself with the promulgation of rules which prescribe desirable behavior but which have no real sanctions. To the extent that the various compulsory marriage preliminaries are contrived to identify problem cases, and to prevent marriages in violation of the rules concerning who may marry whom, they indicate how seriously the various marriage restrictions in a given country are to be taken. We will not be especially concerned here with the law of nullity, which tells us whether or in what respects a marriage entered in violation of the legal rules will be valid. Nullity has ceased to be a major technique for control of marriage formation and is now primarily remedial in function. It is concerned with problems which are for our purposes secondary, that is, with the effects to be given to a marriage entered in spite of attempts to prevent it.

Compulsory marriage preliminaries not only give us a good idea of the weight behind various marriage policies in a legal system, but furnish another kind of clue to the nature of the relation of the state to the family. Marriage provides a convenient opportunity for society to promote a wide variety of policies by making the celebration of marriage depend upon the compliance with whatever conditions the legislature has deemed important. Thus, for example, individuals may be required to undergo a medical examination before they marry, or, as a supposed deterrent to hasty marriages, to allow a specified period of time to elapse between obtaining a marriage license and the marriage itself. In a growing number of American states, the state takes the occasion of the application for a marriage license to require the licensing official to dispense information about birth control and genetically transmitted defects to couples. As we saw above, certain American states have also taken this opportunity to require or offer premarital counseling for underage couples.

England

The law of marriage preliminaries in England is rather complex because there are two parallel systems: one set of civil preliminaries for marriages which are not to be solemnized within the Church of England and one set of ecclesiastical preliminaries. In addition, there are special civil and ecclesiastical procedures which can be used in cases where persons are housebound because of illness or disability or confined in institutions. The surface complexity of the system however, masks the fact that it exercises little real control over the formation of marriage. Neither the state nor the church takes much advantage of the occasion of marriage to promote any particular policies.

Civil Marriage Preliminaries

The usual civil preliminaries[119] involve obtaining a *Superintendent Registrar's Certificate*. To get this certificate of permission to marry, the parties must notify the Superintendent Registrar for the district where each has resided for at least seven days of their intention to marry. They must swear, on pain of perjury, that the residence requirement is satisfied, that any required consents have been obtained, and that there are believed to be no impediments to the marriage. Registrars are authorized to require written evidence of the absence of legal obstacles to the proposed marriage. The notice of intent is entered in a marriage notice book, which is to be conspicuously displayed in the Superintendent Registrar's office and open to public inspection. After twenty-one days have elapsed, the certificate (which is the couple's license to marry) is issued. The marriage can take place at any time within three months of the issuance of the certificate.

Those who are not willing to wait so long may resort to a more expedited procedure, the *Superintendent Registrar's Certificate and License*. This procedure, sometimes called *Special License*, involves practically no publicity, and almost no time for objections to be raised. Although intended to be exceptional, it has come to be used in over a quarter of all English civil marriages. Apart from the fact that it costs more, it differs from the Superintendent Registrar's Certificate process mainly in that the application, while entered on the marriage notice book and open to inspection by the public, is not displayed, and the marriage can take place upon the expiration of only one full day after the day of giving notice.

119. See, generally, *Cretney* 19–24.

Ecclesiastical Marriage Preliminaries

Most Church of England weddings are preceded by the *banns of marriage*. This procedure begins with a written notice of intention to marry, stating the full names of the parties, their places of residence, and how long they have lived there. No declaration concerning capacity to marry or consents is required. Seven days after such a notice is given, the banns are published. This means that the proposed marriage is noted in a church register and is announced publicly at church services on three successive Sundays preceding the wedding. An alternative procedure for couples in greater haste is the *common license*, analogous to the expedited civil preliminaries. It involves little publicity, no waiting period, and no opportunity for objections to the marriage to be raised. But unlike its civil analogue, it is infrequently used and is available only at the discretion of the church authorities.[120]

The most striking characteristic of English marriage formation law as a whole is its lack of compulsion. There is no requirement of any medical test and no statutory requirement for documentary proof. It is optional with each Registrar whether or not to check up on the truth of declarations made in the notice of intention to marry. There seems to be little enthusiasm for introducing medical tests or longer waiting periods, but the Law Commission in 1973 did recommend a uniform system in which all persons intending to marry would have to give notice in a single prescribed form, and would be required to produce birth certificates, evidence of identity, and proof of the termination of any prior marriage.[121] The Commission also raised the question whether the Registrar should have more duties in connection with verifying the information submitted. In this area, however, England is struggling with a policy conflict familiar to Americans. Pointing out that the present provisions for bringing problems to light are "largely nugatory," former Law Commissioner Cretney stated, "The only effective remedy would be the creation of a national register of civil status on the continental pattern. . . . [A]nything less seems an unsatisfactory compromise."[122] Yet the very idea of such a national record keeping system is "anathema to many" in a country traditionally unused to that degree of official regulation.[123]

France

In comparison with the English system, the preliminaries which must be observed prior to the compulsory civil marriage in France are not only more

120. *Cretney* 25–28.

121. Law Commission, *Family Law: Report on Solemnisation of Marriage in England and Wales* (no. 53), Annex Par. 39–41 (London: Her Majesty's Stationery Office, 1973).

122. *Cretney* 38–39.   123. *Id.*

numerous, but are more effective reinforcements of the legal requirements concerning eligibility to marry and choice of spouse. The first step required of a French couple who intend to marry is the production of a medical certificate, not more than two months old, certifying that each has been "examined with a view toward marriage."[124] Unlike some American state laws, which permit a marriage license to be refused if the certificate reveals the existence of certain conditions, French law seeks only to assure that each person is well informed about his or her own physical condition and in possession of information relevant to procreation before he or she marries. The doctor's findings do not appear on the certificate, which says only that the examination took place. The results are made known only to the person examined, not to the future spouse or to any public official. Thus, the medical examination is not meant to be an impediment to marriage. But to ensure that the examination takes place, it is made a necessary prerequisite to the next required step in marriage preliminaries—public notice.

After the medical certificates have been filed, public notice of the intended marriage must take place for a period of at least 10 days before the ceremony. The Civil Code prescribes the manner of giving notice in some detail:

> Before the celebration of the marriage, a notice of the intended marriage must be posted at the door of the city hall (*mairie*) of the commune where the marriage is to be celebrated, and of the place of the domicile or residence of the future spouses. The notice is to contain the first names, surnames, occupations, domiciles and residences of the parties, and the place where the marriage is to be celebrated.[125]

This secularized version of the banns of marriage is supposed to give the relevant community the opportunity to call attention to any impediments to the marriage either through simple notice to public officials, or through formal objections in cases where these are permitted. Dispensations from the waiting period or notice requirements can be granted by local authorities for "serious reasons," which in the former case are apt to be the imminent birth of a child and in the latter that the marriage is the regularization of a union which has long passed in the community for a legal marriage.[126]

Finally, before the marriage can be celebrated, copies of the birth certificates of the parties must be sent to the official who will celebrate the marriage.[127] The certificates, which must not be more than three months old, contain entries on their margin of any marriages previously entered by the

124. French Civil Code art. 63.
125. French Civil Code arts. 63, 64, 166.
126. French Civil Code art. 169; *II Carbonnier* 73.
127. French Civil Code arts. 70, 71.

parties, and the names of former spouses. This will, in certain cases, make the production of divorce decrees or death certificates necessary before the marriage can be celebrated. If a birth certificate cannot be obtained, the information it would have contained must be established by at least three witnesses. Additional procedures are required if a prospective spouse is not of French nationality.

West Germany

Like the French system, the West German law governing marriage preliminaries is characterized by requirements designed effectively to bring to light any impediments to the marriage before the compulsory civil ceremony takes place. And, as in France, it is aided in doing this by a comprehensive system of registration of civil status. In West Germany, the first step required of persons intending to marry is to produce their birth certificates, or authenticated entries or extracts from the Family Book, and any necessary consents from parents or guardians.[128] Furthermore, the Registrar of Civil Status (*Standesbeamte*) is obliged to satisfy himself or herself before the marriage as to whether there is any impediment to the marriage and to require further documentary proof where necessary, as when one of the parties is not of German nationality.[129] Only when the Registrar has accepted the documentary evidence can the parties proceed to the next required step, which is the posting of public notice at a designated place for one week prior to the marriage.[130] Under certain circumstances, this notice can be dispensed with by the Registrar. Since such a notice is unlikely to bring impediments to light except in rather small communities, its abolition has been proposed, but its retention has been defended on the ground that it does assure a minimal period of reflection and preparation.[131]

In the case of the marriage of anyone who is the guardian of a minor child, or of certain other individuals who are under fiduciary obligations, West German law takes the occasion of marriage to require a certificate attesting that those wishing to marry have fulfilled their legal duties or that such duties no longer exist.[132] A marriage entered in violation of this provision is valid, but it may result in the loss of the violator's control over the property of the person for whom he or she is responsible.[133]

128. PStG §5.
129. *Beitzke* 39; EheG §10; PStG §5a.
130. EheG §12; PStG §3; PStG—AVO §12.
131. See F. W. Bosch, "Weitere Reformen im Familienrecht der Bundesrepublik Deutschland?" 1982 *Zeitschrift für das gesamte Familienrecht* 862, 868.
132. EheG §9.
133. *Beitzke* 54–55.

At present, West German law requires no premarital medical examination, but suggestions for reform have included a recommendation for a confidential certificate of the French type, which would leave the freedom to marry unaffected.[134] It has also been proposed that German marriage preliminaries ought to include the dispensation of information about the legal effects of marriage on property, a subject about which persons entering marriage are often ignorant, but which may profoundly affect their lives.[135]

United States

American law concerning marriage preliminaries differs from that of the three countries just discussed in two important ways. First, there is no uniform nationwide law of marriage formation, except insofar as the Supreme Court's recognition of a "right to marry" has placed limits on what the various state legislatures may do in this area. Second, as an aspect of the variety that exists among the states, a few states recognize a form of legal marriage which involves no preliminaries and no formalities: the so-called common law marriage.

All American states and the Uniform Marriage and Divorce Act (UMDA) require a license before formal marriage can take place, and the majority of states impose a short waiting period (usually three days as in the UMDA) between the application for a license and its issuance.[136] The licensing statutes usually require that the parties state under oath their names, ages, any relationship between them, whether they have been previously married, and if so how their marriages were terminated.[137] If the statements of the parties do not reveal any irregularities, the license is issued. The licensing official does not as a rule make any investigation. Indeed, one state attorney general has formally advised clerks that they have practically no discretion to look behind the sworn statements of the parties on the application for a marriage license, except to request proof of age.[138] The Uniform Marriage and Divorce Act has followed this pattern. It does not require documentary evidence of eligibility to marry. In fact the Uniform Law Commissioners rejected the suggestion of the Family Law Section of the American Bar Association that, in line with the practice of some states, a copy of any divorce decree should be required in addition to the simple declaration of the parties regarding previous mar-

---

134. Bosch, above, note 131 at 869.

135. P. H. Neuhaus, "Zur Reform des deutschen formellen Eheschliessungsrechts," 1972 *Zeitschrift für das gesamte Familienrecht* 59.

136. *Clark* 36; UMDA §204.

137. *Clark* 36.

138. "Marriage-Licensing (News Notes)," 5 *Family Law Reporter* 2188 (1979).

riages. The Act continues the practice of most states, which, as in English law, take the information on the license application at face value. In none of the United States is there a system for publicizing the intended marriage. Some states require a physician's certificate stating that each party is free from venereal disease before a marriage license will issue, but the requirement is easily evaded by marrying in another state, and a marriage contracted in violation of the requirement is not invalid.[139] As we have seen, those who drafted the UMDA concluded that a premarital medical examination was unnecessary.

In understanding the law of American marriage formation, it is essential to know that nearly every aspect of a particular state's regulatory scheme can be avoided simply by marrying in another state whose law does not happen to include the requirement that poses an obstacle. Thus, compulsory premarital counseling, waiting periods, restraints on remarriage, and consent requirements have been rejected or abandoned by the American states at least as much out of a sense of their futility as on principle or under the influence of the idea of freedom to marry. Furthermore, noncompliance with the few prescribed procedures for licensing, solemnization, and registration does not necessarily render a marriage invalid. Well-settled case law holds that "substantial compliance" with the statutory formalities is sufficient.[140]

American law as a whole is thus as lax as the English with respect to finding out whether marriage impediments exist. Like England, the United States lacks any system of registration of civil status, which in itself would provide checks on bigamous marriages. In contrast to England, however, the United States has begun to manifest new and distinctively modern types of state interest in its law concerning marriage preliminaries. The moment of licensing is seen as an opportunity to further certain social purposes. For example, several states have adopted laws requiring that birth control information or brochures about genetically transmitted diseases be dispensed to all applicants for marriage licenses.[141] And, as concern about the spread of the AIDS virus mounts, a few states are requiring all marriage license applicants to be tested or to be informed about the disease and available testing services.[142] Another type of interest is manifested in requests on license application forms for

139. *Clark* 34.

140. See cases collected in the draftsmen's comment to UMDA §201.

141. *E.g.*, 16 Georgia Code Ann. §19-3-41 (1982); 10 Hawaii, Rev. Stat. §572–5(d) (1985); 14 Kentucky Rev. Stat. §402.270 (1984); Maryland Code Ann., Family Law §2–405(h) (1984); New Hampshire Rev. Stat. Ann. §457: 28a (1983); 8A South Carolina Code §20-1-240 (1985).

142. As of early 1988, only Illinois and Louisiana required such tests; California, Hawaii, and Virginia required information about AIDS to be given to applicants, and the issue was being debated in the legislatures of several other states.

information which is not concerned with revealing impediments to the marriage but rather with the gathering of data to be used for the study of family life. This kind of innovation poses a problem for law reformers, torn between the wish to protect privacy and the desire to make better laws. Even the Uniform Act, which (its authors claim) "greatly simplified premarital regulation," includes the social security numbers of the parties among the items of required information on the marriage license application.[143] This item was inserted in the Uniform Act, over the objections of commissioners concerned about governmental data gathering, for the purpose of laying the groundwork in the marriage license for the day when the bridegroom, now a deserting husband and father, must be located for the purpose of enforcing support obligations.

The social security number is fast becoming the basis of a *de facto* national system of identification in the United States. From time to time, proposals are made for an outright well-considered system of coordinated birth-and-death records and a national identification system, but national traditions and civil libertarian objections have so far been stronger than the impetus for change. Public and private computerized data banks, however, continue to amass information about individuals, to the point where Americans are subject to many of the disadvantages of computerized collections of personal information without having either the advantages for purposes of law enforcement or the safeguards against abuse provided by the more rational and carefully controlled systems of continental Europe.[144] Meanwhile, the present system, in which information about civil status is difficult for private individuals to obtain, coupled with the ability of Americans to freely drop or assume names, places obvious limits on the degree to which marriage law and family support obligations can be enforced.

Formalities for the Solemnization of Marriage

While the laws concerning marriage preliminaries give some indication of the degree to which various marriage restrictions are in fact policed, the laws specifying certain formalities for the actual celebration of the marriage reveal two entirely different aspects of official involvement in marriage regulation: (1) the extent to which marriage rituals, religious or customary in origin, have been appropriated by the state, secularized, and made uniform for all groups of the population, and (2) the ideology of marriage being communicated by

143. UMDA §202 (1).

144. See, for a highly informative cross-national treatment of this subject, Joseph W. Eaton, *Card-Carrying Americans: Privacy, Security, and the National I.D. Card Debate* (Totowa, N.J.: Rowman & Littlefield, 1986).

the legal system. The laws concerning registration of the marriage once it has been celebrated obviously bear an important relationship to the structure and effectiveness of official record-keeping, which in turn aids in enforcing the system of marriage impediments. So far as the required formalities for the celebration of marriage are concerned, the systems of France and West Germany, where the only possible method of forming a valid marriage is a compulsory civil ceremony, represent a fundamentally different and more thoroughly secular approach than those of England and the United States, where two quite different variants of what one might call *pluralistic systems* are in force.

Pluralism: England and the United States

England

CELEBRATION   Until 1753 marriages could be concluded in England by a simple exchange of consents with no other ceremony. Lord Hardwicke's Act that year tried to put an end to these "clandestine" marriages by making an ecclesiastical ceremony in the Church of England, with publication of banns and registration of the marriage, compulsory for all persons except members of the Royal Family, Quakers, and Jews. This scheme had the awkward effect that Protestant dissenters and Roman Catholics had to marry by the Anglican rite or not at all. When partial secularization of marriage came to England in 1836, it came not in the form of the compulsory civil ceremony for everyone, as in France and Germany, but in a law permitting two parallel marriage systems, those of religious and civil law, to exist side by side. The main lines of the system laid down in the Marriage Act of 1836 still exist today. English couples may marry according to the rites of the Church of England, or civilly, or according to the rites of any non-Anglican religion. Quakers and Jews continue to form a separate category. To see what aspects of marriage ritual are legally required in England, one must examine not one but four separate systems.

Civil Marriage. There has been a growing trend toward civil marriage in England, with approximately half of all marriages there now taking place in the office of a Superintendent Registrar. The trend seems, at least in part, to be due to increased divorce and the restrictions placed by many churches on remarriage of divorced persons. Over two-thirds of first marriages in England are still performed in religious form.[145]

The law regulating the formation of civil marriage still shows vestiges of the old antagonism to secret marriages. The ceremony must take place in the

145. *Cretney* 29–30.

daytime (between 8:00 A.M. and 6:00 P.M.), in an office with open doors, in the presence of a Superintendent Registrar who acts as celebrant and a Registrar who attends to the formalities of registration. The ceremony itself is required by statute to be purely secular. It consists of the exchange of consents in a prescribed form: "I call upon these persons here present to witness that I, AB, do take thee, CD, to be my lawful wedded wife (husband)." [146] The parties must state that they know of no impediment to the marriage. It is apparently the custom, though not required by law, for the Registrars to make the following statement:

> It is my duty to remind you of the solemn and binding character of the vows you are about to take. Marriage, according to the law of this country, is the union of one man with one woman, voluntarily entered into for life to the exclusion of all others. [147]

Cretney remarks dryly that, "Since a divorced person is involved in more than half of all Register Office ceremonies it is not clear that this practice is wholly sensible." [148] He has described the total effect of the ceremony as "bureaucratic" and lacking in solemnity, and the physical surroundings of the Registry offices as "often rather depressing." [149]

Anglican Marriage. Anglican marriages are nearly as common as civil marriage in England. The law leaves the details of the ceremony to the Church of England, providing only that there must be two witnesses and that the marriage rite must be that of the Book of Common Prayer or any other currently authorized ritual.

Non-Anglican Religious Marriage. The form of the non-Anglican religious ceremony is largely left to the parties and the church authorities, but certain aspects of procedure and ritual are legally required. The marriage must be celebrated by an "authorized person" in a "registered building." These requirements are intended to assure that the non-Anglican ceremony is in fact a religious ceremony of some sort and not performed by a secular marriage mill in competition with the Registry office. The ceremony itself must take place during the daytime in a room with open doors in the presence of two or more witnesses and a registrar or "authorized person." At some point in the ceremony the parties must state: "I do solemnly declare that I know not of any lawful impediment why I, AB, may not be joined in matrimony to CD." [150] They must also repeat the civil formula for the exchange of consents.

Quaker and Jewish Marriages. Since Lord Hardwicke's Act, Quaker and Jewish marriages have been in a special category. They must be preceded by

---

146. *Id.*
148. *Id.*
150. *Id.* at 30–32.

147. *Id.*
149. *Id.* at 40.

civil preliminaries, but they need not be celebrated in a "registered building" nor by an "authorized person," and the form of the ceremony is left entirely to the religious rules of these groups.

The pluralistic system just described has not been immune to criticism in England. It has been claimed that the procedures for preliminaries as well as for celebration of marriages are not well understood either by the public or by the persons who administer them, and that administration of the procedures is so lax that persons involved may not fully understand when a marriage, as distinct from, say, licensing, is taking place.[151] A joint working party of the Law Commission and the Registrar General's office once suggested that the introduction of a compulsory civil ceremony would be the simplest and most effective means of solving these problems.[152] Concluding, however, that such a change would be strongly resisted by the churches and the general public, the Law Commission in its 1973 report on the solemnization of marriages recommended that the present pluralist system be retained but that safeguards be added through the introduction of uniform preliminaries and more standard elements.[153] These modest suggestions were never implemented, owing, it seems, to the rather low priority given by Parliament to reconsideration of the law of marriage formation.[154]

REGISTRATION   The Marriage Act of 1836, together with the Births and Deaths Registration Act passed immediately after it, brought into existence the Superintendent Registrars of births, deaths, and marriages. Today all marriages, however concluded, must be registered in their offices. The public record of marriages serves to provide documentation necessary for the parties' own proof of their status for tax or social security purposes, and for the assembly of vital statistics. However, it is not centralized or cross-indexed with other types of records so as to provide a really effective system which would enable third parties or the government to obtain full and accurate information about any given individual's civil status.

United States
The version of pluralism in effect in the United States differs from the English version in two important respects. First, as already noted, a legally valid marriage can be formed in some American states with no formalities whatever. Second, the American system of coexisting civil and religious methods for

151. Id. at 36, 39.
152. Law Commission Report No. 53, above, note 121 at pars. 21–22.
153. *Cretney* 40.
154. *Id.*

concluding marriages does not accord the same degree of deference to religious law and does not reserve the privilege of concluding a marriage outside the office of a public official to those persons who wish to be married in a religious ceremony. In short, the American system as a whole is characterized by a higher degree of informality than the other systems and by the smallest degree of compulsory ritual.

Common Law Marriage. As in England until 1753, couples in some fourteen American states can form a legal marriage (providing there is no impediment) simply by agreeing to be husband and wife and holding themselves out as such.[155] Obviously, where common law marriages are recognized, compulsory marriage preliminaries or formalities do not apply to them. A few states which do not recognize common law marriage recognize a type of legal marriage arising from the registration of a written declaration that a marriage exists.[156]

Formal Legal Marriage. In most American states, the very existence of statutes establishing marriage preliminaries and regulating the solemnization and registration of marriage has been interpreted to exclude the possibility of forming a legal marriage informally. But regulation of the solemnization of marriage is minimal in the United States. A wide variety of civil and religious officials are authorized to perform marriages. Most states require witnesses but do not impose any particular form of ceremony.[157] Every state has provision for recording marriage certificates, but some states permit this record to be kept confidential under certain circumstances.[158] The present legal regulation of marriage in the United States is basically just a matter of licensing and registration. This appears clearly in the Uniform Marriage and Divorce Act, which, in this area, simply restates well-established features of state law. The draftsmen's comment to the "solemnization and registration" provision explains that the provision was "designed to take account of the increasing tendency of marrying couples to want a personalized ceremony, without traditional church, religious, or civil trappings."[159] According to the comment, the provision "authorizes one of the parties to such a [personalized] marriage ceremony to complete the marriage certificate form and forward it to the appropriate official for registration."[160]

Though the Uniform Act and the state laws regulating marriage formation

155. See below, chapter 6, text at note 97.

156. Montana Code Ann. §40-1-311 (1985); Texas Family Code §1.94 (Supp. 1987).

157. Several states expressly provide that no particular form is required except that the parties must declare that they take each other as husband and wife. *Clark* 39.

158. *E.g.*, California Civil Code §4213 (1970), *as amended*, (Supp. 1987).

159. UMDA §206 and Comment thereto.

160. *Id.*

are really just marriage registration laws, few couples actually dispense entirely with a ceremony. A more significant social phenomenon than the desire identified by the UMDA draftsmen of some people to dispense with religious and civil wedding ceremonies is the tendency to dispense with formal legal marriage altogether. This informal marriage behavior regularly gives rise to a variety of legal problems which we will examine in chapter 6.

The marriage registration systems of the various American states operate, as in England, to make records available to the parties and to permit the accumulation of some vital statistics, but in contrast to their continental counterparts, they do not provide a basis for a wholly reliable check on the identity or marital status of any particular individual.

Compulsory Civil Ceremony: France and West Germany

France

Celebration. French revolutionary legislation broke completely with the former ecclesiastical monopoly of marriage, making marriage a civil contract and denying all legal effect to the religious celebration of marriages. In the postrevolutionary era, the civil marriage ceremony was made compulsory in the Civil Code, and it spread from France to many other parts of the world, including most of continental Europe. The secularization of marriage in France had little effect, however, on the custom of having a religious wedding ceremony. It is still very common in France for couples to proceed directly from their civil wedding (which is required by law to take place before any religious ceremony) to a wedding in church.

The French civil ceremony itself, though completely secularized, contains more elements of ritual than its counterpart in any other system. The marriage must be celebrated by the *officier de l'état civil* (often the *maire*) of the commune.[161] The celebrant must formally ask the future spouses (and, if they are minors, their parents, who must be present) to declare whether a marriage contract has been made, and if so the date of the contract as well as the name and address of the notary who has kept a copy of the contract.[162] As part of the ceremony the celebrant must read to the couple certain articles of the French Civil Code.[163] This is what they hear:

> Spouses mutually owe each other fidelity, support, and assistance. The spouses together assure the material and moral direction of the family. They provide for the upbringing of the children and prepare for their future. If the matrimonial agreement does not regulate the

161. French Civil Code arts. 74, 75, 165.   162. French Civil Code art. 75.
163. *Id.*

contribution of the spouses to the expenses of the marriage, they contribute to them in proportion to their respective abilities. The spouses are mutually bound to a community of life.[164]

These provisions are taken from that part of the Code which sets out the "primary matrimonial regime," the set of rules which applies to all marriages and cannot be varied by contract. This obligatory reading from secular scripture at the marriage ceremony is a way in which a certain ideology of marriage is transmitted. However, the message currently enshrined in the Code is not the one which has always been there. A couple today hears that they are to run the household and the family together, but prior to 1970 they would have been told that "the husband is the head of the family." Prior to 1938, they would have heard the original language of the Code Napoleon, indeed the language of Napoleon himself (for these words were included at his personal insistence): "The husband owes protection to his wife, the wife obedience to her husband." After the Code reading, the celebrant must request the parties, one after the other, to declare that they take each other for husband or wife. He or she then pronounces "in the name of the law" that they are united in marriage and draws up the marriage certificate on the spot.[165] This ritual, more elaborate than that required by the other legal systems here examined, has nevertheless drawn the same sort of criticism as has the English civil ceremony for being banal and bureaucratic. Yet here is how Jean Carbonnier, the chief architect of the modern code provisions on the family, sees the civil ceremony:

> Even though secularized, marriage has a sort of religious gravity which is peculiar to it and which separates it from the free union—a gravity based on the idea that man's binding himself until death is an aspect of his intimation of mortality and his struggle against the ephemeral nature of existence. . . . As for the minority who marry only civilly, it is difficult to reconstruct their ethical notions, but no matter how little of the sublime there is in the civil rites . . . with which they content themselves, it is likely that they attribute to marriage at least that sacred value which popular morality accords to any exchange of promises.[166]

To a greater extent than elsewhere, marriage formation law in France seems to be part and parcel of the country's civil religion.

Registration. Unlike England and the United States, France has a system

164. French Civil Code arts. 212, 213, 214, and 215.
165. French Civil Code art. 75.
166. Jean Carbonnier, *Flexible droit: textes pour une sociologie du droit sans rigueur* (Paris: L.G.D.J., 1971), 137.

of marriage registration which, together with a national identity system, permits highly reliable verification of statements made by individuals concerning their civil status and facilitates the policing of the system of marriage impediments. Not only is the marriage certificate itself recorded, but as mentioned above, a note of the marriage is entered on the margin of an individual's birth certificate. This is but one feature of the system, which France gave to the rest of the world, of complete registration under state control of events such as births, deaths, marriages, and divorces which affect a citizen's legal status.[167] As the examples of England and the United States demonstrate, the system which was established, elaborated, and perfected in France and imitated all over the world has not been implemented everywhere with such thoroughness as in its home country. Nor has thoroughness in these matters been seen everywhere as desirable.

West Germany

Celebration. The system of compulsory civil marriage was introduced in all of Germany in 1875 and was maintained in the German Civil Code of 1896 as well as in the present Marriage Law.[168] As in France, the civil ceremony must precede any religious ceremony, and the practice of having two successive ceremonies is common.[169] The current West German version, however, has fewer aspects of obligatory ritual than the French, and the principle of compulsory civil marriage is more controversial. The current Marriage Law provides that a marriage must be concluded before a public official, in the presence of two witnesses.[170] The registrar must ask each of the future spouses whether they wish to enter marriage with the other.[171] After they have assented, he or she is to pronounce "in the name of the law" that they are from then on legally bound as spouses, and to record the marriage.[172] Failure to observe these requirements does not, however, make the marriage invalid. A 1976 amendment added that the spouses must be asked at the time of the ceremony whether they wish to make a stipulation concerning the name they will bear in the future.[173] West German law specifies that the ceremony "shall be appropriate to the significance of marriage" and that it shall be conducted in solemn fashion.[174] The obligatory civil marriage has been criticized as violating the spirit of Article 4 of the West German Basic Law (which guarantees freedom of religion), but the prevailing view is that the complete separation

167. *Rheinstein* 198, 204.
168. H. F. Thomas, *Formlose Ehen* (Bielefeld: Gieseking 1973), 95.
169. *Gernhuber* 107; PStG §67.
170. EheG §§11, 14.   171. EheG §13.
172. EheG §14.   173. EheG §13 A.
174. PStG §8.

of church and state in the present marriage formation law satisfies the Constitution.[175]

Registration. In West Germany registration of civil status is not centralized. As in France, however, it is, together with a national system of identification, organized in such a way as to permit effective verification of vital information about spouses. Registrars of civil status are required by law to keep a marriage book, a family book, a birth book, and a death book.[176] The family book collects and coordinates records of changes in civil status, of deaths, births, marriages, marriage terminations by divorce or annulment, and remarriages, in order to facilitate inquiry into all aspects of a person's current status.[177]

Sweden

In Sweden, as in England, civil marriage was made an alternative to religious marriage, rather than a compulsory procedure. As in England, too, marriages in Sweden must be concluded before a religious or civil authority, not informally. But certain features of Swedish regulation of the formation of marriage set it apart from the other systems described here as pluralistic. In the first place, both the optional civil ceremony and the secular version of the Tridentine decree abolishing informal marriage appeared quite late in Sweden. Civil marriage was made available for marriages between Christians and Jews in 1863 but did not become an option in other situations until 1908.[178] The Swedish law providing that civil or religious celebration is the only means of concluding a valid marriage did not appear until 1915.[179] Prior to that time, the exchange of promises to marry, followed by sexual intercourse, gave rise to certain of the legal effects of marriage. These "uncompleted marriages" were not at all unusual in rural areas.

The most interesting feature of the 1915 legislation on Formation and Dissolution of Marriage was the introduction of some quite modern ideas about marriage itself. The 1915 law prescribed the following formula to be read by the pastor or secular official by whom the marriage is performed: "The purpose of marriage is the welfare of the individuals who desire to enter matrimony. Do you AB take CD as your wife for better or for worse? Do you CD

---

175. Klaus G. Mayer-Teschendorf, "Standesamtliche Eheschliessungsform und Grundgesetz," 1982 *Das Standesamt* 325.

176. PStG §1.

177. PStG §§2, 12.

178. Folke Schmidt, "The Prospective Law of Marriage," 15 *Scandinavian Studies in Law* 191, 196 (1971).

179. *Id.* at 204.

take AB as your husband for better or for worse?" [180] The early twentieth-century Swedish marriage legislation was intended to go well beyond the French revolutionary marriage laws. Not only was marriage to be freed from its religious foundations, but wives were to be liberated from dependence on their husbands. [181] Subsequent Swedish developments have innovated further. In 1969 the Committee for the Reform of Family Law recommended that both civil and ecclesiastical ceremonies be made purely voluntary and that a valid marriage could be formed by simple registration. [182] When this proposal was rejected, the Committee recommended in 1972 that official recognition of religious marriage be eliminated and that marriage be concluded by a formal declaration to the registrars of civil status. [183] Although these proposals were not adopted in the comprehensive revision of Swedish Marriage Law which eventually took place, another change, equally significant on the ideological level, was made. Apparently in the hope of making legal marriage more attractive (or less intimidating) to cohabitants, Swedish law now gives couples the option to request the official performing a civil marriage to omit from the ceremony the exchange of vows for life. [184]

The Ideologizing of Freedom to Marry

The evolution of English, French, German, and American marriage formation law has long been marked by currents favorable to an individual's right to marry and to freely choose his or her spouse. As individuals have gradually achieved independence, for better or worse, from the types of family and group ties that characterized pre-modern society, nearly all elements of political, ecclesiastical, or family control over marriage decisions have disappeared from the law of marriage formation. A long, slow, process of social and economic change has constantly nudged the law in the direction of more freedom to marry. But most of the legal changes took place without any particular reference to the idea that marriage was a fundamental human right. No "right to marry" is to be found expressly stated in the constitutions of France, West Germany, or the United States, or in any English statute, although such a right is mentioned in several twentieth-century international conventions and

180. *Rheinstein* 127.

181. Schmidt, above, note 178 at 197.

182. Note, "Current Legal Developments, Sweden," 19 *International and Comparative Law Quarterly* 164 (1970).

183. Note, "Family Law—Sweden (follow-up)," 22 *International and Comparative Law Quarterly* 766 (1973).

184. Anders Agell, "The Swedish Legislation on Marriage and Cohabitation: A Journey Without a Destination," 1980 *Scandinavian Studies in Law* 9, 13.

declarations.[185] Yet, beginning in the 1960s in France, West Germany, and the United States, courts at the highest level, dealing with the few remaining restrictions on an individual's freedom to marry or to choose a spouse, began to articulate the issues as involving a basic right. In England, the evolution of the law has proceeded along much the same lines as in the other three countries but with much less ideological discussion.

The pronouncements of the French Court of Cassation, the West German Constitutional Court, and the United States Supreme Court, together with their reception in the scholarly writing in each country, crown the developments recounted here, and at the same time create a new atmosphere for the further development of marriage-formation law. In each country that atmosphere is somewhat different.

France

The evolution of the law of marriage formation in the direction of increased freedom to marry and to choose one's spouse can be seen more clearly in the changes that have occurred since 1804 in the French Civil Code than in the law of England, Germany, or the United States. Developments in England and the United States, though similar, have been less visible, having accrued gradually through piecemeal case-law and statutory reforms, rather than being emblazoned upon a national monument, as one may well characterize the Code Napoleon. Since the family law provisions of the German Civil Code (which went into effect in 1900) were already modern in several ways, the contrast between the original code provisions and current law is less great in Germany than in France.

The French civil law scholar who was entrusted in the 1960s with the task of revising many important family law provisions of the Civil Code, Jean Carbonnier, has written: "An affirmation of the liberty of man in the formation of the matrimonial bond is the essence of the French message for the social order. . . . The history of our marriage law for the past one hundred and fifty years is the history of a continuous liberation." [186] The message is

185. *E.g.*, Universal Declaration of Human Rights, adopted by the General Assembly of the United Nations on 10 December 1948 (Art. 16–1: "Men and women of full age, without any limitation due to race, nationality, or religion, have the right to marry and to found a family"); International Covenant on Civil and Political Rights, adopted by the General Assembly of the United Nations on 16 December 1966, Art. 23–2; European Convention for the Protection of Human Rights and Fundamental Freedoms, signed in Rome on 4 November 1950, Art. 12.

186. Jean Carbonnier, "Terre et ciel dans le droit français du mariage," in *Le droit privé français au milieu du XXe siècle. Études offertes à Georges Ripert*, vol. 1 (Paris: L.G.D.J., 1950), 325, 327–28.

rooted in the emphasis on individual liberty in the French Declaration of the Rights of Man and the Citizen of 1789. But in the postrevolutionary era, the legislators were less willing to promote individualism in domestic relations law than in the areas of property and contract. Thus the marriage law of the Code, like that of the *ancien régime*, reinforced paternal authority and treated the family more as a unit rather than as a collection of individuals.

The original scheme of the Civil Code (in which the marriage of a family member was treated as very much the affair of the group which the marriage was destined to perpetuate) has given way over time to a set of provisions which increasingly treat marriage as the affair of the individual spouses. This rise of individualism in French family law has been accompanied, interestingly, by the gradual decline of individualistic notions in French property law. The cross-movements are doubtless related, in the sense that the wider social distribution of both wealth and the risk of economic misfortune has made individualism in family law possible. As Alain Bénabent has put it, "When this role of assuring security is transferred from the family to the state, the social bond becomes stronger but family bonds relax proportionately and we tend to approach the ideal to which the men of 1789 aspired: every individual would have a direct relationship with the state, without 'intermediaries' ".[187] In cross-national perspective, however, although French law does increasingly promote individual freedom in marriage, it still bears more traces than the other three systems of an older social order.

It was not until 1968 that the diverse transforming trends were brought together in an idea of a "right to marry" by the highest French court for private law matters, the Court of Cassation.[188] The groundwork for this decision had been laid by a 1963 Paris Court of Appeals decision. The Paris Court (often an innovator) was the first to articulate the right judicially in France and has given it its fullest expression to date.[189] The 1963 case was a suit by an Air France stewardess seeking damages from the airline for wrongful termination of her employment contract. The company's defense was a clause in the employment contract which purported to give the employer the right to terminate the contract upon the marriage of the employee. The employee had good grounds in both contract law and labor law for resisting this defense, and the court did in fact rest its decision for the employee in part upon those grounds. So it is all the more remarkable that the court went on to say that even if the clause in the contract were not invalid under contract and labor law, it should be held void as a matter of public policy. The court said,

187. Bénabent, above, note 20 at 443.
188. Court of Cassation decision of 7 February 1968, D. 1968. Jur. 429.
189. Paris Court of Appeal decision of 30 April 1963, D. 1963. Jur. 428.

[T]he right to marry is an individual right *d'ordre public* which cannot be restricted or alienated; . . . [A]s a result, in the area of contractual relationships . . . the freedom to marry should in principle be safeguarded and in the absence of obvious and compelling reasons, a no-marriage clause should be declared void as infringing a fundamental personal right.[190]

The court further remarked that such a restriction on marriage, because of its tendency to encourage informal unions (not forbidden by the employment contract), constituted an infringement of good morals.[191] In 1968, the Court of Cassation held that a no-marriage clause in an employment contract was an unreasonable restriction of the "right to marry and the right to work," and in 1975 it gave its approval to the notion that the freedom to marry was a principle *d'ordre public.*[192]

West Germany

The German Civil Code of 1896 (which went into effect on January 1, 1900) is nearly a century younger than the French Civil Code. In contrast to the Code Napoleon, it was the product of many years of careful drafting, public scrutiny of drafts, and extensive revisions. It was a "modern" code, free of such vestiges from earlier times as the French requirement of a formal request by even an emancipated adult son or daughter for parental permission to marry or the elaborate system of formal objections to marriages. Nevertheless, its family law sections expressed the cohesion and authority structure of the family unit more than they did the independent individuality of the persons composing it. As in France, this pattern has altered over the past fifty years, especially in the period following World War II.[193]

In West Germany, the idea of a fundamental right to marry seems to have

190. *Id.* at 428–29. The concept of public order (*ordre public*) is an important one in French law. A great body of legal writing and case law has grown up in the effort to give content to the general language of Article 6 of the French Civil Code which provides that, "One may not derogate by private agreement from laws based on public order (*ordre public*) and considerations of morality (*bonnes moeurs*)."

191. *Id.* at 429.

192. Court of Cassation decisions of 7 February 1968, D. 1968. Jur. 429, and 17 October 1975, D. 1976. Jur. 511.

193. Most of the marriage provisions of the Civil Code were removed from the Code and extensively modified by the National Socialist Marriage Law for Greater Germany (Grossdeutsches Ehegesetz) of 6 July 1938, RGB1.I.807. The 1938 law was modified and reenacted by Allied Control Council Law No. 16 of 20 February 1946, 1946 KRAB1.77. The 1976 Marriage and Family Reform law made major changes in the law governing divorce and its consequences, but marriage formation in West Germany is still basically governed by the Control Council Law, which is referred to in shorthand form as the Ehegesetz (EheG).

been first articulated judicially by the Federal Supreme Administrative Court (*Bundesverwaltungsgericht*) in 1962.[194] It was implicitly accepted by the Federal Constitutional Court (*Bundesverfassungsgericht*) in a 1970 decision, and then emphatically endorsed by the Constitutional Court in 1971.[195] Like the French cases discussed above, the 1962 West German case arose in the employment context. Here, however, the employer was the government, and the plaintiff was a police officer who had married without securing the advance permission he was required to seek under administrative regulations. The Supreme Administrative Court did not invalidate the requirement of permission, but it did hold that the refusal of permission to marry was an infringement of Article 6 of the Basic Law of 1949 under the particular circumstances of this case where a child had already been conceived. The court went on to hold that the plaintiff's marriage without permission was not a "gross violation" of his official duties.

The constitutional article referred to by the Court says nothing about a right to marry. It simply states that: "Marriage and the family enjoy the special protection of the state." [196] However, the Constitutional Court held in 1970 that the constitutionally protected institution of marriage rests "upon the free decision of husband and wife." [197] Then, in 1971, the Constitutional Court discussed the matter more fully in a case involving the question whether a Spaniard, wanting to marry a German woman divorced in Germany from a German husband, had sufficiently complied with the statutory requirement that a foreigner must produce documentary evidence of his capacity (under the law of the country of which he is a national) to marry, given that his future wife's divorce would not have been recognized at that time in Spain.[198] Holding that the denial of permission to marry in these circumstances was in violation of the Basic Law, the Court said that Article 6 guarantees even to a foreigner the "freedom to marry" (*Eheschliessungsfreiheit*) with a spouse of his own choice.[199]

These judicial decisions do not, however, establish an unqualified right to marry. Article 6 is certainly ambiguous so far as marriage formation is con-

194. Bundesverwaltungsgericht decision of 22 February 1962, reported in 1962 *Zeitschrift für das gesamte Familienrecht* 303.

195. Bundesverfassungsgericht decisions of 7 October 1970, reported in 29 *BVerfG* 166 (1971), and 4 May 1971, reported in 1971 *Neue Juristische Wochenschrift* 1509.

196. Grundgesetz (Basic Law) of 1949, Art. 6, I.1.

197. Bundesverfassungsgericht decision of 7 October 1970, above, note 195 at 176.

198. Bundesverfassungsgericht decision of 4 May 1971, above, n. 195. See also Hans Stöcker, "Der internationale Ordre Public im Familien- und Familienerbrecht," 38 *Rabels Zeitschrift* 79–127 (1974).

199. This result is now codified in the 1986 conflict of laws statute, IPR-Gesetz, §13(2)(3) EGBGB, above, n. 96.

cerned. The fact that it places marriage and family under the special protection of the state arguably supports marriage impediments to the extent that they are "protective" of the institution of marriage.[200] Similarly, the right to marry in Article 12 of the European Convention on Human Rights, often cited in West German discussions, seems primarily intended to prevent discrimination against persons or groups of persons in marriage law. It expressly recognizes that there may be differences among the laws of the individual states: "Men and women of marriageable age have the right to marry and to found a family, according to the national laws governing the exercise of this right."[201]

Consequently, in West Germany as in France, it is uncertain what practical consequences flow from the establishment of a right to marry. It is sometimes argued that Article 6 of the Basic Law, together with Article 4 guaranteeing freedom of thought and religion, mean that certain aspects of marriage-formation law are constitutionally required. Some think that the introduction of optional religious celebration of marriage is required by religious freedom; others that religious freedom requires the continuation of the compulsory civil ceremony. Professor Neuhaus has cautioned that it may be unwise to frame these issues as constitutional questions, contending that the "persuasive power of such reasoning is small, and arguments in these terms lead rather to an aggravation of existing differences."[202] From this point of view, the approach which England has so far taken in the area of marriage formation—practical, functional, without sloganizing the issues—has much to recommend it.

United States

Recognition of "the freedom to marry" by the United States Supreme Court came in 1967, in one of the many cases involving issues of racial discrimination which reached the Court in the 1960s. As in France and West Germany, the decision by the highest court had been foreshadowed by decisions of lower (in this case, state) courts.[203] It had roots, too, in the Court's own dicta in previous cases.[204] The case of *Loving v. Virginia* involved a Virginia statute prohibiting interracial marriages.[205] In a unanimous opinion written by

200. *Beitzke* 49–50.

201. European Convention for the Protection of Human Rights and Fundamental Freedoms, Art. 12.

202. P. H. Neuhaus, "Zur Reform des deutschen formellen Eheschliessungsrechts," 1972 *Zeitschrift für das gesamte Familienrecht* 59.

203. The most important of these was *Perez v. Lippold*, 198 P.2d 17 (Cal. 1948).

204. In particular, *Meyer v. Nebraska*, 262 U.S. 390, 399 (1923) and *Skinner v. Oklahoma*, 316 U.S. 535, 541 (1942).

205. 388 U.S. 1 (1967).

Chief Justice Warren, the Court struck down the Virginia statute (and by implication the fifteen other state miscegenation statutes then existing) as violative of the Equal Protection and Due Process clauses of the fourteenth amendment to the United States Constitution.[206] In holding that the statute deprived the Lovings of liberty without due process of law the Court said:

> The freedom to marry has long been recognized as one of the vital personal rights essential to the orderly pursuit of happiness by free men.
> Marriage is one of the "basic civil rights of man," fundamental to our very existence and survival. . . . Under our Constitution, the freedom to marry, or not marry, a person of another race resides with the individual and cannot be infringed by the State.[207]

But for this expansive rhetoric, which, like that of the French and West German courts, went beyond what the decision of the case at hand actually required, *Loving v. Virginia* would have been an unremarkable application of the Equal Protection Clause, a part of the process of securing full equality to members of minority groups. But with this language, the case casts doubt on the validity of much state regulation of marriage.

Loving has a special significance within the American federal system because, by virtue of the legal supremacy of the national Constitution, it potentially subjects to federal reexamination and evaluation a large body of state statutory and case law which had previously been taken for granted. However, as we have seen, state law already had been developing in broadly similar fashion to that of England, France, and West Germany, gradually shedding anachronistic provisions. At the time, one scholar described the *Loving* decision as merely giving constitutional status to a preexisting "profound consensus" in the United States that the state and the law should say "as little as possible about who should marry whom." [208] Whether it really ratified a consensus to that effect or contributed to creating one itself is open to discussion, but the *Loving* decision did accelerate the process of deregulating the forma-

---

206. Section 1 of the fourteenth amendment, added to the U.S. Constitution in 1868, provides: "All persons born or naturalized in the United States, and subject to the jurisdiction thereof, are citizens of the United States and of the State wherein they reside. No State shall make or enforce any law which shall abridge the privileges or immunities of citizens of the United States; nor shall any State deprive any person of life, liberty, or property, without due process of law; nor deny to any person within its jurisdiction the equal protection of the laws."

207. *Loving v. Virginia*, 388 U.S. 1, 12 (1967). The interior quote is from *Skinner v. Oklahoma*, 316 U.S. 535, 541 (1942), which held unconstitutional a law providing for the compulsory sterilization of habitual criminals.

208. Robert F. Drinan, "American Laws Regulating the Formation of the Marriage Contract," 38 *Annals of the American Academy of Political and Social Science* 48, 49 (1969).

tion of marriage. Its influence is apparent in the provisions of the Uniform Marriage and Divorce Act.

Conclusion

The foregoing survey of marriage-formation law is far from demonstrating in itself that the posture of the state with respect to the family is radically changing in the four countries whose law has been examined. But it is an important part of the case to be made. Thus far, we have seen that state involvement in the questions of who can marry, who marries whom, and how they do it is generally diminishing, while some modern forms of state intervention in aspects of marriage formation are increasing. The strength of the trends is not the same in all four countries.

As to the diminution of official interest in who marries whom, marriage restrictions in all four countries are primarily statements of notions about what ought to be. In England and the United States, especially in the latter, the marriage impediments lack teeth. There seems to be no really effective way of preventing anyone who is determined to do so from evading them. As we have seen, the number of restrictions is everywhere being reduced to those involving age, simultaneous polygamy, and marriage among members of the core family. On closer examination, we see that age limits are set so low as to approach complete deregulation, and that even the polygamy and incest prohibitions are not so absolute as they first appear.

So far as the manner in which marriages are solemnized is concerned, only France at present exhibits much official interest in this matter. At the other extreme, in the United States, the state systems are scarcely distinguishable from straightforward marriage registration, and the Uniform Act continues this approach. The UMDA draftsmen claimed to have reduced premarital regulation to a minimum and stated that, as to this minimum, "substantial compliance" is enough.[209] In the other three countries, where it can be said that some sort of marriage ritual is compulsory, dissatisfaction with the official rituals has been registered on occasion, but there has been no serious move toward changing them. England has cast an eye toward the compulsory civil ceremony, West Germany has studied the pluralist compromise, and France has recognized that much of its system is anachronistic, but all are reluctant to alter long-standing arrangements which have in some sense entered into the marriage customs of the countries in question.

The marriage-formation laws of all four countries have been, and will continue to be, affected by their new approach to divorce law. To some, the fact

209. UMDA Prefatory Note, 4; Comment to §201.

that exit from marriage has become increasingly easy means that there is less reason to guard the entrance; to others, the fragility of marriage is all the more reason for vigilance. There is virtually no legal response to the suggestions occasionally made that entry into marriage should be made more difficult. Legislative movement is clearly in the direction of reducing impediments and formalities as well as mitigating the consequences of disregarding them. In the United States, all of these trends are reinforced by the tendency of the law to respond to diversity by becoming "neutral."

As for the increase in peculiarly modern forms of state interest, we have noted the use of the occasion of marriage to communicate certain types of information to the prospective spouses—whether it be the message of equality, as in France, or information about genetic defects and birth control, as in some American states. Social interest in record-keeping and data-gathering is also apparent. Sometimes information-gathering is in pursuit of the vague and benign aim of studying and supporting "the family." Sometimes it is for a more precise instrumental purpose, as is the case with the requirement of the social security number to facilitate enforcement of family support obligations in the United States. Even the reality of the consents exchanged by the spouses can become a public law issue when intent to evade immigration and nationality laws is suspected.

As we begin to reflect in the following chapters on what has happened to marriage itself in recent years, the various regulations concerning entry into the institution will appear to be part of a larger pattern. The ensemble of minor changes in the manner in which the legal institution of marriage is formed is one small but essential aspect of the revolution which is taking place in the way Western governments interact with families in the late twentieth century. As we will see, legal distinctions between being married and being single and between marriage and informal cohabitation are diminishing. In this light then, the ideologizing of the freedom to marry has appeared on the scene just at the moment when legal marriage is losing much of its traditional significance. As marriage impediments and formalities fall away, those exercising the new-found "right to marry" may find that life on the other side of the door which once was not so easy to open is not much different, in a legal sense, from the life they left behind. In crossing the threshold, however, they may encounter an unexpected intimacy with the state.

As for the remaining civil marriage formalities, it is doubtful whether their debasement or disappearance will much affect such a persistent aspect of human behavior. Marriage rites of some sort are practically universal in human societies and, as mating rituals, are common even among animals.[210] In soci-

210. *König* 20–21.

eties where marriage has not been extensively regulated by law, it has nevertheless typically been accompanied by ritual and festivity. One may think of the Roman gifts of fire and water, Michael's capture of Sarah in *The Tinker's Wedding*, or the contemporary marriage palaces of the Soviet Union. Thus the description of legal developments in this chapter is in no way meant to dispute the underlying assumption of Yeats' question, "How but in custom and in ceremony / Are innocence and beauty born?"[211]

211. "A Prayer for my Daughter," *The Collected Poems of W. B. Yeats* (New York: Macmillan, 1956), 185, 187.

3
The Law of the Ongoing Family

I doubt whether there is a country in Europe in which the relation between husband and wife, parents and children, between the family and the outside world, as it actually takes form in life, corresponds to the norms of the positive law.

> Eugen Ehrlich, *Fundamental Principles of the Sociology of Law.* [1]

Legal Images of Family Relations

In almost any continental European treatise on family law, one finds, between the chapter on formation of marriage and the chapters on its dissolution, a rather extensive treatment of a subject that is almost completely neglected in Anglo-American coursebooks and treatises. The subject is the law of the ongoing marriage, or, as it is usually called in continental legal terminology, the legal effects of marriage (*Rechtswirkungen der Ehe; les effets du lien matrimonial*). It encompasses various aspects of how the fact of legal marriage affects the personal status, and the personal and property relationships of the spouses with each other, their children, and the outside world before the marriage has been disrupted by separation, divorce, or death.

The reason these matters are, to a great extent, nonsubjects in Anglo-American law has a great deal to do with the way the common law systems have evolved. English common law was the product of writs developed to deal with recurring types of disputes and of the slow accretion of judicial opinions in individual cases. It was a system of procedures rather than substantive rules. When systematizers and treatise writers tried to make sense of the sprawling, rather disorderly body of law produced in this fashion, they took their categories from the materials at hand—court decisions—generalizing from the types of situations that had given rise to lawsuits. This causes family law in the common law countries even today to have an entirely different appearance from its continental counterparts. As the author of the leading English family law treatise wrote in 1984, "Family law carries to an extreme degree the reluctance of English law to establish clear rights; . . . it is often necessary to ask first what procedures are available to resolve the issue in dispute." [2] Since spouses rarely seek legal intervention during a func-

---

1. Walter Moll, trans. (New York: Russell and Russell, 1962), 491 (Originally published 1936.)
2. *Cretney* 288.

tioning marriage, it is not surprising that little attention has been devoted in case-law systems to this stage of their relationship.

English political traditions, too, help to explain why the common law kept its distance from intrafamily affairs. As John Stuart Mill put it:

> In England, from the peculiar circumstances of our political history, though the yoke of opinion is perhaps heavier, that of law is lighter than in most other countries of Europe; and there is considerable jealousy of direct interference by the legislative or the executive power with private conduct, not so much from any just regard for the independence of the individual as from the still subsisting habit of looking on the government as representing an opposite interest to the public.[3]

Largely due to the influence of Mill and his followers, what had been a long-standing practice of noninterference in private life came in time to be regarded as a principle. The principle retains most of its vigor in the common law systems. On the rare occasions when spouses have asked judges to settle their intrafamily disputes, the courts have tended to respond as the Massachusetts Supreme Judicial Court did in a case in which a husband wanted some say as to whether his wife should have an abortion: "Except in cases involving divorce or separation, our law has not in general undertaken to resolve the many delicate questions inherent in the marriage relationship. . . . Some things must be left to private agreement."[4]

Things proceeded differently, at least in form, on the European continent. The great eighteenth- and nineteenth-century codifications were drafted by men who were determined that their codes would be systematic and comprehensive. Thus, for example, it seemed logical to the draftsmen of the German Civil Code to begin their treatment of family law with engagement, and to proceed from the formation of marriage to the legal effects of the ongoing marriage, and from there to divorce and the legal effects of divorce. In the codifications of the Enlightenment period, a strong attachment to system and theory coincided with an ambition to bring under legal regulation many matters that most of us today would consider to be beyond the power of the law to control, such as personal relationships within the family. Thus, the Prussian Code had specified that the purpose of marriage was the begetting and raising of children, and the French Civil Code provided that wives should obey their

---

3. John Stuart Mill, *On Liberty* (Indianapolis: Bobbs Merrill, 1956), 11–12.

4. *Doe v. Doe*, 314 N.E. 2d 128, 132 (Mass. 1974). The United States Supreme Court later put this result on a constitutional basis, holding that a woman's right of privacy was violated by a statute requiring her to seek her husband's consent to an abortion, *Planned Parenthood of Central Missouri v. Danforth*, 428 U.S. 52 (1976).

husbands, husbands should protect their wives, and children should honor and respect their fathers and mothers.[5]

It is not likely that those who penned such language harbored the illusion that law could compel family members to behave in a certain way.[6] Rather, their idea of law included an element which has found less acceptance in the Anglo-American tradition—the notion that law can persuade as well as command, and that it becomes operative not only through enforcement but also through education. Today, there is also a more modern justification for the explicit and extensive attention still given to the legal effects of marriage on the continent. Countries with national identity systems and comprehensive regulation of civil status feel the need for clear rules regarding an individual's name, nationality, domicile, and residence. In such countries, therefore, the law on the legal effects of marriage is closely linked to a highly developed set of rules on personal status.

Nevertheless, as we will see in this chapter, continental legal norms regarding the ongoing family are a strange kind of law. They tend to take the form of pronouncements of general models for behavior rather than specific rules of conduct with direct sanctions for their violation. At one time, legal norms on the rights and duties of husbands and wives were relevant on the question of whether a spouse had committed "fault" in the sense of the divorce law. But in the age of nonfault divorce, general rules on the husband-wife relationship are often just symbolic representations of an ideal of family life. It is precisely for this reason, however, that any change in this kind of law is particularly interesting. This law which is not "law" in the usual sense provides a window on the process through which the legal system confers and withholds approval of various types of conduct. The process is harder to discern in the Anglo-American systems where the underlying assumptions of family law are rarely made explicit. Generally, though, these assumptions can be perceived through the patterns of outcomes in specific cases.

5. Prussian General Code II.1. §1; French Civil Code, former art. 213 and art. 371.

6. The difficulty of regulating these matters must have appeared along with the first efforts to do so. The Book of Esther tells us that when Ahasuerus, the King of Persia, gave a great feast in order to display the riches and power of his kingdom, he commanded that Queen Vashti be brought out in all her finery. But the Queen refused to come. The King was advised by his wise men that if the Queen went unpunished, all the women in the kingdom would ignore the commandments of their husbands. Accordingly Vashti was banished forever, and it became part of the unalterable law of the Medes and the Persians that wives must obey their husbands. But then and now, as John Stuart Mill pointed out: "The real practical decision of affairs, to whichever may be given the legal authority, will greatly depend, as it even now does, upon comparative qualifications." John Stuart Mill, "The Subjection of Women," in John Stuart Mill and Harriet Taylor Mill, *Essays on Sex Equality*, ed. Alice Rossi (Chicago: University of Chicago Press, 1970), 123, 170.

What stories has the law been telling about families? In Western societies until recently, one set of ideas about family life found universal expression in the law. Beginning in the eighteenth century, Western family law became increasingly marriage-centered, treating the conjugal family of father, mother, and children as a unit, headed by the husband and father. Within this unit, separate spheres of activity were designated as appropriate for women and men. The wife was expected to be the principal caretaker of the home and children, and to collaborate with her husband on the farm, in the craft, or in the shop. The husband, as principal provider, was held responsible for the support of the family, had the final say concerning the place and mode of family life, and the power to deal with all the family property, including that of the wife. Children were subject to paternal authority until they reached majority.

Needless to say, these legal images did not necessarily correspond to the ideas or practices of all groups in society. The law in the eighteenth and early nineteenth centuries tended to express the values of elites—at that time, the professional classes and the gentry. It paid little attention to the needs of ordinary folk. The predominance it accorded to the husband within the conjugal family could always be tempered by private agreement if the wife's family was powerful enough: all of the traditional family law systems provided ways for the husband's powers to be restricted through marriage contracts or family settlements so as to protect the interests of the wife's blood relatives, especially where real estate was involved.

Beginning in the late nineteenth century, traditional family law was periodically readjusted to take account of changes in the economic basis of family life and to adapt to the needs and desires of wider groups in the population. But at last the center could not hold. Laws which might have been appropriate for the family engaged in running a farm or small business together, or for the housewife-breadwinner type of marriage when divorce was rare, no longer worked well when both men and women were in the labor force and divorce had become pandemic. Yet, until the 1960s, nearly every legislative attempt to regulate the family decision-making process gave the husband and father the dominant role.

This chapter describes how the law of the ongoing family has been gradually transformed, and how it continues to change, in England, France, the United States, and West Germany, as new ideas about family life and new patterns of family behavior vie for legal recognition. Without doubt, the most powerful transforming influence, beginning in the mid-nineteenth century, has been the inexorable advance of ideas of equality and individual liberty. With varying meanings and degrees of strength, these ambiguous and emotion-laden concepts have completely reshaped the law of the ongoing family, not only in the countries with which we are primarily concerned here, but also in many other places, such as Greece, Italy, Portugal, Spain, and Switzerland, where they produced an even sharper break with tradition.

Marriage

The French and German Civil Codes dealt elaborately with the personal relationship of husband and wife and, in particular, with the family decision-making process. Let us consider first how marriage was depicted in the French Civil Code of 1804 and how this image of marriage has been revised over the years through amendment or new judicial interpretations of old language. Today, as in 1804, the Code provides that spouses owe each other fidelity, support, and assistance.[7] Originally, they were entitled to expect something more, for as we have already mentioned, the Code provided that "The husband owes protection to his wife, the wife obedience to her husband."[8] These reciprocal duties were spelled out further in an article which read:

> The wife is obliged to live with her husband, and to follow him wherever he judges it appropriate to reside; the husband is obliged to receive her and to furnish her with all that is necessary, according to his ability and his station.[9]

In 1938 the duties of protection and obedience were deleted, but until 1970 the Code proclaimed that the husband was the "head of the family." A wife had to seek her husband's permission to work outside the home until 1965; the husband remained primarily responsible for the support of the family and had the last word concerning where the family would reside until

---

7. French Civil Code, art. 212.

8. *Id.*, former art. 213. The duty of obedience was one of the few provisions of the Civil Code inserted at Napoleon's personal insistence. He is recorded as having said on the occasion: "Women ought to obey us. Nature has made women our slaves! A husband ought to be able to say to his wife: 'Madam, you will not go to the theatre; Madam, you will not see such or such a person; Madam, you belong to me body and soul.'" Recounting this story to an audience of Canadian law students, the French civil law scholar, René Savatier, commented: "When one hears his impassioned tone, one realizes that this was not simply a legal question. It was a domestic matter. Bonaparte was thinking about Josephine! During the Egyptian campaign, there were a certain number of men whom Josephine found pleasing; and this fact rankled in the memories of Bonaparte! So it was the spiteful act of a man who could not succeed in making his wife obey him that was responsible for the insertion of this historic phrase in our Civil Code. . . . One should not attach more importance to it than that. Not even Napoleon had the power to make his wife always obey him!" René Savatier, "La femme et son ménage dans le mariage français," in *Le Droit dans la Vie Familiale*, ed. Jacques Boucher and André Morel (Montreal: Presses de l'Université de Montréal, 1970), 173, 177.

9. French Civil Code, former art. 214.

1975; and the husband remained the manager of the couple's community property until 1985.

Piecemeal amendments, beginning at the turn of the century, eventually removed all vestiges of the married woman's legal incapacity from the Civil Code. The spouses have now been made equally responsible for family support and have been given equal say in choosing a place of residence, raising their children, and managing common property. The great symbolic turning point came in 1970, when the husband was deposed as "head of the family," and the following language concerning family authority was substituted: "The spouses together assure the moral and material direction of the family." [10] The legislature then went on to set forth what it may have expected to become the new organizing principle of French family law: "The spouses are mutually bound to a community of life." [11] But it has not proved easy to give any meaningful content to the idea of marital community. All that the Paris Court of Appeal could find to say in a case involving the question of how the obligation to live in community bore on a disagreement between husband and wife about their place of residence, was:

> [I]t is certain that this community of life will not take on the same form, nor the same intimacy in each household; it is not up to the law, but to each family to work out the modalities of the community of life between spouses who may have serious difficulties and whose personal and material potential may be quite diverse. [12]

The changes wrought by the 1970 law were described by the Minister of Justice at the time as reflecting the evolution of mores and family practices in France. [13] If so, it was an evolution that had been well underway for many years. As early as 1945, the legislature had ignored a compelling argument that the time for such a change was already overdue:

> The power of the head of the family can be justified if the family must defend itself by arms; it can even be understood if, because of the social and economic structure, the man is stronger in a social sense, or acts alone in daily affairs. But this is no longer the case; it is no longer the man alone who earns the living for the family; the wife generally has an education equivalent to that of the husband, and she has equal political rights. The notion of a head of the family is contrary to good sense and contrary to reality.

10. *Id.*, art. 213.
11. *Id.*, art. 215.
12. Paris Court of Appeal decision of 2 February 1973, D. 1973. Jur. 524.
13. Claude Columbet, "Commentaire de la loi du 4 juin 1970 sur l'autorité parentale," D. 1971. Chr. 1, 3.

Real family unity under these circumstances does not depend on the authority given to one of the spouses (such an authoritarian conception can only give rise to conflict); it depends on the unity of the two spouses. If they get along well (and this will be more difficult if you require the submission of one), the family will last; if they do not get along, the exercise of authority which is not accepted will only serve to poison the situation.[14]

It seems likely that what caused the National Assembly to act in 1970 was not logical argument of this sort but rather the jolt they had received from the French worker-student uprising in May of 1968. The reform law was presented as corresponding to the ideas about equality and shared authority held by "young people today."[15] The 1970 draftsmen, no less than their nineteenth-century predecessors, had the notion that law performs a pedagogical role. The Minister of Justice made this explicit:

The Civil Code can fulfill an educational function by encouraging the spouses to exchange their points of view on all the important questions which arise in connection with the running of the household and the education of the children, as well as to come to agreement, before marriage, concerning a common ethic.[16]

In the same vein, the Senate Report on the reform bill stated:

[I]t is good to set down in writing and to proclaim to young husbands, when they present themselves before a public official at the dawn of their married life, that the wife has achieved equality with the husband, and that it is up to him to seek out with her the ways of exercising this right.[17]

German family law has taken a similar course in moving from a patriarchal to an egalitarian model. But it did not have so far to travel, for the German Civil Code of 1896 was quite modern in comparison to the French codification of nearly a century earlier. In the German Civil Code, the husband's powers and rights were predominant but not absolute, and rather than imposing a duty of obedience on the wife, the German Code already prescribed an ideal of *Lebensgemeinschaft*: "The spouses are obliged to live together in a matrimonial community of life."[18] But the division of labor and of decision-

---

14. *Id.* at 5, quoting a speech by Julliot de la Morandière. Cf.: "Things never come to an issue of downright power on one side, and obedience on the other, except where the connexion altogether has been a mistake, and it would be a blessing to both parties to be relieved from it." Mill, above, note 6 at 170.

15. Columbet, above, note 13 at 5.   16. *Id.*

17. *Id.* at 11.   18. German Civil Code §1353.

making power within this community was arranged according to gender. Thus the husband had the right to "decide all matters of matrimonial life," including the family's place of residence, although the wife was not obliged to follow the husband's decision if it was an "abuse" of his right.[19] In addition, he had limited rights to give notice of termination to his wife's employer, and to manage his wife's property.[20]

This legal conception of family life in the Civil Code could not survive the post-World War II period. It was fundamentally at odds with the spirit and letter of the West German Basic Law (Constitution) of 1949, which proclaimed the principle of equality of the sexes and the right of each individual to the "free development of his personality."[21] The Constitution also guaranteed the protection of the private sphere of marriage and the family from interference by the state.[22] Thus, for these three ideals to coexist in harmony, a new understanding of "marriage" and "the family" had to be worked out.

More than a little hesitation characterized the initial West German efforts to implement the equality principle. Foreseeing that the transition would not be easy, the Constitution had provided for a delay of four years before the equality provision would become self-executing. This was supposed to give the legislature plenty of time to make the necessary changes in existing laws. The four years passed, however, with no legislative action at all. Thus the courts in 1953 were faced with the task of implementing the equality principle on their own. Accordingly, they began to strike down provision after provision of the Civil Code. Finally, in 1957, the legislature came up with an Equality Law (*Gleichberechtigungsgesetz*).[23]

But even then, the move toward equality was less than wholehearted. The 1957 law left untouched, for example, several provisions of the Civil Code which indirectly accorded a dominant position to the husband by enshrining housewife-marriage as the cultural ideal. For example, Article 1356 began by stating that "The wife's responsibility is to run the household," and went on to provide that a wife could work outside the home so long as this was compatible with her marital and family duties. Wives did not in fact gain equal legal rights to independent work outside the home until this article was amended in 1976. The West German experience illustrates, among other things, that strong constitutional pronouncements of equality do not transform

19. German Civil Code, former §1354.
20. German Civil Code, former §§1358 and 1363.
21. *Grundgesetz* (Basic Law) of 1949, art. 3(2), art. 2(1).
22. *Id.*, art. 6.
23. Gesetz über die Gleichberechtigung von Mann und Frau auf dem Gebiet des bürgerlichen Rechts (*GleichberG*) of 18 June 1957, BGBl. I.609.

society and law overnight. But the fact that this was the state of West German law until 1976 renders all the more significant the changes brought about by the family law reforms of that year.

In the Social Democratic government's 1976 marriage and divorce law,[24] the model of housewife-and-maintenance marriage was replaced by the idea of marriage as a partnership of spouses pursuing their chosen occupations and arranging their home life by common accord.

> §1356 (1) The spouses conduct the running of the household by mutual agreement. If the running of the household is left to one of the spouses, that spouse manages the household on his own responsibility. (2) Both spouses have the right to be employed. In the choice and exercise of an occupation they must pay due regard to the interests of the other spouse and the family.

Here we have an entirely changed concept of marriage—a community of life in which the partners work out their own roles in consultation with, and having regard to the interests of, each other and the family. This now is the "marriage" which according to Article 6 of the Constitution enjoys the "special protection of the State."

At present, nearly all the old provisions giving preeminence to the husband have been repealed by the Equality Law or by the Marriage and Family Law Reform of 1976, or they have been declared unconstitutional by the courts. The net effect is that the original emphasis in the Civil Code on the community aspect of marriage stands out more clearly than ever, but with new meaning. The *Lebensgemeinschaft* of the 1980s is not that of the 1890s. What "marital community of life" shall mean is now left up to the determination of the parties (as the Constitutional Court said when it removed the barriers to a transsexual's marriage).[25] In view of such statements, and with the drastic curtailment of the role of fault under the 1976 Divorce Reform Law, it might be questioned whether the idea of *Lebensgemeinschaft* has any real content left. Prevailing scholarly opinion holds, however, that the duty of the spouses to live in community is a legal as well as a moral one.[26] Although, as in France, it does not necessarily imply a duty to live together, it has at least

24. Erstes Gesetz zur Reform des Ehe- und Familienrechts (*EheRG*) of 14 June 1976, BGBl. I. 1421.

25. Bundesverfassungsgericht decision of 11 October 1978, reported in 1979 *Neue Juristische Wochenschrift* 595.

26. Dieter Giesen, "Allgemeine Ehewirkungen gem. §§1353, 1356 BGB im Spiegel der Rechtsprechung," 1983 *Juristische Rundschau* 89, 91.

enough substance to support a wife's action to compel the removal of her husband's mistress from the marital dwelling.[27]

The transformation of the ideologies of marriage expressed in French and West German law is a highly visible response to changes in the economic and social roles of women and in ideas about married life. In the uncodified Anglo-American law, however, the process is less readily apparent. No model of married life has been as explicitly enshrined in our law as it was in the French and German Codes,[28] and we have few cases on relationships in the ongoing family. Yet, though Anglo-American family law lacked general, sweeping statements about the nature of marriage and the roles of spouses, it was in fact organized along broadly similar lines to the French and German law. The old common law institution of coverture and numerous specific rules of family law emphasized the unity of the married couple and assigned the husband and father the dominant role in the family.[29] The notion of consortium vaguely expressed the right of the spouses to each other's company, cooperation, and aid. Over time, as on the continent, traditional family law was gradually altered under the influence of the expansion of individualism and egalitarianism, the entry of women into the labor force, and the increase in divorce. In the United States, the combined effects of the Married Women's Acts of the late nineteenth and early twentieth century, the Equal Protection Clause of the Fourteenth Amendment to the Constitution, recent equal rights amendments to many state constitutions, state and federal civil rights legislation, and innumerable court decisions have eliminated or rendered null nearly all vestiges of sexual inequality in matters of domicile, choice of residence, management of property, and so on. A similar evolution has taken place through statutes and case law in England.

But while continental systems keep open the possibility of judicial intervention on occasion in disputes that arise in the ongoing marriage, recent developments in the United States appear to reinforce the traditional approach

27. Decision of Oberlandesgericht-Celle of 29 November 1979, reported in 1980 *Zeitschrift für das gesamte Familienrecht* 242.

28. The words "The husband is the head of the family" did, however, creep into some state statutes during a short-lived flurry of interest in codification in nineteenth-century United States; *e.g.*, former California Civil Code §5101, repealed in 1975.

29. Blackstone's formulation has become (in)famous: "By marriage, the husband and wife are one person in law: that is, the very being or legal existence of the woman is suspended during marriage, or at least is incorporated and consolidated into that of the husband under whose wing, protection and *cover* she performs every thing; . . . and her condition during her marriage is called her *coverture*. Upon this principle, of an union of person in husband and wife, depend almost all the legal rights, duties and disabilities, that either of them acquire by marriage." William Blackstone, *Commentaries on the Laws of England*, vol. 1 (New York: Collins and Hannay, 1832), 442.

of nonintervention. Notable among these developments has been the United
States Supreme Court's decision in *Griswold v. Connecticut*.[30] Like *Loving
v. Virginia*,[31] *Griswold* has become remarkable not for its narrow holding
(that an archaic state law forbidding the use of birth-control devices even by
married couples is unconstitutional), but for the potentially far-reaching implications of its articulation of a constitutional right to marital privacy. *Griswold* seems to raise to the constitutional level the practice and principle of
noninterference with a functioning marriage. The notion of a right of marital
privacy is a convenient way of dealing with a problem which exists in all four
countries but is especially acute in the United States—that of devising family
law which is suited to the needs and desires of persons with different ethnic
and religious backgrounds, different social status, and different standards of
living. The ideas of "neutrality" and "privacy" have permitted American
family law to avoid the appearance of imposing the views of any one group
upon others. In practical terms, these ideas have been most easily translated
into action by the withdrawal of regulation of marital life. Thus, the ideology
of tolerance, the belief system of an influential elite, has become the leitmotif
of American family law.

The trend toward withdrawal of regulation of the ongoing marriage in the
United States is reinforced by the advance of the equality principle. While
equality theoretically can be implemented by extending legal rights and duties
connected with marriage to whichever sex previously lacked them, the
equality principle more often, in combination with other factors, results in
diminished rights and duties for both, draining marriage of much of its legal
content, promoting the idea of marriage as an association of separate individuals, and blurring the distinctions between marriage and other forms of
cohabitation.

In England, the overall development has taken a similar course. The idea
of matrimonial community of life in the English common law was embodied
in the concept of consortium, the right of the spouses to the society and services of each other. At one time, only the husband was viewed as having that
right, but consortium gradually evolved into the notion that " . . . both
spouses are the joint, co-equal heads of the family."[32] Consortium persists as
a symbol of the unity of the married couple, but like the continental idea of
marital community, it does not prevent the spouses from being separately
domiciled and does not signify any particular mode of life. It seems to acquire
legal force in the United States only as an element of damages when a spouse
sues a third party for injuring his or her partner and for the resulting loss of

30. 388 U.S. 1 (1967).   31. 381 U.S. 479 (1965).
32. *Bromley* 94.

companionship. In England, however, the cause of action for loss of consortium was abolished in 1982.

When divorces were available only or mainly for adultery, extreme cruelty, or desertion in the countries that concern us here, court decisions on what sorts of behavior amounted to mental cruelty or constructive desertion shed some light on how one might understand the legal rights and duties of spouses during marriage. Even though the vast majority of fault divorces were on fabricated grounds, people had to concoct stories that would be accepted by tribunals. Today, in countries where fault has been eliminated or downplayed as a ground of divorce or a factor in maintenance questions, divorce law no longer provides much insight into these matters.

In France, however, the idea of marital fault still plays a significant role in divorce, and court decisions continue to provide glimpses of what judges believe spouses are entitled to expect from each other by telling us what kind of conduct justifies the termination of a marriage. We may start with the observation that divorces are now routinely granted in France for conduct that would not have justified a decree earlier in the century. From one point of view, this is simply evidence of the increasing relaxation in France, as elsewhere, of legislative and judicial standards for granting divorces. But in the present relaxed atmosphere, the complaints that plaintiffs make in fault cases sound more authentic, and the reactions of the courts reveal subtle changes that have taken place in ideas about husband-wife relationships. Since 1975, fault divorce has been available in France on the ground of "serious or repeated violation of the duties and obligations of marriage, rendering the continuation of life in common intolerable."[33] The case law on what kind of behavior seriously violates marital duties shows—not surprisingly—that adultery and physical abuse (which used to be separate fault grounds) are still considered to be major marital offenses. But a host of less dramatic insults and injuries have also been held to be sufficient grounds for release from marriage.[34]

Divorces are now granted against spouses who fail to care for their sick partners or who neglect to visit them in the hospital; spouses who are lazy or undependable in carrying out their household responsibilities; spouses who publicly criticize, belittle or insult each other; spouses who are too attached to their own parents or who behave outrageously to their in-laws; spouses who are sullen and spouses who make scenes; "shrewish" wives and "autocratic" husbands. It can violate one's marital duties to spend too much time away

33. French Civil Code, art. 242.
34. The cases are surveyed in Françoise Dekeuwer-Defossez, "Impressions de recherche sur les fautes causes de divorce," D. 1985. Chr. 219.

from home, to be overly absorbed in one's work or hobby, or to be excessively given over to religious activities. In a survey of ten years' accumulation of decisions in fault cases, the author's most surprising discovery was that—without any legislative basis—judges were treating the mere failure of a spouse to express affection or show interest in the other as a marital offense.[35] Although adultery by itself was occasionally held not to justify a decree, divorce was granted in every case where the fault complained of was indifference. Thus, a duty that not even Napoleon thought of imposing on husbands and wives—the duty to love each other—has become central to the modern French legal ideology of marriage. The French fault cases not only display a more relaxed attitude toward divorce, they also, paradoxically, endorse "a very high standard concerning the moral and affective quality of the relationship of the spouses," and a view of marriage as "designed to satisfy the affective needs of the spouses, rather than a . . . structure of rights and obligations."[36]

Parents and Children

The law concerning parents and children in the ongoing family has been profoundly influenced in the four countries with which we are concerned not only by the establishment of equality between parents but also by new ways of envisaging the parent-child relationship. Again, it is illuminating to begin with the law of France as it stood in 1804. The Civil Code originally gave a father unchecked power over a child's person and property until the child reached the age of 21. This *puissance paternelle* included the right to control the child's mode of life and education and to give or withhold consent to the child's marriage or emancipation. Until 1935, a father who had grave cause for dissatisfaction with the conduct of his child could even obtain a court order for the child's arrest and detention in an "appropriate place."[37] In 1942, the role of the mother began to be recognized. The Code was amended in that year to provide that authority over a child "belonged" to both parents, even though it was to be "exercised" by the father in his capacity as head of the family. It was not until 1970, however, that a thoroughgoing revision of the law in this area took place.

The 1970 law was, as we have seen, a landmark in the development of legal equality of the sexes in France. It was, in addition, the culmination of a steady trend to modify the degree and kind of control to which children were subjected. It not only provided that mothers and fathers should exercise their

35. *Id.* at 223.
36. *Id.* at 224–225.
37. French Civil Code, former arts. 375–382.

authority jointly from then on, it replaced the *puissance paternelle* with what is now called *l'autorité parentale*. The change from *power* to *authority* was as significant as that from *paternal* to *parental*. *Puissance*, like the Roman law concept of *potestas*, signified dominion over the children; *authority* in the new law was the name given to a scheme which encompassed parental duties as well as powers. The Code still recites, as it did in 1804, that: "A child of any age owes honor and respect to its father and mother." [38] But now parents have obligations too: to protect the child's "safety, health, and morals," and to furnish him or her with care, supervision, and education.[39] Far-reaching as the 1970 changes were, they nevertheless stopped short of establishing full equality between father and mother. The father's right to administer and receive the income from his children's property remained predominant until 1985, and his right to transmit his surname to his legitimate children remains to this day.[40]

In Germany, the Civil Code of 1896 had already substituted *parental*, for *paternal*, power (*elterliche Gewalt*) and had assigned parents duties as well as rights. But except for a few specific rights given to mothers, parental power over the child's person and property was to be "exercised" by the father, who also was given the last word in the event of disagreements between the parents. An early inroad on this patriarchal model, however, was made in a 1921 statute on the religious upbringing of children.[41] Under this law, which is still in effect, the religious education of a child up to the age of fourteen is supposed in principle to be determined by both parents acting together. In the event of disagreement, the child is to be raised in the religious denomination of the parents at the time of their marriage. If the parents did not have a common religion at that time, the guardianship court can accord the right of decision to one parent. The law goes on to specify that the religious denomination of a child over twelve cannot be changed against his or her will and that a child over fourteen can decide the matter alone.

In other areas, despite the equality command of the 1949 Constitution, the 1957 Equality Law specified that the father's decision would prevail in the event of disagreements between parents regarding the child. It also provided that only the father could act as the child's legal representative. Equality between parents thus had to await a court decision which declared these provisions unconstitutional.[42] The legislature then remained silent on these matters until 1979, when it completely redesigned the legal image of the relationships

---

38. French Civil Code, art. 371.
39. French Civil Code, art. 371–2.
40. See below, text at note 78.
41. Gesetz über die religiöse Kindererziehung of 15 July 1921, RGBl.I.939.
42. Bundesverfassungsgericht decision of 29 July 1959, BGBl.I.633.

between parents and children.[43] The 1979 law replaced the term *parental power* with *parental care* (*elterliche Sorge*) and established mutual duties of parents and children to assist and respect each other.[44] The new law also provided for participation by a child in decisions regarding his or her education and upbringing. It admonished parents to take into consideration the child's aptitudes and needs for independent responsibility at various stages of development and instructed them that their child-raising methods were not to include "humiliating treatment."[45]

The idea that parents should exercise restraint in discipline was extended to include a specific ban on corporal punishment in the much-publicized Swedish no-spanking law, which provides that a parent may not subject a child "to physical punishment or other humiliating treatment."[46] It must be noted, however, that these and most other legal prescriptions regarding the duties and rights of parent and child are (like the legal rights and duties of spouses) without sanction. Unless and until a parent's conduct amounts to child abuse or neglect, no Swedish official will stay the hand of the parent who believes that to spare the rod is to spoil the child. The no-spanking law seems to have been intended mainly to communicate to a large population of foreign workers that most Swedes do not approve of punishment as a method of education.[47] A vast information campaign followed the enactment of this frankly educational law. Its provisions were described in over half a million brochures printed in 10 languages, and the policy was widely discussed in all the mass media.

The changing legal images of parent-child relationships that emerge from Anglo-American common law are similar in their broad outlines to those in the amended French and West German Civil Codes. Parental rights at common law were vested in the father alone, but statutes and case law began to equalize the rights and duties of parents in England and the United States even earlier than on the continent. In both countries, despite lip service paid to the idea of parental authority, current high court decisions have strongly empha-

---

43. Gesetz zur Neuregelung des Rechts der elterlichen Sorge of 18 July 1979 (SorgeRG), BGBl. I.106. See, generally, Uwe Diederichsen, "Die Neuregelung des Rechts der elterlichen Sorge," 1980 *Neue Juristische Wochenschrift* 1.

44. West German Civil Code, §§1626 and 1618a.

45. West German Civil Code, §§1626 II, 1631(2).

46. Bertil Ekdahl, "The Swedish Law on Physical Punishment," in *The Ombudsman and Child Maltreatment* (Stockholm: Save the Children, 1980), 6. Finland followed suit in 1983, and Denmark adopted a similar law in 1985. Matti Savolainen, "Finland: More Rights for Children," 25 *J. Family Law* 113, 118 (1986); Jørgen Graverson, "Denmark: Custody Reform," 25 *J. Family Law* 81, 85 (1986).

47. Ekdahl, above, note 46 at 9.

sized the independent individuality of even a minor child, especially in cases involving adolescent sexuality.

The House of Lords, for example, held in 1985 that a doctor might prescribe contraception, under certain circumstances, to a girl under sixteen without her parents' knowledge or consent, quoting with approval the statement by Lord Denning in a previous case that the legal right of a parent "is a dwindling right which the court will hesitate to enforce against the wishes of the child, and the more so the older he is. It starts with a right of control and ends with little more than advice." [48] The 1985 decision of the Law Lords accords with the view expressed by the Law Commission in 1982 that "the concept of parental rights, in the sense of conferring on a parent control over the person, education, and conduct of his children throughout their minority reflects an outdated view of family life which has no part to play in a modern system of law." [49] The new view of parental rights, as expressed by Lord Fraser in the *Gillick* case, is that they derive from parental duties, exist for the benefit of the child rather than the parents, and are justified only so long as they are needed for the protection of the person and property of the child. [50]

In the United States, the Supreme Court has struck down statutes restricting the access of persons under sixteen to contraceptives [51] and has held that every minor desiring an abortion "must have the opportunity—if she so desires—to go directly to a court without first consulting her parents. If she satisfies the court that she is mature and well enough informed to make intelligently the abortion decision on her own, the court must authorize her to act without parental consultation or consent." [52] That notions of a child's individual liberty can be taken quite far by American courts is evidenced by the decision of a New York Family Court judge that a mother could not invoke the power of the state to have her fifteen-year-old daughter adjudicated as a person in need of supervision simply because the daughter left home when forbidden to continue her relationship with a twenty-one-year-old lesbian. The judge, broadly construing the Supreme Court's abortion and contraception cases involving minors, held that the fifteen-year-old in question had a right to choose her sexual orientation and urged the parties "to reconcile their differences within the framework of this decision." [53]

48. *Gillick v. West Norfolk and Wisbeck Area Health Authority* [1985] 3 W.L.R. 830, 841, quoting *Hewer v. Bryant*, [1970] 1 Q.B. 357, 369.

49. The Law Commission, *Report on Illegitimacy*, Law Comm. No. 118, (London: Her Majesty's Stationery Office, 1982), par. 4.18.

50. *Gillick v. West Norfolk and Wisbeck Area Health Authority*, above note 48.

51. *Carey v. Population Services International*, 431 U.S. 678 (1977).

52. *Belotti v. Baird*, 443 U.S. 622, 647 (1979). But cf. *H. L. v. Matheson*, 450 U.S. 398 (1981), holding that a statutory parental notice requirement does not violate the constitutional rights of an unemancipated, dependent minor.

53. *In the Matter of Lori M.*, 496 N.Y.S.2d 940, 942 (Fam. Ct. 1985).

American courts will not intervene in disputes between parents concerning their children's upbringing except in the context of neglect, abuse, or other emergencies. In the rare cases where courts have been asked to end an impasse regarding less urgent matters, judges have declined to assume jurisdiction so long as the spouses are living together and sharing custody. The leading American case involved a mother and father who were apparently on good terms except for a disagreement about their daughter's education. The New York Court of Appeals declined to settle their argument, saying:

> The court cannot regulate by its processes the internal affairs of the home. Dispute between parents when it does not involve anything immoral or harmful to the welfare of the child is beyond the reach of the law. The vast majority of matters concerning the upbringing of children must be left to the conscience, patience and self restraint of father and mother. No end of difficulties would arise should judges try to tell parents how to bring up their children. Only when moral, mental or physical conditions are so bad as seriously to affect the health or morals of children should the court be called upon to act.[54]

In England, the situation at first blush would appear to be different. If a spouse wishes to bring an issue concerning the care, education, or control of a child before a court outside the context of divorce or separation, he or she may petition under the Guardianship Act of 1973, and the Court may make such an order as it thinks proper.[55] But Cretney in 1984 reported that he could not discover any decisions under this section.[56] The situation in England appears in fact to be much the same as in the United States: except in emergencies, the law will not interfere with parental decision-making processes in the functioning family unit.

Even in France and West Germany, where courts are authorized to intervene in such matters, this power is rarely invoked or exercised. In West Germany, the court's jurisdiction[57] stands in the shadow of Article 6 of the Constitution, which subordinates the interest of the state to the "natural right" of parents to the care and upbringing of their children. As for French law, it provides that, in the first instance, if a mother and father cannot agree about a particular decision, they should continue the practice they have been following.[58] If the parents have had no such practice, or if the practice is alleged to have been ill founded, a parent may invoke the aid of a court. But the judge's first duty in such a case is to try to induce the parents to work out their own

---

54. *People ex rel. Sisson v. Sisson*, 2 N.E.2d 660, 661 (N.Y.C.A. 1936). *Accord: Kilgrow v. Kilgrow*, 107 So.2d 885, 888 (Ala. 1959) (dispute over public vs. parochial school); *Hackett v. Hackett*, 150 N.E.2d 431, *aff'd* 154 N.E.2d 820 (Ohio 1958).

55. Guardianship Act 1973, s. 1 (3).   56. *Cretney* 366–67.

57. West German Civil Code, §1628.   58. French Civil Code, art. 372–1.

solution.[59] If conciliation fails, French courts seem little inclined to become embroiled in disputes between parents in a functioning household. For example, in a case involving a disagreement between parents over whether corporal punishment was appropriate for their four-year-old son, the court simply refused to act, saying that there was no way that it could enforce any order it might issue.[60]

Separateness and Solidarity

In summary, then, we have noted the emergence of new legal images of the family which, in varying degrees, stress the separate personalities of the family members rather than the unitary aspect of the family. In the marital relationship, equality has replaced hierarchy. The law has abandoned its former express or implicit stereotyping of sex roles within marriage and has moved toward a new model in which there is no fixed pattern of role distribution. We have seen a movement in all four systems toward equal sharing of parental rights and obligations. At the same time, there has been a trend toward diminution of the rights of both mothers and fathers, as children are increasingly treated as individuals with rights of their own.

The dominant image of the ongoing family in the French and West German Codes is that of a community of life in which husbands and wives work out their own roles, parents exercise their authority in the interests of their children, and all family members collaborate with and assist one another in accordance with their abilities. In these systems, spousal independence and equality are envisioned as existing within a framework of cooperation. Similar views seem to inform the decisions of English judges in the rare cases where underlying assumptions about such matters are made explicit. The following description of marriage by Lord Denning, however, places somewhat more stress on the separate existences of the spouses than one would see in a continental formulation.

> Nowadays, both in law and in fact, husband and wife are two persons, not one. They are partners—equal partners—in a joint enterprise, the enterprise of maintaining a home and bringing up children. Outside that joint enterprise they live their own lives and go their own ways—always, we hope, in consultation one with the other, in complete loyalty one with the other, each maintaining and deserving the trust and confidence of the other.[61]

59. *Id.*
60. Decision of Juge des tutelles de Chateaudun, reported in 1972 *Gazette du Palais* II.561.
61. *Midland Bank Trust Co. Ltd. v. Green* (No. 3) [1982], Ch. 529, 538–39.

The separateness and individuality of the persons who are associated in families and marriages is an even stronger theme in recent decisions of the United States Supreme Court. In *Eisenstadt v. Baird*, the Court said: "[T]he marital couple is not an independent entity with a mind and heart of its own, but an association of two individuals each with a separate intellectual and emotional makeup." [62] A few decisions still employ the rhetoric of family solidarity. [63] But if one attends to their outcomes, Laurence Tribe seems correct in saying that what the Court has characterized as family rights often turn out to be rights of individuals.

> [T]he stereotypical "family unit" that is so much a part of our constitutional rhetoric is becoming decreasingly central to our constitutional reality. Such "exercises of familial rights and responsibilities" as remain prove to be individual powers to resist governmental determination of who shall be born, with whom one shall live and what values shall be transmitted. [64]

Equality between spouses in a system like the American one tends to be envisioned as existing within a family of independent individuals rather than within a community of life. But it must be stressed that the differences among the four systems in this area are only ones of degree. To take the two polar cases, even American family law is not entirely individualistic, [65] and French family law is far from being wholeheartedly communitarian. [66] The pervasive tension in all systems between the symbolism of family cohesiveness and that of independent individualism carries over into the law of names, to which we now turn. Here, the common law countries have taken a markedly different course from that followed on the continent.

Names

The effect of marriage upon the names of the spouses, like the issue of interspousal decision making, is heavily laden with symbolism. The matter of

62. *Eisenstadt v. Baird*, 405 U.S. 438, 453 (1972).

63. *Griswold v. Connecticut*, 381 U.S. 479 (1965), Marriage promotes "a way of life," a "harmony in living," and a "bilateral loyalty"; *Parham v. J.R.*, 442 U.S. 584, 602 (1979), "Our jurisprudence historically has reflected Western civilization concepts of the family as a unit with broad parental authority over minor children."

64. Laurence Tribe, *American Constitutional Law* (Mineola, N.Y.: Foundation Press, 1978), 987.

65. This point is brought out in the analysis of the family rights cases of the United States Supreme Court by Bruce C. Hafen, "The Constitutional Status of Marriage, Kinship, and Sexual Privacy—Balancing the Individual and Social Interests," 81 *Michigan Law Review* 463 (1983).

66. The theme of individual liberty in French family law is extensively explored by Alain Bénabent, "La liberté individuelle et le mariage," 1973 *Revue trimestrielle de droit civil*, 440.

names concerns not only husbands and wives, but their children and their respective families of origin (especially in societies of patrilineal organization).[67] In many countries, names are important to the state in connection with official identity records.[68] So long as it was the nearly universal custom for a woman to assume her husband's name and rank upon marriage, these interests did not need to be analyzed separately from one another. The social custom of taking the husband's name expressed a wife's integration into her husband's family, and the common family name expressed the unity of the new household. The custom was incorporated into the Prussian General Code of 1794[69] and also into Article 1355 of the German Civil Code of 1896. In England, France, and the United States (except Hawaii), however, women were never required by statute to change their names upon marriage.

The English common law of names, as received in the United States, provides that any person, man or woman, may use any name he or she wishes so long as the use is nonfraudulent.[70] One's legal name is the name by which one is customarily known, but nothing prevents a person from freely changing his or her name from time to time. Formal procedures for changes of name do exist, but they are for the convenience of those who wish to obtain an official record of their name change and need not be followed in order to make the change legally effective.[71] In England, the status of the ancient rules remained clear. There, a married woman is said to have a right, by custom, to assume her husband's name and, if he is a peer, his title and rank.[72] Long before the women's rights movement awakened wider interest in the matter, women's practice of assuming their husbands' names was consistently regarded in England as nothing more than a custom: "[T]here is, so far as I know, nothing to compel a married woman to use her husband's surname, so that the wife of Mr. Robinson may, speaking generally, go by the name of Mrs. Smith if she chooses to do so."[73]

----

67. "Names, whereby men acquire an idea of a thing which one would imagine ought not to perish, are extremely proper to inspire every family with a desire of extending its duration. There are people among whom names distinguish families; there are others where they only distinguish persons; the latter have not the same advantage as the former." Montesquieu, *The Spirit of the Laws*, Book 23, Ch. 4.

68. In continental countries, not only are surnames regulated, but parents are typically forbidden to give their children unconventional first names. See generally, Michael Coester, "Vornamensrecht-international," in *Internationales Handbuch der Vornamen* (Frankfurt: Verlag für Standesamtswesen, 1986), 5–49.

69. Prussian General Code, Part II, art. 192.

70. *Secretary of the Commonwealth v. City Clerk of Lowell*, 366 N.E.2d 717 (Mass. 1977).

71. *Id.* at 724.

72. *Bromley* 95.

73. Vaisey, J., *In re Fry* [1945] Ch. 348, 354.

While this was also the legal situation in all the United States except Hawaii, the *custom* of women taking their husband's surnames upon marriage was so widely followed that many Americans (including lawyers) came to believe that a woman's name changed upon marriage as a matter of law. Indeed, until recently it would have been an interesting question whether this custom had acquired the force of law. But when increasing numbers of women began to depart from the custom, the old common law rules were rediscovered and revitalized. Because of the nearly universal belief that the law required them to use their husbands' surnames, women who started not to do so often ran into difficulties when they tried to register to vote or to get passports or driver's licenses.

Several lawsuits were brought before it became clear that the old common law of names was still valid in the United States. In some states, the attorneys general issued opinions for the guidance of municipal clerks, voting registrars, and motor vehicle registrars who were confused by the sudden influx of demands by married women to obtain official documents in names other than those of their husbands. Guidelines issued in 1975 by the Massachusetts attorney general and secretary of state on "the law as it applies to commonly encountered situations of name choice" tried to make the matter plain:

> [I]t has always been the law of this Commonwealth that any individual, male or female, has the right to choose and from time to time change his or her name. . . . A person may change his or her name simply by using another name. . . . There is no law which requires parents to name their children with a particular surname. Thus, the child of John Doe and Mary Jones may be named Baby Doe, Baby Jones, Baby Doe-Jones or even Baby Smith. The choice is left entirely to the parents.[74]

This instruction was met with disbelief and a wholesale revolt on the part of Massachusetts city and town clerks. They flatly refused to follow the common law on the interesting ground that it was contrary to "custom and usage in Massachusetts for over 200 years." [75] In the litigation that ensued, the Mas-

---

74. Reported in *The Boston Evening Globe*, 10 Dec. 1975, at 47. There appears to be no clear rule in the United States about what happens if the parents cannot agree on the child's surname. In most European countries, a legitimate child takes the name of its father, but under the 1982 Swedish Names Act, if the parents have different last names and do not pick a name for their child within three months of its birth, the child takes the mother's name unless the parents have other children in their custody, in which case the child takes the name of the most recently born sibling. Åke Saldeen, "Sweden," 8 *Annual Survey of Family Law, 1983–1984*, Vol. 8, ed. M.D.A. Freeman (London: International Society on Family Law, 1985), 168, 175.

75. *Secretary of the Commonwealth v. City Clerk of Lowell*, 366 N.E.2d 717, 720,721 (Mass. 1977).

sachusetts Supreme Judicial Court upheld the attorney general on the basis of the "well settled" principle that " 'at common law a person may change his name at will, without resort to legal proceedings, by merely adopting another name, provided that this is done for an honest purpose.' " [76]

Thus one effect of changing mores in the United States has been to breathe new life into long-dormant legal doctrines. Although the great majority of American married women still use their husbands' surnames, the legally supported nonconformity of a significant minority has also begun to erode a traditional social distinction between the married and the unmarried state.

The question occasionally arises whether a husband may under certain circumstances restrain his wife from using his name. But, in both England and the United States, since a woman is free to use any name she chooses, it has been held that an ex-husband cannot prevent his former wife from using his name after divorce, so long as the use is nonfraudulent. [77] The fact that in England and the United States the government does not assert an interest in what people call themselves or their children seems bizarre to most continental Europeans. But our casual approach to these matters is possible because we have no official system of identification. The state of our name law also illustrates why the *de facto* identification system in the United States is based on the social security number rather than names.

In France, one's legal name is that which appears on one's birth certificate. Except in the case of some children born outside legal marriage, this is the father's surname. [78] Marriage does not, however, have the legal effect of changing a woman's name. [79] Most women by custom begin to use the name of their husband upon marriage, but a married woman continues to be referred to by her birth name in deeds, wills, and official documents such as identity cards, passports, and driver's licenses. [80] Marriage does, however, give a woman something like a license to use the name of her husband. This is a significant privilege because France, unlike the United States or England, forbids purely voluntary name change. Furthermore, the name on one's birth

76. *Id.* at 721, quoting *Merolevitz, petitioner*, 70 N.E.2d 249, 250 (Mass. 1946).

77. *Bromley* 95; *Richette v. Ajello*, 2 Family Law Reporter 2716 (Pa. Common Pleas 1976).

78. French Civil Code, art. 334–1. Under a 1985 law, the patrinominal French system has been modified slightly by permitting people, as a matter of "usage," to add their mother's surname to their surname if they desire (and parents of minors to add the mother's name to the father's when they name their children). Raymond Lindon, "La nouvelle disposition législative relative à la transmission de l'usage du nom," D.1986. Chr. 82. See also Michael Coester, "Neues Namensrecht in Frankreich," 1987 *Das Standesamt* 196. See generally, *Cornu* 234–61; *Labrusse-Riou* 225.

79. *Labrusse-Riou* 225.

80. *Cornu* 247.

certificate can only be changed by official action for good reasons and provided no one who already has the proposed new name objects.[81]

The wife's right to use her husband's name is not absolute, however. Shortly after divorce was reintroduced in France in 1884, the Civil Code was amended to require that when a marriage is terminated by a judicial decree, "each spouse is to resume the usage of his own name."[82] Indeed, an exception to this rule introduced in 1976 was very controversial, even though it permits a divorced woman to continue using her ex-husband's name only under special circumstances.

> Art. 264. Following divorce each spouse is to resume the usage of his own name.
>
> Nevertheless, in the case provided for in articles 237 and 238 [unilateral nonfault divorce after long separation] the wife has the right to retain the use of the husband's name if the divorce has been sought by him.
>
> In other cases, the wife may retain the use of the husband's name, either with his permission, or with the permission of the judge, if she demonstrates that it has special importance for her or for the children.

It would be wrong to conclude after reading this statute that a woman who had once secured formal permission from her husband to go on using his name after divorce need never trouble herself about the matter again. In 1980, a remarried journalist whose first husband had given her permission to use his name (by which she was known professionally) was sued by her ex-husband and six of his relatives to restrain her from continuing to use their family name. The court, while stating that such permission once given could not be revoked arbitrarily, held that the circumstances of the case—the woman's remarriage and the fact that she had become notorious for mingling with criminals in the course of producing sensational stories about life in the underworld—justified forbidding her to use the name again for any purpose whatsoever.[83]

Thus, socially, there is both a similarity and a contrast with the American situation. In both countries, the husband's name has been thought to be of such special importance that the wife's freedom of choice concerning the name she will use has met with obstacles. But in America, the wife's right to

81. *Id.* at 244.
82. French Civil Code, former art. 299.
83. Decision of the Tribunal de Grande Instance of Paris, of 10 February 1981, reported in 1981 *Juris-Classeur Périodique* II.19624.

use a name *other* than her husband's has encountered resistance, whereas in France the wife's right to use the name which belongs to her husband and his family has been challenged under certain circumstances. What unites these seemingly contrasting points of view is their common reluctance to let women decide for themselves what name they wish to bear.

In West Germany, when the codification of the customary name practice ran into constitutional difficulties, a search was undertaken for a way to reconcile the goal of expressing family unity through a common family name with the equality principle. West Germany is the only one of the four countries (excluding the American state of Hawaii)[84] in which married women were obliged by statute to assume their husband's name upon marriage. Original paragraph 1355 of the Civil Code, which provided that the family name was the husband's name, was thought to be of doubtful constitutionality after the equality command of the Basic Law became self-executing. But between that time and the adoption of the present name provisions in 1976, the wife's interest in her birth name was taken into account only by permitting her, through a public declaration at the time of marriage, to append her own name to that of her husband and to bear a double name.[85] A husband who wished to add the wife's name to his could do so only through a formal name change proceeding.

Full equality in the matter proved extremely difficult to implement in West Germany. The only way to offer completely equal rights to both spouses in a country where names are crucial to the identity system seems to be to give each spouse the option of retaining his or her birth name. However, the West German legislature has been reluctant to relinquish the idea of the common name as an expression of family unity.

One West German reform proposal (ultimately rejected) would have amended Art. 1355 to provide that the spouses are to bear a common name chosen as follows:

> The spouses are to declare their marriage name at the time of marriage. They are permitted to choose either the birth name of the wife or that of the husband or a double name composed of both, but which can contain no more than two names. The spouse whose name is not the marriage name or part of the marriage name is permitted, by making an official public declaration of his or her intent to do so, to append to the marriage name his or her name or any other name legally used before the marriage, such as that of a former spouse.[86]

84. The Hawaiian statute was eventually repealed.

85. *Beitzke* 64.

86. Quoted in Christof Böhmer, "Die Neuregelung des Eheschliessungsrechts," 1975 *Das Standesamt* 5,9.

This draft would have reorganized the law of marriage formation so that a declaration of the marriage name would have been required prior to marriage. If the spouses did not make a declaration, the marriage name would have been a double name composed of the names of both spouses, with the man's name standing first. This scheme was approved by the Bundestag but not by the Bundesrat, where the majority considered that unless the spouses filed notice of intent to use the wife's name, the family name should be the husband's.

The approach finally settled on in 1976 kept the common name idea and made certain concessions to the conservative elements in the Bundesrat. The registrar must now ask the spouses before the marriage is celebrated whether they wish to make a declaration concerning which marriage name they will bear, the woman's or the man's.[87] If they do not make such a declaration, the husband's name becomes the marriage name of the couple. Either spouse has the option to add his or her own name ahead of the marriage name.

> §1355. (1) The spouses bear a common family name (the marriage name).
> (2) The spouses can designate as the marriage name, by declaration before the Registrar, the birth name of the husband or the birth name of the wife. If they make no designation, the marriage name is the birth name of the husband. The birth name is the name recorded on the birth certificate of the intended spouses at the time of the celebration of the marriage.
> (3) A spouse, whose birth name is not the marriage name, can, by declaration before the Registrar, place his birth name or the name he bears at the time of the celebration of the marriage ahead of the marriage name; the declaration must be publicly attested.

Upon divorce, by new Art. 1355(4) a spouse may resume his or her birth name or the name he or she bore upon entering the marriage by making a public declaration before the registrar of intent to do so, but an ex-spouse can be restrained from using the other spouse's name after divorce in certain circumstances.

More is going on here than appears on the surface. Under Civil Code §1616, the marriage name of the parents is also the legal name of their legitimate children, and West Germany has not even begun to address the issue of the rights in the matter of children's names of the spouse whose name is not chosen as the marriage name. Furthermore, it seems clear that with tradition so strongly in favor of the wife's taking the husband's name, a choice which requires either one partner's name or the other's to be selected as the marriage name is apt to be no choice at all. The option of the double name for both

87. *EheG* §13a(1).

spouses seems to be the only way to square the ideal of a common name with the equality principle (although it seems that some neutral principle should govern the order of names, rather than giving automatic precedence to that of the husband). The present West German law has ended up by derogating from the ideal of the common name *and* by violating the equality principle.[88]

The feelings people have about names, the way names are bound up with a person's identity and with continuity among generations, and the implicit messages about power involved in name change upon marriage have made new developments in this tiny corner of family law controversial. Despite the prevailing customs, we have seen that official approval of the symbolic subordination of the wife to the husband, or absorption of her independent existence into his, is gradually being removed from the law of names. In England, France, and the United States, change of name on marriage is a matter for individual choice. In West Germany, however, the law still seeks to encourage the use of a common name as an expression of family unity and continuity as well as for administrative convenience.

Economic Relations

The law governing family support obligations and family property has, for the most part, been developed for situations of crisis, such as death, divorce, separation, or insolvency. The parts of that body of law dealing with support and property relationships in the functioning household comprise only a small proportion of the whole. For a fuller picture of family property relationships, therefore, the subject matter of the present chapter must be supplemented later with the parts of chapter 5 dealing with the law of succession and the law regulating the economic consequences of divorce and separation.

Let us begin by reviewing the traditional legal approaches to support and property in the ongoing family.[89] On the eve of the Industrial Revolution, the legal systems for regulating family economic relationships in England, France, the United States, and the various regions of Germany, differed in techniques but were similar in their basic characteristics. Husbands had the power to manage all the family property, including the property of their wives, and were expected to provide for the material needs of the members of the household. For those cases where significant property was brought into

88. See Michael Coester, "Fortschritt oder fortgeschrittene Auflösung im Recht des Personennamens," 1984 *Das Standesamt* 298, 302–304. The issue of the constitutionality of Article 1355, as well as of certain aspects of the West German choice-of-law rules concerning children's names, was pending before the Constitutional Court in 1988.

89. What follows is but a brief, schematic, description. For more details, see Max Rheinstein and Mary Ann Glendon, "Interspousal Relations," in *International Encyclopedia of Comparative Law*, ed. Aleck Chloros, Vol. 4 (Tübingen: J. C. B. Mohr, 1980), 31–147.

the marriage by the wife, all the traditional systems were characterized by the development of legal techniques to protect the wife (and the wife's blood relatives) from the consequences of mismanagement by the husband and to assure that title to land remained in the family from whence it came. By aggregating the family assets under the control of the husband and giving him the right to their income, the system helped to provide a capital base for the family enterprise. This was well suited to the needs of the rising entrepreneurial class, and by according special treatment to real estate, it also served the interest of the aristocracy in seeing that family land did not pass out of the blood line.

These traditional systems underwent a first wave of changes in the late nineteenth and early twentieth centuries as the effects of increasing industrialization made themselves felt. The two-earner marriage began to find recognition in the law, first in some of the American states, then in England, then in the German Civil Code of 1896, and in a series of French statutes from 1881 to 1907, with the rest of the American states falling into line along the way. The technique chosen in each system was to give married women the right to dispose freely of at least their own earnings and whatever assets they might have received by gift or by will under stipulations that the assets were to remain subject to their separate control. These innovations were really no more than an extension to the entire population of devices which had been worked out by lawyers for the wealthy. They represented the democratization of the techniques used in marriage settlements in England, *contrats de mariage* in France, and *Eheverträge* in Germany, and of the special legal treatment which had long been accorded to married women traders.[90] It is probable that the early appearance of the first Married Women's Property Acts in the United States was related to the fact that marriage settlements had never been used in the new country to the extent that they were in England. Thus the need for reform arose earlier in America among influential sectors of the population.

The turn-of-the-century reforms, however, proved to be irrelevant to one large group of marriages. When a married woman had no independent means and did not work outside the home, they affected her situation not at all. In the twentieth century, as the situations of many industrial workers improved to the point where one wage-earner could support an entire family, more and more women became full-time homemakers. Unlike their mothers and grandmothers, who had been needed as important collaborators in interdependent family enterprises, they and their children found themselves dependent on

90. Universally, it seems, a married woman merchant was empowered to manage her own business, but her ability to act as a trader depended upon her husband's revocable permission. The withholding or revoking of such permission was widely made subject to judicial review.

husbands and fathers who worked outside the home and who no longer depended on them, except in an emotional sense.[91] This was the beginning of
the end of marriage as a reliable support institution. With increasing marriage
dissolution by divorce and departure, it has become clear what risks the full-
time homemaker role involves for women and their children. The old forms
of economic interdependence had provided a certain amount of security. So
long as divorce was exceptional, and the norms of convention, custom, ethics,
and religion supported the ideal of indissolubility of marriage, economic dependence did not seem dangerous. But as divorce increasingly came to be
considered a right, necessary for each individual's pursuit of happiness or
self-fulfillment, the situation of a married woman without income or resources
of her own became precarious indeed.

The legal systems at first sought to adjust to this new situation by continuing the husband's primary economic responsibility for the family through the
device of alimony. But it soon became apparent that the financial position of
most men, especially if they took on new financial burdens through remarriage, did not in fact allow much security for ex-wives who had devoted substantial parts of their lives to caretaking activities. All four countries are
presently searching for ways to make this choice less dangerous, but not even
advanced welfare states have been able to completely socialize the work of
raising children and caring for the infirm and elderly, and no amount of ex-
hortation seems likely to bring about fully equal sharing of such tasks between
women and men in the near future. To make matters even more complicated,
these countries are also seeking to implement the equality principle, to promote individual independence, and to maintain the ideal of marriage as a
community of life. It is no wonder that the current evolution described here
and in chapter 5 is the story of a groping and hesitant search that has not yet
achieved its goals.

Maintaining the Household

As we have seen, under the traditional systems of the early nineteenth century,
all family income, including any wages earned by the wife, was at the dis-
posal of the husband, who was responsible for the basic needs of his wife and
children. These traditional schemes were usually accompanied by the wife's
legal power to obtain "necessaries" upon the credit of her husband—for example, the married woman's agency of necessity in the common law and the
German homemaker's "power of the keys" (*Schlüsselgewalt*).

The successive alterations in the French Civil Code since 1804 again pro-

91. Judith Blake, "The Changing Status of Women in Developed Countries," *Scientific
American* (September 1974): 144.

vide a good starting point for examining how changes in the social and economic roles of women have made themselves felt in the way the maintenance of the ongoing household is envisaged. Let us recall the Code's original provision:

> The wife is obliged to live with the husband and to follow him to whatever residence he deems appropriate: the husband is obliged to receive her and to furnish her with the necessities of life according to his ability and station.[92]

After married women were given the power to deal with their separate earnings in 1907, this scheme was modified to provide that the wife was obliged to furnish, from any funds subject to her separate administration, a proportionate contribution to the expenses of the household and the upbringing of the children. Then, in 1942, article 214 was amended again to read,

> If the marriage contract does not regulate the contribution of the spouses to the expenses of the marriage, they are to contribute in proportion to their respective abilities.
> The principal obligation to assume these expenses falls on the husband. He is obliged to furnish the wife with the necessities of life according to his ability and station.
> The wife discharges her obligation for the expenses of the marriage by her dowry or separate property brought into the community and by deductions made from the personal funds subject to her separate administration.

In 1965, the idea was belatedly added to the last-quoted paragraph that a wife could also discharge her obligation to contribute to the expenses of the household "through her activity in the home or her collaboration in the profession of the husband." In addition, the married woman's power to pledge her husband's credit for household necessities was replaced by the power of both spouses to bind each other in transactions for the maintenance of the household and the education of the children.[93] At the same time, the wife finally was given the right to engage in an occupation separate from that of her husband without his consent or judicial authorization.

Through this series of changes, one can trace the shift in France from a notion of economic interdependence within the family unit headed by the husband in 1804, through various stages of recognition of the wife's economic activity outside the home, to acknowledgment in 1965 of the economic value of the wife's activity within the home. All these developments took place

92. French Civil Code, former art. 214.
93. French Civil Code, art. 220.

within a framework in which the husband bore primary responsibility for the needs of the family. But in 1975 the mold was broken. The divorce reform law of that year eliminated the husband's primary responsibility for the support of the family and established a new model of interdependence based on the principle that husband and wife are to contribute to household expenses according to their respective abilities.[94]

In West Germany, the 1957 Equal Rights Law established the principle that both spouses are obliged to support the household during their life together and freed the wife to work outside the home without obtaining her husband's permission. But it recast the Civil Code provisions describing the duties of the spouses in a way that was so bound up with the model of housewife-marriage as to render the whole scheme of doubtful constitutionality:

> §1360. The spouses are mutually obliged to adequately maintain the family by their work and property. As a general rule, the wife performs her obligation to contribute to the maintenance of the family through her labor, by running the household. She is obliged to engage in a gainful activity only insofar as the working capacity of the husband and the income of the family do not suffice for the maintenance of the family, and insofar as an inroad into their capital is not commensurate with the circumstances of the spouses.
>
> §1360a. The proper maintenance of the family includes all that is required in the circumstances of the spouses, to cover household expenses and to satisfy the personal needs of the spouses and the support of those common children of theirs who are entitled to be supported.
>
> Maintenance is to be supplied in the manner which is required by the marital community of life. The husband is obliged to make available for the wife's disposition a proper amount in advance for a reasonable period of time. . . .
>
> §1360b. If one spouse has furnished more for the maintenance of the family than he is obliged to provide, it is to be presumed that he did not intend to obtain restitution from the other spouse.

In 1976, this 1957 vision of equality was revised so as to eliminate the explicitly sex-based role allocations. Paragraph 1360 of the Civil Code now reads:

> §1360. The spouses are mutually obliged to adequately maintain the family by their work and property. If the running of the household is left to one spouse, that spouse as a rule fulfills his duty to contribute to the support of the family through work by managing the household.

94. French Civil Code, art. 214, as amended.

A similar evolution has taken place in statutory and case law in the United States. Equality in support duties has been constitutionally mandated since 1979,[95] and Family Expense Acts in most states have long made husband and wife equally liable for basic household expenses.[96]

In England, the traditional common law rules that the husband is obliged to support the wife, that the wife is obliged to render services in the home and that these duties are reciprocal, have never been formally abolished, but they seem to have been rendered largely obsolete by statutes permitting the courts to order either spouse to provide reasonable maintenance for the other in periods of marriage breakdown.[97]

The fact that legal enforcement of family economic obligations generally is not sought in any of the systems treated here until family life has been disrupted means that these legal provisions are to a great extent that special kind of law which exists mainly to express an ideal of proper conduct. The evolving ideal seems to be that in the absence of special circumstances of need, husband and wife do not "support" each other; rather, they contribute according to their abilities to the running of their joint enterprise. During marriage, the spouses are essentially left to work out their own financial arrangements.

The most extreme version of this attitude of noninterference is in the United States. There, except in cases of gross neglect, the courts will not order support so long as the couple is living together.[98] The leading case is *McGuire v. McGuire*, where the Supreme Court of Nebraska held that the longtime wife of a relatively well-to-do farmer had no cause of action for support from him "as long the home is maintained and the parties are living as husband and wife." For several years, the husband, a man of "more than ordinary frugality," had not given his wife any money for clothing or household items. The couple's house had no indoor bathroom, no kitchen sink, and its primitive furnace was in disrepair. While remarking that there was little to be said for the husband's attitude, the court stated: "The living standards of a family are

95. *Orr v. Orr*, 440 U.S. 268 (1979), Alabama statute making husbands but not wives liable to pay support on divorce held to violate the Equal Protection clause. The Court quoted with approval (at pp. 279–80) *Stanton v. Stanton*, 421 U.S. 7, 10 (1975), which held that the traditional notion that "generally it is the man's primary responsibility to provide a home and its essentials," can no longer justify different legal treatment for men and women. *Stanton* had served notice that, "No longer is the female destined solely for the home and the rearing of the family, and only the male for the marketplace and the world of ideas" (421 U.S. 14–15).

96. *Clark* 257–258.

97. *Cretney* 739–40.

98. "Neglect" for these purposes means that the minimal needs of spouse and children for food and shelter are not being met. *Goldstein v. Goldstein*, 6 Family Law Reporter 2041 (Pa. Superior Ct. 1979).

a matter of concern to the household and not for the courts to determine. . . . Public policy requires such a holding." [99]

Matrimonial Property

In Western legal systems it has traditionally been possible for the property relationships of spouses to be arranged, within certain limits, by private agreement between the marriage partners themselves or with the participation of their parents or other members of their families. In recent years, in the four countries with which we are concerned, the spouses' freedom to arrange their property affairs to fit their ideas about married life and their practical needs has increased.[100] But for situations in which the spouses have not made their own arrangements, the law keeps in store a scheme of its own. In continental terminology, the marital property system established by the law itself is called the *legal regime* (*régime légal, gesetzlicher Güterstand*). During a functioning marriage, this background matrimonial property regime is apt to be of little interest to the spouses, although it may be important to their creditors and other third parties. It is when family life is disrupted by divorce; by the death, insolvency, or incapacity of a spouse; or by some other calamity, that marital property law in all systems comes to the fore. Here, however, we begin our study of these issues with a consideration of the basic matrimonial property regimes in the ongoing marriage.

A half-century ago, scholars from eleven different nations assembled in Paris for an international conference on matrimonial property law. The participants reached the unanimous conclusion that the legal matrimonial property regimes of their respective countries were "responding admirably to the desires and needs of the population and that any modification of the legal regime would be difficult or unnecessary." [101] The eleven countries represented by these well-satisfied gentlemen included England, where marital property has since been gradually but fundamentally transformed, and France, where a completely new system of marital property law instituted in 1965 was significantly modified again in 1985. As it happened, Germany and the United States were not represented at the 1937 Paris conference, but since that time all American states have completely revamped their systems, and West German marital property law has been through two major revisions.

The principal motivations for such thoroughgoing changes were (1) to implement more fully the principle of equality of husband and wife; (2) to respond to the ever-increasing incidence of marriage termination by divorce;

99. 59 N.W.2d 336 (Neb. 1953).
100. See below, text at notes 150–164.
101. *Travaux de la semaine internationale de droit 1937* (Paris, 1938), 1.

and (3) to permit a spouse who works inside the home to participate more fully in the acquests of the spouse who works outside the home. The legal problems to which these efforts have given rise are chiefly those of distribution of powers of management between the spouses during marriage, and of financial settlements upon divorce. The latter subject will be treated in chapter 5.

Problems relating to management of the spouses' property have appeared in the French and American community property systems in connection with the need to bring the wife into the system of control of the community fund. In England, West Germany, and the separate property states of the United States, they have taken the form of determining to what extent, if at all, individual spouses are to be restricted in their freedom to deal with their respective funds. The earliest efforts to deal with these issues assumed the model of the housewife-breadwinner marriage and marriage stability. But even as such reforms were taking place, divorce was increasing, and housewife-breadwinner marriage was becoming only one of many marriage models in society.

In the early 1970s, Rheinstein and Glendon studied marital property systems in several industrialized countries to determine the degree to which equality had been implemented; the measure in which each spouse shared in the other's property; and the extent to which marriage models other than the housewife-breadwinner one were recognized. Our comparative analysis of marital property laws and of the technical devices through which changes in them had been effected indicated that the systems had partially converged insofar as separate property systems had adopted devices to increase sharing of property between the spouses, and community property systems had adopted devices to provide for more independence in management.[102] At the same time, we found a growing divergence among systems according to the degree of emphasis they gave to the solidarity of the spouses or to the autonomy of each individual spouse. In some countries, shared ownership and control of property has been seen either as required by one interpretation of the principle of equality, or as desirable in and of itself—perhaps as representing the needs and desires of most married couples, or perhaps as reflecting the extent to which law reformers or legislatures had in mind the model of housewife-breadwinner marriage or an ideal of community. In other countries, law reforms have emphasized the independence of the spouses, either because it corresponded to a different vision of equality, or because it was thought to be desirable in itself. Neither one trend nor the other has clearly prevailed; they are interacting in each system. Here, we will examine the

102. Rheinstein and Glendon, above, note 89 at 169–175.

varying degrees to which current laws affecting the ownership and control of property in the functioning marriage emphasize the common interests of the members of the household or the individual interests of the spouses.

The French and American Communities: Toward More Independence

FRANCE   In France, where the Civil Code of 1804 (drawing on preexisting custom) made a form of community property the legal regime and gave the wife a half-share in the community fund, the goal of sharing was built into marital property law from the beginning. The "community of movables and acquests" of the Code Napoleon included in the common fund all assets of the spouses except (1) immovables[103] owned separately at the time of marriage or acquired thereafter by gift or inheritance; (2) movables acquired by gift with a stipulation that they were to remain separate; and (3) movables of a peculiarly personal nature, such as clothing and tools. But shared ownership did not mean shared control. The husband had exclusive power to manage and dispose of the community fund, limited by certain protective devices that had been established in favor of wives and, after 1907, by the wife's power to control her own earnings. Thus, the problem in the 1960s seemed to be how to bring about full equality in control, as well as ownership, of the community property.

The Nordic countries had confronted this problem early in the twentieth century. To require that both spouses join in every transaction seemed so cumbersome as to be unworkable, but to give up community property would have gone against ingrained tradition. Hence, the idea of *deferred community* was developed. In a deferred community property regime, so long as the marriage lasts (or, more correctly, so long as the regime operates), each spouse independently manages all the assets he or she brings in, but when the marriage (or the regime) comes to an end, the funds which remain are shared equally as if there had been a community scheme all along. In outline form, such a system had already existed in Costa Rica, and as a legal system for certain groups in Hungary, and as an optional system in Austria. But Sweden and the other Nordic countries modernized it and made it their basic legal pattern. Since then, deferred community has been widely regarded as a model where demands for equality have required changes in an existing scheme of shared ownership.

When France embarked on its first major matrimonial property law reform in 1965, deferred community was thought by many to strike the ideal balance between concern for the rights of married women and the widely held French

103. In the Romano-Germanic legal systems, *immovables* and *movables* correspond roughly to what we call *real* and *personal* property in the common law systems.

conception of marriage as a union of the financial, as well as other, interests of two people. But most French legal scholars, law reformers, and legislators were not yet ready to break with the tradition of the husband's headship of the community. So the choice was made instead to modify the community property system by reducing the scope of the common fund and increasing the participation of the wife in its control. The community of movables and acquests became a *community of acquests* only, thus excluding all property, real or personal, acquired before marriage, and all property acquired thereafter by gift or inheritance.[104] That part of the community property represented by a spouse's earnings remains subject to the separate management of that spouse unless or until they are invested or converted into other assets.[105] Each spouse has exclusive powers to deal with his or her separate property, that is, all property brought into the marriage or acquired thereafter by gift or inheritance.[106]

After a couple has lived together for some time, it can become quite difficult to distinguish separate from community property. A crucial feature of all community property systems, therefore, is the legal presumption that any given asset is co-owned unless it can be shown to be the separate property of one spouse. In the light of this presumption, the difference between the post-1965 community of acquests and the 1804 community of movables and acquests is less great than might first appear. Proof of separate ownership is ordinarily available only in the case of land, buildings, and other assets for which documents of title are required. Therefore, nearly all assets of an average couple who started married life with little property will be deemed to be co-owned under the regime of community of acquests, just as they were previously.

With respect to the management powers of the spouses, the 1965 law retained the husband as sole manager of the community property (except for that part represented by the wife's separate earnings). But his powers were greatly circumscribed. He had to obtain the wife's consent to transactions of major importance involving the community fund (and his consent was required for the same group of transactions concerning the wife's reserved fund). In practice, except for couples engaged in a joint business, the assets subject to the husband's sole control consisted mainly of those which had been acquired through his own gainful activities, or property which could be traced to such assets. But where the wife assisted her husband in a family farm or

104. French Civil Code, art. 1401. This pattern is the most prevalent marital property regime in the world, having spread from Spain to most of Latin America and eight American states, and from the Soviet Union to most of the socialist countries.
105. French Civil Code, art. 224.
106. French Civil Code, art. 1428.

shop, whatever income she generated was part of the ordinary community property administered by the husband.

The residual inequalities of the system were significant. Once a working wife invested her earnings or used them to acquire assets, the property so acquired became subject to the exclusive control of the husband. The contributions of women who assisted their husbands in family enterprises were not considered "earnings" at all. Such women, like full-time homemakers, participated in management only indirectly through possession of a veto over certain major conveyances. Legislation in 1980 and 1983 began to remedy these inequities for the wives of farmers and small entrepreneurs, but the era of piecemeal solutions finally came to an end in 1985.

By that time, the discrepancy between French marital property law and the equality norms contained in international conventions to which France had subscribed had become embarrassing.[107] Law reformers were nevertheless still reluctant to adopt the unfamiliar deferred community system. Against the background of a long community tradition, separate property was out of the question. Yet requiring both spouses always to act in concert seemed impractical. The decision was made, therefore, to give each spouse the power to administer and dispose of community property by acting alone.[108] Exceptions to this basic principle were made in two directions. If one spouse is engaged in a separate profession, he or she has the *exclusive* power to carry out all necessary transactions connected with it. Both spouses must act together, however, in important transactions of the type for which the husband formerly had to have his wife's consent, such as major gifts of community property and sales or encumbrances of community real estate or businesses. In explaining why the list of transactions for which the consent of both spouses is required was not expanded in 1985, the minister of justice emphasized the importance of preserving the freedom of action of the individual spouses:

> [The addition of more consent requirements] would have significantly diminished the scope of the reform. What indeed would women have gained from a law which would have given them equality only on condition of acting with the consent of their husbands?. . . . I believe it is indispensable to preserve, to the greatest extent possible, the autonomous powers of action of each spouse. At a time when the . . . number of marriages is constantly dropping and many observers consider that [marriage] is facing serious competition from free unions, it would be an error to institute a real diminution of the legal capacity of both spouses.[109]

107. A. Colomer, "La réforme de la réforme des régimes matrimoniaux, ou: vingt ans après (premières réflexions sur la loi du 23 décembre 1985)," D. 1986. Chr. 49.

108. French Civil Code, art. 1421, as revised.

109. Quoted in Colomer, above, note 107 at 54–55.

This sounds quite gallant until one realizes that in practice the double-consent requirement would have weighed most heavily on spouses who have significant income and property, usually husbands (and on third parties—banks and creditors—dealing with husbands). This is not to say that imposing full comanagement would be an effective or desirable way of improving the economic position of married women. But it does show what vision of equality guided the 1985 reforms. Since the husband's earnings are still the main source of income in most French households, the 1985 law, like the reforms at the turn of the century, benefits mainly married women with significant income or property of their own. In the type of marriage that is now becoming the norm in all industrialized countries—in which the wife is the primary homemaker and a secondary earner—the French reform leaves husbands in full control over the principal resources of the family. Indeed, their power has in a sense been expanded, because most of the old protective devices for wives established in the days when French marital property law was explicitly gender-based have been eliminated as inconsistent with the equality principle.

We see, then, in French law the increasing influence of an abstract formal idea of equality, which favors the individual liberty of each spouse and which seems to assume *de facto* equality. But it would be an error to suppose that French marital property law has moved so far along these lines as to eliminate what is "communitarian" about its system. For, to a greater extent than in any of the other countries with which we are here concerned, French law contains devices to help assure that there will be a community fund to be divided when the marriage comes to an end through divorce or death. In the first place, either spouse may be liable to the other for damages for mismanagement of the community property.[110] Although this is not an insignificant restraint on the freedom of action of the spouses, its potential impact is importantly tempered by the principle that either spouse can freely dispose of that part of the community property represented by his or her earnings, after having made the necessary contributions to household expenses.[111] Thus, for example, in a 1984 case, a wife failed in her efforts to invalidate very substantial gifts made by her husband to his mistress from his current earnings over a period of years during which he had apparently also provided adequately for his wife and son.[112] A second device to protect community prop-

110. French Civil Code, new art. 1421.
111. French Civil Code, new art. 1423.
112. *Consorts Le Berre v. Dame Patrin*, Court of Cassation decision of 29 February 1984, D. 1984. Jur. 601. See also *Veuve Pelletier v. Consorts Menager*, Court of Cassation decision of 12 December 1986, D. 1987. Jur. 269, where the Court held that a husband did not need his wife's consent to designate or change the beneficiary on a life insurance policy purchased from his earnings.

erty from dissipation is the provision of Art. 220–1 that if either husband or wife defaults seriously in his or her duties so as to jeopardize the family's interests, the president of the local trial court may order "all the urgent measures that those interests require," and in particular may forbid him or her to dispose of his own property or that of the community without the consent of the other. This article was once applied to authorize the wife of a corporation president to have shares of stock, belonging to the community and registered in the husband's name, transferred to her control and registered in her name on the books of the corporation, where the husband was shown to be "captivated by a young mistress" and to be endangering the interests of the family.[113]

In certain cases, a spouse may also seek a court order authorizing him or her to exercise the powers of the other.[114] Such authorization may be obtained if a spouse becomes legally incompetent, or where a spouse's management of community property is manifestly inept or fraudulent. The spouse so authorized can carry on the day-to-day exercise of the other spouse's powers and, with the special authorization of the court, can perform even the acts for which joint consent would otherwise have been required. Another remedy for mismanagement is to sue to put an end to the community. If, "due to the disorder of one spouse's affairs or his mismanagement or misconduct, it appears that to maintain the community imperils the interests of the other partner, he or she can sue for the separation of property."[115]

Finally, the matrimonial home and its contents receive special treatment in French law regardless of title and regardless of what matrimonial property regime the couple has chosen. Neither spouse may dispose of the "rights which assure the family's lodging and furniture" without the consent of the other.[116] If one spouse attempts to convey such property to third parties, the other has one year within which to bring an action to avoid the transfer.

The first three of the five foregoing protections are characteristic of devices traditionally used in community systems to preserve the community fund. Involving as they do restraints on individual action (even, in the case of Art. 220–1, of one's freedom to deal with his or her own separate property), they have tended to be phased out from those systems (such as those in the Nordic countries or the American community property states) which are moving furthest toward equality in the sense of individual autonomy. In the separate property systems, restraints on a spouse's freedom to deal with property are exceptional and tend to be limited to a few special situations, such as the

---

113. *Ribatto v. Ribatto*, Decision of the Tribunal de Grande Instance of Digne, 1 July 1972, D. 1973. Jur. 259.

114. French Civil Code, art. 1426.   115. French Civil Code, art. 1443.

116. French Civil Code, art. 215.

protection of the family home and the protection of a surviving spouse against complete disinheritance.

AMERICAN COMMUNITY PROPERTY SYSTEMS   In the eight American states where a form of community of acquests has been the system of marital property either from the beginning of settlement or from a very early date (Arizona, California, Idaho, Louisiana, Nevada, New Mexico, Texas, and Washington) a series of reforms appeared at the turn of the century restricting the broad powers of the husband and providing protection to the wife against abuses of his managerial power. As in France, these laws required the wife's consent for certain important transactions and gave her managerial power over her own earnings. In a second wave of changes, beginning in the late 1960s, the American community systems deposed the husband as head of the community and provided for schemes of comanagement.[117] In Arizona, California, Idaho, Louisiana, Nevada, New Mexico, and Washington, either spouse, acting alone, may deal with community property, joinder of both spouses being required only for certain important transactions, such as purchase, conveyance, or encumbrance of community real estate.[118] In most of these states, as in France, if one spouse is the primary manager of a community business, that spouse is expressly authorized to deal with the business assets in the ordinary course of management without the other spouse's consent.

Texas has taken a somewhat different approach. There, each spouse during marriage has the sole power to deal with those community assets that he or she would have owned if single.[119] But if such community property is "mixed or combined" with community property subject to the sole control of the other spouse, then such mixed property becomes subject to the "joint management" of both spouses, unless the spouses provide otherwise in writing. Joint management means that both spouses must join in any transaction affecting such property, not that either can act for the other. Community property other than that which each spouse would have owned separately if single is also subject to the "joint management, control and disposition" of the spouses unless they provide otherwise. Presumably, this would subject all joint acquisitions of the spouses (such as those earned in a family business) to joint

---

117. The last to do so was Louisiana, which clung to its tradition of male headship of the community until the United States Supreme Court held it unconstitutional in *Kirchberg v. Feenstra*, 450 U.S. 455 (1981).

118. Arizona Rev. Stat. Ann. §25–214 (1976); California Civil Code §5125, 5127 (West Supp. 1987); Idaho Code §32–912 (1983); Louisiana Civil Code, arts. 2346, 2347, 2850 (West 1985); Nevada Rev. Stat. §123.230 (1986); New Mexico Stat. Ann. §§40-3-13, 40-3-14 (1987); Washington Rev. Code Ann. §26.16.030 (West 1986).

119. Texas Family Code Ann. §5.22 (1975).

control. Cooperation of both spouses is also necessary for disposition of the marital homestead whether it is an asset of the community fund or the separate fund of one of the spouses.

Apart from consent requirements, most American community systems do not have anything resembling the complicated network of restraints which French law has established to protect the community. Indeed, the scope given to mutual representation, especially in Idaho, gives each spouse considerable power to diminish the community fund to the other's detriment. Only the matrimonial home is singled out for special legal protection. California in 1986 moved in the French direction, however, by establishing a cause of action for mismanagement of community property and giving each spouse the right to an accounting from the other during the marriage.[120]

Anglo-American Individualism: Toward More Sharing

In the preceding section we saw how equality in management was introduced into marital property systems in which shared ownership of certain assets is a standard feature. In the Anglo-American systems established by the various Married Women's Property Acts around the turn of the century, where separate ownership is the distinctive feature, equality (in the sense of each spouse's right to manage and dispose of his or her own property) was built in. The issue here has been whether and how to give to each spouse a share in the acquests of the other.

The American and English married women's legislation, by giving wives the same powers over their earnings and assets as those possessed by men and single women, transformed the traditional common law system into what continental legal scholars call the *regime of separation of assets* (*séparation de biens*, *Gütertrennung*). The common law, however, has no special term for its rules governing the property relationships of husband and wife. An English or American lawyer contemplating the system simply observes that in a marriage, a husband owns and controls his property, and a wife owns and controls hers, and that the fact that they are married to each other has certain effects in the event of death, divorce, or insolvency, and also affects their tax situation.

At first glance, the separate property system appears to be both simple and just. The spouses are equal in a strict formal sense; their property is neatly divided into his or hers. On closer inspection, it is not always simple in practical application, nor does it necessarily function in accordance with presently prevailing ideas of fairness. Complexity creeps in because in most households the assets of the spouses tend to be mingled rather than kept separate or neatly

120. California Civil Code §§5125–5125.5 (West Supp. 1987).

earmarked. Fairness is problematic where the husband is the sole or the principal breadwinner, and where, as a consequence, the bulk of the assets are in his name when the marriage or marital harmony has come to an end, or when one of the parties becomes insolvent. These problems have given rise to much discussion in England and the United States.

ENGLAND   In a separate property system there is no doubt that the acquests made from a spouse's earnings and to which title is taken in that spouse's own name are his or hers alone. But in the course of living together, husbands and wives jointly acquire assets, make gifts to each other, and use many items in common—all in serene disregard of such notions as title and without keeping track of the precise contributions each has made. Thus considerable uncertainty surrounds the ownership rights of the spouses during marriage. The basic approach to sorting them out was laid down in the leading English case, *Pettitt v. Pettitt*, where Lord Upjohn said:

> [T]he rights of the parties . . . must be judged on the general principles applicable in any court of law when considering questions of title to property, and though the parties are husband and wife these questions of title must be decided by the principles of law applicable to the settlement of claims between those not so related, while making full allowances in view of the relationship.[121]

The application of general principles of property law to marital disputes means that the answer to any controverted question about who owns what as between husband and wife depends in the first instance upon the intent with which the property was acquired.[122] Given the difficulties of ascertaining or proving states of mind (especially where the parties may never have focused clearly on the question of ownership), the cases often seem to be resolved by the court's own idea of what would have been a "reasonable" intent in view of the circumstances at the time of acquisition. Some judges have been quite candid about this. Lord Diplock, for example, stated in *Pettitt* that where the parties have not formed a common intention, the court will "impute to them a constructive common intention which is that which in the court's opinion would have been formed by reasonable spouses."[123] The prevailing view, however, is that courts must decide such cases only on the basis of the evidence of the parties' intent and reasonable inferences therefrom.[124] No matter

121. [1970] A.C. 777, 813.
122. *Pettitt v. Pettitt*, [1970] A.C. 777; *Gissing v. Gissing*, [1971] A.C. 886. It also means that precedents in marital and cohabitation cases are often used interchangeably.
123. *Pettitt v. Pettitt*, [1970] A.C. 777, 823.
124. *Cretney* 643–44.

how they describe what they are doing, it is apparent that English judges have a great deal of discretion in these cases.

Under present English case and statutory law, a *prima facie* case of co-ownership in equity can be made out, regardless of how title is taken, by showing (1) that the property was acquired through the direct cash contributions of both spouses; (2) that the property was acquired from a joint fund to which both spouses contributed directly in cash; or (3) that one spouse contributed in money or money's worth to the improvement of real or personal property of the other.[125] Contribution by the spouse who is not the title holder, however, may be exceedingly hard to show in all of these situations, just as proof of intent at the time of acquisition is difficult in most cases. Especially troublesome in all separate property jurisdictions is the problem of determining whether and how indirect contributions or contributions of substantial physical labor, as distinct from cash, should be recognized in property division. The English cases, as John Eekelaar has pointed out, tend to exclude homemaking activities from consideration, with the result that the wives who have relied the most on their partner's statements of intention are the least likely to be held to have acquired property rights.[126] (In community property jurisdictions, of course, the presumption that all property is co-owned provides a clear starting point from which to approach such questions.)

When and if it can be established that both spouses have a beneficial interest in an asset, the further problem arises of determining the exact share of each spouse. If it can be shown that the parties contributed in distinct and unequal shares, it will be presumed that they are tenants in common in equity, in shares proportionate to the amounts they advanced.[127] But the problem becomes more complex when, as is often the case, the parties' financial affairs cannot be so neatly sorted out. In the usual case, the English courts have developed a doctrine of *joint enterprise*, which normally results in equal division of the acquisition or its proceeds. But there seems to be no presumption in favor of equal division of property acquired through joint contribution. The case law, with varying approaches sometimes taken by individual judges within a single case, is highly uncertain. A recent Law Commission proposal would help to tidy up this disorderly corner of property law. The commissioners favor a law providing that "where money is made available directly or

125. See generally *Cretney* 635–60.

126. Eekelaar is highly critical of English marital property law both for the artificiality of the search for intent that it requires and for the low value it implicitly places on child-raising and homemaking. John Eekelaar, "A Woman's Place—A Conflict Between Law and Social Values," *The Conveyancer and Property Lawyer*, (March-April 1987), 93.

127. E.g., *In re Rogers' Question* [1948] 1 All E.R. 328 (C.A.); *Walker v. Hall*, [1984] Fam. 21.

indirectly by one spouse, for the joint purposes of the spouses, . . . that money, and any property acquired with it shall in the absence of any agreement to the contrary, written or otherwise, be owned equally by the spouses." [128] This proposal to, in effect, codify the better case law would introduce a limited form of co-ownership within the framework of a joint purpose test, but would not seem to change the uncertain situation of a spouse who makes nonfinancial contributions through child care or housework.

The rights of third parties are also affected by the present confused state of the law, especially since the House of Lords held, in a case that caused great consternation to conveyancers and lenders, that the beneficial rights of a spouse whose name does not appear on the title to real estate can bind third parties, so long as that spouse is in "actual occupation" of the property in which he or she has acquired an interest through contributions. [129]

Joint tenancies do not completely eliminate these problems. Property acquired through the earnings of one spouse and held in the names of both may turn out to be held on a resulting trust for the funding spouse, or may be treated as a gift of a one-half interest from the funding spouse, or merely as subject to a contingent right of survivorship. In case of litigation, the question is again ultimately one of intent.

Singled out for special treatment in the English system is the matrimonial home. However, there is no unified, comprehensive regulation of a spouse's rights in the family homestead. Rather, a patchwork of statutory provisions has been put together in response to certain recurring problems. We will mention here only the most important of these statutes. The Matrimonial Homes Act of 1967 gives a nonowning spouse a "right of occupation" in the marital home which, if publicly registered, will be valid against purchasers and mortgagees of the owner-spouse. This measure was passed to give a deserted wife a means of protecting herself in the situation where the owner-husband attempted to sell the home out from under her. But the public registration requirement rendered it virtually a dead letter. In 1976, Parliament addressed a different problem: whether one spouse could exclude the other from the matrimonial home in situations of domestic violence. The Domestic Violence and Matrimonial Proceedings Act of that year gave courts the power to order even an owner-spouse to leave the household under certain circumstances. At present, petitions to oust one spouse from the family home during the marriage are governed by the Matrimonial Homes Act 1983, which authorizes a court

128. Law Commission, *Transfer of Money Between Spouses—The Married Women's Property Act 1964*, Working Paper No. 90 (London: Her Majesty's Stationery Office, 1985), par. 5.24.

129. *Williams & Glyn's Bank Ltd. v. Boland*, [1981] A.C. 487.

to make such orders with respect to the marital home "as it thinks just and reasonable having regard to the conduct of the spouses in relation to each other and otherwise to their respective needs and financial resources, to the needs of any children, and to all the circumstances of the case." [130] The 1983 Act also clarified the rights of a tenant's spouse. If the marital home is rented, and the lease is in the name of only one spouse, the nonlessee spouse is protected against eviction by the lessee, and is also entitled to the protection of the Rent Acts, which contain an elaborate system of regulation of the landlord-tenant relationship, including security of tenure. One can thus say that, at least as to one type of property, the matrimonial home, the English separate property system has been significantly modified.

At one time, it seemed that England might go further in implementing the idea of sharing between spouses by adopting some form of community property. In 1956, seven of the nineteen members of the Royal Commission on Marriage and Divorce (Morton Commission) had advocated that step, but the majority rejected it as too unfamiliar and novel to be suitable for England.[131] Nonetheless, the idea persisted. In 1969, a member of Parliament introduced a bill for the establishment of a unified matrimonial property system with community features. The bill was withdrawn upon the Government's undertaking to request the Law Commission to study the subject and prepare systematic family property legislation. The Law Commission initially seemed to be leaning strongly in favor of some form of community property.[132] But by 1973, when it issued its First Report on Family Property, a very different frame of mind had taken hold. The Law Commission confined itself to recommending the introduction of a principle of co-ownership limited to the matrimonial home.[133] Meanwhile, the Matrimonial Proceedings and Property Act of 1970, consolidated in the Matrimonial Causes Act of 1973, had implemented sharing in another way by giving the courts broad discretion to redistribute the spouses' property upon divorce, rather than simply restoring to each spouse what was "his" and "hers." Since English courts also have power to reallocate the spouses' property upon death,[134] the impetus for considering a shift to community property largely disappeared.

In 1978 and 1982, the Law Commission reiterated that the system of pro-

130. Matrimonial Homes Act 1983 s. 1 (3).

131. *Report of the Royal Commission on Marriage and Divorce* (Morton Commission) (London: Her Majesty's Stationery Office, 1956), pars. 644, 650–653.

132. The Law Commission, *Family Property Law*, Working Paper No. 42 (London: Her Majesty's Stationery Office, 1971).

133. The Law Commission, *First Report on Family Property Law*, Law Commission No. 52 (London: Her Majesty's Stationery Office, 1973).

134. See below, chapter 5, text at note 136.

tection of a spouse's rights in the matrimonial home should be reinforced and simplified by establishing a statutory scheme of equal co-ownership and a requirement, similar to those found in American statutes known as *homestead laws*, that no sale or encumbrance of the marital home could be valid without the consent of both spouses.[135] In order to protect third parties, however, the Law Commission also recommended that these co-ownership and consent rights would have to be publicly registered if they were to be valid against purchasers or lenders. These recommendations have failed to attract significant parliamentary support. The *Boland* decision,[136] therefore, is left in place with the result that, in practice, purchasers and lenders routinely must obtain consents or waivers from anyone in occupation who might have a beneficial interest in property being used as a dwelling. The protection thus afforded to a nonowner spouse has been reinforced by the courts' willingness to inquire into the genuineness of a wife's consent to transactions involving the family home.[137] Thus, *Boland*, by requiring the wife's involvement in transactions that previously she could not affect, has had some unanticipated but significant effects on power relations within the family.[138]

UNITED STATES   Marital property law in those jurisdictions of the United States which do not have community property has diverged in some respects from the direction taken in England, especially when property disputes arise upon the death of a spouse.[139] But in the rare cases where determination of who owns what must be made during the ongoing marriage, the problems and approaches in the United States are basically similar to those in England. As in England, the extent of the ownership rights of each spouse depends on the intent with which each asset was acquired and thus may remain uncertain until a court has spoken. Neither the source of funds nor the form in which title is held is necessarily dispositive of these issues. In some jurisdictions, evidence of joint use and possession of furniture and other household items raises a presumption of co-ownership;[140] in other jurisdictions, the issue is one of fact and intent with respect to each asset in each case.[141]

135. The Law Commission, *Third Report on Family Property*, Law Commission No. 56 (London: Her Majesty's Stationery Office, 1978); *The Implications of Williams & Glyn's Bank Ltd. v. Boland*, Law Commission No. 115 (London: Her Majesty's Stationery Office, 1982).

136. See above, n. 129.

137. See *Kingsnorth Trust v. Bell*, [1985] Fam. 948.

138. I am grateful for this information to Professor John Eekelaar.

139. See below, chapter 5, text at note 148.

140. E.g., *In re Estate of Smith*, 232 N.E.2d 310 (Ill. App. 1967); *DiFlorido v. DiFlorido*, 331 A.2d 174 (Pa. 1975).

141. *Avnet v. Avnet*, 124 N.Y.S.2d 517 (N.Y. Mun. Ct. 1953); *Susan W. v. Martin W.*, 3 Family Law Reporter 2250 (N.Y. Sup. Ct. 1977).

   In practice, the custom of holding savings and real estate in joint tenancies with right of survivorship has become so widespread in the United States as to amount to a form of quasi-community property, entered into voluntarily with respect to particular assets. In most cases, these devices operate smoothly and efficiently to assure complete ownership to the surviving spouse without the expense and delay of probate. But when disputes arise, evidence is admissible to show that the intention was to create some other relationship, such as an agency, or that the funding spouse had put the property in joint names only as a will substitute, with no intent to make a present gift.[142]

   Even though both spouses are in principle free to deal with their property as they wish, their powers are somewhat restricted in many states by statutes and case law doctrines developed to rotect the other spouse's rights to a share in inheritance and by homestead laws which require the consent of both spouses to conveyances or encumbrances of the land on which the family home is located. Homestead laws also assure a spouse a certain amount of protection, which varies from state to state, from execution on the matrimonial home by creditors.

   Because courts in most American jurisdictions have extensive powers to disregard title to property upon divorce, and because of the generous protection afforded to surviving spouses in nearly all states, there has been little attention paid until recently to the property rights of spouses in the ongoing marriage, except by creditors. In 1983, however, the National Conference of Commissioners on Uniform State Laws proposed a Uniform Marital Property Act which applies only to the property relations of spouses during marriage. The Act, which as of 1988 had been adopted only in Wisconsin, makes the spouses equal co-owners of all property acquired during marriage except by gift or inheritance. As in community property systems, all property is presumptively co-owned. Management and control of the spouses' property, however, remains essentially the same as in a separate property system, except that both spouses have a duty to act in good faith, and the consent of both is required for large gifts of co-owned property. The Act says nothing about how property shall be divided upon divorce or death, but it has an indirect effect in these situations by ensuring that when the relevant procedures are called into play, they will at least begin on the assumption that the marital acquests are co-owned in equal shares.

   Thus, the Act has the curious effect of introducing systematic regulation of marital property only where such regulation is least needed—during the marriage. The system it establishes resembles deferred community in that it

   142. E.g., *Doucette v. Doucette*, 279 N.E.2d 901 (Mass. 1972); *Blanchette v. Blanchette*, 287 N.E.2d 459 (Mass. 1972).

leaves the individual spouses relatively free to deal with their own incomes; but unlike community property laws generally, the Act does not assure the spouses that their rights to separate and community property will be respected on divorce. In contrast to the authors of the U.M.P.A., most English and American law reformers have attempted to mitigate the sometimes harsh effects of the system of strict separation of title through revising the law of succession and divorce. In both England and the United States, proposals to establish more direct sharing by one spouse in the acquests of the other during the marriage have met with a cool reception.

In sum, then, an English or American property owner does not ordinarily gain or lose ownership rights upon marriage and is relatively free to deal with his or her own property during marriage, but he or she does become subject to a system of legal rules that promote sharing of property when the marriage comes to an end. Sometimes these rules are considered to be a recognition of the activity of one spouse in the home and to compensate not only for this activity but for opportunities lost. Sometimes they are thought of as an expression of the presumed intent of husbands and wives to pool their fortunes on an equal basis, share and share alike. Whatever their rationale, numerous devices designed to introduce increased sharing of property on death and divorce have penetrated separate property systems. In so doing, they have transformed these systems into something resembling what several community systems have become when they introduced separate management as a means of implementing equality. The main difference is that the common law systems have tended to rely more heavily on judicial discretion in case of disputes, while the continental systems make more use of fixed rules.

The West German Zugewinngemeinschaft: Equality, Independence, and Solidarity

The movement of the English and American separate property systems toward increased sharing and of the French and American community property systems toward increased independence has brought both systems close to the accommodation of these two goals worked out in the Nordic countries and West Germany. In the Nordic countries, where the starting point was a form of community property, each spouse is in sole control of his or her own property and responsible for his or her own debts so long as the marriage or the regime exists, just as if the regime were that of separation of assets. But once the marriage or the regime terminates, the funds of the two spouses are pooled, and the common mass is evenly divided. Hence the name *deferred community*. This scheme of marital property is supplemented by inheritance rights of the surviving spouse and by the possibility of a maintenance award upon divorce.

In West Germany the starting point was different. In the late nineteenth century, when the married women's separate property acts were being passed in England and the United States, the matrimonial property provisions of the German Civil Code were being prepared. The property system selected for the legal regime in the Code of 1896 was the *Güterstand der Verwaltung und Nutzniessung*, which, like the turn-of-the-century French and Anglo-American reforms, gave married women the right to their own earnings and property. This regime, which remained the legal regime (through both the Weimar Republic and the Third Reich) until 1953, was a system of separation of ownership under which the husband had the right to administer, possess, and keep the income from most of his wife's real and personal property. He could not, however, transfer ownership of her assets. With respect to one important category of her property, the *Vorbehaltsgut*, the wife had not only the title but also the exclusive right to administer, possess, and dispose. The *Vorbehaltsgut* consisted of the wife's profits and earnings acquired in the exercise of a separate occupation. It also included objects exclusively destined for her personal use, any property designated by the marriage contract as *Vorbehaltsgut*, and any assets acquired by the wife through gift or inheritance granted under the express condition that they should remain subject to her control.

West Germany began to review the Civil Code provisions on matrimonial property, along with family law in general, after the adoption of the 1949 Constitution. But no new property regime was adopted by the legislature before the 1953 deadline for implementation of the equality command. Since the existing legal provisions were clearly not in conformity with the Basic Law, the task fell to the courts to equalize the property relations of husband and wife. Almost unanimously they held that the only regime satisfying the equality rule that could be judicially imposed was the regime of separation.[143] As a result, West Germany for a while became a separate property jurisdiction.

Even though the goal of equality thus had been fully achieved, the West Germans were not satisfied with the system. A need was felt to give married women more of a share of the family property than they had received either under the new system of separation or under the old system of the Civil Code. After extensive comparative studies, a new matrimonial property regime was worked out and was put into effect by the 1957 Equality Law. It was called the *Zugewinngemeinschaft* (*community of gains*, or *of increase*).

The new system was patterned on the Nordic deferred community, but un-

143. Max Rheinstein, "The Law of Family and Succession," in *Civil Law in the Modern World*, ed. Athanassios Yiannopoulos (Baton Rouge, La.: Louisiana State University Press, 1965), 27, 34.

like its model, the *Zugewinngemeinschaft* excludes the value of gifts, inheritances, and premarital assets from the property to be shared (so long as their origin can be traced). Another difference was introduced in order to simplify the liquidation. The fund to be shared is not the spouses' property as such, but the *Zugewinn*: the *increase* of the monetary value of their estates that has occurred during the marriage (or, more precisely, during the existence of the marital property regime, which may be terminated by agreement or by court decision even while the marriage continues). The increase, if any, of one spouse's estate is compared with the increase, if any, of the estate of the other. A partner whose increase is greater than the other's must pay to the other one-half of the difference.[144] Thus, the basic difference between the West German and the Nordic systems is that the former provides merely a share in the marital increase rather than a share of the total combined assets of both parties. The sharing of the *Zugewinn*, or increase, is reduced to an arithmetical operation resulting in mere money claims.

During the parliamentary debates, the influence of the West German notaries brought about another deviation from the Nordic model. In the Scandinavian countries, sharing occurs in the same manner in the case of death as in the case of divorce or other termination *inter vivos*. In the course of the deliberations of the West German Bundestag, however, the above-described scheme of equalization claim was rejected as unnecessarily complicated for the most frequent case of marriage termination: the death intestate of one spouse. In this case, sharing was believed to be adequately provided by the simpler method of giving the surviving spouse a fixed share in lieu of any claim of equalization.[145]

So far as freedom of disposition during marriage is concerned, neither spouse, in principle, has any interest in specific assets of the other. There are only two limitations on a spouse's ability to deal with the assets subject to his or her control. Neither spouse can engage in a transaction involving his or her estate in its entirety (*Vermögen im Ganzen*) or household goods (*Hausrat*) without the other's consent.[146] In order to be treated as involving a spouse's estate in its entirety, a transaction does not need to include each and every asset. The term may apply to the matrimonial home, but only if the home constitutes the main economic value owned by the spouse.

The deferred community, with its accommodation of individual liberty, equal rights, and property sharing, has appealed to law reformers in many countries. It has been adopted as the basic marital property regime in the

144. West German Civil Code § 1378(1).
145. This is regulated in West German Civil Code § 1371. See below, chapter 5, text at note 157.
146. West German Civil Code § 1365, 1369.

Nordic countries, Israel, Quebec, West Germany, and Switzerland, and it has been approached in fact, though not in name, through reform of the management schemes of community property systems in France, the Netherlands, and many Latin American countries.

Convergence and Divergence

We have seen that the marital property systems of England, France, West Germany, and the United States have come to resemble each other in a number of ways. In all of them the spouses are formally equal, and each spouse has substantial freedom to deal with his or her own earnings.[147] Despite their rhetoric, none has done much to improve the day-to-day position during marriage of a spouse who has no income.[148] Significant differences among the systems remain, however. In the first place, we have seen that while all systems impose some limits on the freedom of spouses to deal with property during marriage, the restraints in the French system are more substantial than in other systems and thus more geared toward assuring that there will be some property left to divide when the marriage or the property regime is terminated. Second, there are important differences among the systems in the degree of certainty the spouses have during marriage about what their rights will be when the marriage comes to an end. In France and three American community property states, husbands and wives know that their equal co-ownership during marriage will be reflected in fixed equal property rights upon death and divorce. In West Germany, they know they will have fixed equal shares in the marital gains. By contrast, in most of the United States, while fixed rules govern the rights of surviving spouses, the courts have wide discretion to reallocate property upon divorce regardless of title or when or how it was acquired. In England, these broad discretionary judicial powers extend even to reallocation of property upon death. Another major difference is that it is relatively simple to opt out of the statutory marital property regime by contract in France or West Germany, while the process is considerably more difficult and its effectiveness more doubtful in the United States and England.

If we turn to the social and economic context within which marital property

147. The first empirical study of the effects of introducing increased autonomy in collection and spending of income has concluded that such rules regularly disadvantage the economically weaker spouse, especially when marital problems arise. Monique Gysels, Jean Van Houtte, and Mieke Vogels, "(In)equality of Husband and Wife in Patrimonial Matters: An Empirical Investigation of the Effects of a Progressive Matrimonial Law in Belgium—A Research Note," 15 *International Journal of the Sociology of Law* 29 (1987).

148. West German Civil Code §1360a at least recognizes the problem by providing that the spouses are obliged to make available the cash required for running the household a reasonable time in advance.

law operates, we become aware of a larger similarity among all four systems. Because of changes in the nature and forms of wealth, marital property law is losing much of its accustomed subject matter and is, once again, becoming only marginally relevant to the lives of great numbers of couples. The fact that the great majority of couples spend what they earn on food, shelter, clothing, and a few modest conveniences or luxuries leaves a restricted field of application to marital property law as traditionally conceived and validates the decision of nearly all modern legal systems to create in practice, and often in law, a special "mini-regime" of marital property for the marital home and household goods.

Meanwhile, for most people, government entitlements and job-related rights such as salaries, pensions, insurance, and other benefits have become more important than land, traditional investments, and other forms of personal property. As Charles Reich put it in a now-famous law review article:

> [T]oday more and more of our wealth takes the form of rights or status rather than of tangible goods. An individual's profession or occupation is a prime example. To many others, a job with a particular employer is the principal form of wealth. A profession or a job is frequently far more valuable than a house or a bank account, for a new house can be bought, and a new bank account created, once a profession or job is secure. For the jobless, their status as governmentally assisted or insured persons may be the main source of subsistence.
>
> The kinds of wealth dispensed by government consist almost entirely of those forms which are in the ascendancy today. To the individual, these new forms, such as a profession, job, or right to receive income, are the basis of his various statuses in society, and may therefore be the most meaningful and distinctive wealth he possesses.[149]

These trends do not mean that family law is losing any of its economic emphasis. Rather the emphasis has shifted from rights in traditional property to the issue of rights in a spouses' earning power and benefits, especially after divorce.

Contract as an Ordering Mechanism

No single matrimonial property regime will be appropriate for each and every couple. Not only do different couples have different needs and desires, but the requirements of the same couple with respect to their economic relationship may change over the course of their marriage. Thus it becomes important

149. Charles Reich, "The New Property," 73 *Yale Law Journal* 733, 738–39 (1964).

to know whether and to what extent couples may contract out of the basic regime and arrange (and rearrange) their economic relations to suit themselves. Traditional marital property systems had left ample room for prenuptial marriage contracts or settlements, but at the same time they made it difficult for a couple—once married—to undo the prenuptial bargain struck between their respective families. Thus the English married woman's separate estate in equity typically included restraints on alienation and anticipation. The French Civil Code of 1804 simply provided that prenuptial contracts could not be changed at all after the celebration of the marriage.[150]

Today, all systems accept that the spouses themselves should have substantial freedom to order their affairs in the way they deem suitable, and the problem has become what limits should be imposed on that freedom in order to protect the economically weaker party. The issues in this area are less complicated in civil law countries, no doubt because the use of marriage contracts is not so unusual in those countries as it still is in England and the United States, and it is facilitated by statutes and notarial practice. Both the French and West German civil codes spell out the details of the principal alternative marital property regimes, which are of course mainly of interest to the relatively affluent. The existence of these statutory options means that couples who elect to have separate property in France or a traditional form of community property in West Germany do not incur the trouble, expense, and risks of inventing their own marital property systems from scratch and need not be greatly concerned about how a court will interpret the terms of the regime they choose. The likelihood of subsequent litigation about capacity and voluntariness is minimized by surrounding the execution of marriage contracts with formalities comparable to those required for witnessed wills in the American legal system.

The situation in the common law countries is quite different. Couples in the separate property jurisdictions of the United States and England encounter little difficulty when they make agreements establishing co-ownership of specific assets, such as homes and bank accounts. Joint tenancies and tenancies in common are familiar and effective ways to introduce islands of community property into systems of separate ownership. But marriage contracts are not widely used, and American and English law has done little to facilitate them. Contracts regarding spouses' rights in inheritance generally have been upheld, but until quite recently, the common law was hostile to agreements by which spouses or prospective spouses attempted to specify in advance of separation what their respective property and support rights would be in the event of divorce. In England, it is still said to be the case that an agreement between

150. French Civil Code, former art. 1395.

spouses regarding the effects of a future separation is void as tending to encourage divorce (unless the husband and wife were separated at the time and the agreement was made as part of a reconciliation attempt).[151] Even in the latter situation, such an agreement can be set aside or varied by an English divorce court[152] or avoided for unconscionability.[153]

Most American states in recent years have abandoned the position that prenuptial agreements looking toward divorce are against public policy.[154] Thus the most pressing problem in this area has become determining what limits should be placed on the enforcement of such contracts. All states agree that the spouses' freedom of contract has to be subordinated to the need to provide adequately for their children. Beyond this, however, there is great confusion in the law. As the prefatory note to the 1983 Uniform Premarital Agreement Act states, "There is a substantial uncertainty as to the enforceability of all, or a portion, of the provisions of [premarital] agreements and a significant lack of uniformity of treatment of these agreements among the states." [155] American courts have tended to consider some or all of the following factors in deciding whether and to what extent they will implement the parties' agreements: whether there was fair disclosure of the extent of the parties' wealth at the time of the contract; whether the contract is "fair," "reasonable," or "unconscionable" (with some courts seeking to evaluate these qualities as they were at the time of contracting and others at the time of attempted enforcement); how the provisions of the contract compare with the legal support obligations that they would displace; and whether enforcement of the contract would make one of the spouses a public charge.[156] Under the Uniform Marriage and Divorce Act, a marriage contract is just one factor among several that a court is to "consider" in determining whether its division of the spouses' property is equitable.[157]

The Uniform Law Commissioners have attempted to introduce some coherence into the situation by providing in the Uniform Marital Property Act (UMPA) that spouses can agree before or during marriage with respect to

151. *Cretney* 896.

152. Matrimonial Causes Act 1973, s. 25(1).

153. *Cretney* 896–897.

154. *E.g.*, the early and influential decision in *Dawley v. Dawley*, 551 P.2d 323. (Cal. 1976), where traditional public policy objections were brushed aside, and "realistic planning that takes account of the possibility of dissolution" was expressly approved.

155. UPAA, 9B Uniform Laws Annotated (St. Paul, Minn.: West, 1987), 369. UPAA was adopted in nine states as of 1987.

156. See, for illustrations, Homer Clark, "Antenuptial Contracts," 50 *University of Colorado Law Review* 141 (1979); J. Thomas Oldham, "Premarital Contracts Are Now Enforceable Unless . . . ," 21 *Houston Law Review* 757 (1984).

157. UMDA §307A.

property rights on death or divorce or modification or elimination of spousal support, subject to a requirement of good faith and subject to the rights of creditors, bona fide purchasers, and children entitled to support.[158] With respect to *prenuptial* agreements, the Act (deliberately tracking the Uniform Premarital Agreement Act) provides that such contracts will not be enforceable if they are not voluntary, or if they are unconscionable when made, *and* if the agreement was not accompanied by a fair disclosure, *and* the spouse attacking the agreement neither waived disclosure nor was on notice of the extent of the other spouse's assets.[159] The spouse against whom enforcement is sought has the burden of proof on all these points. Where *postmarital* agreements are concerned, the UMPA imposes a higher standard: an agreement unconscionable when made will not be enforced.[160] Finally, the UMPA provides that if the contractual provisions on support would render one spouse eligible for public assistance, the court may require the other spouse to pay enough support to avoid such eligibility.[161]

Under these provisions, a spouse who wishes to minimize the chances that a contract governed by this or a similar statute will be held unenforceable would be well advised to see that the other spouse was independently represented. But the risks for the relationship of the parties from two lawyers vigorously contending for their clients in this situation are not negligible. In civil law countries, this problem seems to be satisfactorily handled by execution of the contract before a legal specialist known as a notary who advises both parties and whose authentication lends great evidentiary weight to the instrument, but one wonders whether conflicts of interest do not arise from time to time. The common requirement of judicial approval of any change in the contract further promotes the widespread confidence in civil law countries that such agreements will be enforced as written. Third parties are protected by registration requirements.

Since most attacks on the enforceability of marriage contracts involve circumstances surrounding their execution, American law reformers might do well to consider introducing a system of heightened procedural formalities for marriage contracts similar to those currently available in many states for authenticated wills. This would minimize the danger that marriage contracts could be successfully challenged on grounds of involuntariness or lack of disclosure years after their execution—when memories have failed, one party is dead, or the spouses are engaged in a marital dispute. Even if most of the present uncertainties concerning the initial validity of American marriage contracts could be cleared up, however, behavior of the parties that is at vari-

158. UMPA §§2, 3, 8(e), 9(c), 10(b).   159. UMPA §10(g).
160. *Id.* §10(f).   161. *Id.* §10(i).

ance with their agreement over a long period of living together may affect its enforceablity later on.[162]

In Anglo-American discussions of the role which law ought to have in interspousal personal and economic relations during the ongoing marriage, some writers have seen private contractual regulation of these matters as the ideal way to preserve the neutrality of the state, promote sex equality, and respect individual liberty.[163] Many of the proponents of marriage contracts, however, appear to disregard the fact that such agreements are nearly always used to insulate the property of the economically stronger spouse, who in most cases will have the better bargaining position. Leaving this practical problem aside, we have seen that, as a matter of law, relegating interspousal economic relations to private contract in common law systems is not so simple as it has been made to sound. The problems proliferate when a partner seeks to use an interspousal contract for noneconomic purposes. Contract law furnishes little support for the idea that courts should become involved in enforcing agreements about the duration of marriage, the number and spacing of children, the duties of the spouses, or the division of labor and decision making within the family. It is axiomatic that no legal system attempts to enforce every promise or every bargain fulfilling all the formal requirements of a contract.

> [T]he law has not made contracts out of all promises. The reason why it has not is probably a reason of public policy. Some promises are not of enough importance to make it worthwhile to make contracts out of them. The legal enforcement of all promises is expensive. No more expense should be incurred for the enforcement of promises than the needs of our social order make imperative. There is a social interest in personal liberty; and personal liberty, even the personal liberty to lie, ought not to the delimited unless the social interests of other people are thereby injured enough so as to warrant the delimitation of personal liberty.[164]

"Contracts" which purport to regulate who will wash the dishes and take out the garbage are but modern variants of the contract professor's hypotheti-

---

162. Cases are beginning to appear which suggest that a course of conduct of ignoring or failing to abide by or to insist on the terms of the contract may ground claims of abandonment, estoppel, or waiver. 56 *American Law Reports* 4th 998 (1987).

163. *E.g.*, Marjorie M. Schultz, "Contractual Ordering of Marriage: A New Model for State Policy," 70 California Law Review 204 (1982); Lenore Weitzman, "Legal Regulation of Marriage: Tradition and Change, A Proposal for Individual Contracts and Contracts in Lieu of Marriage," 62 *California Law Review* 1169, 1170 (1974).

164. *E.g.*, Hugh Willis, "Rationale of the Law of Contracts," 11 *Indiana Law Review* 227, 230 (1936).

cal promise to go out to dinner. In all legal systems, happily, there is a wide range of obligations whose sanctions are left to the realms of custom, manners, and ethics. Furthermore, the general retreat of the state from involvement in the arrangement of interspousal relations in the ongoing marriage which we have observed in the law of England, France, the United States, and West Germany is not likely to be halted in favor of enforcing private bargains about personal rights and duties in marriage.

The Ongoing Family and the Outside World

We have thus far confined our discussion to the legal relationships of members of the ongoing family with each other. If we consider briefly the changing legal treatment of their relationships with third parties, be they private individuals or agencies of the state, we find further evidence of an increasing tendency to diminish the legal effects of marriage and to assimilate the status of marriage either to that of being single or to the situation of unmarried cohabitants.

One type of third party who takes more than a passing interest in the degree to which marriage constitutes a community of life is a creditor, who would always prefer to have recourse against two individuals rather than just the one originally dealt with. In the Anglo-American systems of separation of assets, the starting point is, and has been since the Married Women's Property Acts, that each spouse is liable only for his or her own transactions. The mingling of affairs typical of persons who live together immediately poses problems, however, concerning the rights each spouse may have in property apparently belonging to the other or in assets whose title is not clearly apparent, and the extent to which those rights can be attached by third parties. In a separate property system, such problems are resolved by the application of the same general principles of the law of property that would apply to two strangers. Creditors of married persons are assisted, however, by the policy in favor of protecting good-faith reliance on appearances. Thus, creditors of either spouse are able to reach everything held in their debtor's name and also their debtor's interest in jointly held property. But if they attempt to reach any equitable interests their debtor may have acquired by virtue of contributions to the acquisition of property held in the other spouse's name, they encounter the same difficulties of proof that the debtor-spouse would have.

An exception to treating spouses as any other cohabitants exists in many American states where family expense statutes or common law doctrines make both spouses liable for a variety of debts incurred in connection with maintaining the household or raising the children. In some states, however, the spouse who has not engaged in the transaction cannot be held liable for such expenses so long as payment can be obtained from the other. Furthermore, American courts will increasingly look behind the formal marriage bond to the reality of the relationship in determining whether or not to apply rules that are premised on a notion of family solidarity. Thus married but separated spouses have been held not liable for necessaries supplied to the other.[165]

In England, the Matrimonial Proceedings and Property Act of 1970 abolished the married woman's agency of necessity by which at common law she had had the power to pledge her husband's credit for such items as housing, food, clothing, medical attention, and education for the children. Today, if an English spouse is to be liable for such transactions of the other, it is on the general agency principle of apparent authority, which applies not just to married people but to all who have given a third party reason to believe that someone has authority to pledge their credit.[166] The presumption of authority thus applies not only to a wife but to anyone who has apparent power to make purchases for the household.

The situation under the West German version of deferred community is broadly similar. Obligations incurred by one spouse can be enforced against his or her property only, unless they were for household expenses. But, in favor of a creditor of either spouse, movable assets which are in the possession of either or both are rebuttably presumed to be owned by the debtor-spouse. If the spouses do not live together, the presumption does not apply to assets in the possession of the spouse who is not the debtor. Assets which exclusively serve the use of one spouse are presumed to be owned by that spouse.[167]

The situation under the French community property regime contrasts with both the Anglo-American and the West German systems. In France, as a consequence of the regime of co-ownership, a creditor of one spouse may have recourse in some situations not only to the separate assets of the debtor but also to the fund which is co-owned, even where the debt involved is not a household expense.[168] In France, a creditor may also resort to the totality of the community fund for obligations of support due from either the husband or wife; obligations which encumber an inheritance or a donation of personal property acquired by either spouse during marriage, if the movables thus acquired have been so intermingled with the community that they can no longer

---

165. *National Account Systems v. Mercado*, 11 Family Law Reporter 1024 (N.J. Super. Ct. 1984).

166. *Bromley* 121–23.

167. West German Civil Code, §1362.

168. French Civil Code, art. 1409.

be distinguished; and, most importantly, obligations which are incurred by either spouse during the existence of the regime.[169] In some cases, a spouse will be entitled to recompense from the other, but this is not the concern of the creditor. Creditors thus receive substantial protection in France against possible surprises arising from the complexity of the property relationships which may exist between the spouses themselves.

While creditors are probably the third parties most concerned with enforcing legal rights *against* spouses, the spouses themselves are often interested in suing a variety of individuals for harm done to one of the spouses or even to the marital relationship itself. The community aspect of marriage comes to the fore when a spouse sues a third party who has injured or killed his or her partner. On the other hand, there is a definite trend to deny a spouse any civil remedy against a third party for diverting the affection of the other spouse. In many places, such actions have been abolished because they are thought to be especially susceptible to abuse by spiteful persons or even to encourage blackmail. In the United States, one state court has even held that the tort of criminal conversation (adultery) is unconstitutional as a "violation or infringement of the right to privacy of individuals to engage in natural consensual sexual relations."[170] In England, the "heart balm" actions of enticement, harbouring, and damages for adultery, were abolished in 1970.[171] According to Professor Bromley, "it was doubtful whether it was any longer socially desirable to give either spouse a remedy if the loss of the other's consortium was due to the latter's voluntary act, even though the defendant had induced or encouraged it."[172] In France, under general principles of tort law, similar causes of action still exist but seem not to be much utilized.[173] In West Germany, lawsuits against a third party for disturbing the marriage relationship (*Ehestörungsklage*) are still permitted, but their continued existence is highly controversial.[174]

Another area in which there are signs of a tendency to emphasize the individuality of each spouse rather than the solidarity of the married couple is that of taxation. Here, as in many other areas, Sweden has taken the most radical steps. In 1960, in reaction to a significant number of "tax divorces" which married couples had undergone in order to gain more favorable tax treatment, Sweden established a system of separate taxation for married couples in which the taxation of each spouse in principle follows the rules applicable to single

169. French Civil Code, arts. 1409, 1411, 1413.
170. *Kyle v. Albert*, 2 Family Law Reporter 2361 (Pa. Ct. Common Pleas 1976).
171. Law Reform (Miscellaneous Provisions) Act 1970 s. 4, f(a) and (c).
172. *Bromley* 103–104.   173. *II Carbonnier* 22, 68.
174. *Beitzke* 74–76.

persons.[175] In England, France, the United States, and West Germany, married couples in principle receive more favorable treatment than single taxpayers through income splitting, split rates, or through using different tax scales for married and single persons. In particular situations, however, each of these systems contains anomalies which can result in a "marriage penalty." In the United States, for example, married couples in which only one partner works outside the home receive more favorable treatment than single taxpayers, but many married couples with two incomes pay a higher rate than they would if they were cohabiting. As two-earner families have become the norm, there has been increasing discontent with the system. But tax law reform efforts in this area have foundered on the fact that it is impossible to create a system of taxation which is perfectly neutral regarding married and single persons; two-earner marriages and one-earner marriages; married couples and cohabiting couples; and childless couples and couples with children.

The tendency to treat the spouses as separate individuals in their relations with the outside world continues in numerous other ways: in the law of evidence; in the reexamination of antinepotism and conflict-of-interest rules; in the law governing such aspects of personal status as nationality, residence, and domicile; and, above all, where government benefits are concerned. In this latter area, the fluidity of modern family relationships makes systems of derivative rights difficult to design and administer. Thus, governmental social policies, benefit programs, and services tend to be geared primarily toward individuals in need rather than to families as social groups requiring attention and support.

Legal Ideas and Family Life

The modern law of the ongoing family has internalized a high degree of tension between the ideas of the family as involving cooperation and community of interest on the one hand and as facilitating the personal fulfillment of its individual members on the other. Since we have noted that this body of law is, in great part, a peculiar type of law without sanctions, it is time to ask about the relation of the imagery it embodies to the way family life is lived in Western societies.

The social science that is mediated through television, newspapers, and magazines assures us one day that families are here to stay, and warns us the next that they are in grave peril. Some see the changes of the past twenty years as unremarkable; others claim they are unprecedented. How is one to

175. Jacob Sundberg, "Marriage or No Marriage: The Directives for the Revision of Swedish Family Law," 20 *International and Comparative Law Quarterly* 223 (1971).

interpret the data? Louis Roussel of the French National Demographic Institute, after comparing the major trends in family behavior in the industrialized countries (North America, Europe, Japan, Australia, and the Soviet Union), concluded that something quite unusual in population history had indeed occurred beginning around 1965.

> It is rare in the history of populations that sudden changes appear simultaneously across the entire set of demographic indicators. More often, change appears first in one area and then with time, a general adjustment takes place, establishing a new equilibrium. Thus, for example, the decline of the death rate in the eighteenth century progressively entailed a general transformation of individual behavior and the relations between generations. What we have seen between 1965 and the present, among the billion or so people who inhabit the industrialized nations, is, by contrast, a general upheaval in the whole set of demographic indicators.
>
> In barely twenty years, the birth rate and the marriage rate have tumbled, while divorces and illegitimate births have increased rapidly. All these changes have been substantial, with increases or decreases of more than fifty percent. They have also been sudden, since the process of change has only lasted about fifteen years. And they have been general, because all industrialized countries have been affected beginning around 1965.[176]

Roussel relates these changes in behavior to still greater changes in the realm of ideas. Profound alterations in the way we think about marriage, sexuality, and family life have placed us in the midst, not merely of a demographic transition, but of a cultural transformation. One of the elements of this cultural shift, according to Roussel, has been "the banalization of behavior previously considered illegitimate." Thus, abrupt increases in nonmarital cohabitation and births outside formal marriage are revealing indicators of, among other things, a decreasing identification of legitimacy with legality. As for the marriage-centered family, the traditional conjugal unit concerned with reproduction and the survival of its members has lost ground to families based on marriage for the pursuit of reciprocal, or merely individual, gratification. Different marriage models, with varying emphases on family solidarity, child-raising, the relationship of the married couple with each other, or the interests of the individual spouses, are associated with different probabilities regarding divorce and numbers of children.

176. Louis Roussel, "Démographie: Deux Décennies de Mutations," paper presented at the Fifth World Conference of the International Society on Family Law, July 8–14, 1985, Brussels, Belgium.

> Obviously . . . reality is complex, and everyone adapts the different
> models current in society in a unique manner. But in our current
> social situation one's choice of marriage model, like one's choice of
> marriage partner, can always be reconsidered. Thus very logically
> linked together are the privatization of the family, the pluralism of
> its models, and the mobility of emotional investments. One can
> easily see that the models involve different kinds of demographic
> behavior: not that the choice of a family type mechanically entails
> this or that type of behavior, but that the adoption of one model
> rather than another implies different probabilities concerning mar-
> riage, divorce, remarriage, and the rate and schedule of fertility.[177]

The most dramatic shift that has taken place in the past twenty years, then,
is not in outward behavior but in the *meanings* that people attribute to marriage, to family relations, and to life itself. The ambivalence that exists with
respect to these matters in society and within individuals is mirrored faithfully
in modern family law.

This ambivalence has no doubt contributed to the tendency we have observed in all four legal systems for the state to refrain from intervening in
most intrafamily disputes and to abstain from endorsing any very specific set
of ideas about marriage and family life. Where general ideas about the conduct of family life are expressed in the law, they are bland and "neutral,"
capacious enough to embrace a variety of attitudes and life styles. The modern
ideas of freedom to marry, individual self-determination, family and individual privacy, sex equality, and tolerance of diversity all come together to
promote or reinforce deregulation. This withdrawal or abstention from legal
concern with the ongoing family in turn contributes to a certain blurring of
distinctions between legal marriage and other forms of cohabitation and between being married and being single.

From one point of view, this can be seen as a belated atonement for the
legal hubris of the Enlightenment. The law has decamped from ground that
in truth it never firmly held. To the extent it has abandoned its high-minded
aspirations for the family in the name of high-sounding ideas about the relationship of law to society, however, it may be involved in a newer sort of
hubris. Deregulation in the name of freedom, as Max Weber pointed out long
ago, means leaving the realm abandoned by the law to be governed by the
play of private power relations.[178] In the areas of procreation and the family,
where women and children have generally been the weaker parties, withdrawal of regulation thus may operate to shore up the traditionally dominant

177. *Id.*
178. *Weber* 188–191.

position of men, despite the new legal rhetoric of equality. Underneath the mantle of privacy that has been draped over the ongoing family, the state of nature flourishes. Recognizing this, all modern legal systems acknowledge that intervention in the ongoing family is often necessary to protect women from violence and children from neglect and abuse.[179]

The idea of sex equality also has its problematic side. Family law has been reorganized so that husband and wife, mother and father, have become genderless "spouses" and "parents" whose rights and duties are exactly alike. The discrepancy between the imagery in the law and the actual circumstances of most families, however, is quite striking, especially in those households—the majority—where children have been or are being raised. As we shall see in chapter 5, all legal systems have felt the need to compensate for this discrepancy to some extent upon divorce through mechanisms that enable them to take account of the fact that women ordinarily are secondary earners, with major responsibility for child-raising and other caretaking tasks, while men generally have higher incomes, more job security, and better fringe benefits. Norms portraying the spouses as perfect equals in the home and on the job are, from one point of view, exhortations with the benevolent aim of improving the position of women and encouraging more *de facto* equality between spouses. But the question arises in particular cases whether the law should be interpreted with reference to an ideal that is not yet established, or in the light of the existing circumstances of most men and women. In West Germany, for example, a local statute in Nordrhein-Westfalen has long provided that homemakers who work full-time outside the home are to have one extra day off a month to help them cope with running their households. After the 1976 marriage law equalized the duties of the spouses, a hospital discontinued giving its married women employees the "housework day" off, claiming that it was no longer needed now that working wives could expect their husbands to share the household tasks. Less optimistic about the effect of a mere legal change, the Federal Supreme Court for labor cases disagreed, citing surveys that showed that most husbands of working women were not yet fulfilling their legal duty to assume equal responsibility for housework.[180]

Taken together, the various recent changes in the law concerning the effects of the ongoing family display some of the same curious irony that characterizes modern marriage-formation law. Like the freedom to marry, the heightened symbolism of marriage as a community of life and of family privacy has

179. Franklin E. Zimring, "Legal Perspectives on Family Violence," 75 *California Law Review* 521 (1987).

180. Bundesarbeitsgerichtshof decision of 26 October 1978, reported in 1979 *Zeitschrift für das gesamte Familienrecht* 424.

appeared just at a time when marriage has less legal content than ever and when many of the legal effects of marriage are being diminished or assimilated to those of informal unions. Despite the rhetoric of partnership and community, concrete legal changes in each system have moved in the direction of emphasis on the separate and equal individuality of the family members—most decisively in the United States, least so in France. Stamped on the reverse side of the coinage of individual liberty, family privacy, and sex equality, are alienation, powerlessness, and dependency.

The law, torn between promoting modern ideals and attending to human needs, displays the same ambivalence that is deeply embedded in our culture and in the hearts of individuals. It is likely that most persons still entertain ideals of family solidarity and cooperation, and that these ideals guide a functioning family, more or less. It is also likely that these ways of imagining family relations will undergo revision in times of stress. The lack of firm and fixed ideas about what family life is and should be is but an aspect of the anguish of modernity. And in this respect, the law seems truly to reflect the fact that in modern society more and more is expected of personal relationships at the very time that social conditions have rendered them increasingly fragile. Thus, it is appropriate for us now to turn from a body of law which to a great extent represents society's aspirations for the marriage-centered ongoing family to the law of marriage dissolution, which deals with the situations in which these hopes are not fulfilled.

4
Divorce

Divorce and Marriage Breakdown

Marriage termination, like marriage itself, is both a legal and a social phenomenon. Just as the tinkers Michael and Sarah were married in a sense that any anthropologist would recognize, despite their failure to have a wedding, so a couple that has ceased to pursue a life in common has dissolved their marriage whether or not they proceed to a formal divorce. Marriage dissolution in the social sense, like marriage itself, is often a gradual process of transformation of status. In some societies, therefore, it may be hard to pinpoint the moment when a couple ceases to be married.[1] On the other hand, even where legal divorce is not available or affordable, termination of the marital status may be marked by an event. Among rural folk in early modern England, ritual wife-selling and a ceremony known as "jumping the broom" were widely believed to terminate a marriage and free the spouses to enter new unions.[2] In the United States, the term "poor man's divorce" came into being to describe marriage dissolution by the simple departure of a husband (or wife) in the days when access to the judicial system seemed foreclosed to large groups of the population for financial reasons. Informal methods of dissolving marriage have by no means been confined to premodern societies or to the poor. In divorceless countries, such as France throughout most of the nineteenth century and present-day Ireland, there is always a certain amount of marriage dissolution, often followed by the formation of new *de facto* marriages. There has never been a society where divorce, or some functional equivalent, did not exist.[3]

The subject of this chapter, however, is legal divorce. Legal marriage dis-

---

1. See, for example, the description of customary divorce in Owen Jessep and John Luluaki, *Principles of Family Law in Papua New Guinea* (Waigani: University of Papua New Guinea Press, 1985), 54–57.

2. Stephen Parker, "The Marriage Act 1753: A Case Study of Family Law-Making," 1 *International Journal of Law and the Family* 133, 140 (1987).

3. *König* 66–67.

solution performs a double function in societies where marriage itself is legally regulated. It releases the spouses from the marriage bond, thus enabling them to remarry, and it terminates or alters the legal effects of marriage. The present chapter is concerned primarily with the regulation of the circumstances under which termination of the marriage bond is permitted. In the following chapter, we turn to the more complex subject of the effect of divorce on the economic relations among the members of the family.

No aspect of modern family behavior has received more public attention than the sharp rise in divorce rates that began in the mid-1960s in most of the industrialized countries, nor is any development in family law more familiar than the widespread liberalization of the grounds of divorce that took place mainly in the 1970s. Within a relatively short period of time, marriage was transformed all over the developed world from a legal relationship terminable only for serious cause to one that is more or less terminable at will. Among the most dramatic changes was the introduction of civil divorce in the predominantly Catholic countries of Italy and Spain and its extension to Catholic marriages in Portugal. In Europe, only Ireland remains without legal divorce, 63 percent of the voters having rejected it, at least for the time being, in a 1986 referendum. The countries with which we are here concerned, like most other nations, have replaced or completely reformulated their old, strict divorce laws. The chief common characteristics of the new laws are the recognition or expansion of nonfault grounds for divorce and the acceptance or simplification of divorce by mutual consent. Behind these broad similarities, however, there are significant differences, both practical and ideological, among the new, liberal divorce statutes of England, France, West Germany, Sweden, and the American states.

England: Divorce Reform Act, 1969

Prelude

Judicial divorce did not exist in England until the passage of the Matrimonial Causes Act of 1857, which went into effect in 1858.[4] Previously, the exclusive route to divorce had been a special act of Parliament, a system which allowed only a wealthy few to end one marriage and enter another. Its availability was further limited by the practice of Parliament to admit petitions only on the ground of adultery. For women, access to divorce seems to have been especially difficult. There are only four reported cases of parliamentary divorces on a wife's petition.[5] Apart from transferring jurisdiction from Parliament to

4. *Cretney* 107.
5. *Bromley* 204 n. 10.

the courts, the 1857 statute made little change in this state of affairs. As Cretney put it, the Matrimonial Causes Act extended the possibility of divorce from the very rich to the rich.[6]

Following the prior parliamentary practice, the 1857 law made divorce available only on grounds of adultery, which was judged according to different standards for men and women. A man could divorce his wife for a single act of adultery, but a woman could divorce her husband only if his adultery was aggravated by special circumstances such as desertion or extreme physical cruelty. It was not until 1923 that a woman was finally enabled to divorce her husband for adultery without aggravating circumstances, and not until 1937 was divorce made available on the following grounds besides adultery: desertion for three years; cruelty; and supervening, incurable insanity.[7] The introduction of this latter ground marked the initial recognition in England of the ideas that one spouse might divorce the other without charging him or her with "fault," and that a marriage might end through misfortune as well as misconduct.

More significant changes took place in the aftermath of World War II. The divorce courts suddenly became more accessible to the general population when the Legal Aid and Advice Act went into effect in 1950.[8] Then began that process, so well documented by Max Rheinstein, through which the strict divorce laws on the books of various countries were converted by the courts into systems of relatively easy divorce by mutual consent.[9] By the 1960s, divorce in England had been so thoroughly (though quietly) transformed that over 90 percent of divorces there were uncontested.[10] In many of the remaining cases, there was no real dispute about the divorce, but cross-petitions had been filed by both spouses, each seeking for economic reasons to have the other appear as the guilty party of record.[11] In England, as elsewhere, the high postwar incidence of divorce cases and the obvious collusion involved in most of them, raised the question of whether any changes should be made in the law. All aspects of the matter were examined in the report of the Morton Commission of 1956[12] and in reports by a Church of England group and the Law Commission, both of which were published in 1966.[13]

The searching, meticulous, and extensive studies done by the latter two groups on the social and legal aspects of divorce law reform had great influence, not only on the course eventually taken by English law, but also on the

6. *Cretney* 107.   7. Matrimonial Causes Act 1937, s. 2.
8. *Rheinstein* 320.   9. *Id*. at 247–60.
10. *Field of Choice* par. 120.   11. *Bromley* 217.
    12. *Report of the Royal Commission on Marriage and Divorce* (Morton Commission), Cmnd. 9678 (London: Her Majesty's Stationery Office, 1956).
    13. *Putting Asunder* and *Field of Choice*.

thinking of law reformers in other countries. It is interesting to note the contrast between how the case for eliminating fault from divorce laws looked to the Morton Commission in 1956 and how it appeared just 10 years later to the Law Commission and to the Archbishop of Canterbury's Group. Only one member of nineteen on the Morton Commission thought that fault should be eliminated from the divorce laws. Of the remaining eighteen members who believed fault grounds should be retained as the basis of the law, nine were of the view that marriage breakdown should not be introduced even as an additional ground for divorce. The nine members who were *for* breakdown as an added ground thought that it should be available in principle only where husband and wife had lived apart for seven years *and* the petition was not opposed by the defendant spouse. It was due to the introduction in Parliament in 1963 of a bill providing for divorce along the lines advocated by these latter nine that the matter once more came in for intensive study.[14]

The 1966 report of the Archbishop of Canterbury's Group, *Putting Asunder*, began by drawing a clear distinction between what was required by religious law and what might be an appropriate basis for divorce in the secular law of the state.[15] The group saw its task as that of developing a Christian position with respect to a social problem affecting both believers and nonbelievers. Their report expressed dissatisfaction with the existing system of collusive divorce. To the surprise of many at the time, it came out in favor of reorganizing the law, with breakdown of the marriage as the exclusive ground for divorce. But to guard against abuse, the report cautioned that courts should not take the parties' word for it that their marriage was no longer viable. Rather, the fact of breakdown should be established by an elaborate judicial inquest.[16] The report of the Law Commission, which appeared later in the same year, considered the views of the Church of England along with other proposals. The commissioners agreed with the Archbishop's Group that the matrimonial offense principle did not provide a satisfactory basis for a good modern divorce law, but they pointed out that judicial inquiry into the fact of breakdown in every case would be too expensive and time-consuming to be practicable. As the Law Commission saw it, the "field of choice" for reform could be narrowed down to three possible schemes: (1) Marriage

14. *Rheinstein* 323.
15. "Today, it is manifestly impossible that the Church should accept the matrimonial law of the land as satisfactory for its own purposes." *Putting Asunder* 7. "When . . . a modern court 'dissolves' a marriage, it is not making a pronouncement about the *vinculum matrimonii* in the traditional Christian sense of that term; for it does not take cognizance of any such thing. What it dissolves is the legal complex of rights and duties that make up legal status of marriage." *Id.* at 11.
16. *Id.* at 67–70.

breakdown, but without the extensive inquest desired by the Archbishop's Group, might be established as the sole ground for divorce, with a period of separation sufficing to prove breakdown unless evidence to the contrary were produced. The Commission judged that such a system would not be feasible as the *sole* ground for divorce if the required period of separation were much more than six months. Surmising that Parliament would probably not adopt a law which afforded a divorce so quickly in all cases, the Commission went on to set forth two alternatives: (2) Mutual-consent divorce might be added to the existing grounds for divorce. It could not be the sole ground, because it would be undesirable to permit a spouse who had been guilty of conduct which would have justified divorce on fault grounds to block a divorce by withholding consent. Finally, the Commission suggested that (3) marriage breakdown might be added to the other grounds, with divorce on this basis being available only after a period of separation. Where the other spouse consented, or at least did not oppose the divorce, this period would be two years. When the spouses had lived apart for five or seven years, the commissioners recommended that divorce should be granted even over the objections of the defendant spouse.[17]

All three of the Law Commission's proposals contradicted certain basic ideas of the Archbishop's Group: the first because it did not provide for adequate judicial inquiry; the second because it gave the parties themselves too much control over the termination of their marriage; the second and third because they retained fault grounds alongside nonfault grounds, thereby perpetuating the defects of the old fault-based law.

The 1969 Reform

In November 1966, the members of the Law Commission entered into discussions with the Archbishop's Group concerning the points of difference between their two reports. As a result of these discussions, the Law Commission put forward proposals that became, with slight modifications, the Divorce Reform Act 1969, which went into effect on 1 January 1971. (This delay was to enable Parliament to reform the law of financial provision in a statute which went into effect at the same time as the divorce law.)[18]

The Divorce Reform Act was a compromise. Section 1(1) of the act declares that the sole ground of divorce is the "irretrievable breakdown" of the marriage. But Section 1(2) makes it clear that the reform law did little more

---

17. *Field of Choice* par. 20.
18. The Divorce Reform Act 1969 and the Matrimonial Proceedings and Property Act 1971 were consolidated in the Matrimonial Causes Act 1973, which has since been amended by the Matrimonial and Family Proceedings Act 1984.

than tack separation grounds onto the traditional offense grounds, for "break-down" can only be proved in five ways, three of which involve fault. In the fault sections, however, the emphasis was subtly shifted from the blame-worthiness of the spouse committing the marital offense to the effect his or her conduct has on the other spouse. Section 1(2) provides:

> (2) The court . . . shall not hold the marriage to have broken down irretrievably unless the petitioner satisfies the court of one or more of the following facts, that is to say
>
> (a) that the respondent has committed adultery and the petitioner finds it intolerable to live with the respondent;
>
> (b) that the respondent has behaved in such a way that the peti-tioner cannot reasonably be expected to live with the respondent;
>
> (c) that the respondent has deserted the petitioner for a continuous period of at least two years immediately preceding the presentation of the petition;
>
> (d) that the parties to the marriage have lived apart for a continu-ous period of at least two years immediately preceding the presenta-tion of the petition and the respondent consents to a decree being granted;
>
> (e) that the parties to the marriage have lived apart for a continu-ous period of at least five years immediately preceding the presenta-tion of the petition.[19]

Even when one of these five fact situations has been proved, the divorce in theory can be denied unless the court is satisfied on all the evidence that the marriage has in fact broken down irretrievably. Reflecting to some extent the views of the Archbishop's Group, the statute requires the court "to inquire, so far as it reasonably can, into the facts alleged" by the petitioner or respon-dent.[20] As we shall see, however, this provision has been rendered nearly null in practice. As originally enacted, the statute also made divorce completely unavailable during the first three years of marriage, unless "the case is one of exceptional hardship suffered by the petitioner or of exceptional depravity on the part of the respondent."[21] As written, the 1969 act had something for everyone—attention to the behavior of the spouses as well as to the state of the marriage and the appearance of taking both marriage and its termination very seriously, while permitting a dignified exit when the marriage had died.

The modest innovations of the act were simply that mutual-consent divorce (which, disguised as fault divorce, already accounted for the overwhelming

19. Matrimonial Causes Act 1973, s.1(2).

20. *Id.* , s.1(3).

21. Matrimonial Causes Act 1973, s.3. This section was repealed by the Matrimonial and Family Proceedings Act 1984. See below, text at note 47.

majority of marriage dissolutions) was brought out in the open and permitted
after a two-year separation, and that unilateral divorce was permitted after a
five-year separation. The idea of unilateral nonfault divorce (some called it
"Casanova's charter")[22] was sufficiently controversial that special provisions
for the protection of the respondent had to be included to secure its adoption.
Where breakdown is sought to be proved by five years' separation, the court
must dismiss the petition if it believes the respondent's allegation that the
dissolution of the marriage will result in "grave financial or other hardship"
to him or her and that it would "in all the circumstances be wrong to dissolve
the marriage."[23] Also, where the divorce is sought on the basis of two or five
years' separation, the court may refuse to make the decree absolute until it is
satisfied that the financial provision, if any, for the respondent is "reasonable
and fair, or the best that can be made in the circumstances."[24] A court may
not, in any case, pronounce an absolute decree unless it has made an order
with reference to arrangements for any children of the marriage.[25]

The Aftermath of Reform

After the 1969 act had been in effect for a few years, it became clear that in
many ways it was not fulfilling the hopes and expectations that either the
Archbishop's Group or the Law Commission had entertained in 1966. Both
groups had agreed that when a marriage had failed to the point where there
was no reasonable likelihood of the parties again living together as husband
and wife, the legal tie should be dissolved in a way which involved "maximum fairness, and the minimum bitterness, distress and humiliation."[26] But
marital fault has remained the most frequently used way of proving "breakdown" under the act. Consistently over the years, over two-thirds of all divorces in England have been based on allegations of fault, with unreasonable
behavior the most frequent claim, closely followed by adultery.[27] The five-
year separation ground seems to have had its day shortly after the act went
into effect, when it was used to formalize long-standing separations. Its use
has rapidly dwindled since then. The enduring popularity of fault grounds is
apparently attributable to the fact that they offer the quickest and easiest path
to divorce. Accordingly, they are employed when both parties are in haste to
get on with their lives or when one party's impatience has resulted in a trade-
off of financial advantages to the other. Fault grounds are also sometimes

22. According to *Bromley* 213.   23. Matrimonial Causes Act 1973, s. 5.
24. *Id.* , s. 10(2)–(4).   25. *Id.* , s. 41.
26. *Field of Choice*, par. 15. Cf. *Putting Asunder* 23–24.
27. In 1984, the figures were as follows: behavior, 37 percent; adultery, 30 percent; two
years' separation, 24 percent; five years' separation, 7 percent; desertion, 1 percent. Susan Maidment, "Family Law Practitioner," 135 *New Law Journal* 1028 (1985).

employed when the spouses have not been able to agree on financial or child-custody matters. In such cases, the parties may file cross-petitions alleging fault as part of their jockeying for position with respect to the ultimate judicial settlement of these matters.[28] Conduct remains relevant to some extent on custody and financial provision issues, which are called *ancillary*, but are actually at the center of most disputes between divorcing spouses. A number of English family law experts maintain that even in an uncontested case, the allegation of fault "encourages hostility, or at the very least, fails to encourage cooperation between the parties."[29]

Along with the desire to eliminate from marriage dissolution the bitterness which fault divorce was thought to engender or at least exacerbate, both the Archbishop's Group and the Law Commission had thought that the divorce law should perform a positive social function by facilitating and encouraging reconciliation between estranged couples.[30] The Divorce Reform Act accordingly had introduced provisions designed to aid in bringing such couples together.[31] Within a few years, however, it was agreed that efforts in that direction had been largely futile. Cretney has written that these provisions have "an exceedingly limited effect in practice."[32] Others have dismissed them as a "dead letter"[33] and a "sham."[34]

Another feature of the act which reflected strong views of the Law Commission and the Archbishop's Group was the provision that unilateral divorce should be denied where it would result in "grave financial or other hardship" to the respondent.[35] There have been few cases, however, where a decree has been refused under this provision, and no reported case where hardship other than financial has been accepted as a bar to divorce.[36] As Cretney says, "The section seems . . . likely to be used primarily to protect middle-aged and elderly wives against the loss of pension rights, and then only very sparingly."[37]

28. See *Cretney* 216.

29. John Eekelaar and Eric Clive, *Custody after Divorce* (Oxford: Centre for Socio-Legal Studies, 1977), par. 1.7; *Cretney* 215. This was also the view taken by the Matrimonial Causes Procedure Committee in its 1985 Report discussed in John Eekelaar, "Divorce English Style—A New Way Forward?" 1986 *Journal of Social Welfare Law* 226, 227.

30. *Field of Choice* pars. 29–32; *Putting Asunder* 63–64.

31. Matrimonial Causes Act 1973, s. 6.

32. *Cretney* 188.

33. Joseph Jackson, Book Review, 89 *Law Quarterly Review* 422, 424 (1973).

34. M. D. A. Freeman, "The Search for a Rational Divorce Law," 1971 *Current Legal Problems* 210.

35. *Field of Choice* par. 119; *Putting Asunder* 53.

36. *Cretney* 167–68.

37. *Cretney* 172.

The provision of the act that has been most drastically undercut over the years, however, is the direction to the court to inquire into the facts of each case to see whether the marriage has really broken down. Despite the statutory requirement of judicial inquest, English courts from the first demonstrated no more inclination to look into this matter than they had shown to investigate the reality of "fault" in an uncontested case. A 1973 Bristol University study of undefended divorce petitions in three county courts found that the great majority of cases (85 percent) took less than ten minutes each.[38] In two of the three courts studied, 61 percent of the cases took less than five minutes, and in the courtroom of one judge, the average case time was four minutes. Furthermore, regardless of how the hearing was conducted, "the result was invariably the same. A decree was granted."[39] The use of court time for these perfunctory hearings and the attendant burden on legal aid funds increasingly were perceived as wasteful and as serving no useful purpose.

It is thus not surprising that the requirement of a hearing in uncontested cases was quietly done away with through changes made in court rules in the 1970s. The court rules established a new "special procedure"[40] under which a registrar now merely reviews the parties' affidavits, certifies satisfaction with the allegations in support of the petition, and forwards the file to a judge for automatic issuance of a decree. The parties need not appear in court either to testify or to hear the decree pronounced. No evidence, apart from the affidavits, need be furnished. All that is required is to fill in the forms correctly.[41] Thus, without any action by Parliament, judicial inquest divorce has been converted unobtrusively into a summary administrative procedure, a kind of registration divorce.

This radical development, so distant from the vision entertained by the law reformers of the 1960s, is now firmly entrenched. In 1979, the Court of Appeal abandoned all pretense that adjudication was taking place in any but the tiny minority of divorce cases that are contested. Denying a respondent husband leave to file a late answer to his wife's petition for divorce after the registrar had certified her petition to the court for issuance of a decree, Ormrod, J., stated, "It is impossible to regard the issuance of the decree by the judge as anything more than a formality."[42] The court took the occasion

---

38. Elizabeth Elston, Jane Fuller & Mervyn Murch, "Judicial Hearings of Undefended Divorce Petitions," 38 *Modern Law Review* 609, 626, 636 (1975).

39. *Id.* at 635.

40. Described in detail in *Cretney* 179–188.

41. *Id.* at 120.

42. *Day v. Day*, [1980] Fam. 29.

to make perfectly clear the nature of the system that the courts themselves had created by exercising their power to issue procedural rules.

> The first point to be made is that its description has become a complete misnomer. It is no longer the "special procedure"; it is now the ordinary procedure for dealing with undefended causes of all kinds, and therefore of great importance to very large numbers of ordinary people who can no longer obtain legal aid for this part of the divorce process. It has been progressively extended until under the Matrimonial Causes Rules 1977 it now applies to all classes of undefended causes, including those in which a notice of intention to defend has been received but no answer has been filed.
>
> [Respondent] made a valiant effort to maintain that the decision still remained in the judge but in our view so to hold would be to create a legal fiction. The registrar certifies that the petitioner has proved the contents of the petition and is entitled to a decree. The requirements of the Matrimonial Causes Act 1973, s.1(4) therefore have been complied with, and subject to ss.3(3) and 5 of the Act, a decree must be granted. Sub-section (4) refers to the "Court," not to a "Judge."[43]

Despite this far-reaching judicial reorganization of the system of divorce established by the 1969 act, Parliament has not shown the slightest inclination to force a return to more elaborate divorce proceedings. That issue was decided, *sub silentio*, when Parliament chose to ignore the report and recommendations of the highly regarded Finer Committee on One-Parent Families[44] for, among other things, a comprehensive but costly family court system. In 1985, the report of the Matrimonial Causes Procedure Committee recommended in effect that Parliament ratify the Special Procedure by permitting the registrar, in undefended cases not involving minor children, to grant the decree rather than sending the case to a judge for formal approval.[45]

So far as marriage dissolution as such is concerned, the only legislative change that has taken place since 1969 was the abolition of the bar on divorce within the first three years of marriage. Not only had this restriction come to seem unecessarily hard on couples whose union appeared early on to have been a mistake, but judges were beginning to profess themselves at a loss to decide what circumstances should be held to justify lifting the bar. In a case involving a husband whose homosexuality first became evident to his wife on

43. *Id.* at 32–33.
44. *Report of the Committee on One-Parent Families* (Finer Report), 2 vols., Cmnd. 5629 (London: Her Majesty's Stationery Office, 1974).
45. John Eekelaar, "Divorce English Style—A New Way Forward?" 1986 *Journal of Social Welfare Law* 226, 234–35.

their honeymoon when he became impotent and turned his attentions from her to a young male cousin, Ormrod, J., noted that judges were "troubled" about what meaning to give to "exceptional depravity" in an era of changing notions of sexual morality.[46] In 1984, Parliament relieved the judges of this vexing problem by substituting a one-year mandatory bar for the three-year discretionary one.[47]

One day, perhaps, Parliament will consider whether to move to a system of outright unilateral divorce with no inquest, as the Law Commission proposed in 1988. Stressing the desirability of eliminating litigation over fault, the Law Commissioners recommended that divorce should be made available to either party after a one-year delay.[48] As we have seen, however, the eventual adoption of such an approach, should it occur, would effect little change in practice.

If the matter does come up for reconsideration in England, the comparative law context will be considerably different from what it was in 1969. At that time, there were no working models of "pure" nonfault or unilateral divorce statutes. The Law Commission in 1966 had been influenced strongly by the fact that systems of mixed fault and nonfault grounds were operating in Australia, New Zealand, and the United States. In 1975 however, Australia abandoned the mixed-grounds approach and substituted a system of irretrievable breakdown to be established by the simple fact of twelve months' separation.[49] In the United States, marriage breakdown was established as the sole ground of divorce in 1970 in both the California divorce law and in the Uniform Marriage and Divorce Act (UMDA), and, by late 1987, laws of this sort had been adopted by a total of nineteen American jurisdictions.

Increasingly, since 1969, the matter of marriage termination as such is coming to be seen in England, as elsewhere, as less important than the treatment of economic and child-related matters in connection with divorce. With respect to those issues it is by no means clear that the trend is toward the elimination of fault from consideration. English judges, responding, in the view of one commentator, to a widespread popular desire "for blame to be formally recognised" in divorce proceedings, have been hearing evidence in the so-called ancillary matters of a type that the Law Commisssion would banish forever from the divorce itself.[50] Another range of issues is suggested

46. *C. v. C.*, [1979] 1 All E.R. 556 (C.A.).

47. Matrimonial and Family Proceedings Act 1984, s. 1.

48. Kay Jones, "The Law Commission or the Law of the Folk?" 138 New Law Journal 460 (1988). The case for such a move had been made several years before in John Eekelaar, "The Place of Divorce in Family Law's New Role," 38 *Modern Law Review* 241, 252 (1975).

49. Henry Finlay, "Reluctant, but Inevitable: The Retreat of Matrimonial Fault," 38 *Modern Law Review* 153, 157–58 (1975); Australia, Family Law Act 1975, No. 53 of 1975 s. 48, 49.

50. See Jones, above, note 48.

by the view frequently expressed both among the learned writers and on the part of divorcing couples,[51] that the process neither gives enough attention to the welfare of children nor provides adequate supervision of financial arrangements. But reforms to remedy these problems would be expensive, and the state's interest in divorce in England at the moment seems to be dominated by short-run considerations of cost. The current climate of economic austerity in Britain is chilly toward proposals that would involve substantial commitments of judicial time and public funds. The fact is that the most revolutionary change in divorce law there, marriage termination by registration, took place—without reports, debates, or discussion—not in furtherance of any particular family policy, but as a bureaucratic response to over-crowded courts and the need for economy.

As we turn now to examine the form that liberalization of the grounds of divorce took in other countries, it is worth restating that English ideas were highly influential in this process. The studies that preceded the cautious English Divorce Reform Act of 1969 explored every major issue that legislatures elsewhere would face in deciding how to modernize their divorce laws. The shared premises of the Archbishop's Group and the Law Commission—that society has no special interest in permanently maintaining the legal shell of a failed marriage and that the role of the law in such cases is to manage the dissolution process with the minimum human cost—became the leading ideas of divorce-law reform everywhere.

France: Divorce Reform Law, 1975

Prelude

Up to 1 January 1976, when the 1975 divorce law went into effect in France, the grounds for divorce had been virtually unchanged for ninety-two years. Prior to that, however, the legal pendulum had swung from one extreme to the other. In the late eighteenth century, French revolutionaries had made an all-out assault on ecclesiastical regulation of marriage in the name of individual liberty. Since marriage was held to be a civil contract, it followed that it should be terminable by mutual consent; and because marriage was a restraint on one's freedom, the principle of individual liberty seemed to require that either spouse should be able to emancipate himself or herself through divorce.[52] Thus, the 1792 divorce law made divorce available on a variety of grounds, including mutual consent and incompatibility of temperament.[53]

51. See Elston, Fuller, and Murch, above, note 38 at 637.
52. Alain Bénabent, "La liberté individuelle et le mariage," 1973 *Revue trimestrielle de droit civil* 440, 486.
53. *Rheinstein* 201; *Gaudemet* 390.

Though time-consuming and cumbersome, the mere possibility of unilateral divorce on this ground represented a momentous break with traditional thinking about marriage. But the revolutionary law was far from reflecting the dominant point of view in France, and divorce for incompatibility disappeared when the Civil Code was adopted in 1804. Indeed, were it not for the personal interest that Napoleon himself took in the divorce provisions of the Code, it is doubtful whether divorce by mutual consent would have survived either.[54] When the Napoleonic period came to a close, the uneasy balance in the realm of ideas, politics, and law between "*les deux Frances*"—the France that was oriented to conservative, Catholic, family-centered tradition, and the France drawn to the liberal-individualistic ideas of the Enlightenment—shifted again.[55] In 1816 divorce was completely abolished, its demise heralded by a member of the Law Commission as follows: "For twenty years in France men have made laws like themselves—feeble and fleeting. Let us now finally establish those eternal laws which constitute men rather than being constituted by them."[56]

The eternal law lasted for quite a while, as these things go. It was not until 1884 that divorce was reintroduced by the *Loi Naquet* (so named after its author). This time it was made available only on grounds of adultery, sentence for a serious crime,[57] and grave violation of marital duties.[58] This scheme of *divorce-sanction*, severe in form, but increasingly lenient in practice, lasted without substantial change until 1975, by which time there was wide consensus in French society on the need for, although not the direction of, revision.

When the government of Giscard d'Estaing prepared to make good its promise to reform the divorce laws, it discovered that in the France of the 1970s there were still "*deux Frances.*" The revolutionary spirit was enjoying a revival in some of the learned writing,[59] and had inspired the proposals of

54. *Rheinstein* 211. It is said that Bonaparte insisted on the inclusion of divorce by mutual consent among the grounds for divorce in the Civil Code because he wanted to divorce Josephine in order to be able to enter a marriage that would produce an heir. He also seems to have wanted the Code to provide the French people with a method of divorce that would not involve dishonor and embarrassment. As it happened, he himself never used the divorce provisions of the Civil Code. The dissolution of his marriage was pronounced by *Senatus-Consult.* Denise Roughol-Valdeyron, "Le divorce par consentement mutuel et le Code Napoléon," 1975 *Revue trimestrielle de droit civil* 482, 484–487.

55. *Rheinstein* 195.

56. Roughol-Valdeyron, above, note 54 at 487.

57. "*La condamnation de l'un des époux à une peine afflictive et infamante*" under former Article 231 was understood to mean sentence to death or lengthy imprisonment.

58. "*Excès, sévices ou injures*" [excesses, cruelty or abuse], amounting to a serious or repeated violation of marital duties," under former Article 232 came to be interpreted by French courts in much the same way as American and English courts interpreted cruelty, establishing a kind of judge-made mutual-consent divorce. *Rheinstein* 214, 217, 219.

59. E.g., *Bénabent*, above, n. 52.

the socialist and communist parties to replace fault divorce with divorce on some objective ground, such as permanent disruption of the life in common.[60] The idea of divorce upon the unilateral allegation of marriage breakdown was also favored on pragmatic grounds by the Association Nationale des Avocats de France.[61]

Such proposals encountered predictable and substantial opposition from the strongholds of conservative family policy. Doubts about them were also raised by public opinion surveys made at the behest of the government for the express purpose of aiding in the preparation of reforms. The surveys revealed considerable ambivalence within the population at large on the subject of divorce.[62] The responses suggested that this division of opinion was not just a reflection of age, sex, regional, class, educational, or income differences. As Rheinstein had remarked in his 1971 study of marriage stability and divorce in several countries, the two Frances coexist in the minds and hearts of individual French men and women.[63]

Thus it is not surprising that unilateral nonfault divorce was rejected as the guiding principle of the reform, but was introduced alongside slightly reformulated fault grounds. The authors of the law were well aware of the kinds of arguments that had won the day for pure nonfault divorce in Sweden, in several American states, and in the West German reform proposal then pending before the Bundestag.[64] But they believed that in France such legislation would be seen as authorizing "divorce by repudiation, a tragedy for the wife, and an object of horror for our Western societies."[65] Divorce on fault grounds, the object of so much criticism from French practitioners and aca-

---

60. Raymond Lindon, "La nouvelle législation sur le divorce et le recouvrement public des pensions alimentaires," 1975 *Juris-Classeur Périodique* I. 2728, pars. 22, 38.

61. Pierre Chaumié, "À propos du projet de loi sur le divorce," 1974 *Gazette du Palais. Doctrine*. 786–801.

62. "There are different feelings about divorce, which can give rise to different forms of the institution. Public opinion, for its part, is divided with respect to the idea of reform. One can discern one bloc—young (is it their age or their generation?)—which is disposed to go very far; another bloc is opposed to any innovation; and between the two the "centrists" who, while manifesting an attachment to the principle of indissolubility of marriage or at least to the exceptional character of divorce, take indulgent positions with respect to concrete situations described to them. It seems, in any event, that the general widespread sense of justice, which supported the reforms on behalf of children, (and therefore the reform of the law of filiation), is not so easily identified when it is the parents who are at issue." Jean Carbonnier, "La question du divorce: mémoire à consulter," D. 1975. Chr. 115, 116.

63. *Rheinstein* 195.

64. During the drafting process, the systems of nine countries (not including the United States) were studied and extensive sociological investigations were undertaken. Carbonnier, above, note 62 at 116.

65. *Id.* at 117.

demics alike, was retained in the reform law because, as Carbonnier, the principal draftsman, explained:

> There are some marital conflicts which the popular mentality contin-
> ues to characterize in terms of culpability and to resolve in terms of
> sanctions—all the more vigorously when, in the popular view, the
> faults which have caused the divorce are those which flaunt the very
> duties which constitute marriage. To underestimate the force of these
> elementary reflexes would gratuitously compromise the reception of
> the reform in the nation.[66]

Thus the choice was made for a mixed-grounds compromise, or, as Carbonnier put it, a "pluralistic system of grounds for divorce."[67]

The 1975 Reform Law

Like the code draftsmen of 1804, the reformers of 1975 offered a number of
avenues to divorce—so many, in fact, that the statute has been described as
establishing divorce *à la carte*. Unlike other mixed-grounds statutes, however, the 1975 French law accompanies each form of divorce with its own set
of procedural rules and a distinctive array of legal consequences. Divorce by
mutual agreement is organized as the preferred form of divorce, while the
other types (fault divorce; "resignation" divorce; divorce after legal separation; and divorce for prolonged disruption of the life in common) are made
available for exceptional cases.[68] In this respect, too, there is a historical reso-
nance between the new divorce law and the Code Napoleon. For under the
divorce provisions of the Code of 1804, which were in force only until 1816,
divorce by mutual consent was also established as the "civilized" form of divorce which the draftsmen hoped would be the most frequently utilized.[69]

The various bases for divorce will be examined here in the order in which
they are set out in the Code, as amended, under the headings of "Divorce by
Mutual Consent," "Divorce for Prolonged Disruption of the Life in Common," and "Divorce for Fault." Contrary to the great tradition of French
cuisine, the *pièce de résistance* comes first.

---

66. *Id.* at 118.

67. *Id.*

68. Law No. 75–617 of 11 July 1975, (J.O. 12 July 1975, p. 7171(1)), amending the French
Civil Code; and Decree of 5 December 1975, D. 1975. Leg. 426 on divorce procedure. References herein are to Civil Code articles 229–259–3 as amended.

69. Roughol-Valdeyron, above, note 54 at 487, recounts that the reporter for the divorce
provisions of the Code stated to the Tribunate: "All the law of divorce is there [in the mutual
consent provisions]. Recourse to specific grounds is never frequent in our mores—our manners
may not be good, but they are polite. . . . We earnestly sought for a device which would conceal
all evils and cure them without publicity."

Divorce by Mutual Consent

The Code provides for an active and a passive form of divorce by mutual consent. They have been characterized by the commentators as *divorce-convention* and *divorce-résignation*, (*agreement divorce*, and *accepted divorce*). In the former the divorce is sought on the joint petition of the spouses, whereas in the latter the divorce is sought by one spouse and accepted by the other. As one writer has put it, the latter ground is for spouses who want to leave marriage "by the same door, but not hand in hand." [70]

Divorce-Convention

The form of mutual-consent divorce in which the spouses jointly petition for termination of their marriage is the one that was most favored by the authors of the reform law and that secured the widest base of support in the legislature.[71] The three articles of the Civil Code which now govern "divorce by agreement" follow:

> Art. 230. When the spouses petition together for a divorce, they need not make known the cause; they must only submit for the approval of the judge the draft of an agreement which will regulate the consequences.
> The petition may be presented either by the respective lawyers of the parties, or by one lawyer chosen by common accord.
> Divorce by mutual consent may not be sought during the first six months of marriage.
>
> Art. 231. The judge is to examine the petition with each of the parties, then to call them together. Then he is to call in the lawyer or lawyers.
> If the spouses persist in their intention to divorce, the judge is to advise them that their petition should be renewed after a three-month period of reflection.
> In the absence of a renewal within the six months following the expiration of this period of reflection, the joint petition will lapse.
>
> Art. 232. The judge is to pronounce the divorce if he is convinced that the intention of each spouse is real and that each of them has given his consent freely. In the same judgment he is to approve (*homologue*) the agreement governing the consequences of the divorce.
> He can refuse his approval and the granting of the divorce if he judges that the agreement does not sufficiently protect the interests of the children or of one of the spouses.

70. Lindon, above, note 60 at par. 34.

71. *Id.* at par. 138. The National Assembly and the Senate voted on the law section by section rather than as one single piece of legislation.

This procedure was designed to eliminate the necessity of a ritual recitation of reasons for divorce in open court by spouses who had already come to agreement on the divorce and its economic and child-related aspects. A major reason for reform in France, as elsewhere, had been dissatisfaction with the necessity, under the fault system, for testimony concerning details of the spouses' personal lives even where the divorce was uncontested.[72] But in bringing mutual-consent divorce into the open, the new law also brings it and, most importantly, its economic aspects under judicial control. It thus stands in marked contrast to the old system of disguised mutual-consent divorce, which involved no judicial review of the parties' agreement and no safeguards for weaker parties.[73]

This is not, therefore, a speedy form of divorce. The petition must be accompanied not only by a draft agreement on the eventual consequences of divorce but by a temporary agreement covering the period leading up to the divorce.[74] Then the Code provides for four successive court appearances: the judge meets first with each spouse separately, then with both together, and finally with both spouses and their lawyers or lawyer. In the course of these discussions, the judge indicates to the parties whether he or she believes their agreement is adequate and in what respects it may need to be modified. After these meetings, there is a mandatory three-month waiting period, after which, if the suit is to be pursued, the parties must act affirmatively to reactivate their petition.

When the petition is renewed, judicial approval of the agreed-upon divorce is not automatic. The parties must present a report on how their temporary agreement has worked out, as well as the final draft of their agreement concerning property division, and, where relevant, other economic matters and child custody.[75] In deciding whether to approve the final agreement, the judge will take into consideration how the temporary agreement has operated. There are two bases on which the judge can withhold approval under Article 232—those relating to the quality of the intention and consent of the spouses and those relating to the adequacy of their agreement in protecting the interests of any children or of one of the spouses. Article 232 gives the court so

---

72. Carbonnier wrote: "It is notorious that we already have in France, de facto, divorce by mutual consent, in the innumerable cases of 'divorce by accord' where the spouses collaborate to simulate wrongs and injuries. The comedy discredits the law and (as sociological inquiry has revealed) leaves the spouses with bitter memories. To introduce a procedure of joint petition thus would be a healthy step." See above, note 62 at 117.

73. Jacqueline Rubellin-Devichi, *L'évolution du statut civil de la famille depuis 1945* (Paris: C.N.R.S., 1983), 32–35.

74. *Bénabent* 201.

75. *Id.* at 203.

much discretion, according to writers close to the practice, that, through successive denials of approval, it can in effect force the parties into an arrangement which the court itself has indirectly authored.[76] Bénabent reports that
"in practice, a judge who is prepared to refuse to approve an agreement will
indicate to the spouses the points as to which modifications seem necessary. . . . It is then up to the spouses to decide for themselves whether these
changes are acceptable."[77]

Divorce-Résignation

Under the heading of "Divorce by Mutual Consent," the Code also sets forth
the rules governing "divorce sought by one spouse and accepted by the
other." The four articles pertaining to this type of divorce follow:

> Art. 233. One spouse may petition for divorce by setting forth the
> fact of a set of acts, proceeding from both spouses, which make the
> continuation of their life in common intolerable.

> Art. 234. If the other spouse acknowledges the facts before the
> judge, the judge is to grant the divorce without ruling on the alloca-
> tion of fault. A divorce granted in this manner produces the legal
> effects of a divorce granted for shared fault.[78]

> Art. 235. If the other spouse does not acknowledge the facts, the
> judge is not to grant the divorce.

> Art. 236. The allegations made by the spouses may not be used as
> evidence in any other legal action.

Thus, under this system, when one spouse alleges certain facts and the
consequent insupportability of continuing the life in common, and the other
spouse acquiesces, the economic and other consequences of divorce are left
to be decided by the judge. As with divorce by agreement, four separate
preliminary meetings with the judge are required after the petition has been
filed. It was not expected that this form of divorce would be widely used. It
was apparently included with the idea that certain spouses, while not opposing
a divorce, would prefer for religious or ethical reasons not to participate
actively.[79] But only infrequently has it occurred that a defendant is so indifferent to the effects of divorce as to completely abandon them to judicial
discretion.[80]

76. *Id.* at 202; Lindon, above, note 60 at par. 145.
77. *Bénabent* 204–5.
78. Regulated by French Civil Code, art. 245.
79. Lindon, above, note 60 at par. 131.
80. *Bénabent* 207.

Divorce for Prolonged Disruption of the Life in Common

There are two forms of divorce which can be sought unilaterally without allegation of fault, even by a spouse who may have committed fault. Rather
than breakdown or "irreconcilable differences," the French formula for this
type of divorce is "prolonged disruption of the life in common." The principal form of this ground contemplates the situation where the disruption of the
life in common has been accompanied by a *de facto* separation of six years;
the second form is for cases where one spouse has been mentally ill for at
least six years. The relevant code sections follow:

> Art. 237. One spouse may petition for divorce, by reason of the
> prolonged disruption of the life in common, when the spouses have
> been separated in fact for six years.
>
> Art. 238. The same is the case where the mental faculties of the
> other spouse have been so seriously impaired for a period of six years
> that the community of life no longer exists between the spouses and
> cannot, according to the most reasonable conjectures, be reestab-
> lished in the future.
>
> The judge may on his own motion dismiss this petition, without
> resorting to the provisions of Article 240, if the divorce would entail
> risk of too serious consequences for the illness of the other spouse.
>
> Art. 239. The spouse who petitions for divorce for disruption of
> the life in common is to assume all of the costs of the suit. In the
> petition he is to specify the means through which he will fulfill his
> obligations to his spouse and children.
>
> Art. 240. If the other spouse establishes that the divorce would
> entail, either for him, taking account of his age and of the duration
> of the marriage, or for the children, material or moral consequences
> of exceptional hardship, the judge is to dismiss the petition. He can
> even dismiss it on his own motion in the situation provided for in
> Article 238.
>
> Art. 241. The disruption of the life in common can be invoked as
> a ground of divorce only by the spouse who presents the initial peti-
> tion, called the principal petition.
>
> The other spouse can then present a petition, called the cross-
> petition (*demande reconventionnelle*), by alleging the fault of the
> spouse who took the initiative. This cross-petition can only be for
> divorce and not for legal separation. If the judge accepts the cross-
> petition, he dismisses the principal petition, and grants the divorce
> on the ground of fault of the spouse who took the initiative.

Like the similar provision of the English Divorce Reform Act of 1969, this
provision of the French divorce reform bill was controversial. It attracted the

label, which its government sponsors vigorously disavowed, of "divorce by repudiation."

In France, as in England, this form of divorce provoked lively debate centering about the hypothetical situation of the blameless wife who devoted herself for years to homemaking and childraising only to be put aside in favor of a younger woman.[81] The government had to tread a difficult path, denying on the one hand that this ground permitted unilateral repudiation, but explaining that broad social concerns made it desirable to permit one spouse under some circumstances to divorce a blameless partner: "Is it advisable to promote illegitimate unions, by preventing the legal reconstitution of a new home? In the present state of the mores and living conditions, the law no longer is responding to these concerns."[82] The mental impairment ground, new to French law, was likewise controversial, the original version passing the Senate but not the National Assembly.[83] After a modification (Article 238) giving to the judge the power to dismiss the petition on his or her own motion, it was adopted. But in one of the two Frances, it was seen as undermining the notion that spouses take each other for better or worse, in sickness and in health.

These sections of the new law bear the imprint of then- President Giscard d'Estaing, who was perhaps inspired by the example of Napoleon when he undertook to redraft them and permitted a photograph of a page of the draft law with his handwritten additions to be published in *Paris-Match*.[84] The changes he made were in fact quite important. As originally drafted, the bill sponsored by the government had three sections on unilateral nonfault divorce. The first provided that one spouse could seek a divorce for prolonged disruption of the life in common. The second specified that a spouse might seek such a divorce in cases where the spouses had lived apart for six years, and the third, that a spouse might seek such a divorce in cases where the mental faculties of the other spouse had been gravely impaired for six years.[85] In that scheme, the first article seemed to announce a general principle of which the following two articles were but particular applications, illustrating but not limiting the scope of the principle. As the sections were reformulated by Giscard, however, it is clear that there is now no divorce for prolonged disruption except where the marriage has been broken down for at least six years.

As in England, the battle on the question of principle—whether a spouse who may have brought about the disruption of the life in common nevertheless

---

81. Lindon, above, note 60 at pars. 90, 95, 110.
82. *Id*. at par. 102.
83. *Id*. at pars. 76–86.
84. *Id*. at pars. 25–27.
85. *Id*.

should be allowed to divorce a partner who has committed no marital fault—was resolved in the affirmative. But in France, strong opposition to this form of divorce was overcome only by setting its price tag very high. The provisions governing divorce for prolonged disruption tacitly assume that the petitioner is at fault and should pay handsomely to regain his or her liberty.[86] As Article 239 hints, and as we shall see when we examine the economic effects of this type of divorce in the following chapter, the economic disadvantages to the plaintiff may well be greater than those involved in the system of fault divorce, where the consent of a reluctant spouse can (usually) be purchased.

Another brake on this form of divorce is a mandatory conciliation procedure, which can consume more than six months.[87] And lest anyone assume that divorce is always available to anyone who waits six years and is willing to foot the bill, the hardship clause of Article 240 gives the judge discretion to deny the divorce if it would entail "material or moral consequences of exceptional hardship" for the unwilling spouse or for the couple's children.

Divorce for Fault

The French divorce-reform law, in retaining fault-based divorce, did not simply reenact the former provisions under which divorce could be granted for specified categories of fault: adultery, sentence for serious crime, or serious violation of marital duties. Instead, fault divorce was completely reformulated and is now available on one generally stated ground, plus the rarely used ground of sentence for a serious crime. Adultery has disappeared as a separate ground automatically entitling the aggrieved partner to a divorce. As under the prior law, the plaintiff's own commission of marital fault does not bar him or her from obtaining a divorce. Divorces under such circumstances are now treated under the heading of "shared fault," rather than (as before) "reciprocal fault."

The new style of fault divorce is regulated by the following four articles:

> Art. 242. Divorce can be sought by one spouse for acts imputable to the other spouse when these acts constitute a serious or repeated violation of the duties and obligations of marriage and render intolerable the maintenance of the life in common.

> Art. 243. It can be sought by one spouse when the other has been sentenced in a criminal case to one of the punishments set forth in Article 7 of the penal code.

86. *Bénabent* 211.
87. French Civil Code, arts. 251–252–1.

Art. 244. The reconciliation of the spouses taking place after the occurrence of the facts alleged bars them from being invoked as cause for divorce.

The judge in such case is to declare that the petition is inadmissible. A new petition can however be presented on the basis of facts occurring or discovered after the reconciliation, the earlier facts then being admissible in support of this new petition.

The temporary maintenance or resumption of the common life are not to be considered a reconciliation if they result only from necessity or from an attempt at conciliation or from the requirements of the upbringing of the children.

Art. 245. The faults of the spouse who took the initiative in the divorce do not prevent the examination of his petition; they can however, deprive the acts with which he reproaches the other spouse of that character of seriousness which would have made them a cause for divorce.

These faults can also be invoked by the other spouse in support of a cross-petition for divorce. If both petitions are accepted, the divorce is granted for shared fault.

Even in the absence of a cross-petition, the divorce can be granted for shared fault of both spouses if the trial reveals fault attributable to both of them.

Because all French divorce law from 1884 to 1976 was fault-based, there is an abundant settled case law (*jurisprudence constante*) in this area. The case law interpreting the language of former article 232, *"excès, sévices ou injures*, constituting a serious or repeated violation of the marital duties" continues to be relevant in interpreting the new general ground based on "acts constituting a serious or repeated violation of the duties and obligations of marriage." However, as before, the general language has been given widely varying interpretations, often meaning one thing in Paris to a busy judge who may have been divorced, and quite another in the provinces.[88] Fault divorce necessitates four meetings on the same schedule as for the preliminaries to a mutual-consent divorce.[89] In keeping with the central place given in the new law to divorce by mutual consent, the spouses are authorized, at any time before judgment is rendered, to transform a fault action (or any other type of divorce action) into a divorce based on agreement and to proceed under the system laid down in Articles 231 and 232.[90] If the spouses do proceed to judgment on fault grounds, and if the divorce is granted on the basis of

88. *Bénabent* 181.   89. Articles 251, 252.
90. Article 246.

evidence of serious marital offenses, the parties may request the judge to issue a decree stating simply that a cause for divorce existed, without setting forth the specific wrongs on which it was based.[91]

Legal Separation

Legal separation was enormously important in French law, as might be imagined, in the period from 1816 to 1884 when divorce, in the sense of release from the matrimonial bond with permission to remarry, did not exist.[92] The same law which repealed the divorce provisions of the Civil Code in 1816 reenacted them *in haec verba* as the grounds for legal separation, omitting only the ground of mutual consent.[93] Thus a considerable body of case law was built up which long continued to influence the cases on divorce when that institution as such was reintroduced in 1884. The institution of legal separation has remained important for that part of the population which, for religious reasons, is reluctant to use the divorce law. The approach to legal separation under the new law is basically similar to the mode of regulation under the prior law. As before, legal separation is available on the same basis as divorce. Thus with the addition of the new divorce grounds, the availability of legal separation has been broadened. The right of either party to convert the legal separation into a divorce after three years is continued from the prior law in substantially the same language. Legal separation by mutual consent, however, can only be converted to divorce if both spouses agree.

The Aftermath of Reform

In the first decade after the divorce reform law went into effect, French men and women did not show the same enthusiasm for open mutual-consent divorce as had the legislature, but its use has gradually increased. Although fault grounds are still the most common basis for divorce, they are preferred by a much narrower margin than in England, where mutual-consent divorce must be preceded by a two-year separation.[94] In France as a whole, nearly half of all divorces are based on consent grounds, and in Paris, the majority of divorces are now granted on this basis. Fault divorce (understood as including disguised consent divorces) is still going strong, however, the more so the further one is from the capital. When a fault divorce is truly contested,

91. Article 248–1.
92. *Rheinstein* 216.
93. *Id.*
94. In 1984, 51 percent of all divorces in France were on fault grounds; 48 percent were granted under the mutual consent procedure; and 1 percent were on the ground of prolonged disruption of the life in common. *Statistique annuelle: Les procès civils*, vol. 4 (Paris, Ministère de la Justice, 1986), Table D1.

there continue to be (as under the old law) considerable differences among judges in the way they evaluate the seriousness of the conduct alleged. This is shown by a significant variation in the percentages of fault divorces granted and denied from court to court and region to region.[95] As for divorce on prolonged disruption grounds after six years' separation, its opponents need never have feared that it would take the country by storm. After an initial period when it was invoked in a number of cases involving long-dead marriages, its use has dwindled to only 1 percent of divorces. This, of course, is similar to what happened in England.

The most striking aspect of the French "liberalization" of divorce is that the move away from fault has not, as in many other countries, made divorce easy to obtain or relegated it entirely to the realm of private ordering. If anything, the matter of marriage termination is treated—legally—with greater seriousness than before, although the 1975 statute on its face appears less harsh than its predecessor. This attitude of gravity without severity is most evident in the way that the granting of divorce is linked to regulation of its consequences. The authors clearly wished to avoid replacing the old collusive fault divorce system with an equally perfunctory consensual one. Carbonnier, in an article discussing some of the problems involved in drafting the reform law, wrote:

> All divorce by mutual consent must steer between two dangers: either it is very accommodating in accepting the reality of the consents, and the risk is great that the better-armed of the spouses surprises, extorts or buys the consent of the other; or it multiplies the precautions, the formalities and the delays, and the spouses (who are by hypothesis in agreement to divorce) prefer to bring a simulated lawsuit, rather than to confront this procedure fraught with complications.[96]

One is tempted to say that Carbonnier sought to avoid both dangers by providing *no* form of divorce which was not fraught with complications. Even though part of the impetus for divorce reform was the slowness of divorce procedures under the former law, the multiplication of stages of litigation, the increase in the tasks of judges (combined with the shortage of judicial personnel), and the rigorous new sets of rules for dealing with the economic aspects of divorce have in fact added to its complexity.[97]

There is nothing in the French divorce law that can be compared to divorce by mail or registration divorce, and there is no form of divorce that is really rapid. Alain Bénabent, a scholar-practitioner, reports that it is rare for a di-

95. *Bénabent* 181.
97. *Bénabent* 190.

96. Carbonnier, above, note 62 at 119.

vorce case to be terminated in less than a year, and that contested fault cases can drag on for years.[98] Mandatory conciliation procedures, though generally recognized as ineffective, serve to prolong the process, as does the more-than-cursory judicial examination of the spouses' arrangements concerning finances and children. The fastest form of divorce, "resignation" with the consequences left up to the judge, is favored by persons impatient to remarry, but involves great risks for anyone with a substantial interest in the economic outcome.[99]

Divorce on the prolonged disruption ground not only requires six years of separation, but is somewhat chancy, owing to the hardship clause. French judges are much more ready than their English counterparts to deny divorces on this basis, especially in the provinces.[100] The Court of Cassation has accorded great deference to the discretion of lower courts in the matter, holding that what amounts to exceptional hardship is a question of fact in each case and within the "sovereign power of appreciation of the trier of fact."[101] This means that considerable regional variation in results will be tolerated. For example, in 1984 a trial court in Perpignan (near the Spanish border) dismissed a husband's petition for divorce because it appeared that the wife, "who suffers already from having been abandoned by her husband, would be subject to disapproval within her customary milieu (a Catholic community) by reason of the granting of a divorce, even though it would not have been based on [her] fault."[102] Other courts have denied divorces for such reasons as that the defendant-wife was "beyond reproach," or that she had "run the household and raised six children," or that "she had lost three children and had then been subjected to the indignity of seeing her husband turn to another woman."[103] Many provincial courts seem, without statutory authority, to be applying a test like the one that was written into the English statute but largely ignored by English judges: they deny the divorce if it appears to them that it would "in all the circumstances be wrong." Unlike English judges, they do not view hardship as an exclusively economic concept. Indeed most denials are based on the "moral" consequences of divorce for the mental or physical well-being of the nonconsenting spouse.[104] Parisian courts, on the other hand,

98. *Id.* at 206.
99. *Id.* at 216, 220.
100. See above, notes 36 and 37.
101. Court of Cassation decision of 18 April 1980, 11 *Bulletin Civil* No. 73; Court of Cassation decision of 28 April 1980, 11 *Bulletin Civil* No. 90.
102. Reported in D. 1984. Jur. 520.
103. Olivier Guillod, "La clause de dureté dans quelques législations européens sur le divorce," 1983 *Revue internationale de droit comparé* 787, 808.
104. *Bénabent* 221–22.

interpret the hardship clause quite restrictively, with the approval of most French family law scholars.

It does not seem likely that the balance that was worked out in 1975 between a liberal ideology of marriage and a concern to protect dependent wives and children will be altered in any significant way in the near future. For the time being, the French system represents a modern approach to divorce that contrasts strikingly with the less carefully thought-out rush to the no-fault bandwagon in many American states. France has made divorce available on unilateral application, but under such conditions that no one would think of describing it as "divorce on demand." It has also made open mutual-consent divorce respectable without thereby establishing divorce by registration. It is, of course, possible that over time divorce for prolonged disruption (with the waiting period shortened or removed) could become divorce on demand and that mutual-consent divorce could be converted into a mere postal procedure. But for that to happen, ideas about law and morality, as well as about public and private responsibility for the casualties of marriage breakdown, would have to change to a degree that is not currently foreseeable.

West Germany: Marriage and Family Law Reform, 1976

Prelude

Unlike the English and French statutes which replaced very old, traditional divorce laws, West Germany's 1976 reform repealed a thirty-eight-year-old law which was not too different in substance from either the 1969 English act or the 1975 French law.[105] Like the more recent English and French liberalization efforts, the prior German law had permitted divorce on proof of "marriage breakdown" (*Zerrüttung*) following a period of separation, as well as on proof of fault. As under the modern English and French laws, divorce for marriage breakdown could be denied if special circumstances made it unjust in a given case. Divorce on the nonfault ground of insanity had been available in Germany from the time of the German Civil Code. Thus, it is particularly interesting to examine the events and the thinking that led up to the relatively liberal 1938–1946 law, and to see why further and more fundamental change was thought necessary in the 1970s.

Prior to the legal unification of the German empire that occurred when the

---

105. The Marriage Law for Greater Germany (*Grossdeutsches Ehegesetz*) of 6 July 1938, RGB1.I 807, was reenacted with minor changes as Allied Control Council Law No. 16 of 20 February 1946 (referred to herein as *EheG*). The 1938 law is discussed in detail in Magdalene Schoch, "Divorce Law and Practice under National Socialism in Germany," 28 *Iowa Law Review* 225 (1943).

Civil Code came into force on 1 January 1900, there had been three major legal approaches to divorce in the various regions of Germany.[106] One of these patterns was that of the Code Napoleon, which had been mantained in effect in the Rhineland and was also the law of the Grand Duchy of Baden. Another was that of the so-called common law of Germany (*gemeines Recht*), which referred questions of marriage and divorce to ecclesiastical law, that is, to canon law for Catholics and to Protestant ecclesiastical law for Protestants. Hence, in places such as Southern Bavaria, where common law applied, marriage was indissoluble for Catholics, and divorce was available to Protestatnts only on narrow fault grounds (not by mutual agreement as was the case under the Code Napoleon). The third approach was that of the Prussian General Code of 1794, which was in effect in about half the territory of Prussia and in a few small territories outside it.

Under the Prussian Code, marriages could be dissolved not only for fault, as under Protestant law, but also by mutual consent and even upon unilateral application. As the Prussian Code is known to have been influenced in several respects by the secular thought of Frederick the Great, and Frederick is known in turn to have been an admirer of Voltaire, its divorce provisions have often been thought to embody the same spirit of individual liberty that animated the French divorce law of 1792. Heinrich Dörner's research indicates, however, that the nonfault divorce provisions of the Prussian Code were probably not based on the idea of marriage as a civil contract; nor were they designed to liberate individuals from restraints on their personal freedom. Rather, they seem to have been inspired by Frederick's pronatalist thinking.[107] Dörner has traced the Code's principle of free divorce to a cabinet directive of 1783 in which Frederick wrote that divorce

> must not be made too difficult, lest the population be hindered. For when two spouses are so angry and irritated with each other that no further connection between them is to be hoped for . . . then also will they produce no children with each other, and that is detrimental to the population. On the other hand, if such a pair is divorced, and the wife then marries another fellow, then surely children are likely to come along.[108]

The language of the divorce provisions of the Prussian General Code lends itself to the interpretation that their purpose was to encourage population growth. Mutual-consent divorce was made available only where the marriage

---

106. *Rheinstein* 293–294.

107. Heinrich Dörner, *Industrialisierung und Familienrecht* (Berlin: Duncker and Humblot, 1974), 59.

108. *Id.*

was "entirely childless" (*ganz kinderlose*).[109] Unilateral divorce was to be granted only when the petitioner could prove "the existence of such a violent and deeply rooted aversion, that no hope remains for reconciliation and for achievement of the purposes of the state of marriage."[110] Under the Prussian Code, there was no doubt about the chief purpose of marriage: it was expressly stated to be the procreation and upbringing of children.[111]

These three contrasting treatments of divorce in Germany had to be replaced by a single pattern when the country was legally unified. The pattern selected by the draftsmen of the Civil Code resembled the one chosen by the French when divorce was reintroduced into the French Civil Code in 1884. Basically, divorce was to be granted only for the misconduct of one spouse.[112] An exception was made for the case of insanity. Thus divorce was made possible for Catholics in former regions of the common law, but was rendered more difficult for residents of those regions where the Code Napoleon or the Prussian Code had been in force. However, studies of divorce in Germany for the period beginning nineteen years before the new Code went into effect and ending sixteen years afterwards indicated that the new law had no appreciable influence either on the incidence of divorce or on the behavior of judges.[113]

Unlike France and England, Germany did not retain the fault principle as the main basis of its divorce law until well into the second half of the twentieth century. In 1938, under the National Socialist regime, a new marriage law for Greater Germany was prepared. It had been the original idea of the draftsmen of the National Socialist divorce law to eliminate the concept of fault entirely and to have only one ground of divorce—the breakdown of the marriage to such a degree that the marriage had become "valueless to the *Volksgemeinschaft*," the community of all racially pure Germans.[114] But such a radical innovation did not seem immediately feasible, so the provisional decision was made to modify the old fault grounds and to add new grounds.[115] Among these new bases for divorce was breakdown of the marriage as evidenced by a period of separation. When the 1938 Marriage Law came under review in the "denazification" process after World War II, the Allied Control Council substantially reenacted it, adding a hardship clause to the breakdown ground.

109. Prussian General Code, Part II, Title I, §716.

110. *Id.*, §718a.

111. *Id.*, §1 ("Der Hauptzweck der Ehe ist die Erzeugung und Erziehung der Kinder.")

112. German Civil Code, former §§1564–1587. The grounds for divorce included adultery, bigamy, insanity, unnatural practices, attempt on a spouse's life, wilful desertion, and a general fault ground.

113. *Rheinstein* 295–301.

114. Schoch, above, note 105 at 234–36.

115. *Id.* at 237.

Only a few provisions, such as divorce for "unreasonable refusal to beget offspring," were thought to be so closely related to National Socialist ideology that they had to be eliminated.[116]

The 1938 law, as reenacted in 1946, became the divorce law of West Germany until the 1976 reform law went into effect in 1977. The 1938–46 statute provided for divorce upon proof of two types of matrimonial misconduct: adultery, and other "violations of matrimonial duties" so serious that they have led to disruption of the marriage and made restoration of the life in common an unreasonable expectation.[117] In addition, divorce was made available in two types of cases where neither partner could be charged with fault. In one of these, divorce could be granted on the ground of the physical or mental condition of the defendant.[118] In the other, a version of breakdown divorce was provided on proof of three years' separation, without reference to misconduct of the defendant:[119]

> §48. (1) If the marriage partners have not kept a common household for three years and if, owing to a deep-rooted incurable breakdown (*Zerrüttung*) of marital relations, restoration of the life in common cannot be expected, either of the marriage partners can petition for a divorce.
>
> (2) If the spouse petitioning for divorce is wholly or predominantly responsible for bringing about the breakdown, the divorce cannot be granted against the other spouse's opposition, unless the opposing spouse lacks attachment to the marriage, and such readiness to continue it, as may fairly be expected of him or her, (amended in 1961).[120]
>
> (3) The petition for divorce must not be granted if a true understanding of the interests of one or more minor children of the marriage requires the maintenance of the marriage (added by the Allied Control Council Law of 1946).

In 1946 the breakdown principle—even the cautious version which appeared in the 1938 German law—was still novel enough to attract the attention of the English, French, and Soviet members of the quadripartite Committee on the Reform of German Law, established by the four allied powers to purge German law of National Socialist ideology. They were ini-

---

116. Ernst J. Cohn, *Manual of German Law*, vol. 1, 2d ed. (Dobbs Ferry, N.Y.: Oceana, 1968), 229.

117. *EheG* §§42, 43.

118. *EheG* §§44, 45, 46.

119. *EheG* §48.

120. The law of 11 August 1961, BGBl.I 1221, merely ratified the existing judicial practice, which had made it difficult for a plaintiff to overcome the defendant's opposition in contested cases, *Rheinstein* 287. Ironically, soon after the amendment, the Bundesgerichtshof abandoned its earlier restrictive attitude and began to interpret §48(2) liberally so as to deny few divorces.

tially of the view that the breakdown ground, like certain racial and eugenic aspects of the Marriage Law, should be deleted.[121] The American member of the Committee eventually persuaded his colleagues that the provision was not tainted—in part by pointing out that the American state of Louisiana, which had long permitted nonfault divorce after three years' separation, could hardly be said to be under the sway of National Socialist ideas.[122]

Despite the fact that section 48 of the Allied Control Council Law of 1946 was the best-known and most-discussed feature of West German divorce law, it did not play a very significant role in practice for reasons which eventually produced agitation for further reform in Germany. Awareness of the German debate might have given pause to the English in 1969 and to the French in 1975. In the first place, in West Germany by that time, as in England, France, and the United States, over 90 percent of all divorces were uncontested, chiefly because the spouses had reached agreement on the essential points at issue between them.[123] But such consensual divorces were generally disguised as divorces for marital misconduct, rather than being based on the breakdown of the marriage. The main reason for this was that section 48 was the long road (three years) to a divorce, whereas fault divorce involved no waiting period. The breakdown ground played a constantly diminishing role in practice: in 1950, it accounted for 12.2 per cent of all divorces; by 1968, the percentage was only 4.4.[124] The general misconduct clause permitting one spouse to obtain a divorce if the other's behavior had seriously disrupted the marriage was by far the most popular ground for divorce, accounting for 93 per cent of all divorces in West Germany by 1968.[125]

The plans of the Social Democratic government for a divorce-law reform which would strengthen the breakdown principle and eliminate the fault principle were explained in a 1970 speech by the Minister of Justice, Gerhard Jahn:

> The parties involved, as well as the courts, must be relieved of the need to search for responsibility in a sphere that cannot be clarified and to find in this search the justification for a divorce. They must confine themselves to the objective and more easily demonstrated establishment of whether a marriage has in fact broken down.[126]

121. Max Rheinstein, "The Law of Family and Succession," in *Civil Law in the Modern World*, ed. Athanassios Yiannopoulos (Baton Rouge: Louisiana State Univ. Press, 1965), 27, 46.
122. *Id.*
123. *Rheinstein* 287–88; Dieter Giesen, "Divorce Reform in Germany," 7 *Family Law Quarterly* 351, 360 (1973).
124. *Rheinstein* 393.
125. *Id.*
126. Quoted in Michael Bohndorf, "Recent Developments in German Divorce Law," 19 *International and Comparative Law Quarterly* 705, 710 (1970).

A discussion draft of a reform bill, based on the report of a commission appointed in 1968 to examine the questions of divorce and support law reform, was circulated in 1970, and a draft law was introduced by the government in the Bundestag in 1971.[127]

From the time the government's draft bill on divorce (and many other aspects of family law) was introduced until the eventual adoption of a compromise version in 1976, divorce was the subject of widespread and highly publicized discussion. It was debated two dozen times in the legal committee of the Bundestag and no less then forty-five times in the subcommittee on divorce-law reform.[128] Less controversy was generated by the proposed changes in the grounds for divorce than by the projected innovations with respect to postdivorce economics.[129] But an important element of the debate concerned whether the traditional ideology of marriage was at stake.

A compromise bill appeared certain of adoption in December 1975, having passed the Bundestag on December 11 and needing only the approval of the Bundesrat. But before the Bundesrat could act, an intervening by-election in Lower Saxony suddenly gave the Christian Democrats a one-vote majority in the Bundesrat which served to defeat the bill—by one vote—in January 1976.[130] This gave the Christian Democrats the leverage they needed to secure a few important last-minute modifications in conference committee before the bill was finally adopted.

The Marriage and Family Law Reform, 1976

The West German Marriage and Family Law Reform Law[131] begins with the words, "Marriage is concluded for a lifetime" (*Die Ehe wird auf Lebenszeit geschlossen*).[132] Following this optimistic, if somewhat anomalous, opening statement (inserted at the last moment to gain the support of the Christian Democrats), the Reform Law replaced all specific grounds for divorce with a single nonfault ground. The new ground is called *Scheitern* (literally, *foundering*, as of a ship upon the rocks; figuratively, *failure*), rather than *Zerrüttung* (*breakdown*) of the marriage. The basis for divorce was set forth in five sections:

> §1564. A marriage can be terminated only through judicial decision upon the petition of one or both spouses. The marriage is dis-

---

127. *Rheinstein* 392.
128. *The German Tribune*, 21 December 1975, 4.
129. *Rheinstein* 394–95.
130. *The Boston Globe*, 31 January 1976, 2.
131. Herein, *EheRG*. By this statute, divorce law was, for the first time since 1938, reinserted in the Civil Code; references are made hereafter to specific provisions of the Code.
132. West German Civil Code §1353.

solved by the legal force of the judgment. The conditions under which divorce can be sought are set forth in the following provisions.

§1565. (1) A marriage can be terminated, if it has failed (*wenn sie gescheitert ist*). A marriage has failed, if the community of life of the spouses no longer exists and it can not be expected that the spouses will restore it.

(2) If the spouses have lived apart for less than one year, the marriage can only be dissolved if the continuation of the marriage would pose an insupportable hardship for the petitioner for reasons which repose in the person of the other spouse.

§1566. (1) It is irrebuttably presumed that the marriage has failed, if the spouses have lived apart for one year and both spouses petition for divorce or the respondent consents to the divorce.

(2) It is irrebuttably presumed that the marriage has failed, if the spouses have lived apart for three years.

§1567. (1) The spouses are living apart if no household community exists between them and one spouse perceptibly refuses its restoration by rejecting the marital community of life. The household community no longer exists in such case even if the spouses live apart within the marital dwelling.

(2) Cohabitation for a short time, that should serve the reconciliation of the spouses, does not interrupt or stop the time periods specified in §1566.

§1568.(1) The marriage may not be dissolved, although it has broken down, if and so long as the maintenance of the marriage is especially necessary for exceptional reasons in the interest of minor children produced by the marriage, or if and so long as the dissolution, for the respondent who opposes it, would pose such exceptional hardship by reason of extraordinary circumstances, that the maintenance of the marriage, even taking into consideration the interests of the petitioner, appears exceptionally required.

(2) Paragraph (1) is not applicable if the spouses have lived apart for more than five years.[133]

It will be noted that, unlike the English and French statutes, the 1976 West German Reform Law retains no fault grounds. Further, it does not require any period of actual separation before a divorce can be granted. The marriage can be found to have "failed" even though the parties are still living under the same roof.

Under the general clause of paragraph 1565(1), a spouse can obtain a divorce by convincing the court that the marriage has failed. This general rule is qualified by 1565(2), which was added in the haggling that went on between

133. §1568(2) was held unconstitutional in 1980 and repealed in 1986. See below, n. 134.

the government coalition and the opposition between January and April 1976 as a concession to the Christian Democratic and Christian Social Unions, who then held the upper hand in the Bundesrat. Where the couple has not been separated for one year, the marriage can be dissolved only if it has broken down *and* its maintenance, for the divorce-seeking partner, "would pose an insupportable hardship" for reasons attributable to the other spouse. This obviously opens the door to evidence of fault, a least in a small class of cases.

If the divorce is by mutual consent (either on joint petition or with the consent of the respondent), and the parties have lived apart for one year, the presumption of failure is conclusive, and the court must grant the divorce under paragraph 1566(1). If only one spouse seeks the divorce, and if the spouses have lived apart for three years, the petitioner is aided in making out his case of marriage failure by the irrebuttable presumption established in paragraph 1566(2). The irrebuttable presumption in this case, however, will not automatically lead to divorce. The hardship clause in paragraph 1568 permits the court, in exceptional circumstances at least, to deny a divorce even where a marriage has failed.

As originally enacted, the statute meant that a divorce could not be denied (even though this might result in grave hardship) after the couple had lived apart for five years. This absolute outer limit of five years in paragraph 1568(2) made the West German Reform Law ideologically quite different from the English and French divorce laws. In 1980, however, the Federal Constitutional Court ruled that the five-year cutoff was unconstitutional under Article 6 of the West German Basic Law, which provides that "Marriage and the family are under the special protection of the state." [134] The court held that, even after five years' separation, a spouse opposed to a divorce must at least be given an opportunity to try to prove that a divorce decree would produce extraordinary hardship. In 1986, the legislature repealed paragraph 1568(2) to conform the Code to the court's decision.

Unlike the English and the French, and perhaps with awareness of the poor success of conciliation and reconciliation efforts in other countries, the West Germans repealed their mandatory reconciliation provisions, and rejected proposals for compulsory counselling or conciliation as useless and impracticable. [135]

The Aftermath of Reform

The West German Reform Law, like the English and the French, was a compromise. But in concept it differed in significant ways from the two earlier

134. Bundesverfassungsgericht decision of 21 October 1980, reported in 1981 *Neue Juristische Wochenschrift* 108.

135. *Rheinstein* 395.

reforms. The principle of elimination of marital misconduct from consideration was much more fully accepted, as was the principle of availability of
unilateral divorce. In actual operation, however, the West German law is more
akin to the French statute than the English. Like the 1975 French reform law,
it represents a considerable increase in judicial control over the effects of
divorce, to the point where some scholars have complained that divorce is
now harder to obtain than it was before the law was "liberalized." Müller-
Freienfels, for example, has written that the law "has made divorce more
economically difficult, even economically impossible," and F. W. Bosch has
claimed that, "the consequences of marriage dissolution are now more onerous than before." [136] As we shall see in chapter 5, empirical research in West
Germany indicates that such claims are somewhat exaggerated, but it is
clearly the case that the effects of divorce are now receiving a higher degree
of judicial attention than previously.

The focus of the West German law, as in all the discussions that led up to
it, is much more on the satisfactory resolution of the economic consequences
of divorce than on the fact of divorce itself. The role of the judge in ascertaining the fact of breakdown is curtailed by the irrebuttable presumptions, although not to the point of establishing mail-order divorce. Judicial inquest
into the fact of breakdown was completely eliminated under paragraph
1566(1) in mutual-consent divorces after a one-year separation. But the personal appearance of the spouses is still required, in principle, in every case.

Over the first decade of operation, there were few surprises so far as the
grounds of divorce are concerned. The removal by the Constitutional Court
of the five-year outer limit on the operation of the hardship clause has turned
out to be primarily of symbolic significance. The clause is rarely invoked,
and divorces are almost never denied on this basis. [137] Most divorces, as before, are uncontested. As expected, most petitions are brought under paragraph 1566(1) on the basis of mutual consent after a year of living apart. It
seems, however, that many spouses who are in full agreement on divorce
choose nevertheless to petition under the general breakdown provision
(§1565), rather than the mutual-consent provisions (§1566), in order to avoid
the more burdensome regulations laid down in the procedural rules for
mutual-consent divorce. The Code of Civil Procedure provides that spouses
seeking a divorce on the mutual-consent ground must present the court with a
detailed agreement on all the consequences of divorce—allocation of the
dwelling and household effects, spousal and child support, marital property

136. Wolfram Müller-Freienfels, Review Essay, 33 *American Journal of Comparative Law*
733, 744 (1985); F. W. Bosch, "Ruckblick und Ausblick," 1980 *Zeitschrift für das gesamte
Familienrecht* 739, 746.
137. Guillod, above, note 103 at 808.

and pension division, custody and visitation—and that the divorce cannot be granted until all these matters are settled.[138] In other types of divorce, only child custody and pension-splitting must be arranged before the divorce can be granted. An empirical study of these procedures in operation has reached the conclusion that "simple" consent divorces have been rendered unnecessarily complicated and costly through insufficiently differentiated procedural rules.[139]

The breakdown principle and, in the words of *Die Zeit*, "the withdrawal of the modern State with its civil marriage law from the sphere of marital privacy"[140] seem to have been fully accepted. The battle over the economic aspects of divorce, however, rages on. As we shall see in the following chapter, although fault has been largely eliminated from the grounds of divorce, it has made a surprising comeback in support law. In its shift of emphasis from the fact of marriage termination to the financial problems associated with the breakup of a household, the West German law leads naturally to a consideration of Swedish law, where this trend has reached its furthest point.

Sweden: The Family Law Reform, 1973

Prelude

As we have just seen, the West German divorce reform of 1976 was of a prior law which appeared liberal in comparison with pre-1969 English law, pre-1975 French law, and the laws of many American states prior to the reforms of the 1970s. The Swedish divorce reform of 1973, however, was of a statute which had long been thought to be even more remarkable for the ease with which it made divorce available without allegation of fault and even upon unilateral application.

The pre-1973 Swedish law was adopted in 1915[141] in reaction to a situation which had developed under the exclusively fault-based divorce law of the Swedish Code of 1734. That eighteenth-century code, in accordance with the ecclesiastical law of the Lutheran State Church, had permitted divorce only for adultery or desertion.[142] But the king was empowered to relax the strict

138. West German Code of Civil Procedure, arts. 623, 630.
139. Lutz Müller-Alten, *Ehescheidung und Scheidungsverträge* (Frankfurt: Haag & Herchen, 1984).
140. *Die Zeit*, 23 April 1976, 1 (overseas edition).
141. Reenacted with slight modifications as the Marriage Code of Sweden (*Giftermalsbalken*) of 11 June 1920, and amended by the Law of 5 June 1973, No. 645.
142. Folke Schmidt, "The 'Leniency' of the Scandinavian Divorce Laws," 1963 *Scandinavian Studies in Law* 107, 110–111.

requirements of the Code. According to Folke Schmidt, by the end of the eighteenth century, enlightened Swedish monarchs were quite liberal in granting divorces.[143] Obtaining a royal dispensation, however, was a time-consuming process. Thus, in Sweden, as in other countries where divorce was not easily available, other means to dissolve marriages were found. For spouses who were in agreement on divorce and relatively well-to-do, the answer was the "Copenhagen divorce," described as follows in an 1879 Swedish parliamentary law committee report:

> The matter is arranged thus, that one of the spouses, e.g. the husband, travels to the nearest foreign city, usually Copenhagen. Then the wife sues him in court for divorce on the ground that he maliciously and wilfully deserted her, and went abroad with the intention not to be and cohabit with her any more. Having been served the writ, the defendant admits the circumstances of the case by attorney, whereupon the court grants its decree of divorce without more ado. . . . With the rapid communications of today, all this can be managed within the period of a few weeks.[144]

For those who could not afford the trip to Copenhagen or who could not obtain the agreement of the other spouse, there was always the possibility of entering an informal union, or "Stockholm marriage," as it was known because of the frequency of such arrangements among the working class in the capital city.[145]

A law revision commission charged with looking into the matter of divorce reform in 1913 came to the conclusion (as had a Swiss commission as early as 1907) that the basis for divorce should be the breakdown of the marriage:

> Ordinarily, it is not desirable, either from the point of view of the community or with regard to the spouses, that in such situations [of breakdown] a marriage can be held together by force. The State can enforce the external bond alone; but a community of life which carries into effect the moral content of a marriage cannot be enforced by external pressure.[146]

The minister of justice, referring to the Copenhagen divorce and the delay involved in divorce by royal writ, said, "Here we have an abuse to be countered, but also a need which should be recognized."[147] Accordingly, in 1915

143. Folke Schmidt, "The Prospective Law of Marriage," 1971 *Scandinavian Studies in Law* 191, 198.
144. Quoted in Schmidt, above, note 143 at 111–12.
145. *Rheinstein* 139.
146. Quoted in Schmidt, above, note 143 at 117.
147. *Id.*

a law was passed to eliminate the practice of ritual trips to Copenhagen and to make divorce simpler and more expeditious. The law had wide support and met little opposition from the Lutheran clergy.[148] It abolished the royal divorce jurisdiction entirely and made divorce available on a nonfault basis as well as on several fault grounds besides the old ones of adultery and desertion.

The nonfault grounds introduced in 1915 permitted divorce on application by either spouse in the following situations: (1) where the two spouses acting together had obtained a judicial decree of separation on the ground that they were unable to continue living together because of profound and lasting breakdown of their marriage and had lived apart for one year thereafter; (2) where one spouse had obtained such a decree of separation, and the spouses had lived apart for one year thereafter (the petitioner in this case had to prove the breakdown was caused by differences in temperament and outlook, but this burden was said not to be heavy); (3) where the spouses had in fact lived seperately for three years even though there had been no decree of separation.[149]

Where both spouses acted together, the court was not permitted to look behind the allegation of breakdown and had no discretion to deny a divorce after the period of separation. In cases where one spouse acted alone, there was a clause permitting the court to deny a divorce if special circumstances made it proper to continue the marriage even though it had broken down.[150] Denial of a divorce under this clause, however, was "almost unheard of." [151] In the entire history of the act, there seem to have been only two published cases where a divorce decree was refused.[152]

Under the 1915 law, mutual consent with legal separation for one year was by far the most frequently used basis for divorce, but the number of divorces sought on fault grounds was sufficiently high to indicate that these grounds remained important, either because fault divorce continued to be a speedier route than separation, or because a decree based on one spouse's fault still gave the other some advantage in economic or child-related matters.[153]

The Swedish divorce law just described, under which unilateral divorce was obtainable with little difficulty, was described in Max Rheinstein's 1971 comparative study of divorce law as the fullest legal expression to date of eudemonistic liberal individualism.[154] The Swedish example was followed by

148. *Id.* at 112.   149. *Rheinstein* 141–42.
150. *Id.*   151. *Id.*
152. Jacob Sundberg, "Facteurs et tendences dans l'évolution moderne du droit de la famille des pays nordiques," in *Famille, droit, et changement sociale dans les sociétés contemporaines* (Brussels: Bruylant, 1978), 49.
153. Schmidt, above, note 142 at 121; *Rheinstein* 142–143.
154. *Rheinstein* 126.

Norway in 1918 and by Denmark, Finland, and Iceland in the 1920s. In both law and practice, divorce was readily available in the Nordic countries. It is therefore interesting to consider why Sweden decided that further liberalizing changes were desirable in 1973.

The Divorce Law Reform, 1973

Legislative cooperation with a high degree of coordination in the handling of problems of private law has long been characteristic of the Nordic countries. Thus it was a noteworthy event when the Swedish minister in charge of family law announced at the 1969 meeting of the Nordic Council that Sweden was about to become a "pioneer country." As Professor Sundberg has described it, the Swedish "pioneer" concept resembled the American idea of the fifty states as "laboratories" where various legal approaches to common social problems can be tested.

> Mr. Lidbom announced that he did not regret but rather rejoiced "when the one or the other Nordic country tries to find new ways to solve social and economic problems by legislation. It is often found that new creations that are inserted into one country's legal system eventually are also adopted by the neighboring countries." [155]

Thus the ground was prepared for a divorce reform in Sweden that would not be, as was the 1915 marriage law, the product of coordinated effort with the other Nordic countries. Later in 1969, the minister of justice, Herman Kling, appointed a committee to prepare new marriage legislation and laid down certain directives to guide their work. He charged the committee that, "[L]egislation should not under any circumstance force a person to continue to live under a marriage from which he wishes to free himself," [156] and that, "A new [family] law should . . . as far as possible be neutral as regards different forms of cohabitation and different moral ideas." [157]

In harmony with these directives, the Committee on Reform of Family Law produced a draft based on the principles that, "not only entry into marriage but also its continued existence, should be based on the free will of the spouses" and that "the wish of one of the spouses to dissolve the marriage should always be respected." [158] But, as we have seen above, the divorce process in Sweden already conformed substantially to these principles.

155. Quoted in Sundberg, above, note 152 at 55.
156. Quoted in Jacob Sundberg, "Recent Changes in Swedish Family Law: Experiment Repeated," 23 *American Journal of Comparative Law* 34, 44 (1975).
157. Quoted in Note, "Current Legal Developments—Sweden," 19 *International and Comparative Law Quarterly* 164 (1970).
158. Quoted in Note, "Sweden—Family Law," 22 *International and Comparative Law Quarterly* 182, 183 (1973).

The changes made by the 1973 law did not constitute major departures from the prior practice. The main difference was in tone and ideology. The divorce provisions of the Swedish Marriage Code now read as follows:

Section 1. If the spouses are agreed that their marriage shall be dissolved, they shall be entitled to a divorce. It shall be preceded by a reconsideration period if both spouses request one or if either of them is living on a permanent basis with a child of his or her own who is under 16 years of age and of whom that spouse has custody.

Section 2. If only one of the spouses wishes the marriage to be dissolved, that spouse shall only be entitled to divorce following a reconsideration period.

Section 3. The reconsideration period shall begin when the spouses make a joint application for divorce or when notice of one spouse's petition for divorce is served on the other spouse. If the reconsideration period has run for at least six months, a decree of divorce shall be granted if either of the spouses then submits a separate petition for such a decree. If such a petition is not submitted within one year from the start of the reconsideration period, the question of divorce shall lapse. If the proceedings for divorce are disallowed or the case is withdrawn, the reconsideration period shall terminate.

Section 4. If the spouses have lived apart for at least two years, either of them shall be entitled to divorce without a preceding reconsideration period.

Section 5. If a marriage has been entered into despite the fact that the spouses are related to one another in the direct ascending or descending line or are sister and brother of the whole blood, either of the spouses shall be entitled to divorce without a preceding reconsideration period. The same shall apply if the marriage was entered into despite the fact that one of the spouses was already married and the earlier marriage had not been dissolved.

In the event of bigamy, either of the parties to the earlier marriage shall be entitled to have it dissolved by divorce without a preceding reconsideration period.

In cases referred to in the first paragraph, proceedings for divorce may also be instituted by a public prosecutor.[159]

The principal changes from the prior law can be summarized as follows: (1) all fault grounds have been eliminated; (2) unilateral divorce is now made

---

159. Marriage Code of 11 June 1920 §§1–5, as amended in 1973 and 1987, SFS 1987:230 (trans. Martin Naylor). For the history of the 1973 reform, see Lars Tottie, "The Elimination of Fault in Swedish Divorce Law," in *Marriage and Cohabitation in Contemporary Societies*, ed. John Eekelaar and Sanford Katz (Toronto: Butterworths, 1980), 131–36.

a matter of unqualified legal right; (3) no reasons for the divorce need be given, no "breakdown" of the marriage need be alleged, and therefore the court need not even go through the motions of making findings concerning these matters; (4) provisions of the prior law requiring that efforts be made to bring the spouses to a mediator are eliminated; (5) divorce is available without any waiting period unless one spouse is opposed or one spouse has custody of children under sixteen, in which cases a six-month period of consideration must be observed.[160] After six months, the court must grant the divorce upon the request of either spouse. There is no discretion to deny a divorce on hardship grounds.

Despite the rhetoric that preceded its adoption, there seem to have been practical as well as ideological reasons for moving to a more streamlined form of divorce in Sweden. By 1973, marriages were being formed and dissolved outside legal categories at rates unprecedented in modern times. It is probably not an accident that relatively rapid divorce on demand was accepted first in that country where informal cohabitation has made the most important claims upon the legal system. One has the impression that in Sweden the introduction of unilateral divorce, like the elimination of the vow for life from the marriage ceremony, is in a curious way almost a conservative measure, intended to "save" legal marriage by winning back persons who live in informal unions. To the extent that it does promote formal marriage, it also serves, of course, the interest of the bureaucratic state in orderly record-keeping and expeditious dispute settlement.

The other Nordic countries, to varying degrees, have adopted similar approaches. The one most resembling the Swedish system is a new Finnish divorce law that went into effect in 1988. Except for making the six-month period of consideration mandatory in all cases, it follows the Swedish statute rather closely, making divorce available without inquest, reasons, or substantial delay.[161] In Denmark, Iceland and Norway, uncontested divorces have long been under the jurisdiction of administrative, rather than judicial, tribunals,[162] so that in this sense a major step in the process of dejuridification of divorce was taken there long ago. In Norway, as of this writing, further liberalizing reforms were pending.[163] It seems fair to say that divorce, as such,

160. Under §5.1, the period of reconsideration must also be ordered if both spouses request it. There is no requirement that the spouses live apart during this period.

161. I am grateful to Matti Savolainen of the Finnish Ministry of Justice for this information.

162. See Torben Svenne Schmidt, "The Scandinavian Law of Procedure in Matrimonial Causes," in *The Resolution of Family Conflict*, ed. John Eekelaar and Sanford Katz (Toronto: Butterworths, 1984), 77.

163. Peter Lødrup, "Norway: Reforming the Law of Divorce," 25 *Journal of Family Law* 199 (1986–87).

is almost a dead subject in the Nordic countries, with legal attention having shifted decisively from the terminating event to its economic and child-related consequences.

The United States: The "No-Fault" Movement, 1969–1985

Like the Nordic countries, the American states have long engaged in cooperative law-reform efforts, notably through the work of the National Conference of Commissioners on Uniform State Laws, which was founded in 1892 with the preparation of uniform divorce legislation as one of its chief stated aims. But uniformity in American divorce law has proved an elusive goal. For most of the twentieth century, divorce was based on fault in the great majority of states. The various jurisdictions differed, however, in the degree of rigor with which their divorce laws were applied. A few states, with lenient laws or tolerant judicial attitudes, or both, served as divorce havens where the well-to-do could quickly and quietly dissolve their marriages. Gradually, courts in other jurisdictions became unwilling, or lacked the time, to inquire into the grievances of the ever-growing numbers of spouses who were seeking uncontested divorces under strict fault-based statutes. By the 1960s in the United States, as elsewhere, at least 90 percent of all divorces were unopposed and were being processed on an assembly-line basis.[164] This dual law of divorce, with the strict law on the books flagrantly at odds with relatively easy mutual consent divorce in practice, troubled many observers. Max Rheinstein was almost alone among academics in having a good word to say for what he called a form of "democratic compromise" that had worked reasonably well to accommodate the ideal of marriage as a commitment for better or worse with the need felt by many people for a way to terminate unhappy unions and to begin a new life.[165]

In the 1960s, the Uniform Law Commissioners and a California governor's commission began work with a view toward eliminating the need to recite instances of marital misconduct in court. Herma Hill Kay, a key member of both groups, has recounted how the California Commission was influenced by the report of the Archbishop of Canterbury's Group, and how the California work in turn influenced the Uniform Act.[166] In 1969, California became the first American state to enact a divorce law from which fault grounds were completely absent. The California Family Law Act, which went into effect in 1970, made divorce available on the basis of "irreconcilable differences" that

164. *Rheinstein* 63.
165. *Id.* at 252.
166. Herma Hill Kay, "An Appraisal of California's No-Fault Divorce Law," 75 *California Law Review* 291–92, 298 (1987).

had caused the "irremediable breakdown" of the marriage and also on an insanity ground.[167] The Uniform Law Commissioners, after much internal strife, completed their work in 1970, producing a statute which made "irretrievable breakdown" of the marriage the sole ground of divorce.[168] Breakdown grounds caught on quickly. By 1985, when South Dakota became the last American jurisdiction to repeal an exclusively fault-based statute, many states had followed the California lead. Many more, however, had modernized their law simply by adding nonfault to fault grounds and eliminating the old traditional defenses of recrimination and collusion.

As of 1987,[169] eighteen states and the District of Columbia had adopted "pure" nonfault divorce laws. The other states had some form of mixed grounds compromise: fault grounds combined with breakdown, separation, incompatibility, or mutual consent. In eight of these compromise states, the waiting period for use of the nonfault ground was more than a year, so that this small group could be said to have adopted a relatively conservative approach to divorce. The same is true of the two states, New York and Mississippi, where the mixed-grounds statutes permit nonfault divorce only if both spouses consent. What differentiates most of the mixed-grounds statutes in the United States from the English and French compromises, however, is that in twenty-two of these states, the waiting period for divorce on unilateral application, without fault, is only a year or less. Since the average American divorce (with negotiation and the inevitable delays of litigation) takes at least several months, these statutes are functionally equivalent to the pure nonfault statutes like California's, many of which also impose a waiting period of a few months between petition and divorce. Thus, in forty-one American jurisdictions, one spouse can terminate a marriage without the other's fault or consent and without delay beyond that normally attendant on civil litigation. No state's divorce law has a hardship clause. A small, but growing, group of states has moved even further toward free terminability of marriage by establishing a summary termination procedure for the simplest kinds of uncontested divorces where no minor children are involved.[170]

Certain features that had been included in the early no-fault statutes in order to win legislative acceptance quickly became dead letters. In form, most of

167. California Civil Code §4506 (West, 1983).

168. UMDA §302.

169. See the useful summary of state divorce law in Doris Freed and Timothy Walker, "Family Law in the Fifty States: An Overview," 20 *Family Law Quarterly* 439, 461–62 (1987).

170. For example, California Civil Code Ann., Title 3, §§4550–4556 (Deering, 1984); Nevada Rev. Stat., Ch. 125.181–125.184 (1986); Oregon Rev. Stat. §107.485 (1983). The Oregon and California statutes make summary divorce available only to couples who have not accumulated substantial property and who have been married less than ten and five years, respectively.

these statutes require, as did the English Divorce Reform Act, a judicial inquest into whether the marriage has actually broken down.[171] They envision a hearing in open court at which evidence will be heard on the state of the marriage. But the same judges who had been processing "cruelty" cases at five minutes a clip were not about to begin second-guessing the spouses themselves on whether their marriage had really "broken down." Conciliation provisions, likewise, had been tactically useful in allaying some legislators' fears about making divorce too easy, but have played little role in practice. Many have now been repealed.

As a practical matter, the federal system in the United States makes it difficult for any one state to maintain for long a system of divorce which is much stricter than that in other states. Although it is not as easy for a couple to get divorced in another state as it is to cross state lines to get married, migratory divorce is always a possibility. Thus, such provisions as a hardship clause or a bar on divorce in the first three years of marriage would be extremely hard to enforce under American conditions. The divorce statutes of many states attempt to make sure that a divorce is not granted until financial and custody issues have been arranged and approved by the court, but this type of provision is not always workable. Even if judges were willing to take the time to carefully inquire into such arrangements, there are some interstate cases where the court dissolving the marriage does not even have jurisdiction over the couple's property or children.

On the surface, the American no-fault statutes appear to involve the state in marriage termination to a greater degree than the 1973 Swedish divorce law does. A reason (breakdown of the marriage) must be given, and a court must certify that the reason exists. But in practice these differences evaporate. The fact of the matter is that there are ways in which American law has taken the idea of individual freedom to terminate a marriage even further than has Sweden. The United States Supreme Court has obliquely hinted at the notion of a constitutional right to divorce, holding in *Boddie v. Connecticut* that welfare recipients cannot be denied access to divorce courts because of their inability to pay court fees and costs.[172] And in *Zablocki v. Redhail*, the Court came close to establishing a constitutional right to marry as many spouses in succession as one wishes.[173] More importantly, as we shall see in the following chapter, divorce has become financially easier (for the economically stronger spouse) in the United States than in most other countries because of the relatively less rigorous American system for assuring that a former provider will continue to shoulder substantial economic responsibility for dependents.

171. *E.g.*, UMDA §§302 and 305.   172. 401 U.S. 371 (1971).
173. 434 U.S. 374 (1978).

Free Terminability as an Attribute of Marriage

The redefinition of marriage from a relationship that could be legally terminated only for grave reasons, if at all, to one which is increasingly terminable upon the request of either party did not take place overnight in Western nations. In fact, the revolution in divorce law was already under way well before legislatures began to change the law on the books. In many countries, mutual-consent divorce through collusion had been judicially tolerated for years, and fault grounds had been expanded by judicial interpretation, chiefly by reading *cruelty* to include mental cruelty. Furthermore, not all divorce legislation prior to the wave of changes in the 1970s was exclusively fault-based. Though mutual-consent divorce was rather promptly expunged from the Code Napoleon, it was retained in the version of that Code that had been received in Belgium and Luxembourg. The nonfault ground of insanity was long recognized as a basis for divorce in several countries and in some of the United States. Australia and a few American states even permitted divorce after a period of separation or on grounds of incompatibility, as well as on fault grounds. Germany from 1938 on, and Sweden since 1915, had permitted divorce on the ground that the marriage had "broken down" in addition to fault grounds. But in general, for one spouse to get a divorce when the other was unwilling and had committed no marital offense (in the technical sense of the divorce laws) was difficult and time-consuming, even where legally permitted. When the spouses had reached agreement, as they eventually did in all but a small percentage of cases, fault grounds everywhere were the express route to divorce.

By the 1960s, consent divorce disguised as fault divorce was a routine legal procedure in many countries, and divorce had become a relatively common way of terminating a marriage. It was at about this time that dissatisfaction began to appear in some quarters with the fact that the legal system required an "innocent" spouse to prove that the other spouse had committed one of the marital offenses listed in the statutes—typically, cruelty, adultery, or desertion. The major criticisms leveled at the fault system were that it tended to aggravate and perpetuate bitterness between the spouses and that the widespread practice of using perjured testimony in collusive divorces promoted disrespect for the legal system. It was argued that no social interest was served by forbidding the legal termination of a dead marriage and the remarriage of the parties to others. Reformers suggested too that divorce could play a positive role—in terminating conflict and regularizing *de facto* family situations.

The next step in the modernization of divorce was taken by legislatures. When California became the first Western jurisdiction completely to eliminate fault grounds for divorce, the move was thought by some to prefigure the direction of reforms in other places. But it soon became clear that this purist approach would not be politically viable in most jurisdictions. The majority of countries, like England and France, chose instead to modernize their systems simply by adding nonfault grounds to the traditional grounds. Typically, the breakdown or separation grounds in these compromise statutes are hedged in by various safeguards for dependents and by waiting periods, ranging in length from a few months in some American states to several years in many European countries. Several countries have granted courts the power to deny a unilateral nonfault divorce altogether if legal dissolution of the marriage would involve exceptional unfairness or hardship for the nonconsenting spouse.

Among the countries whose law we have examined here, Sweden, West Germany, and nineteen American jurisdictions have eliminated fault as a basis for divorce. As we have seen, however, the abolition of fault in West Germany is less than complete and, in principle, a three-year period of separation is required before a spouse wishing to terminate a marriage against the will of the other can benefit from a presumption that the marriage has broken down. Even then, a divorce may, in theory, be denied. Thus Sweden and the forty-one American jurisdictions where the breakdown ground is available to either spouse within a year or less have gone furthest toward making marriage a relationship freely terminable at the will of one spouse.

In practice, there is one great similarity among the divorce laws of the five countries discussed here. Under all of these laws, divorce is readily available when the spouses reach an agreement on all issues, as they eventually do everywhere in the great majority of cases. But differences among the various sets of divorce grounds affect even those cases that are ultimately settled out of court. The laws differ from country to country in the amount of leverage they afford to one or the other spouse in making an advantageous settlement, in the degree of control the judge is required or permitted to exert over the terms of divorce, and in the messages they communicate about marriage itself and the rights and duties of husbands and wives. The hardship clauses, for example, in the English, French, and West German statutes rule out the notion that divorce can be viewed there in some sense as an individual's "right." This is strongly reinforced by the long separation periods required—five, six, and three years—before an unwilling and legally "innocent" spouse loses his or her right to effectively contest a divorce in those countries. Long waiting periods are often combined with other legal provisions which, as we will see in the following chapter, can aid a reluctant spouse in extracting better economic terms in exchange for agreement to a quicker divorce. In any event, a legal system that requires a spouse to wait for several years to divorce a nonconsenting husband or wife is obviously promoting a different ideology of marriage from that fostered in a country where a divorce is available on one party's demand in a year or less.

Given these differing legal approaches to divorce, one might wonder whether there is any correlation between them and the incidence of divorce in a given country. TABLE 4.1 shows the evolution of divorce rates in the five countries with which we are here concerned from 1920 to 1984. It will be noted that divorce rates had begun rising before the liberalized laws went into effect in the 1970s. Beginning in the late 1960s, the rates climbed rather steeply until the 1980s, when they seem to have stabilized at relatively high levels. Rates in the United States have consistently been higher than in the other countries treated here. The relatively low Swedish rate must be understood in a social context in which much marriage (and therefore divorce) behavior is informal and therefore not reflected in the rates.

Table 4.1 Divorce Rates, 1920–1985

	1920–24	1930–34	1940	1950	1960	1970	1975	1980	1985
England & Wales	0.07	0.1	0.18	0.7	0.51	1.17	2.43	3.01	3.20
France	0.67	0.51	0.28	0.84	0.61	0.79	1.27	1.59	1.95
Germany	0.59	0.67	0.75	—	—	—	—	—	—
West Germany	—	—	—	1.57	0.83	1.24	1.73	1.56	2.10
Sweden	0.25	0.40	0.55	1.14	1.20	1.61	3.14	2.41	2.37
United States	1.48	1.47	2.00	2.55	2.18	3.51	4.82	5.19	4.96

Rates per 1,000 mid-year population; final civil divorce decrees granted.
Source: United Nations Demographic Yearbooks 1953, 1962, 1968, 1972, 1980, 1986
(New York: United Nations).

The sharp rise in divorce rates over the past two decades has been widely perceived as cause for concern. At the same time, however, it is almost universally accepted that divorce is better understood as a symptom than as a cause of marriage breakdown. If marriage stability rather than divorce is a problem in modern society, it seems to follow that public concern should be with marriage breakdown and its causes rather than divorce as such.[174] The search for causes of marriage breakdown, however, seems to lead down a blind alley. One can, of course, identify a group of social factors characteristically found present in societies where marriage breakdown is common. Such factors turn out, however, to be mainly matters over which law has little or no control, or as to which most persons would not want to see legal control: life styles in which work, home, and leisure are separate, and family members spend large parts of their day apart; improved educational and employment opportunities for women; family pressure; age at marriage; longer life expectancies and the consequent longer duration of marriages; chronic unemployment; separations such as those caused by military service; availability of social assistance; and other well-known aspects of

174. *Rheinstein* 247–307. See also *König* pars. 98, 101.

modernization.[175] Yet, one cannot entirely discount the possibility that legal changes facilitating divorce may themselves have contributed to some extent to a "cognitive restructuring" of the idea of marriage.[176]

It helps to gain some perspective on high modern rates of divorce if we recall that men and women today live much longer on the average than they did in former times. Recent work of social historians indicates, for example, that from the sixteenth to the nineteenth century, marriages were dissolved by death about as often as they now are by divorce, and that remarriage was about as common as it is today.[177] Lawrence Stone has pointed out that in early modern England, nearly a third of all marriages lasted less than fifteen years before one partner died, and that death rates among the peasantry in France were even higher.[178] This leads, according to Stone, to "one very firm conclusion about the premodern family, namely that it was, statistically speaking, a transient and temporary association, both of husband and wife and of parents and children." [179] Stone believes that English marriages must have lasted longest in Victorian times, before declining mortality was offset by rising divorce rates.[180]

Thus it is not the perishability of marriage (or even the frequency of remarriage) that is modern, but the role that individual choice now plays in both the formation and the dissolution of marriage. This expanded role for choice was in turn made possible by the declining role played by marriage and the family as determinants of an individual's economic security and social standing.[181] Marriage law has moved from a situation once characterized by a family or parental role in the selection of a spouse, to the gradual introduction of a veto by the child, then to choice of one's own spouse limited by the retention of a parental veto, then to unfettered choice, and now finally to a situation where people may and often do try to "correct" their original choices. The fact that marriage in itself is no longer so important as a determinant of wealth, rank, and status has made it easy for "freedom to marry" to be established as a

175. *König* 67–8.

176. *Commaille* 233–37.

177. Micheline Baulant, "The Scattered Family: Another Aspect of Seventeenth Century Demography," in *Family and Society*, ed. Robert Forster and Orest Ranum (Baltimore: Johns Hopkins University Press, 1976), 104, 105; Natalie Zemon Davis, "Ghosts, Kin, and Progeny: Some Features of Family Life in Early Modern France," 105 *Daedalus* 87–114 (1977); *Stone* 54–60.

178. *Id.* at 56.

179. *Id.* at 55.

180. *Id.* at 56.

181. See, generally, Mary Ann Glendon, *The New Family and the New Property* (Toronto: Butterworths, 1981).

fundamental legal principle and has likewise facilitated the free terminability of marriage.

As free exit becomes established as an attribute of marriage, either in fact or in law, it inevitably interacts with the increasing freedom of entry we observed in chapter 2, and the increasing withdrawal of regulation of the ongoing marriage that was traced in chapter 3. The trends react upon and reinforce each other. When marriage relations became less important economically, and when mate selection began to be left up to the man and woman involved, relations within the conjugal family became simultaneously closer and more unstable. Paradoxically, what Lawrence Stone has called the "intensely self-centered, inwardly turned, emotionally bonded, sexually liberated, child-oriented" family of the late twentieth century exists under conditions which are also conducive to the relatively easy detachment of family members from the home and from each other.[182]

The same factors that facilitate free terminability of marriage in practice have contributed to the decline of legal regulation of divorce. It is not unusual, even in societies where legal divorce is unknown, for termination of the married state to be marked by a rite of some sort. But the complexity of divorce rituals usually bears a direct relationship to the elaborateness of the marriage rite.[183] Thus, where the marriage rite is attended with great pomp and ceremony, the chances are that the reverse rite, divorce, will be also. Our analysis of the corresponding legal developments seems to bear this out. In chapter 2 we saw a steady movement toward reducing legal regulation, especially the compulsory ceremonial aspects, of the formation of marriage. Now we have seen that modern divorce proceedings often do not resemble a regular lawsuit so much as what would appear to an anthropologist to be a ritual change of status, unless the circumstances of the couple require their economic affairs to be disentangled.

Why are marriage and divorce ceremonies more elaborate in some times and places and simpler in others? René König tells us that in societies where families have a high degree of involvement in, and control of, marriage formation, a spouse or a couple wishing to terminate the marriage is usually expected to produce arguments and reasons, presumably in order to neutralize objections from the interested relatives.[184] He also notes that emphasis on property exchange before a marriage and on property relations during marriage is characteristically associated with elaborate procedures for undoing

182. *Stone* 682.
183. *König* 58–59.
184. *König* 59–60. See, for contemporary examples, Jessep and Luluaki, above, note 1 at 54–56.

such arrangements.[185] Thus we should not be astonished to find that under modern conditions, legal attention has been redirected from the termination of the marriage bond as such to the winding up of the spouse's economic affairs and to the welfare of any children they may have. Deregulation of marriage has not been accompanied by a withdrawal of state involvement in the economic and child-related aspects of marriage dissolution. The issues of property division, support, and custody are the most controversial ones in family law today, and it is to them we now turn.

185. *König* 59–62.

5
The Legal Effects of Marriage Termination

Marriage Termination by Divorce

Although the developments described in the preceding chapters can be seen as moving toward the withering away of marriage as a legal institution, this in no way implies the withering away of the state's involvement in family life. This becomes plain when we turn our attention to the economic and child-related consequences of marriage dissolution. In most countries, official interest in these areas is greater than ever, but it is being manifested in new ways.

Legal retrenchment in the areas of marriage and divorce has exposed several problems of family policy which are serious, controversial, and unresolved. Accordingly, the move toward free terminability of marriage has everywhere been accompanied by revision of the laws governing the effects of divorce. But no country has achieved a satisfactory resolution of the interrelated problems of spousal and child support, property division, and child custody. Perhaps no such resolution is possible in societies where serial family formation is common among persons of modest means. As we shall see, however, some countries seem to have done better than others, at least in alleviating the financial difficulties of female-headed one-parent households.

As we begin to consider the different ways in which five legal systems handle the effects of divorce, it is well to keep in mind that a number of theoretically distinct problems are closely intertwined in practice in this area. Although lawyers habitually distinguish for analytical purposes among divorce as such, spousal support, custody, child support, and property division, issues in these areas are inseparable from each other in real lawsuits. For example, as we have already noticed in chapter 4, to the extent that one spouse or the judge has the power to delay or even occasionally prevent a divorce until the desired financial or child custody arrangements are agreed to, one cannot say that the divorce itself is separate and distinct from the consequences of divorce. Furthermore, while the question of whether and how continuing support arrangements after divorce should be made is conceptually different from the problem of how the property of the spouses should be allocated, the two issues are often collapsed together in the law (as in England and many American states) or in practice. Similarly, while the basis of spousal support is analytically (and morally) distinct from that of child support, the two must nearly always be treated together in cases where young children are present, because support of a child frequently involves custodial care, and the custodian is typically one of the ex-spouses. Sometimes the distinction between spousal support and child support is deliberately effaced, as when child support is labeled as spousal support or vice versa, in order to gain more favorable tax treatment. Thus, in the discussion that follows, we will present an overview of each country's "package" of laws dealing with the economic and child-related consequences of divorce. But we must also attend to the formal distinctions made among spousal support, marital property division, and child support, because it is often here, at the level of the principles announced (if not implemented) in the law, that changes have occurred with far-reaching implications for the bargaining process through which the overwhelming majority of divorces are arranged. Finally, it is important to bear in mind that each country's support and property-division law exists in a complex relationship with that country's social-assistance law.

As with other areas of family law we have examined, it is useful to begin by briefly considering how turn-of-the-century legal systems approached the aftermath of what was then a relatively uncommon event—divorce. The spouses' property, in traditional legal systems, was divided according to ownership; that is, by restoring to each partner his or her own property in separate property systems, and by dividing the common assets equally in community systems. Marital misconduct was irrelevant to this process, but it was crucial for determining whether a husband could be ordered to make alimony payments after divorce. The legal treatment of spousal support everywhere generally followed the lines that had been laid down for it in the immediate ancestor of secular divorce: ecclesiastical separation from bed and board. A legally innocent ex-wife was entitled in principle to continuing maintenance from her legally guilty ex-husband. Custody of minor children, which had belonged to fathers so long as children were perceived as economic assets, had already begun to be regularly given to mothers by the early twentieth century, and child support to be awarded for their basic needs.

As divorce became more frequent, dissatisfaction with this traditional pattern mounted. At the level of principle, the emphasis on technical fault in support law and on ownership in marital property law was thought to neglect issues of need and dependency. Furthermore, in practice, spousal and child support were often insufficient and precarious. All the traditional systems had in common with each other (and with modern systems) a basic reliance on private agreement as the principal mechanism for adjusting economic and child-related disputes upon divorce, and to a great extent, these agreements were unsupervised by courts. Thus, weaker parties were protected, if at all, mainly by the leverage afforded to an "innocent" spouse by the possibility of withholding consent to a fault divorce until appropriate financial arrangements were made. (An economically weaker party who could be shown to have committed marital fault, or who simply wanted to divorce a legally innocent partner, was, of course, in a poor position indeed.) Starting in the late 1960s, as fault began to be eliminated or downplayed in divorce law, the need for change began to seem acute. Once the process of reexamining the law in this area began, the new postulates of sex equality seemed to require the elimination of old, gender-based support rules where they still existed. Of the countries whose law is examined here, England was the first to try to adapt marital property and support law to a new system of divorce law.

England

The entry into effect of the English Divorce Reform Act of 1969 was postponed for two years so that a new system for regulating the economic effects of divorce could be prepared to accompany it. This new system, as worked out in the Matrimonial Proceedings and Property Act of 1970, came into force with the Divorce Reform Act in 1971.[1] The Matrimonial Proceedings and Property Act of 1970 sounded the death knell for the old marital property system of separation of assets, so far as divorce was concerned. Instead of trying to ascertain and restore to each spouse what was his or hers, English courts were authorized, after 1971, to order one spouse to make "financial provision" for the other by way of periodical payments, a lump sum, a transfer or settlement of property, or various combinations of these devices. In this new system, title to assets could be disregarded, as could the distinction between support and property division. Courts were directed simply to decide whether to order "financial provision" and were given great discretion as to how it should be paid and in what amounts.

Until the act was amended in 1984, the courts were supposed to exercise their discretion in such a way

> as to place the parties, so far as it is practicable and, having regard to their conduct, just to do so, in the financial position in which they would have been if the marriage had not broken down and each had properly discharged his or her financial obligations and responsibilities towards the other.[2]

1. The two statutes are now consolidated in the Matrimonial Causes Act 1973, as amended in 1984.
2. Matrimonial Causes Act 1973, former s. 25.

To guide the court in carrying out this direction, the statute provided that the following factors relating to the needs and resources of the spouses should be taken into consideration: the present and probable future financial situation of the spouses; their financial needs and obligations; their standard of living during the marriage; their ages; their mental and physical health; the duration of the marriage; and the loss of marriage-related benefits (such as pensions) in the future. The contributions of the spouses to the marriage were to be taken into account at this time, and the statute expressly stated that these contributions included housework as well as financial payments.[3]

Because of the broad discretion and flexible powers this statute and its amended version have conferred on the courts, English spouses can anticipate that upon the termination of their marriage by divorce, a court ordinarily will effect some kind of redistribution of their property. But beyond this, predictability is not one of the chief features of such a system. As Lord Denning has described its operation, the decision-maker

> takes the rights and obligations of the parties all together and puts the pieces into a mixed bag. Such pieces are the right to occupy the matrimonial home or have a share in it, the obligation to maintain the wife and children, and so forth. The court then takes out the pieces and hands them to the two parties—some to one party and some to the other—so that each can provide for the future with the pieces allotted to him or to her. The court hands them out without paying any too nice a regard to their legal or equitable rights but simply according to what is the fairest provision for the future, for mother and father and the children.[4]

Palm-tree justice along these lines is administered by the matrimonial registrars, court officials who examine the evidence in contested cases and make awards, subject to the right of appeal to a judge.[5] As a body of decisions in appellate cases accumulated over the years, it became apparent that certain rules of thumb were being developed by the courts. These clues from the case law enabled solicitors to give their clients some idea of what to expect if a given case had to be decided by adjudication rather than through negotiation.[6] One thing became clear early on: the original statutory direction to restore divorcing spouses to the position they would have occupied if there had been no breakdown of the marriage was wholly unrealistic in all but the rare case.[7] Similarly, the hopes of Parliament and the Law Commission that financial

3. Matrimonial Causes Act 1973, s. 25.
4. *Hanlon v. The Law Society*, [1981] A.C. 124, 146.
5. *Cretney* 179.
6. *Cretney* 827–51.
7. *Cretney* 761.

provision could often be made in the form of a lump-sum payment proved impossible to realize in most situations.

Variations among registrars[8]—and the wild-card conduct factor in section 25—render the outcome of contested divorce cases in England unpredictable to a degree that continental observers find surprising.[9] Even though one can expect in a general way that a court will order some combination of property transfer and periodic maintenance, and will try to give possession of the marital home to a custodial parent,[10] the precise status of the couple's property and the amount of support that will be awarded are in doubt until a decree is issued.[11] The ideal of individualized justice (which is the main justification for a system of broad discretion) seems impossible to achieve, while the degree of uncertainty the system entails seems unnecessarily high.

In an effort to prevent the conduct factor from getting out of hand, Lord Denning recommended in a 1973 case that marital misconduct should not be held to justify reduction of financial provision, unless it was "both obvious and gross," as distinct from "what was formerly regarded as guilt or blame."[12] But judges will differ even as to what is obvious and gross, or—as the statute now puts it—what is so "inequitable" that it should not be disregarded. A hearing on financial provision can thus come to resemble a postmortem examinaton of the parties' marriage. The English system contrasts in this respect with most community property systems, where as we shall see, the common fund is equally divided, irrespective of the marital (as distinct from economic) misconduct of the parties. In such systems, conduct is treated as relevant, if at all, only in deciding questions of maintenance and fitness for custody.

By the 1980s, "serious and sustained criticism" of the 1970 act prompted the Law Commission to take another look at financial provision on divorce.[13] Some of this criticism concerned the law's potential for arbitrariness and raised the question whether it adequately protected custodial parents and chil-

8. These are documented in the empirical study by W. Barrington Baker, John Eekelaar, Colin Gibson, and Susan Raikes, *The Matrimonial Jurisdiction of Registrars* (Oxford: Centre for Socio-Legal Studies, 1977).

9. See the comments of Jacques-Michel Grossen, "Comparative Developments in the Law of Matrimonial Regimes," 60 *Tulane Law Review* 1199, 1205 (1986).

10. *Cretney* 751–52.

11. For trenchant criticism, see Ruth Deech, "Financial Relief: The Retreat from Precedent and Principle," 98 *Law Quarterly Review* 621 (1982).

12. *Wachtel v. Wachtel*, [1973] Fam. 72, 90.

13. Law Commission, *The Financial Consequences of Divorce: The Basic Policy: A Discussion Paper*, Law Com. No. 103 (London: Her Majesty's Stationery Office, 1980), and *The Financial Consequences of Divorce. The Response to the Law Commission's Discussion Paper, and Recommendations on the Policy of the Law*, Law Com. No. 112, (London: Her Majesty's Stationery Office, 1981).

dren. But most of the complaints involved what many regarded as an implicit assumption that a husband should continue to support his wife after divorce.[14] In 1984, acting on the recommendation of the Law Commission, Parliament made one important, and several minor, changes in the act. Stephen Cretney (who was the member of the Law Commission primarily responsible for family law from 1978 to 1983) has written that the 1984 amendments were not meant to bring about a radical restructuring of financial provision law, but rather to effect a certain shift of emphasis.[15]

The main change made in 1984 was at the level of principle. The direction to try to place the parties in the positions they would have been in had the marriage not broken down was removed. In its place, the new principle was laid down that the courts were to give "first consideration" to the welfare of any minor children in making financial arrangements:

> s. 25. (1) It shall be the duty of the court in deciding whether to exercise its powers . . . and, if so, in what manner, to have regard to all the circumstances of the case, first consideration being given to the welfare while a minor of any child of the family who has not attained the age of eighteen.

Parliament then took account of some of the criticisms that had been made by ex-husbands and second wives, adding several new provisions directing the court to consider making awards in such a way as to recognize and promote the potential of both spouses for independence and self-sufficiency. These provisions appear in section 25(2)(a) on earning capacity and in a new section 25A. The rest of section 25, as amended, now reads in relevant part:

> s. 25 [continued]
> (2) As regards the exercise of the powers of the court . . . in relation to a party to the marriage, the court shall in particular have regard to the following matters—
> (a) the income, earning capacity, property and other financial resources which each of the parties to the marriage has or is likely to have in the foreseeable future, including in the case of earning capacity any increase in that capacity which it would in the opinion of the court be reasonable to expect a party to the marriage to take steps to acquire;
> (b) the financial needs, obligations and responsibilities which each of the parties to the marriage has or is likely to have in the foreseeable future;

14. *Cretney* 762–64. According to Law Commissioner Brenda Hoggett, an organization of divorced husbands and second wives (The Campaign for Justice in Divorce) was "largely responsible for building up the pressure for reform." "Recent Reforms in Family Law: Progress or Backlash?" 11 *Dalhousie Law Journal* 5, 17 (1987).

15. *Cretney* 757.

(c) the standard of living enjoyed by the family before the break-down of the marriage;

(d) the age of each party to the marriage and the duration of the marriage;

(e) any physical or mental disability of either of the parties to the marriage;

(f) the contributions which each of the parties has made or is likely in the foreseeable future to make to the welfare of the family, including any contribution by looking after the home or caring for the family;

(g) the conduct of each of the parties, if that conduct is such that it would in the opinion of the court be inequitable to disregard it;

(h) in the case of proceedings for divorce or nullity of marriage, the value to each of the parties to the marriage of any benefit (for example, a pension) which, by reason of the dissolution or annulment of the marriage, that party will lose the chance of acquiring.

(3) As regards the exercise of the powers of the court . . . in relation to a child of the family, the court shall in particular have regard to the following matters—

(a) the financial needs of the child;

(b) the income, earning capacity (if any), property and other financial resources of the child;

(c) any physical or mental disability of the child;

(d) the manner in which he was being and in which the parties to the marriage expected him to be educated or trained;

(e) the considerations mentioned in relation to the parties to the marriage in paragraphs (a), (b), (c) and (e) of subsection (2) above. [Subsection (4) on support of children who are not the children of both spouses is omitted].

New section 25A specifies how the policies of promoting a "clean break" and spousal self-sufficiency may be implemented by making orders of limited duration, or even by dismissing support petitions, where this is not inconsistent with the direction in section 25(1) to consider first the interests of children:

25A. (1) Where on or after the grant of a decree of divorce or nullity of marriage the court decides to exercise its powers . . . in favour of a party to the marriage, it shall be the duty of the court to consider whether it would be appropriate so to exercise those powers that the financial obligations of each party towards the other will be terminated as soon after the grant of the decree as the court considers just and reasonable.

(2) Where the court decides in such a case to make a periodical payments or secured periodical payments order in favour of a party to the marriage, the court shall in particular consider whether it

would be appropriate to require those payments to be made or secured only for such term as would in the opinion of the court be
sufficient to enable the party in whose favour the order is made to
adjust without undue hardship to the termination of his or her financial dependence on the other party.

(3) Where on or after the grant of a decree of divorce or nullity of
marriage an application is made by a party to the marriage for a
periodical payments or secured periodical payments order in his or
her favour, then, if the court considers that no continuing obligation
should be imposed on either party to make or secure periodical payments in favour of the other, the court may dismiss the application
with a direction that the applicant shall not be entitled to make any
further application.

The 1984 changes, with the exception of the new requirement of first consideration for children, did not represent major departures from the prior law.
It will be noted, for example, that although the idea of trying to restore the
status quo ante has been abandoned, "the standard of living enjoyed by the
family before the breakdown of the marriage" is still a factor to be weighed
in determining what is appropriate financial provision under section 25(2)(c).
The conduct factor was retained but recast in section 25(2)(g) to provide that
conduct should be treated as relevant, but only where it is of such a nature
that it would be "inequitable" to ignore it. Meanwhile, however, English
courts seem to be increasingly willing to investigate the conduct of both parties in some detail in order to determine whether or not it would be inequitable
to disregard their behavior.[16] New section 25A is very cautious in the degree
to which it promotes the idea of a "clean break" and is of limited practical
importance in view of the relative infrequency of spousal support orders.[17]
Even after the 1984 amendments, it seems that English law still implicitly
presumes a continuing obligation of support after divorce, unlike many other
countries which have embraced the principle of self-sufficiency as their starting point. Still, as Law Commissioner Brenda Hoggett observed, the old direction to try to restore the parties to the position that they would have been
in had the marriage not broken down did at least encourage fair sharing of
marital property, and its withdrawal leaves the statute without any general
standard for doing justice between the spouses.[18]

The new statutory emphasis on the interests of children has the potential to
bring about major changes in practice, but whether it will do so in fact re-

16. E.g., *Leadbeater v. Leadbeater*, [1985] F.L.R. 789.

17. John Eekelaar and Mavis Maclean, *Maintenance after Divorce* (Oxford: Clarendon Press,
1986), 90–102.

18. Brenda Hoggett, above, note 14 at 19.

mains to be seen. In a sense, Parliament has only recognized, belatedly, the position advanced by the Archbishop of Canterbury's Group in 1966:

> The needs of any children of a marriage to be dissolved should as a rule be made first charge on all available assets, with the object of enabling them to be brought up with as nearly as possible the same standard of opportunity as they would have enjoyed had the marriage not failed. To that end, it would in some circumstances be necessary to award a spouse, *qua* guardian of children, a level of maintenance that would not otherwise be due; for provision for children should always include suitable provision for the person given the care of them.[19]

Increasingly, legal scholars, too, have been advocating a nuanced and differentiated approach to financial provision on divorce, with a special set of principles and rules for cases involving minor children.[20] Such cases, in England as in most countries, constitute the majority of divorces,[21] and in England as elsewhere, although custody, under the standard of the general welfare of the child, may be awarded to either parent, to both jointly, or to a third party,[22] mothers are the custodial parents in the vast majority of cases.[23]

To some extent, English courts in cases involving minor children had already been according primary importance to the needs of the children, especially where the matrimonial home was concerned.[24] The 1984 amendments, however, were meant not only to ratify and encourage this trend but also to ensure adequate recognition of the custodial parent's role and to endeavor to make payment of financial provision more acceptable to the noncustodial par-

19. *Putting Asunder* 73–74.

20. The argument that the law should distinguish between the economic effects of divorces of couples where children are present (or have been raised) and other types of divorce has been made frequently by John Eekelaar, most recently in John Eekelaar and Mavis Maclean, above, note 17 at 141–49. See also, Mary Ann Glendon, "Property Rights upon Dissolution of Marriages and Informal Unions," in *The Cambridge Lectures: 1981*, ed. Nancy Eastham and Boris Krivy (Toronto: Butterworths, 1983), 245, 253; "Fixed Rules and Discretion in Contemporary Family Law and Succession Law," 60 *Tulane Law Review* 1165 (1986); "Family Law Reform in the 1980s," 44 *Louisiana Law Review* 1553, 1560 (1984).

21. In England, nearly 60 percent of divorces occur in families with children under sixteen. Susan Maidment, "Family Law Practitioner," 135 *New Law Journal* 1028 (1985).

22. Guardianship of Minors Act 1971, s.1.

23. Eekelaar and Maclean, above, note 17 at 71.

24. Jacqueline Priest, "The Matrimonial and Family Proceedings Act 1984: A Guide," 15 *Family Law* 8, 9 (1985); John Eekelaar, "Some Principles of Financial and Property Adjustment on Divorce," 95 *Law Quarterly Review* 253 (1979); Eekelaar and Maclean, above, note 17 at 105. For the various ways in which the courts exercise their powers to award the use of the matrimonial home to the custodial spouse while preserving fairness between the spouses, see *Cretney* 838–841.

ent.[25] Whether the new attention to children's interests will make a significant difference in the financial well-being of female-headed families will depend, in large part, on whether courts will begin to make awards that reflect the actual costs of maintaining children, which, it seems, have often been underestimated.[26]

From a comparative perspective, what is most striking about the overall English approach to financial provision on divorce is its heavy reliance on judicial (registrars') discretion. Even if one can assume that the decision makers who hold such extensive powers over the economic relations among family members are men and women of competence and integrity, a discretionary distribution scheme does very little to facilitate the negotiating process through which most divorces are in fact fought out and eventually settled.

With respect to the all-important question of how English financial provision law works out in practice, the studies so far yield a rather bleak picture of the circumstances of one-parent families headed by divorced mothers. The ongoing research of John Eekelaar and Mavis Maclean at Oxford has documented a general movement into poverty by custodial mothers and their children. Four out of five such families in their sample were below the poverty line and fewer than one in ten enjoyed an average standard of living.[27] The average income of a divorced parent caring for children was considerably lower than that of the parent without children in his household.[28] Eekelaar and Maclean have pointed out that until the 1984 amendments, child support was envisioned legally and in practice as merely something to be "tacked on" to other financial arrangements between the spouses,[29] and that its amount usually bore little relation to the resources actually required by a child.[30] If one is optimistic, one may hope that the statutory shift in emphasis in 1984 may alter both of these practices. One hopeful sign is the 1985 report of the Matrimonial Causes Procedure Committee. If the Committee's proposals are eventually adopted, the statutory policy of focusing attention on the interests of children will be reinforced. The changes proposed by the Committee would require an expedited hearing in such cases and would subject them to a more

25. *Cretney* 810.
26. *Id.* at 818–20.
27. Eekelaar and Maclean, above, note 17 at 71–72.
28. *Id.* at 102.
29. John Eekelaar and Mavis Maclean, "The Evolution of Private Law Maintenance Obligations: The Common Law," (Paper delivered at the Fifth World Congress of the International Society on Family Law, 8–14 July, 1985, Brussels, Belgium).
30. The Eekelaar-Maclean study found that child support typically represented a small percentage of fathers' incomes, exceeding 10 percent in only a third of the cases studied. Eekelaar and Maclean, above, note 17 at 102.

elaborate screening process.[31] This could have the practical result that divorce decrees would not be given, even when the spouses were in agreement, until a registrar found that suitable finanical arrangements for their children had been made.[32]

As of 1988, however, there was some reason to doubt whether the courts would give full scope to the potentially transformative statutory direction to consider children's interests first. The language of the 1984 amendments could be interpreted to require that all support and property issues be arranged so as to provide the best possible outcome for any children involved, giving the interests of children priority, if necessary, over those of the parents. The Court of Appeal, however, stated in 1987 that if the statutory language *first consideration* had been intended to mean that children's interests were "paramount," or that they should have priority over "all other considerations pointing to a just result, Parliament would have said so."[33] The court continued:

> It has not. So I construe the section [as] requiring the court to consider all the circumstances . . . always bearing in mind the important consideration of the welfare of the children, and then to try to attain a financial result which is just as between husband and wife.[34]

Even if this less than whole-hearted endorsement of the children-first principle does not represent the last word on the judicial fate of the 1984 reforms, the principle will not automatically improve the situations of one-parent families. Eekelaar and Maclean have raised the hard questions that would remain even if judicial practices changed: Will noncustodial parents really comply with child-support orders promptly and fully—as Parliament and the Law Commission hoped—if and when those orders begin to reflect the real cost of maintaining the child at a level that bears a reasonable relation to the prior living standard of the family and the present circumstances of the ex-spouses?[35] If not, what steps will Parliament take next?

France

An unusual feature of the 1975 French Divorce Reform Law, with its varied menu of divorce grounds, is that it establishes different systems of economic consequences for different categories of divorces. But the reform left marital

31. John Eekelaar, "Divorce English Style—A New Way Forward?" 1986 *Journal of Social Welfare Law* 226, 235.

32. *Id.* at 230.

33. *Suter v. Suter and Jones*, [1987] 2 All E. R. 336, 342.

34. *Id.*

35. Eekelaar and Maclean, above, note 29.

property law basically unaffected. Except in the case of divorce on joint petition, the parties need not even wind up their matrimonial property regime
before their marriage terminates. When they do liquidate the regime, of
course, any assets acquired by gainful activity during the marriage will normally be divided equally between husband and wife, unless they have made
some other arrangement by marital contract or divorce settlement. The role
of divorce law is thus confined to determining whether and how economic
transfers besides the division of marital property should be made from one
ex-spouse to the other.

Under the former law, where divorce was exclusively fault-based, spousal
maintenance was available only to the "innocent" spouse who obtained the
divorce. This approach has now been abandoned in favor of a new set of
principles. Except for the special case of divorce for disruption of the life
in common, the purpose of the 1975 law, so far as the economic effects of
divorce are concerned, is said to be to try to minimize "après-divorce"
contact and conflict between the ex-spouses.[36] To this end, the starting
point announced in Civil Code article 270 is that in principle, "divorce
puts an end to the duty of support." The economic effects, if any, are
to be regulated by a new technique called the "compensatory payment."[37]
But the basic mechanism for adjusting post-divorce financial matters, in
the French as in the other systems examined here, is now (as it was in
the past) the parties' own agreement. In France, however, the judge's role
in approving such agreements is not perfunctory. The views of a judge
expressed at the outset of a case can play a significant role in shaping the
agreement, and as a rule, he or she spends a good deal of time in the final
interview with the parties and their counsel. One French judge has remarked that "the spouses are very often astonished at the interference by
the magistrate in the arrangements they have made between themselves."[38]
Nor will the judge be superficially informed about the case. The applicable
provisions of the Code of Civil Procedure require that the spouses make
available to the court in advance specified information concerning their financial circumstances, including (since 1984) their tax returns for the preceding few years.[39]

    36. Jean Carbonnier, "La question du divorce—mémoire à consulter," D. 1975, Chr.
115, 118.
    37. See below, text at note 43.
    38. Yvonne Jougla, "Le point de vue du juge," in *Le régime matrimonial à l'épreuve du
temps et des séparations conjugales*, ed. Jacques Foyer and Catherine Labrusse-Riou (Paris:
Economica, 1986), 113, 115.
    39. French Code of Civil Procedure, art. 1075, as amended by decree of 13 July 1984.

Divorce on Joint Petition

The submission of an agreement on the effects of divorce is expressly required by the provisions of the 1975 law governing the economic consequences of the form of divorce which was meant to be preferred: divorce by mutual consent on joint petition of the spouses. Just as the divorce itself is grounded in an agreement approved by the judge, so are its economic effects. Recall from the preceding chapter that the judge can refuse approval and thus delay the divorce if he or she finds that the agreement does not adequately protect the interests of either spouse or the children. The sections on the economic effects of divorce on joint petition repeat this idea in more precise terms:

> Art. 278. In the case of joint petition, the spouses are to fix the amount and the details of the compensatory payment[40] in the agreement which they submit for the approval of the judge. The judge is invariably to refuse approval of the agreement if it allocates the rights and obligations of the spouses inequitably.
>
> Art. 279. The agreement once approved has the same executory force as a judicial decision. It can be modified only by a new agreement between the spouses which must likewise be submitted for approval. The spouses nevertheless have the option to provide in their agreement that either of them may, in the case of unforeseen change in their resources and needs, petition the judge to modify the compensatory payment.

Because divorce on joint petition is the sole form of divorce in which the spouses *must* liquidate the marital property regime at the time of divorce, and because such liquidation can be quite time-consuming, and perhaps because the judge has a good deal of power to influence the mode of division, a significant number of couples who are in agreement on divorce elect not to proceed this way.[41] The problems with leaving the marital property to be dealt with later, however, can be severe, at least for persons with significant property. It can mean that prolonged litigation on property issues may take place after divorce, or that the regime will have to be wound up under pressure when one of the ex-spouses dies or urgently needs to sell some of the community property.[42] The requirement that *all* the effects of divorce be settled at the time the divorce is granted on joint petition is thus simultaneously one of the virtues of the legislature's preferred route and one of its disadvantages.

In cases where the spouses are not able to come to agreement, or where

---

40. See below, p. 210.
41. Philippe Remy, "L'état du droit positif," above, note 38 at 123–24.
42. M. Barat, "Le point de vue du juge," above, note 38 at 147–48.

they choose some other form of divorce, or where one spouse opposes the divorce and has not been guilty of "fault," the divorce will be governed by a different set of rules from those just outlined. Depending on the circumstances, the parties may be required to pay, or may be entitled to receive, "compensatory payment," or support, or sometimes civil damages. Since spousal support is exceptional in practice, and civil damages even more so, the most important of these rules are those governing compensatory payment.

The System of Compensatory Payment

The idea of the compensatory payment (*prestation compensatoire*) is to remedy "so far as possible" the disparity which the termination of marriage may create in the respective living conditions of the spouses. Thus, in theory, it is different from support or property division. Unlike alimony under the prior law, it is not in the nature of a penalty on the person against whom the divorce was pronounced. Nor does it imply continuing economic responsibility of one spouse for another. And it is independent of the liquidation of the marital property regime. It depends on the establishment of the fact of a disparity between the situations of the ex-spouses, and its aim is to enable both of them to live under approximately equivalent material conditions.[43] The types of divorce in which the compensatory payment is called into play are the form of mutual-consent divorce in which the respondent neither cooperates with nor opposes the petitioner; divorce for shared fault; and fault divorce granted for the fault of one spouse only. In the case of fault divorce granted for the fault of one spouse only, the compensatory payment is available to the plaintiff, but not, as a rule, to the defendant, although an exception can be made if the denial of a payment in such a case would be manifestly inequitable.[44]

Compensatory payment is never mandatory. The code section which determines whether a compensatory payment is to be made provides as follows:

> Art. 270. Except where it is pronounced by reason of the disruption of the life in common, divorce puts an end to the duty of support established in Article 213 of the Civil Code; but one spouse may be required to make to the other a payment designed to compensate, so far as possible, for the disparity which the disruption of the marriage creates in the conditions of their respective lives.

43. *Bénabent* 250.

44. "Nevertheless, he [the spouse at fault] may obtain a payment in an exceptional case if, taking account of the duration of the life in common and his collaboration in the profession of the other spouse, it would appear manifestly contrary to equity to refuse him all monetary compensation following divorce." French Civil Code, art. 280–1, line 2.

The judge who decides that such a disparity exists must then determine the amount of the compensatory payment according to the following guidelines:

> Art. 271. The compensatory payment is to be fixed according to the needs of the spouse to whom it is made and the resources of the other, taking account of their situations at the time of the divorce and of developments in the foreseeable future.
>
> Art. 272. In the determination of needs and resources, the judge is to take into consideration notably:
> —the age and the state of health of the spouses;
> —the time already devoted or which they will have to devote to the upbringing of the children;
> —their professional qualifications;
> —their existing and foreseeable economic entitlements;
> —the possible loss of such entitlements in connection with terminable pensions;
> —their wealth, in income as well as capital, after the liquidation of the matrimonial regime.

Because these sections require the judge to make guesses about the future, and since the succeeding section provides that in principle the compensatory payment is unmodifiable,[45] the compensatory payment sections have been criticized for requiring judges "to foresee the impossible and yet forbidding them to make any mistakes."[46] From a comparative perspective, one can see in these sections the nascent acknowledgment in France of the ideas that the spouses (but not the children) are basically on their own after divorce, and that if, after a reasonable transition period, resources derived from an ex-spouse are insufficient, the dependent spouse must meet her needs either through her own efforts or public assistance.[47] The compensatory payment seems to be the germ, though not the full expression, of the "severance pay" idea which has become influential in Sweden, West Germany, and some of the United States, and which found a limited place in the English 1984

45. "The compensatory payment is a fixed sum by nature. It cannot be modified even in case of unforeseen change in the resources and needs of the parties, unless the absence of modification would have consequences of exceptional gravity for one of the spouses." French Civil Code, art. 273.

46. Raymond Lindon, "La nouvelle législation sur le divorce et le recouvrement public des pensions alimentaires," J.C.P. 1975. I. 2728, par. 180.

47. The draftsman clearly felt the time was not ripe to go much further: "There is no reasonable question here of that radical liberalization which would consist of treating divorce as a social risk, whose cost should be spread over the society in general. Thus the effort at liberalization today is for practical reasons confined within the boundaries of private law, which unavoidably impairs its efficacy." Carbonnier, above, note 36 at 118.

amendments. Pensions, it should be noted, are treated as one factor to be considered in determining the compensatory payment; they are not separately regulated as quasi-marital property, as in West Germany.

In keeping with the aim to minimize postdivorce conflict, the 1975 law specified not only that the compensatory payment should in principle be non-modifiable, but that it should be made in a lump sum. The rules which are to guide the judge are as follows:

Art. 274. When the assets of the spouse who owes the compensatory payment permit, the payment is to take the form of a lump sum.

Art. 275. The judge decides on the method according to which assets are allocated or charged for the lump sum:

1. Payment of a sum of money;

2. Transfer of property in kind; movables or immovables, but where usufruct only is concerned, the judgment operates as a forced assignment to the creditor-spouse;

3. Deposit of revenue-producing securities into the hands of a third party charged with the duty of paying income to the creditor-spouse for the period fixed;

The divorce decree can be made conditional on the effective payment of the lump sum or on the establishment of the guarantees provided for in Article 277.

Art. 275–1. If the debtor-spouse of the compensatory payment does not presently dispose of liquid assets, he may be authorized, subject to the guarantees provided for in Article 277, to make up the lump sum in three annual payments.

Art. 276. In the absence of a lump sum, or if the lump sum is insufficient, the compensatory payment can take the form of periodic payments.

Art. 276–1. The periodic payments are to be granted for a time equal to or less than the life of the creditor-spouse.

They are to be indexed; the index is to be determined as in the case of support payments.

The amount of the payments prior to being indexed can be made uniform for their entire duration or may vary in successive stages according to the probable evolution of needs and resources.

Art. 276–2. At the death of the debtor-spouse, the responsibility for the periodic payments passes to his heirs.

Art. 277. Independently of any statutory or court-ordered security interest, the judge may require the debtor-spouse to give a pledge or other security to guarantee the periodic payments.

Despite the clear preference of the legislature for a once-and-for-all financial settlement which would avoid postdivorce disputes and enforcement problems, lump-sum payments in practice have turned out, as in England, to be feasible only in the relatively few cases involving well-to-do individuals. The situation which the law contemplates as the exception—the compensatory payment made in periodic installments—thus has in fact turned out to be the rule in the majority of cases where the payment is allowed. Unlike spousal support under the old law, however, the compensatory payment is not granted for an indefinite duration. Even when it is paid out over time, with the payments indexed to the cost of living, it is of a notional fixed sum. Nevertheless, as was perhaps foreseeable, French judges have been treating the compensatory payment very much like modern maintenance, even making short-term "rehabilitative" orders in cases where the wife seems able to regain self-sufficiency.[48]

Economic Effects of Divorce for Prolonged Disruption of the Life in Common

The general principle that divorce ends the marital duty of support does not apply in divorces based on prolonged disruption of the life in common, nor does the system of compensatory payment operate in these cases.[49] In fact, it does not seem to be an exaggeration to say that the system of economic effects prescribed under the 1975 law for divorces permitted on prolonged disruption grounds amounts to the full continuation of the matrimonial duty of support. In the first place, the plaintiff in this kind of divorce must assume all costs.[50] The sections regulating the other economic consequences reinforce the impression that the legislature intended to make anyone wishing to terminate a marriage to an unwilling and legally guiltless partner pay, and keep paying, for the privilege. There is no evidence here of any effort to reduce postdivorce contact between the spouses. Indeed, the system is the inverse of the compensatory payment. Support continues indefinitely; it is to take the form of periodic payments; and it is always modifiable:

> Art. 281. When the divorce is granted for disruption of the life in common, the spouse who took the initiative in the divorce remains completely bound to the duty of support.
>
> In the case of Article 238 [impairment of a spouse's mental faculties], the duty of support includes everything that is necessary for the medical treatment of the ill spouse.

48. Alain Bénabent, "Bilan de cinq ans d'application de la réforme du divorce," D. 1981. Chr. 33, 35–36.

49. The statute did not make this entirely clear, but the issue was resolved by the Court of Cassation decision of 18 April 1980, D. 1980. I.R. 439.

50. French Civil Code, art. 239.

> Art. 282. The performance of the duty of support is to take the form of periodic alimony. This may always be modified in accordance with the resources and needs of each spouse.
>
> Art. 283. Periodic alimony terminates as a matter of law if the spouse who is the creditor contracts a new marriage.
>
> It is terminable if the creditor is living in open and notorious concubinage.

Accordingly, in this form of divorce, the ex-spouses are bound together economically for better or worse, in sickness and in health, unless the creditor spouse remarries or cohabits with someone. Even when death does them part, support lives on if it is the debtor-spouse who has died, for Article 284 makes alimony a responsibility of the heirs of the deceased debtor. It terminates only upon the death of the creditor spouse. Exactly contrary to the scheme of the compensatory payment, Article 285 provides that in an exceptional case, the duty of support can be fulfilled by a lump-sum payment rather than through a periodic allowance.

In many ways this kind of divorce resembles a continuation of a limited form of marriage, with permission for the man, but not the woman, to add another spouse. This impression is reinforced by an amendment to the Social Security law which provides that when an insured does not remarry after divorce granted on his or her initiative for prolonged disruption of the life in common, the ex-spouse will be deemed a surviving spouse for social security purposes.[51] If the insured does remarry, then the death benefits are made payable to the ex-spouse and the current spouse in proportion to the duration of each marriage.[52]

Action for Damages

Under general principles of French tort law, a spouse in any type of divorce action may bring a civil action for damages against the other spouse for such violations of marital duties as assault and battery, defamation, and adultery.[53] Under the pre-1975 fault-based divorce law, the spouse who obtained the divorce could also seek damages for reparation of "the material or moral prejudice caused by the dissolution of the marriage."[54] The 1975 law also specifically authorizes a damage action, but limits it to the case of the plaintiff in a divorce granted for the exclusive fault of the defendant. Under the prior law, "material and moral prejudice" was interpreted to be separate and distinct from the loss of support which may be occasioned by divorce. The case

51. French Social Security Code, art. 351–2.
52. *Id.*
53. *Labrusse-Riou* 352.
54. French Civil Code, former art. 301.

law on this point, which is presumably still relevant, authorized compensation (sometimes very substantial) for such harms allegedly resulting from the divorce as the loss of esteem suffered by a divorced person, loneliness, or the loss of social position by one who has become accustomed to a high standard of living.[55]

Child Custody and Support

The provisions governing the award of child support are the same for all types of divorce and are virtually unchanged from the prior law. The basic sections are brief. The Code specifies that divorce does not have any effect on the parents' obligation to support their children and that the spouse with whom the children do not habitually reside remains bound to contribute to their maintenance and upbringing in proportion to his or her resources and to those of the other parent.[56] It then provides as follows:

> Art. 293. Contribution to the support and education of children . . . is to take the form of periodic payments to the parent who exercises parental authority or with whom the children customarily reside. . . .
> The modalities of and security for these payments are to be fixed by the decree or, in cases of divorce on joint petition, by the spouses' agreement, approved by the judge.

The Court of Cassation has made clear that child support cannot be left entirely to the agreement of the spouses. Even in a divorce on joint petition, the agreed amounts can always be modified.

In 1987, the word *custody* was removed from the Civil Code provisions regarding the consequences of divorce. The situation of children on divorce is now governed by a provision which permits the judge to order that the parental authority will continue to be exercised jointly by both parents or by one parent alone.[57] If the parental authority is to be exercised jointly, the judge indicates with which parent the child will "reside." Whether this will prove to be more than a cosmetic change is hard to say. In France, as elsewhere, children remain with their mothers after divorce in the great majority (about 85 percent) of cases.[58] As Bénabent has pointed out, the French treatment of

55. *Bénabent* 257; *Labrusse-Riou* 351–52.

56. French Civil Code, arts. 286, 288.

57. French Civil Code, art. 287, as amended by Law No. 87–570 of 22 July 1987, J.O. 24 July 1987, p. 8253. For a critical commentary, see Guy Raymond, "De la réalité de l'absence du couple conjugal à la fiction de l'unité du couple parental," J.C.P. 1987. I. 3299.

58. Marie-France Nicolas-Maguin, "À propos de la garde conjointe des enfants de parents divorcés," D. 1983, Chr. 111.

child support and custody has been characterized by a high degree of flexibility, which entails, as a corollary, great power for the judge and considerable vagueness in the law.[59]

In practice, child support is awarded in about three-quarters of all divorce cases involving minor children, and is collected through a relatively efficient system in which direct deduction from the payor's wages plays a major role.[60] Even so, the amounts awarded are often less than needed for the child's maintenance; about one-quarter of child support orders are never paid, and another quarter are paid sporadically.[61] In cases of default, a 1984 statute effective in 1986 provides for public authorities to make substitute monthly payments up to a certain maximum amount and to take over the task of collecting the unpaid support.[62] As is typical in the countries treated here, in France only about one divorced wife out of ten receives either support for herself or a compensatory payment.[63]

In France, as elsewhere, ways have had to be found to depart from the ordinary rules of marital property where the family home is the main asset and the minor children reside with one parent. Judges have discretionary power to award possession of a rented home to one of the spouses, regardless of whose name is on the lease, "in the light of the social and family interests involved," with compensation where appropriate to the other spouse.[64] In the case of a home owned by both husband and wife, the judge, in liquidating the marital regime, may award the dwelling to one and compensation to the other.[65] Where funds are inadequate to compensate the other spouse in this way, the home may have to be sold, except when the compensatory payment system can be used to justify a transfer of his interest without reimbursement.[66] Even where the home is owned by one spouse alone, the nonowner may be awarded possession by way of a "forced lease," with rent to be fixed by the judge, if a minor child or children reside with the nonowner spouse or if the nonowner is the respondent in a divorce for disruption of the life in common.[67]

59. *Bénabent* 235.

60. Anne Boigeol, "Le recouvrement des pensions alimentaires en France," (Paper delivered at the Fifth World Congress of the International Society on Family Law, 8–14 July, 1985, Brussels, Belgium).

61. Bernard Guibert and Evelyne Renaudat, "L'intervention de l'État dans l'obligation alimentaire (premières leçons de la loi du 22 décembre 1984)," 27 *Annales de Vaucresson* 123, 150 (1987); "Pensions: l'argent ne rentre pas," *L'Express*, 14 February 1986, 54.

62. Law No. 84–1171 of 22 December 1984, J.O. 27 December 1984, 3983.

63. Boigeol, above, note 60.   64. French Civil Code, art. 1751.

65. *Id.* at arts. 832, 1476, and 1542.   66. *Bénabent* 247; *Labrusse-Riou* 382.

67. French Civil Code, art. 285–1.

West Germany

Like French law, West German law distinguishes between property and support issues in divorce. The former are governed by the marital property law provisions of the Equality Law of 1957 and a system of pension-sharing established in 1976, while the latter are regulated by the 1976 divorce law as amended in 1986. Spousal support, in theory, plays a subordinate role in this scheme, supplementing the systems of marital property and pension-sharing in situations of special need. Whereas in most other countries, the marital home and household goods are comprehensively regulated, West German law regarding these matters shows an uncharacteristic lack of system and thoroughness. Despite their great practical importance, problems in this area are still basically governed by an old 1944 ordinance, revised in 1976.[68] This ordinance, which allows the courts a certain amount of discretion in allocating the marital dwelling and household goods upon divorce, leaves it primarily up to the judge in each individual case to harmonize the treatment of this type of property with the rules of marital property and support law.

It will be recalled that in 1957, the West German legislature implemented the constitutional principle of equality in marital property law by establishing a marital property regime (the *Zugewinngemeinschaft*) that leaves the spouses essentially free to deal with their own assets so long as the regime continues, but upon divorce requires an equal sharing of the increase in the value of the estates of each spouse occurring during the marriage.[69] Spouses who do not wish to have their property relations regulated by the statutory regime are free, within certain limits, to adopt an alternative regime by contract.

Upon divorce, the statutory regime requires an "equalization of increase" (*Zugewinnausgleich*) in all cases where one spouse, by his or her gainful activity during the marriage, has increased the value of his or her estate more than the other spouse has. The gains of the two spouses are compared, the smaller increase is subtracted from the larger one, and half the difference is paid by the spouse who has had the larger increase to the other spouse. Unless an increase can be shown to be attributable to a premarital asset or to a gift or inheritance received during the marriage, it is presumed to be a marital in-

68. Verordnung über die Behandlung der Ehewohnung und des Hausrats of 21 October 1944. See, for discussion by two family court judges of this complicated subject: Gerd Brudermüller, "Die Zuweisung der Ehewohnung an einen Ehegatten," 1987 *Zeitschrift für das gesamte Familienrecht* 109; Hans-Ulrich Graba, "Das Familienheim beim Scheitern der Ehe," 1987 *Neue Juristische Wochenschrift* 1721. Disputes concerning the marital home and household goods during separation but before divorce are separately regulated in West German Civil Code §§1361a and 1361b, as amended in 1986.

69. West German Civil Code, §§1363–70, 1372–84.

crease subject to division. Unlike France, the Federal Republic does not bring about the sharing of marital acquests by partition of common assets. The equalization of increase is effected by arithmetical computation; it results in a money claim and is discharged by payment of a sum of money. Like the community of acquests, however, the system was intended to, and does, take account upon divorce of the contributions of a part-time or full-time homemaker to the family. The flat rule of fifty-fifty division can be varied only if it would result in "gross unfairness" (*grobe Unbilligkeit*) under the circumstances of the case.

A problem with the 1957 marital property system was that it did not apply to a kind of savings that was coming to represent a very significant asset of many married persons—pension rights. Housewives often had no job-related benefits, except those derived from their husbands, and such derivative rights were generally destroyed by divorce. The reform law of 1976 addressed this problem by establishing a system of equalization of benefits (*Versorgungsausgleich*) under which pension rights of all sorts accumulated by the spouses during the marriage are computed, compared, and divided equally upon divorce.[70] The division is accomplished by transferring half of the difference in value between the respective entitlements of the spouses to the spouse with the lower value. If he or she does not yet have a pension account, one is set up, usually in the general social security system.[71] In cases of exceptional hardship or inequity, the equalization of security benefits can be omitted or postponed by the court.[72]

Viewed as a matter of policy, the equalization of benefits is an extension of the principle of equalization of marital property increase, but there are differences in the operation of the two processes. *Zugewinnausgleich* takes place on divorce only where the couple has been living under the basic statutory regime of matrimonial property, and not where a different marital property regime has been chosen by matrimonial contract, or where the statutory regime has been terminated by operation of law or judicial decree. *Versorgungsausgleich* applies in all divorces, irrespective of whether the parties have been living under the statutory marital property regime, unless the equalization of benefits was specifically excluded by a contract executed before a notary at the time of the marriage or at a later time.[73] While a divorce proceeding is pending, spouses are normally given considerable latitude to make their own arrangements concerning property equalization and postdivorce

70. West German Civil Code, §§1587–1587p, as amended in 1983 and 1986.

71. *Id.* at §1587b.

72. *Id.* at §§1587c–1587d.

73. *Id.* at §§1408, 1587o. Such exclusion is invalid if less than a year elapses between the contract and the filing of a divorce suit, §1408 par. 2.

support, but their freedom to modify the *Versorgungsausgleich* during the pendency of a divorce proceeding is more limited. *Versorgungsausgleich* is generally to be initiated by the court on its own motion. Any agreement suggested by the parties on the equalization of benefits in connection with the divorce must not only be executed before a notary but submitted to a family court judge for approval.[74] Approval may be withheld if the judge finds that the agreement, viewed in conjunction with the support and property arrangements made by the spouses, will not provide appropriate security against old age or incapacity for a spouse who would otherwise be entitled to pension equalization, or that the agreement does not produce an appropriate equalization between the spouses.

As mentioned above, support law was supposed to play a supplementary role in the West German system of regulating the economic effects of divorce. In this respect, the 1976 West German family law reform on the surface appeared to represent much more of a break with the past than did the 1975 French divorce law or the 1970–1984 English reforms. Until 1976, in West Germany (as in other traditional Western systems), the post-divorce support rights of the parties depended in important respects on the judicial determination of "guilt." If a husband was found to be at fault, he was obliged to maintain his wife at the economic level enjoyed during their married life— insofar as her own resources were insufficient to do so.[75] A wife found to be at fault was required, under the prior law, to maintain her husband after divorce only if he were incapable of supporting himself, and even then only at a subsistence level.[76] The 1976 reform law replaced these rules with a fundamentally different system. Not only is regulation of support made independent of guilt in principle, but as a general rule, spousal support is not to be available after divorce except as needed to help an economically weaker partner adjust to a new situation and to become self-sufficient. It was expected that the amount received by each spouse when the marital property regime was terminated would aid in this readjustment period. A duty of support continuing beyond the transitional period exists only in cases enumerated by the law.

The basic principle is stated in paragraph 1569: "If a spouse cannot take care of his support after divorce by himself, he has a claim for support against the other spouse according to the following provisions." Thus support, as distinct from the sharing of marital property increase and the equalization of benefits, will be granted only if a spouse meets one of several enumerated conditions. Civil Code paragraphs 1570 through 1576 specify the six classes of spouses who may claim support.

74. *Id.* at §1587o.
76. EheG, former §58.

75. EheG, former §58.

The first and most important category in practice is composed of spouses caring for a child of the marriage:

> §1570. A divorced spouse can claim support from the other so long and insofar as employability cannot be expected of him on account of the care or upbringing of a common child.

The second and third categories concern spouses who cannot be self-supporting because of age or physical or mental incapacity.[77] The fourth category of claims relates to a spouse's unemployability; or inability to find employment suitable for a person of his age, ability, and training; or inability to earn sufficient income.[78]

The fifth category of cases in which postdivorce support may be claimed concerns spouses who need temporary support in order to finish an interrupted course of studies or to secure more advanced training in a professional field, particularly where their employment opportunities have been impaired by what the law refers to as "marriage-conditioned delays," such as the devotion of years to child care or the interruption of studies upon marriage.[79]

The sixth and last category of eligibility for postdivorce spousal support is more general, leaving open the possibility of an award of maintenance where an ex-spouse cannot be expected to be employed for other "grave reasons." Recognizing the potential this general clause offers for reintroduction of the marital misconduct factor, the legislature provided that "grave reasons" that may have led to the breakdown of the marriage shall not be decisive in themselves. On the other hand, such evidence is not totally excluded from the decision to grant a support claim:

> §1576. A divorced spouse can claim support from the other, insofar and so long as employment cannot be expected of him for other grave reasons, and the denial of support, considering the interests of both spouses, would be grossly unfair. Grave reasons should not be taken into consideration solely because they have led to the failure of the marriage.

This section is applied, for example, in situations where a spouse, at a sacrifice to his or her own professional development, has devoted years to working in the business of the other spouse.[80]

So far as the amount of support is concerned, paragraph 1578(1) lays down, as a general principle, that support is to be determined with reference to the

77. *Id.* at §§1571, 1572.   78. *Id.* at §§1573, 1574.
79. *Id.* at §1575.
80. Uwe Diederichsen, "Ehegattenunterhalt im Anschluss an die Ehescheidung nach dem 1. EheRG," 30 *Neue Juristische Wochenschrift* 353, 357 (1977).

marital standard of living. But criticism similar to that which led to the removal of the principle of restoration to prebreakdown conditions from English law in 1984, prompted the West German lawmakers in 1986 to give the courts power to reduce support to an "adequate" standard after a period of time.[81] At the same time and for the same reasons, they provided that the support rights of a spouse who is unable to find suitable employment or to earn a sufficient income could be terminated after a specified period.[82]

Even though a claimant meets the threshold requirements for postdivorce support, he or she may be denied it on other grounds. A court may refuse the claim of a spouse otherwise entitled to support who has sufficient personal resources to be self-supporting, or for whom the allowance of support would be "grossly unfair" under all the circumstances of the case. The question of what constitutes unfairness sufficient for denial of support to an otherwise eligible spouse is treated in paragraph 1579. As in England, an effort was made to exclude ordinary marital misconduct from consideration. As originally enacted, paragraph 1579 provided as follows:

§1579(1). A support claim does not exist insofar as the claim against the liable spouse would be grossly unfair, because

1. the marriage was of short duration; the duration of the marriage includes the time during which the claimant was entitled to support under §1570 on account of the care or upbringing of a common child,

2. the claimant has been guilty of a felony or a serious intentional misdemeanor against the obligor spouse or a near relative of the obligor spouse,

3. the claimant has maliciously brought about his own state of need, or

4. another ground exists, as grave as those set out in numbers 1 to 3.

In the first decade under the new divorce law, the general language of paragraph 1579(4) was used by the courts to deny support in a wide variety of cases. This broad judicial view of unfairness apparently met the approval of the legislature, which took the occasion of the 1986 amendments to codify this developing case law. Paragraph 1579 now includes, in addition to the first three examples of gross unfairness listed above, cases where

4. the claimant has maliciously compromised important financial interests of the obligor spouse,

81. On the difficulties of determining what is an adequate (*angemessene*) postdivorce standard as distinct from an adequate marital standard, see Dieter Schwab, "Mass für Mass," 1986 *Zeitschrift für das gesamte Familienrecht* 128.

82. West German Civil Code, §1573(5).

5. the claimant has neglected his obligation to contribute to the support of the family for a long period of time before separation,

6. the claimant is responsible for obvious and serious misconduct toward the obligor spouse, or

7. another ground exists, as grave as those set out in numbers 1 to 6.

Thus, ten years after the switch to pure nonfault divorce, fault was firmly reinstated as a major factor in maintenance issues in West Germany. However, the 1986 legislature also altered the opening section of paragraph 1579 to make it clear that the needs of any child of the couple must be met before the custodial parent's support may be curtailed under this section.[83]

The 1986 amendments to spousal support law were made in response to widespread complaints about allegedly excessive support obligations, especially where the couple had been married but a short time, or where the wife's conduct seemed to make it unfair to require the husband to continue to support her. But questions have been raised as to whether the criticisms of the 1976 act were well founded. It does seem to be the case that spousal support, when granted, was for an unspecified duration and was geared to the marital standard of living.[84] But spousal support appears to be awarded no more frequently in West Germany than in most other countries. A study by Beatrice Caesar-Wolf and her associates at the University of Hannover revealed that in most cases virtually all the effects of divorce are settled by the parties in "court-induced" agreements.[85] As for the contents of these agreements, the Hannover study casts doubt on whether support burdens on former providers were as heavy as had been claimed. Spousal support, for example, figured in only 11 to 14 percent of the cases in the Hannover sample. The *Zugewinnausgleich* took place in only about 10 percent of the cases, either because there was no increase to be shared or because the spouses had renounced their rights. The strict rules regarding pension benefits resulted in a settlement in favor of the wife in nearly half of the cases studied, but this benefit too was frequently renounced. Thus, as in England, much of the hue and cry about the obligations and rights of divorcing spouses towards each other seems to have been misdirected.

83. For speculation about how this will work out in practice, see Dieter Henrich, "Die negative Härteklausel (§1579 BGB n. F.) und die Belange des Kindes," 1986 *Zeitschrift für das gesamte Familienrecht* 401.

84. Meo Micaela Hahne, "Zur Auslegung der §§1578 Abs. 1 Satz 2 und 3 und 1573 Abs. 5 BGB i.d. F. des Unterhaltsänderungsgesetzes vom 20 Februar 1986," 1986 *Zeitschrift für das gesamte Familienrecht* 305.

85. Beatrice Ceasar-Wolf, Dorothee Eidmann, Barbara Willenbacher, "Die gerichtliche Ehelösung nach dem neuen Scheidungsrecht: Normstruktur und Verfahrenspraxis," 5 *Zeitschrift für Rechtssoziologie* 202–246 (1983).

In practice, the main support issue is child support, which was awarded in 69 percent of the cases in the Hannover study.[86] It is worth noting that West Germany has an innovative approach to a child-support problem that is receiving increased legal attention everywhere—the liability, if any, of parents for the educational expenses of children who are no longer minors. In the Federal Republic, as in most European countries, university tuition and other fees are nominal, but books and living expenses are the responsibility of the student. A 1971 West German statute provides that young persons desirous of obtaining higher education in keeping with their "inclination, capacity, and performance" may obtain an advance payment for necessary expenses from a government agency, which then may seek to recoup the amount from the parents.[87]

The West German approach to support of minor children is also noteworthy because it seems to avoid many of the difficulties American states have encountered in trying to devise systems for imposing and collecting support that are realistic and fair. In awarding support, almost all West German courts adhere to the standards set down in unofficial guidelines known as the *Düsseldorf Tables*.[88] These tables, which are constantly adapted to changing conditions, are very realistic about the actual costs of raising children at various age levels.[89] This means that, in practice, child support in West Germany may consume a heftier proportion of a noncustodial parent's income than would typically be the case in England or the United States. The widespread adherence of West German judges to the tables and the courts' own practice of issuing guides for handling certain typically recurring problems[90] enable lawyers to predict with considerable assurance how much support a client can expect to pay or receive.[91] For these reasons, and because of its efficient support-collection system, West German support law bears a certain affinity to that of Sweden. West Germany, however, has been less willing than Sweden to redistribute the costs of divorce among the society at large. Thus Müller-

---

86. *Id.* Child custody in West Germany follows a familiar pattern. Although custody may be given to either parent or, since 1982, to both jointly and is awarded according to the "welfare of the child," most cases are uncontested and mothers retain custody 79 percent of the time. *Id.* at Table 8.

87. Law on Educational Advancement (Bundesausbildungsforderungsgesetz) of 28 August 1971, BGBl.I.1409, as amended 6 June 1983, BGBl.I.646.

88. Dieter Schwab, "Les obligations alimentaires entre époux divorcés dans le droit de la République Fédérale d'Allemagne" (Paper delivered at the Fifth World Congress of the International Society on Family Law, 8–14 July, 1985, Brussels, Belgium).

89. See, for example, the tables reproduced in Philipp Wendl and Siegfried Staudigl, *Das Unterhaltsrecht in der familienrichterlichen Praxis* (Munich: Beck, 1986), 130.

90. Schwab, above, n. 88.

91. The situation seems to be similar in the Netherlands according to John Griffiths, "What do Dutch Lawyers Actually do in Divorce Cases?" 20 *Law and Society Review* 135 (1986).

Freienfels has written that the 1976 divorce reform law "is not only more onerous for the wealthier spouse on account of a heavier support duty and the equalization of pensions, it also furnishes the maximum relief to the State at the expense of the former husband."[92] In legal systems where the state (i.e., taxpayers) does extensively subsidize child raising, however, it does not follow that noncustodial parents are relieved of responsibility for child support. The case of Sweden makes this clear.

Sweden

More thoroughly than any other country whose law we have examined here, Sweden has implemented the idea of a "clean break" between the spouses when their marriage is dissolved. The liquidation of the matrimonial property regime settles the marital accounts once and for all; postdivorce spousal support is legally available only in exceptional cases and rare in practice.

The Swedish deferred community-property regime, like those in the other Nordic countries, is a universal community; that is, it includes *all* the property of the spouses whenever and however acquired. Thus, if the spouses have not chosen some other arrangement by contract, their total assets will be divided equally upon divorce. After much study and debate, the Swedes decided to retain this traditional system in their new Marriage Code, adopted in 1987 to go into effect in 1988.[93] It was considered to be fair for long marriages, and has the virtue of being simple to administer because it does not require property to be classified as belonging to the community or to the individual spouse. But certain changes have been made over the years to adapt this most inclusive of community property regimes to modern conditions.

The most important change was to extend the special set of rules for the marital home and household goods to cases where these have been designated as the separate property of one spouse by marriage contract. No matter what marital property regime the spouses have chosen or how title is held, the dwelling and its necessary accoutrements may be awarded upon divorce to the spouse who "needs it most," usually the custodian of minor children, provided that this step is found to be reasonable in all the circumstances.[94] If the value of the property so awarded exceeds what would otherwise be due to the recipient, however, he or she may have to pay compensation to the other spouse. A second modification of marital property law was required in order to deal with the fact that equal division of a universal community can be unfair where the marriage was short and most of the common assets were brought

92. Wolfram Müller-Freienfels, "Les effets du divorce dans le nouveau droit allemand," in 1979 *Annales de la Faculté de Droit de Strasbourg* 29, 69.

93. Äktenskapsbalk of 14 May 1987, SFS 1987:230.

94. *Id.*, at Ch. 11 §8.

in by one spouse.[95] The new Marriage Code, therefore, provides that courts need not follow the equal division rule in cases where its application would be "inequitable." With respect to pensions, however, the new code specifically provides that they are "special property" of the individual spouses and not divisible on divorce—exactly contrary to the approach in West Germany and to the trend in several American states. Further underlining the independence of the spouses within the framework of a form of community property, the 1987 statute abolished nearly all restrictions on the power of the individual spouses to deal with their property as they please during the marriage. Consent requirements are retained only for transactions involving land or the marital home and household goods.

Spousal support supplements the marital property system only by way of exception. In the 1969 directives for the reform of Swedish family law, the minister of justice laid down the starting point that there should be no maintenance between spouses after dissolution of marriage.[96] In Sweden, alimony had already long been available only on the nonfault basis of one spouse's need and the other's ability to pay and had played a very limited role in practice. Thus it was not a startling change in 1978 when the alimony section of the Marriage Code was amended to conform to the ideology of the governing party and the existing practices of the courts. The section, as further amended in 1987, now provides as follows:

> Section 7. Following a divorce, each spouse shall be responsible for his or her own support.
>
> If a contribution to the support of either spouse is needed for a transitional period, that spouse shall be entitled to receive maintenance from the other spouse on the basis of what is reasonable in view of the latter's ability and other circumstances.
>
> If either spouse has difficulty in supporting himself or herself after a marriage of long duration has been dissolved or if there are other extraordinary reasons, that spouse shall be entitled to maintenance from the other spouse for a longer period than is stated in the second paragraph.[97]

Research conducted by Anders Agell and others at the University of Uppsala found that even before these new rules went into effect, spousal support to the custodian of young children was awarded in only one case out of ten,

95. Note that the regime of community of acquests neatly disposes of this problem, in all but a rare case, because it automatically links the scope of property-sharing to the duration of the marriage.

96. Note, "Current Legal Developments—Sweden," 19 *International and Comparative Law Quarterly* 164 (1970).

97. Swedish Marriage Code, Ch. 6 §7. See generally Anders Agell, *Paying of Maintenance in Sweden* (Uppsala: Institute of Law Research and Law Reform, 1983), 3.

and was limited to a fixed transitional period in about half of these.[98] Only one in twenty spouses was granted alimony for more than four years, and most of these cases involved older women whose marriages had lasted a long time.[99]

Child support, by contrast, plays an important role and is subject to detailed regulation. Apparently the availability of a variety of forms of public family assistance in Sweden does not diminish, but rather intensifies, the interest of the state in private arrangements for child support. Far from letting former providers off the hook, the Swedish welfare state has insisted, despite its generous assistance to one-parent families, that *primary* responsibility for the economic well-being of children remains with the parents. After divorce, as during the marriage, both parents are jointly responsible for child support, having regard for the needs of the children and the resources of the parents.[100] Determination of the amount of child support takes place under guidelines established in 1978 with the aim of introducing more uniformity into the system and more realism into the calculation of what a support debtor can reasonably be expected to pay.[101] Periodically updated supplementary guidelines keep judges informed about the costs of raising children and advise them on how to apply the statutory model to particular cases.[102] In general, a child is entitled to share the standard of living of its parents; but the noncustodial parent is entitled to keep a reasonable amount for his or her own basic needs and his or her contribution to the needs of a new family.[103]

The child-support amount, once calculated, is indexed to the rate of inflation and is modifiable under changed circumstances. In case of default, if the debtor is employed, support payments can be deducted directly from his earnings. The Uppsala study (of collections before the 1978 rules went into effect) found that despite a highly efficient collection process, no payments at all were made in a hard core of about 15 percent of the cases. These debtors were apparently unable to pay due to unemployment, poverty, or new obligations. On the other hand, the study is encouraging about what can be accomplished with a rigorous system of enforcement. Over 90 percent of the sums owed were collected in over 60 percent of the cases studied, and over 60 percent were collected in 80 percent of the cases.[104] (Mothers, as elsewhere, are the custodial parents in the great majority of the cases.)[105] Like France, West

98. *Id.* at 9.

99. *Id.*

100. Swedish Code on Parents and Children, Ch. 7 §1.

101. Agell, above, note 97 at 4.   102. *Id.* at 22–23.

103. *Id.* at 5, 22–24.   104. *Id.* at 14–15.

105. Jan Trost, "Children and Divorce in Sweden," 12 *Journal of Comparative Family Studies* 129, 131 (1980). A 1983 law provides that divorce leaves the subsisting joint custody of the

Germany, and a growing group of other West European countries, Sweden pays a "maintenance advance" to dependents of a defaulting support debtor and assumes the burden of collection in such cases.[106] To a greater extent than most other non-Nordic countries, however, Sweden alleviates the support burden on both parents by providing generous child allowances, housing allowances, and public health insurance.

The United States

The legal approaches of the various American states to the economic aftermath of divorce resemble the English pattern in their lack of emphasis on distinctions between marital property and support law.[107] They are more similar to the continental approaches, however, in the degree to which they have accepted the principle of spousal self-sufficiency after divorce. The Uniform Marriage and Divorce Act (UMDA) is illustrative of a number of American trends. Although adopted in its entirety by only a handful of states, it has been widely influential as a source of ideas and as a model for law revision. Its authors hoped that financial matters between the spouses could be arranged in a one-time property settlement, with periodic support being called into play only when necessary:

> The Act authorizes the division of the property belonging to either spouse, or to both spouses, as the primary means of providing for the future financial needs of the spouses, as well as doing justice between them. Where the property is insufficient for the first purpose, the Act provides that an award of maintenance may be made to either spouse under appropriate circumstances to supplement the available property. But because of its property division rules, the Act does not continue the traditional reliance upon maintenance as the primary means of support for divorced spouses.[108]

To this end, the Uniform Act, like the law of the great majority of the American states and England, gives the courts broad discretion to redistribute *all* of the spouses' property, without regard to title, in the manner that seems fair to the judge:

---

parents in place as it existed during marriage. This law is described in Åke Saldeen, "Sweden," *Annual Survey of Family Law*, vol. 8 (London: International Society of Family Law, 1983–84), 168–74.

106. Agell, above, note 97 at 7–8.

107. Some states, like England, do not even make a formal distinction between property division and support, *e.g.*, Massachusetts General Laws, Ch. 208, §34.

108. UMDA, Draftsmen's Prefatory Note, 5.

Section 307. *Disposition of Property.*

(a) In a proceeding for dissolution of a marriage the court, without regard to marital misconduct, shall finally equitably apportion between the parties the property and assets belonging to either or both however and whenever acquired, and whether the title thereto is in the name of the husband or wife or both.

Section 307 goes on to list several factors which the court must take into consideration in allocating the spouses' property:

In making apportionment the court shall consider the duration of the marriage, any prior marriage of either party, any antenuptial agreement of the parties, the age, health, station, occupation, amount and sources of income, vocational skills, employability, estate, liabilities, and needs of each of the parties, custodial provisions, whether the apportionment is in lieu of or in addition to maintenance, and the opportunity of each for future acquisition of capital assets and income. The court shall also consider the contribution or dissipation of each party in the acquisition, preservation, depreciation, or appreciation in value of the respective estates, and as the contribution of a spouse as a homemaker or to the family unit.

The UMDA authors, fearing that this free-wheeling approach might not appeal to legislatures in all states, particularly those with community property traditions, provided an alternative section in which the fund to be redistributed is limited to the marital acquests.[109] They need not have been concerned. With the enthusiastic support of not entirely disinterested groups of divorce lawyers, discretionary distribution statutes spread like wildfire through the state legislatures. In a few places, the courts simply assumed the power to disregard title on divorce without statutory authority. By 1987, all the former separate property states and all but three[110] of the community property states had adopted, by legislation or court decision, some form of discretionary distribution of property on divorce.[111] There are, of course, variations from state to state. The laws differ, for example, on whether and to what extent fault may be taken into consideration; on how free the spouses are to contract out of the system; on whether all assets or only acquests made during the marriage are subject to division; and on whether the court should begin with a presumption in favor of equal division.

Once the principle of discretionary distribution of property was established,

---

109. UMDA §307, Alternative B.

110. California, Louisiana, and New Mexico.

111. See the summaries of state divorce laws in *Family Law Reporter: Reference File* (Washington, D. C.: BNA, loose-leaf), 400:001–453:001.

the question arose in the United States, as elsewhere, of how pensions and other job-related rights should be treated. Starting in the 1970s, American courts began routinely to consider pension rights as marital property. At present, a number of special statutes accord rights to divorced spouses in various kinds of benefits earned by the other spouse during the marriage.[112]

For those great numbers of folk who consume what they earn and have no significant property, old or new, periodic support of one ex-spouse from the earnings of the other remains the only mechanism for making some kind of financial adjustment between husband and wife upon divorce. Among the states, the approaches to spousal support range from that of Texas, where permanent alimony cannot be given at all, to those of a few states where marital misconduct is an absolute bar to alimony, to the majority of jurisdictions, where the courts have broad powers to award spousal support as they deem equitable under the circumstances.[113] Commonly, statutes governing spousal support provide the court with guidelines for the exercise of their discretion. In these guidelines, maintenance is commonly, but not always, made independent of marital fault. Even where legislatures have attempted to eliminate marital misconduct from consideration, however, fault often continues to play an indirect role in the economics of divorce. In cases where young children are present, putting the fitness of the mother as custodian into question has been a common way for husbands to try to force reductions in demands for support and property division. Furthermore, in recent years, damage actions between spouses for torts (such as assault and battery) committed during the marriage, long a familiar feature of the French legal landscape, have begun to be prosecuted with success in some American courts.

Support guidelines usually emphasize the needs of the support debtor and the ability to pay of the support creditor. The most recent American statutes, like the French, Swedish, and West German laws, treat spousal support as in principle what it is in fact—a temporary and exceptional consequence of divorce. The Uniform Marriage and Divorce Act contains a typical set of guidelines for spousal maintenance. They make maintenance available only in specifically enumerated situations of need and treat it as essentially temporary and rehabilitative, aimed at making the recipient self-sufficient through entry

112. For example, divorced spouses whose marriages lasted at least ten years are entitled to share in the ex-spouse's social security benefits. 42 United States Code §§402, 405, 416, 1302. A number of federal statutes pertaining to retirement benefits, military pensions, and civil service pensions either authorize or require some degree of pension splitting on divorce. See the statutes collected in *Family Law Reporter: Reference File* (Washington, D. C.: BNA, loose-leaf), 105:001–115:015.

113. See the fifty-state survey by Doris Freed and Timothy Walker, "Family Law in the Fifty States: An Overview," 20 *Family Law Quarterly* 439, 493–507 (1987).

or reentry into the labor force as soon as possible after the divorce. Thus one trend makes alimony exceptional and temporary and therefore would seem to limit its availability; while another might seem to widen its potential scope by making it independent of misconduct and available on the basis of need.

The spousal support section of the Uniform Marriage and Divorce Act well illustrates the ambivalent attitudes that characterize law reform in this area. The section begins with the general proposition that there is no continuing financial responsibility of one spouse for the other after divorce, but it immediately qualifies this proposition so that most older divorced wives and most divorced mothers of young children are excepted from the application of the principle:

> Section 308. *Maintenance.*
> (a) In a proceeding for dissolution of marriage . . . the court may grant a maintenance order for either spouse, *only* if it finds that the spouse seeking maintenance [*emphasis supplied*]:
> (1) lacks sufficient property to provide for his reasonable needs; and
> (2) is unable to support himself through appropriate employment or is the custodian of a child whose condition or circumstances make it appropriate that the custodian not be required to seek employment outside the home.

The authors' official comment to the section underscores the objective of promoting individual self-sufficiency:

> [T]he court may award maintenance only if both findings listed in (1) and (2) are made. The dual intention of this section and Section 307 [Property Division] is to encourage the court to provide for the financial needs of the spouses by property disposition rather than by an award of maintenance. Only if the available property is insufficient for the purpose and if the spouse who seeks maintenance is unable to secure employment appropriate to his skills and interests or is occupied with child care may an award of maintenance be ordered.

The section is typical of several modern tendencies in its sex-neutrality, its express exclusion of marital misconduct, and its enumeration of specific criteria to guide the court's exercise of its discretion:

> Section 308 [continued]: (b) The maintenance order shall be in amounts and for periods of time the court deems just, without regard to marital misconduct, and after considering all relevant factors including:
> (1) The financial resources of the party seeking maintenance, in-

cluding marital property apportioned to him, his ability to meet his needs independently, and the extent to which a provision for support of a child living with the party includes a sum for that party as custodian;

(2) the time necessary to acquire sufficient education or training to enable the party seeking maintenance to find appropriate employment;

(3) the standard of living established during the marriage;

(4) the duration of the marriage;

(5) the age and the physical and emotional condition of the spouse seeking maintenance; and

(6) the ability of the spouse from whom maintenance is sought to meet his needs while meeting those of the spouse seeking maintenance.

In practice, in the United States as elsewhere, spousal support plays a relatively minor role. In 1985, only about 15 percent of all divorced or separated women had been awarded alimony, and of these, 27 percent had never received payments.[114]

So far as child support is concerned, the Uniform Marriage and Divorce Act is again typical of state statutes on this subject:

Section 309. [*Child Support.*] In a proceeding for dissolution of marriage . . . or child support, the court may order either or both parents owing a duty of support to a child to pay an amount reasonable or necessary for his support, without regard to marital misconduct, after considering all relevant factors including:

(1) the financial resources of the child;

(2) the financial resources of the custodial parent;

(3) the standard of living the child would have enjoyed had the marriage not been dissolved;

(4) the physical and emotional condition of the child and his educational needs; and

(5) the financial resources and needs of the noncustodial parent.

The court's powers extend to making a property transfer in favor of the child:

Section 307. . . .

(b) In the proceeding, the court may protect and promote the best interests of the children by setting aside a portion of the jointly and separately held estates of the parties in a separate fund or trust for

114. Bureau of the Census, *Child Support and Alimony: 1985*, Current Population Reports, series P-23, no. 152 (Washington, D. C.: U.S. Government Printing Office, 1987), 6.

the support, maintenance, education, and general welfare of any minor, dependent, or incompetent children of the parties.

This power, however, is rarely used.

In the United States, as elsewhere, mothers remain the physical custodians of minor children in the great majority of cases[115] and in general, fulfill their support duties through services and care, rather than cash payments. The amounts of child support customarily awarded from noncustodial parents have been low, typically covering less than half the costs of raising a child, and representing only about 13 percent of the father's income.[116] Even these low amounts have been hard to collect, especially if the support debtor is in a different state. In 1985, only 61 percent of single-parent families were awarded child support; of these, over one-quarter never received any payments, while another quarter received less than the full amount due.[117]

Part of the problem in the United States seems to be that judges, in exercising their virtually uncontrolled discretion, tend to protect the former husbands' standard of living at the expense of ex-wives and children.[118] A second problem is the system's heavy reliance on private ordering with very little judicial supervision of the spouses' agreements on child support. The difficulties of interstate enforcement in a federal system provide an added layer of complication.

It is ironic, as Harry Krause has pointed out, that the Swedish comprehensive welfare state imposes and enforces clear primary responsibility for child support on parents, while the United States, despite its theoretical devotion to

115. Paul Glick, "American Household Structure in Transition," 16 *Family Planning Perspectives*, no. 5 (September/October 1984). This is so even where joint legal custody has been granted.

116. Bureau of the Census, *Child Support and Alimony: 1983*, Current Population Reports, series P-23, no. 141 (July 1985). The average payment declined 12.4 percent between 1983 and 1985, *New York Times*, 23 August 1987, 26.

117. *Id.*

118. Numerous studies document that custodial parents, usually mothers, bear the main economic responsibility for children after divorce and that the standard of living of the custodial parent's household typically declines after divorce, while that of the noncustodial parent rises. See especially Lenore Weitzman, *The Divorce Revolution: The Unexpected Social and Economic Consequences for Women and Children in America* (New York: Free Press, 1985), 324–43. See also David Chambers, *Making Fathers Pay: The Enforcement of Child Support* (Chicago: University of Chicago Press, 1979), 42–58; Lenore Weitzman, "The Economics of Divorce: Social and Economic Consequences of Property, Alimony and Child Support Awards," 28 *University of California Los Angeles Law Review* 1181, 1265–66 (1981); S. Hoffman and J. Holmes, "Husbands, Wives, and Divorce," in *Five Thousand American Families—Patterns of Economic Progress*, ed. G. Duncan and J. Morgan, vol. 4 (Ann Arbor, Mich.: Institute for Social Research, 1976), 23–75; Robert E. McGraw, Gloria J. Sterin, and Joseph M. Davis, "A Case Study in Divorce Law Reform and Its Aftermath," 20 *Journal of Family Law* 443 (1981–82).

private initiative, tends to view postdivorce poverty as a welfare problem.[119] With the Child Support Enforcement Amendments of 1984, however, the United States belatedly took a step toward more effective, European-style approaches. This law required the states, as a condition of eligibility for federal AFDC[120] funds, to adopt legislation by October 1987 providing for automatic wage-withholding when there has been a default in child support for a month or more.[121] Automatic withholding is mandatory in all cases involving clients of state enforcement agencies, and will be available in nonwelfare cases if it is provided for in the support decree. The states are also required to establish nonbinding guidelines for support amounts. The question here, as in England, is whether this heightened emphasis in the law on the needs of children will bring about changes in judicial attitudes or result in significant increases in the amounts of child support agreed upon by parents.

The Costs of Changed Marriage Behavior: Public or Private Responsibility?

Lines of Convergence

The foregoing survey of the legal effects of divorce reveals certain broad similarities in support law, custody law, and marital property law among the various legal systems. Most strikingly perhaps, support law gives us yet another example of a complete reversal of principle in less than a century, most countries having moved, in varying degrees, from the idea of marriage as involving a continuing economic responsibility of the husband for the wife to the position that each spouse ought to be responsible for himself or herself after divorce unless special needs exist. The shift of attention in support law to the needs of the spouse claiming support has rendered the role of fault problematic. While there seems to be general agreement that marital misconduct should not be an absolute bar to recovery of support by an ex-spouse who is otherwise eligible to receive it, it has proved difficult to completely eliminate fault from consideration, especially where the behavior in question is of an egregious sort.

Modern support law, like modern divorce law, promotes an altered ideology of marriage. In place of the homemaker-breadwinner model, support law now presupposes a partnership of two equal individuals who may have been economically interdependent in marriage, but who are at least potentially independent upon divorce. If one of the spouses is not in a position to provide for her own needs immediately, the role of support law is increasingly

119. Harry Krause, "Reflections on Child Support," 1983 *University of Illinois Law Review* 99, 118.

120. Aid to Families with Dependent Children.

121. Child Support Enforcement Amendments of 1984, 42 U.S.C. §§651–667.

seen as that of temporarily aiding in the transition to self-sufficiency. Except
perhaps in England, rules governing postdivorce spousal maintenance insist
on treating as exceptional the cases which are in fact the most common—
those where a spouse's potential for economic independence has been or is
currently being compromised by the time he or she has devoted to child care.
In practice, as we have seen, spousal support after divorce is relatively infre-
quent everywhere.

Modern child custody law takes the vague notion of the interests or welfare
of the child as its basic reference point. In recent years, there has been an
increasing tendency to assume that a child's interests are promoted by encouraging, or at least not discouraging, shared legal custody after divorce. Despite
variations in custody law on this and other points, however, mothers everywhere remain the physical custodians of minor children in the overwhelming
majority of cases.

Our examination of how marital property systems function on divorce
showed fewer similarities among countries, but even here there are substantial
points of convergence. The distinction between separate and community property systems upon divorce has been nearly obliterated in the United States,
where all but three states now permit courts to extensively disregard title in
settling the economic affairs of the spouses. The theoretical boundary between
support and property division—even in countries where a clear legal distinction is made between them—tends to dissolve in practice if the courts have
power to order support (or compensatory payment) to be made out of a
spouse's separate property. Finally, we noted a tendency everywhere for the
family home and household goods to be treated as a special category of marital property regardless of other features of the system.

The development of these "mini-regimes" of marital property for the home
and household goods is highly significant. Most divorces involve relatively
young couples with minor children. Such couples typically have few assets
other than the family dwelling, which may be leased, mortgaged, or owned.
One way or another, courts everywhere, with more or less aid from legislation, endeavor to preserve the marital home or its use for the needed period
of time for the custodial spouse and children. Thus, in terms of the outcomes
in a very large group of cases, one can say that a new marital property regime
has emerged—one which applies in the majority of divorces—and that its
basic features are similar everywhere. Only Sweden has cast it in statutory
form: possession of the home and its contents are to be awarded to the spouse
"who needs it most."

This development represents a practical recognition of the inappropriateness of the principles of independence and self-sufficiency—to which all systems are more or less committed—to the mine-run of cases where children

are involved and the spouses are of modest means. Deep in the capillaries of each system, where court personnel struggle on a daily basis with such cases, judges everywhere seem to be engaged in similar tasks, regardless of the legal framework within which they are operating. They are trying to put together the best possible package—from property, income, and in-kind personal care—to provide for the basic needs of children.

There are two main points to be made about this. The first will be mentioned only briefly, since I have written about it at length elsewhere.[122] Experience under the new laws governing the legal effects of divorce indicates that *in most cases*, division of marital property cannot be the primary mechanism for arranging the spouses' financial affairs after divorce. Support laws that start from the principle that no support should be available treat as exceptional what is in fact statistically the most frequent case: that of a spouse whose capacity for self-support is impaired because of her child-care responsibilities. The idea of making a clean break is wholly unrealistic in those cases where minor children are present and in many cases where one spouse devoted years to raising children who are now grown.

In other legal areas where a body of law meant to apply to an "ideal" situation has proved to be ill-adapted to superficially similar but economically different situations that come within its scope, legislatures have stepped in to make the necessary adjustments. Thus, consumer law has grown up within systems of commercial law designed mainly for merchants dealing with each other, and corporation law regulates closely held corporations separately from publicly held ones. The time has come to recognize in similar fashion that many rules of marital property and support law which may be well suited to the situations of childless couples are inappropriate to the circumstances of families with children.

The second general point to be made about current legal efforts to deal with the problems of divorces involving minor children is that, in assembling a package to provide for the needs of the ongoing custodial unit after divorce, each country parcels out economic responsibility somewhat differently among the custodial parent, the noncustodial parent, and the society as a whole. This leads us to consider some of the ways in which the systems we have examined diverge from one another.

Patterns of Divergence

Among the five countries whose law is examined here, it is possible to discern three different approaches to the problems of continuing dependency after

---

122. Mary Ann Glendon, *Abortion and Divorce in Western Law* (Cambridge,: Harvard University Press, 1987), 91–104, and articles cited therein.

divorce: the continental pattern, as exemplified by France and West Germany; the Nordic pattern, of which Sweden is our example; and the Anglo-American pattern. The patterns are differentiated from one another primarily by the way they allocate responsibility for postdivorce support in cases involving minor children.

As we have seen, the French and West German systems emphasize the financial obligations of former providers, supplemented where necessary by the state. They put teeth into provisions protecting dependent family members by having the judge actively supervise the financial arrangements made by the parties upon divorce.[123] While the French and West German divorce laws differ from each other in numerous details, in general it can be said that the same legislation which permits freer terminability of marriage in these countries also makes it quite difficult for either spouse to be free of family economic responsibilities after divorce.[124] This is not to say, however, as some West German critics have suggested, that the burdens on the former providers are especially onerous, at least when compared to those of the custodial parent.

The Swedish manner of regulating the consequences of divorce is characteristic of the approach of the Nordic welfare states. The emphasis here is on spousal self-sufficiency, with child support computed in such a way as to exact a fair contribution from the noncustodial parent without unduly burdening him or his new family. Absolutely indispensable to such an approach is the absorption by the society as a whole of much of the cost of divorce through generous programs of public benefits for families with children.[125]

What is curious about the way the American states handle postdivorce finances is that they endorse a Nordic degree of commitment to spousal independence and self-sufficiency at the theoretical level, but fail to establish the conditions necessary to realize this ideal in practice. Widely lacking in the United States (and England) are the following features of most Nordic and continental systems: genuine judicial supervision of the spouses' financial ar-

123. Marie-Thérèse Meulders-Klein, "Financial Agreements on Divorce and the Freedom of Contract in Continental Europe," in *The Resolution of Family Conflict: Comparative Legal Perspectives*, ed. John Eekelaar and Sanford N. Katz (Toronto: Butterworths, 1984), 297.

124. See generally Catherine Labrusse-Riou, "Securité d'existence et solidarité familiale en droit privé: Étude comparative du droit des pays européens continentaux," 1986 *Revue internationale de droit comparé* 829–65.

125. See Anders Agell, "Social Security and Family Law in Sweden," in *Social Security and Family Law with Special Reference to the One-Parent Family: A Comparative Survey*, ed. Alec Samuels, vol. 4 (London: United Kingdom Comparative Law Series, 1979), 149, 158–60. The relative generosity of the Swedish benefit-service package is described in Sheila B. Kamerman and Alfred Kahn, *Income Transfers for Families with Children: An Eight-Country Study* (Philadelphia: Temple University Press, 1983), 60, 71.

rangements for children; mechanisms to ensure that child support is fixed at realistic and fair levels; highly efficient collection systems; "maintenance advance" systems in which the state not only collects unpaid child support, but partially absorbs the risk of nonpayment by advancing support up to a fixed amount in cases of default. Notably absent, too, from the American scene is the relatively generous package of public benefits and services for one-parent families that exists in Sweden and, to a lesser degree, in France and West Germany.

Though England still retains in its divorce law something of the notion of continuing responsibility for dependents after divorce, the situation of one-parent families there is in most respects similar to their situation in the United States. One of the main factors that sets these countries apart from France, West Germany, and Sweden is the level of public assistance available to single-parent families. In England and the United States, an unmarried, unemployed mother of two lives on half of the net average production worker's wage, while her French, Swedish, or West German counterpart lives on 67 to 94 percent of what an average production worker earns in those countries.[126]

One should not, of course, let the differences from country to country obscure the fact that custodial parents everywhere shoulder the main burdens of divorce. No country has completely solved the economic problems associated with marriage breakdown. The modest income and assets of most families, the frequency of marriage dissolution and the formation of new families, the many disadvantages of working single mothers in the job market and the marriage market, and the strained resources of all welfare states make it unlikely that any entirely satisfactory solution to these problems can be found. But some countries do more than others to ensure a decent minimum subsistence to families that are raising children. France and West Germany stress the responsibility of the former provider. Sweden, while strictly enforcing child-support obligations, assumes substantial public responsibility for the welfare of one-parent families. The situation in England may move in the continental direction in view of the 1984 reorientation of its divorce law. As for England's levels of public assistance, they are, while low, relatively generous in view of the size of that country's gross national product. Thus it is the United States which stands at an extreme point on the spectrum of countries discussed here, having embraced free terminability of marriage and spousal self-sufficiency after divorce, while failing to assure either public or private responsibility for the casualties.[127]

126. Alfred J. Kahn and Sheila Kamerman, "Social Assistance: An Eight-Country Overview," 8 *Journal of the Institute for Socioeconomic Studies* 93, 102 (1983–84). See also Kamerman and Kahn, above, note 125 at 310.

127. This puzzle is the subject of Glendon, above, n. 120.

Marygold Melli has suggested that the real "divorce revolution" in recent years has been a revolution in consciousness—a heightened awareness "of the failure of our divorce system to apportion fairly the economic burdens of marital dissolution." [128] The postdivorce plight of dependent women and custodial mothers and children, she suggests, has become a social problem because it has begun to be described as such, not because it is something new. [129] Effective ways of dealing with this problem—now that it has been widely recognized—seem likewise to require as a first step an exercise of the legal imagination directed toward what fair and sensible postdivorce arrangements would look like. It seems likely that laws which can capture and articulate widely shared sentiments about the value of child-raising can thereby increase, at least to a modest degree, their own effectiveness in dealing with postdivorce dependency. Conversely, laws which implicitly tap into the all-too-familiar currents of egoistic individualism, or into even darker pools of resentment and group bias, will contribute in their way to the perpetuation of the problem.

Marriage Termination by Death

In contrast to divorce law, the law of inheritance has made the transition to modernity with relative ease and to the apparent satisfaction of most persons affected by it. When a marriage comes to an end with the death of one of the spouses, the companionability that sociologists tell us is characteristic of the modern couple's relationship finds its fullest expression in the legal systems surveyed here. In the gift and inheritance law of these countries, to varying degrees, solidarity and sharing between spouses are implemented and encouraged, the ideology of community and cooperation seems to rule supreme, and the special place accorded to legal marriage appears secure.

The Shrinking Circle of Heirs

One of the great transforming trends that has marked the development of Western family law over the past two centuries has been the gradual attenuation of legal bonds among family members outside the conjugal unit of husband, wife, and children. Nowhere is this more visible than in the law of inheritance, where the position of the surviving spouse has steadily improved everywhere at the expense of the decedent's blood relatives. At the same time, however, inheritance law has an ever-dwindling role to play in family wealth

---

128. Marygold S. Melli, "Constructing a Social Problem: The Post-Divorce Plight of Women and Children," 1986 *American Bar Foundation Research Journal* 759, 771.
129. *Id.* at 760–61.

transmission. Increasingly, family wealth is passed on through lifetime transfers; children receive their "inheritance" in advance in the form of educational and other assistance in their formative years, and spouses provide for each other through survivorship arrangements, life insurance, and so on.[130]

But within inheritance law as such, the rules governing the devolution of property when a person dies without a will strikingly illustrate the movement of modern marriage into the foreground of family relationships. Intestate succession law is the body of law that determines how property will be distributed if a person did not make other arrangements or if the arrangements attempted were not legally valid. In Western liberal democracies, the purpose of such rules is essentially to carry out the desires of the typical decedent. That is, intestate succession law is not designed to promote any specific social aim, such as redistribution of wealth; rather, it is the legislature's attempt to draft the will the average person would have made. The most remarkable changes that have taken place in intestate succession law over time are in the way it strikes the balance between the surviving spouse and the decedent's blood relatives. At the same time, tax law (which can be decisive for the estate planning of the well-to-do) increasingly encourages dispositions in favor of the surviving spouse by giving such dispositions preferred treatment.

How far-reaching these changes are is apparent in view of the fact that, before twentieth-century reforms of succession laws, inheritance, in the proper sense of the word, between husband and wife was still exceptional.[131] Marriage was not seen as a reason for shifting family wealth, especially land, from one blood line to another. In the Anglo-American separate property systems, the survivor could take a share, or in some cases all, of the personal property, but the marital estates of dower and curtesy kept what was once the most important form of property, land, in the family of origin by giving the surviving spouse only a life interest in the real property of the decedent.[132] In the various community property systems (except for the few places, such as the Nordic countries, where the community included *all* property of the spouses), land was kept within the family from whence it came by giving the surviving spouse a share only in the property that had been earned and saved during the marriage (community of acquests), or perhaps also in all the per-

130. John H. Langbein, "The Twentieth-Century Revolution in Family Wealth Transmission," 86 *Michigan Law Review* 722 (1988).

131. Max Rheinstein and Mary Ann Glendon, *The Law of Decedents' Estates* (Mineola, N.Y.: Foundation Press, 1971), 35.

132. The wife's dower right entitled her to a life estate only in one-third of each parcel of the husband's inheritable freehold estates. The husband's curtesy right gave him a life estate in all of the wife's land, provided, however, that the wife had given birth to a live child at some time during the marriage.

sonal property (community of movables and acquests and, in practical effect, community of acquests as modified by the presumption that all movables are presumed to be assets of the community unless their separate character can be proved).

These traditional systems have been altered (in varying degrees, depending on the country) by a widespread trend toward expanding and strengthening the surviving spouse's rights in intestacy. The tendency to view a marriage that lasts until death as a union of the economic interests of the spouses is reflected in current testamentary and *inter vivos* gift behavior, as well as in succession law reforms. Both custom and law reveal a preference for the surviving spouse over children of the marriage and other blood relatives of the decedent. This preference is weaker in some systems, like the French, and very strong in others, like those of the American states. The traditional ideas that family wealth should be preserved for transfer from one generation to another and that a surviving spouse should not take such wealth away from the children are weakening, but they still exist, more so in parts of Europe than in the United States, and more so among certain groups of society than others. The resulting transformation of the surviving spouse's position is substantial when compared with the not-too-distant past.

The Surviving Spouse

In the brief summaries below, we will examine the legal position of the surviving spouse first in intestate succession law. Because the proportion of an estate allocated to the surviving spouse in intestacy often varies according to the number and degree of closeness of other heirs, we will assume in each case that the decedent left behind a spouse and two children of the marriage. Then we will turn to testate succession and the problem of whether and to what extent a surviving spouse may be disinherited by the decedent.

England

In England, if the predeceasing spouse does not leave a will and the estate is less than £75,000, the survivor is entitled to take it all, plus certain personal belongings of the decedent which do not form part of the "estate," such as clothing, furniture, jewelry, household goods, and cars. If the value of the estate exceeds £75,000, and (as we are supposing) issue survive, the surviving spouse takes the personal chattels and £75,000 outright plus a life interest in half of the excess over £75,000.[133] The remainder goes to the issue. As part of the general policy of protecting a spouse's right to occupy the matrimonial

---

133. Administration of Estates Act 1925, s. 33(2), as amended. The Lord Chancellor has authority to increase the base amount periodically to take account of inflation.

home, the law also gives the survivor the right to have the home appropriated to his or her share of the estate.[134] If the value of the home is greater than the spouse's intestate share, he or she will be required to pay the difference in value to the estate. In 1988, the Law Commission, concerned that the rules of intestate succession might be more reflective of the needs and desires of members of an earlier generation than of contemporary men and women, announced its intent to survey public opinion on the subject. It called for a re-examination of this entire body of law, especially with a view toward increasing the share of the surviving spouse.[135]

So far as testate succession is concerned, an English spouse who wishes to leave more or less than the intestate share to the other spouse is free to do so by making a will. Unlike the French and West German systems, where a parent is forbidden to disinherit his or her children completely, English law permits husbands and wives to give or leave their entire estates to each other even if there are surviving children. Freedom to *dis*inherit a spouse was at one time restricted in English law by the marital estates of dower and curtesy, but after 1833, dower and curtesy did not operate in testate succession. So, for over a hundred years, complete freedom of testation prevailed in England. In 1938 this power to cut off one's closest relatives without a penny was curtailed somewhat by a statute providing that a court might, in its discretion, award maintenance from the estate to a spouse or certain other dependents where the will deprived them of a "reasonable share" of the decedent's property. From 1938 to 1975, however, the most a spouse aggrieved in this manner could receive was an allowance of support out of the decedent's estate.

In 1974 the Law Commission brought to Parliament's attention the fact that changes in the divorce law had brought about a situation where divorced spouses were entitled to greater financial protection than widows and widowers.[136] The Law Commission's recommendation that the court's power to make provision for spouses on death should be as wide as its power to do so upon divorce was implemented in 1975.[137] The system of discretionary awards was retained, but since 1975 a surviving spouse's claim is no longer limited to "maintenance." The court has the same power as under the divorce law to

134. *Cretney* 700.

135. The Law Commission, *Distribution on Intestacy*, Working Paper No. 108 (London: Her Majesty's Stationery Office, 1988).

136. The Law Commission, *Second Report on Family Property: Family Provision on Death*, Law Com. No. 61 (London: Her Majesty's Stationery Office, 1974).

137. Inheritance (Provision for Family and Dependants) Act 1975. See generally, Richard Schaul-Yoder, "British Inheritance Legislation: Discretionary Distribution at Death," 8 *Boston College International and Comparative Law Review* 205 (1985). For a critique of the vagueness of the standards of the act in operation, see J. Gareth Miller, "Provision for a Surviving Spouse," 102 *Law Quarterly Review 445* (1986).

award "reasonable financial provision" by means of a lump sum, periodic payments, or a combination of both. What is "reasonable" is to be determined by taking all the circumstances of the case, including conduct of the parties, into consideration, pursuant to guidelines similar to those in the divorce law. Like the 1938 act, the 1975 law applies in any situation where the surviving spouse is left without adequate provision, whether this results from the oversight or deliberate act of the predeceasing spouse, or merely from the operation of the intestate succession laws.

One of the most interesting changes made by the 1975 inheritance legislation was to broaden the category of persons entitled to claim maintenance from a decedent's estate. While "reasonable financial provision" is available only to a spouse, various other family members had been permitted from the beginning to apply for allowance of support. Since 1975, this latter class of claimants includes any person whom the deceased "treated . . . as a child of the family." Others who may be awarded support are divorced former spouses who have not remarried[138] and any person who was being "maintained . . . wholly or partly" by the deceased before his death. This latter provision, to which we will have occasion to refer in the following chapter, was intended to cover the case of nonmarital cohabitation.

The United States

In the United States, the surviving spouse has clearly become the favorite in inheritance. The movement in this direction began in the first half of the twentieth century, when a number of states increased the size of the fractional share to be awarded to the surviving spouse in intestacy from a third to a half of the estate where children also survived. But a fractional share, being dependent on the size of the estate, will often turn out to be quite small and will be inappropriate in most cases where the children are minors. The Uniform Probate Code and the newer intestate succession laws of what is now a majority of the states were therefore drafted so as to permit the surviving spouse to take all of a small or medium-sized estate. This was accomplished, after the manner of English law, by defining the intestate share as a fixed amount plus a fraction of the remainder of the estate, the size of the fraction varying according to the number of competing claimants and their relationship to the decedent.[139] The fixed amount is set high enough so that the surviving spouse

138. Divorced spouses were added to the list of applicants in 1958, but the Matrimonial and Family Proceedings Act 1984 provided that divorce decrees could validly bar the making of such applications. Inheritance (Provision for Family and Depenants) Act 1975, s. 15, as amended.

139. *E.g.*, Uniform Probate Code, §2–102 (which instead of the usual one-third to one-half, gives the survivor $50,000, plus, in the case where there are surviving issue of the marriage,

takes all or practically all of an average estate to the exclusion of children of the marriage.[140] (Children from a prior marriage of the decedent are sometimes the subject of special provisions.) Generous homestead laws and surviving spouse allowances also can operate upon death to effect the transfer of all or nearly all of a small estate directly to the surviving spouse.[141]

Prior to 1978, evidence of the preferences of married persons in the United States concerning distribution of their property at death came from studies of testamentary behavior and the accumulated experience of the estate planning bar. But there was a lingering doubt whether the data yielded by will studies accurately represented the wishes of the average intestate decedent, since persons who leave wills tend to be older, wealthier, and of higher income and occupational status than those who do not.[142] In 1978, however, a well-designed, broadly based survey of popular beliefs and preferences about property distribution at death was published by the American Bar Foundation. The survey confirmed the results of the will studies and—somewhat to the surprise of the researchers—revealed that the majority of respondents wanted the surviving spouse to take the *entire* estate to the exclusion of the decedent's issue *or* family of origin.[143]

Asked to imagine a situation where they would be survived by their spouse and their parents or siblings, a large majority of the persons surveyed favored giving their entire estate to the surviving spouse.[144] These responses did not vary significantly according to how long the persons interviewed had been married or whether they had children themselves, nor were there significant differences between responses from separate and community property states. There were so few differences in attitudes towards property distribution at death that could be attributed to age, education, income, wealth, or occupational

---

one-half of the balance). The Code has been adopted in some 14 states and is under consideration in several more. 8 *Uniform Laws Annotated* (Estate, Probate and Related law) (St. Paul, Minn.: West, 1980).

140. See Uniform Probate Code, §2–102, Commissioners' Comment: "This section gives the surviving spouse a larger share than most existing statutes on descent and distribution. In doing so, it reflects the desires of most married persons, who almost always leave all of a moderate estate or at least one-half of a larger estate to the surviving spouse when a will is executed."

141. Rheinstein and Glendon, above, note 131 at 103–104.

142. Mary Louise Fellows, Rita Simon, and William Rau, "Public Attitudes about Property Distribution at Death and Intestate Succession Laws in the United States," 1978 *American Bar Foundation Research Journal* 321, 324–25, 336.

143. *Id.* at 321.

144. 70.8 per cent of respondents favored giving their entire estate to their spouse as opposed to their mother. The authors believed that people would feel a greater obligation to their mother than to a father or sibling. If this is correct, the figure cited is probably conservative. *Id.* at 351.

status that the authors of the survey concluded that the "values underlying respondents' choices are both consensual and cultural, rather than class-based or economic in nature." [145]

The study obviously challenges the premise on which nearly all American intestate succession law is based, namely that while the surviving spouse should take all of a modest estate, wealthier decedents would probably want at least part of their estates to go to their family of origin. In fact, the survey not only revealed a decisive preference for the surviving spouse to take everything, no matter what the size of the estate, but also showed that the wealthier the respondents were, the more they tended to favor the surviving spouse! [146]

Where the choice concerned only the surviving spouse and the issue (children and other descendants) of the persons interviewed, the responses supported the finding of the will studies that most persons in that situation still want their surviving spouse to take the entire estate. [147] In this case, however, the majorities in favor of the surviving spouse were not so great as they were when the competitors were from the decedent's family of origin. Yet, since the aim of intestate succession law is to approximate the desires of typical decedents, both the will studies and the American Bar Foundation survey suggest that the present laws in the majority of states limiting the surviving spouse to a fractional share or a fixed dollar amount with a further fractional share are not meeting this aim. Only three American states, Arizona, Montana, and Wisconsin, give a surviving spouse the entire estate in intestate succession where parents or issue of the marriage survive.

The bar foundation researchers strongly recommended revision of existing intestate succession laws to give the entire estate to a surviving spouse (leaving those who desire some other pattern free to establish one by will or *inter vivos* arrangement). The recommendation made one exception, however, for the increasingly common situation where the decedent dies survived by a current spouse and a child or children of a previous marriage. In this case, the authors of the survey suggested that giving 60 to 70 percent of the estate to the surviving spouse, with the remainder shared equally by all of the decedent's children, legitimate or illegitimate, from prior or current marriages, would conform to the preferences of most respondents.

In cases where one spouse disinherits or provides inadequately for the other, the difference between the law of the American states and that of England is striking: in every American state a widow or widower has certain property rights which cannot be defeated by will. The major legal techniques by which surviving spouses are protected against disinheritance are dower,

145. *Id.* at 385.   146. *Id.* at 353.
147. *Id.* at 356, 359.

indefeasible share, community property, homestead, and family allowances. Except for the indefeasible share, these techniques operate in both testate and intestate succession and protect surviving spouses to some extent against creditors of the decedent as well as disinheritance. Often these techniques are combined in a single state.

The oldest technique, dower, is today of diminishing importance; where it survives, it usually bears little resemblance to its original common law form. At the time when it was virtually the only device protecting a wife from disinheritance, it was a fixed property right which attached to the husband's real estate upon marriage, and it operated upon the husband's death to give the widow a life interest in a third of his lands. The fact that it only gave her a life estate and only applied to real property limited its effectiveness, especially as personal property acquired more importance. Furthermore, since dower was immune to *inter vivos* transfers and encumbrances by the husband, it was perceived as a clog on the marketability of land, even though in practice wives were often induced to sign away their dower rights when the husband wanted to sell, or borrow money on the security of, property subject to dower. Because of all these defects, the states came to see other protective devices as more appropriate to modern conditions than common-law dower. Many states abolished dower entirely, as England had done in the nineteenth century, and others modified its incidents, extending it to husbands and eliminating its immunity to transfers by the owner-spouse during the marriage.

The most common modern substitute for dower in the American states is the forced share, a device long used in many European systems to reserve a portion of a decedent's estate for certain designated takers. In American law, the forced share operates in favor of the spouse rather than descendants and ascendants, as, for example, in the French system. In some states, the forced share is a fraction of the intestate share; in others it is a fixed sum of money, with or without a fractional share in the surplus. The precise extent of the forced share in any state will of course reflect the way the legislature of that state balances the principle of freedom of testation against the policy in favor of protecting surviving spouses (and protecting the public purse). To Europeans, it must seem strange that policies in favor of protecting other dependents play almost no part, except in the community property state of Louisiana where children are forced heirs.

The American system of indefeasible share has some defects in comparison with the reserved share as it was developed in the civil law systems. Its principal weakness is that it can be defeated by lifetime transfers that deplete the estate. Thus, if one spouse gives away all his or her property shortly before death, the forced share of the survivor is a share of nothing. To cure this defect, the Uniform Probate Code and a small but steadily increasing number of states have taken steps to protect the surviving spouse by statute against such *inter vivos* transactions, and the courts in a number of states have developed doctrines through which assets transferred to the detriment of the survivor can sometimes be reached. A disadvantage of the forced-share system, in contrast to the English system of discretionary awards, is its lack of flexibility to deal with individual situations. Occasionally, the English approach is proposed as a replacement or supplement to present American systems, but it has found no acceptance.[148] Thus far, American legislatures have been unwilling to accord judges the power to rearrange estate plans and redistribute estates in accordance with their own notions of what is reasonable and fair.

The total picture of the protection of the surviving spouse in the United States must include the often generous allowances of support during the administration of the estate (the only protective device that exists in Georgia); the protection of rights in the marital home through homestead legislation; the fact that in community property states the survivor automatically receives half the marital acquests; and finally, the fact that federal estate and gift tax laws provide incentives to pass one's entire estate to one's spouse. Taken together, all these legal devices reveal in the law of the United States the fullest expression to be found in the countries here examined of the idea of solidarity between spouses in the case of marriages that terminate by death.

France

Where the marriage of a couple subject to the rules of the French statutory community of acquests is terminated by death, the matrimonial regime is dissolved, an inventory is made, a balance sheet drawn up, and the assets and liabilities of the community equally divided. The operation is the same as in the case of divorce, except that the division is between the survivor and the estate of the deceased, rather than between the two ex-spouses. All surviving spouses, whether married under the community property regime or not, have the right to receive from the decedent's estate the funeral expenses, and the costs of food and lodging for a period of a year after the death. If the predeceasing spouse owned separate property, his or her estate includes such property as well as his or her half of the community property. Thus, the rights supplementing the survivor's right to his or her "own" half of the community can be quite important.

Whether the surviving spouse as such has any rights in the estate of the deceased depends on what other persons rank as heirs, and on whether or not the decedent left a will. Under the Civil Code of 1804, a surviving spouse

---

148. A case against such proposals is presented in Mary Ann Glendon, "Fixed Rules and Discretion in Contemporary Family Law and Succession Law," 60 *Tulane Law Review* 1165, 1185–97 (1986).

was called to intestate succession only in default of collaterals within the twelfth degree. Since that time, the position of the spouse has improved, but not to the point where it is equivalent to that in the other countries studied here. Where (as we are supposing) the decedent leaves descendants as well as his spouse, a surviving spouse in France is entitled only to the usufruct of (a life interest in) one-quarter of the estate.[149] If the decedent left no descendants, brothers or sisters, descendants of brothers or sisters, ascendants, or illegitimate children conceived during the marriage, the surviving spouse can take one-half of the estate outright.[150] Only if there are no relatives at all, or if the survivors are collaterals more remote than those just mentioned, does the spouse take the entire estate.[151] This pattern is in sharp contrast to the situation of an American widow or widower. As we have seen, American intestate succession law usually secures all of a modest estate to the survivor outright even when he or she is in competition with issue of the decedent.

In the area of testate succession, French and Anglo-American laws differ as well. The differences in this area are partly attributable to the context of the different matrimonial property laws. In every common law jurisdiction (and in West Germany), a surviving spouse is protected to some extent against disinheritance. In French law, however, freedom of testation is limited only in favor of descendants and ascendants. Where the decedent is survived by two children (as we are supposing), their reserved share of the estate is two-thirds.[152] The remaining one-third is the *quotité disponible*, of which the testator is free to dispose by will as he or she wishes.

If a testator with children wishes to leave the *quotité disponible* to his or her surviving spouse, he or she may choose among three alternatives: (1) give the entire *quotité disponible* to the spouse outright (where two children survive, this would be one-third of the estate); or (2) give the survivor one-quarter of the estate outright and the income from the remaining three-quarters; or (3) give the survivor the income of the entire estate.[153] The latter two options have been available only since 1963, when they were introduced by a statute that was seen as marking a major advance in the rights of spouses. Under the prior law, the only alternatives to giving the surviving spouse the *quotité disponible* were to give him or her one-fourth of the entire estate outright plus one-fourth in usufruct; or to give him or her the usufruct of one-fourth of the entire estate. At the same time that these amounts were increased

149. French Civil Code, art. 767.

150. French Civil Code, art. 766.

151. French Civil Code, art. 765.

152. French Civil Code, art. 913. One child's share would be one-third of the estate. The share of three or more children would be three-quarters.

153. French Civil Code, arts. 1094, 1094–1.

in favor of the spouse in 1963, the descendants were given the right to have the usufruct converted to an annuity, provided (1) that they give sufficient security to guarantee the annuity and (2) that the property which is subject to the usufruct is not the residence of the surviving spouse nor the furnishings of such a residence.[154]

Thus, since 1963, one can see in French law more attention to the surviving spouse at the expense of the traditional concern for heirs in the blood line of the deceased. Nevertheless, the maximum amount available to be willed to the surviving spouse is still far less than that available under the law of the American states, where (except in Louisiana) it is the entire estate. The difference between French and American law is somewhat less remarkable, however, when we recall that in France most surviving spouses—under the community regime—have already received one half of the community fund. Perhaps it is the American failure to secure a share of parental estates to children that ought to appear remarkable.

On this point it seems clear, however, that we are dealing with real cultural differences. In France, even the very limited expansion of surviving spouses' rights in 1963 was criticized in some quarters. A 1974 article by a French notary warned that the introduction of forced inheritance by the surviving spouse would encourage divorce. His reasoning shows that the strength of the blood tie is not a negligible factor in contemporary French discourse about succession:

> One must never forget when one speaks of the surviving spouse as a forced heir, that there will always be a fundamental and irreversible difference between the spouse and the other forced heirs. The others are the ascendants and the descendants of the decedent. Their right to a forced share is an unquestionable right, because it is founded on a blood tie, which no one, not even the future decedent, can destroy. It is different with a spouse. The inheritance rights of a spouse are derived from marriage, in the absence of divorce or legal separation. The protection that one might wish to assure to a surviving spouse can only boomerang against him because of the fragility of the basis of such a right.[155]

On the other hand, the widespread use of the optional regime of universal community as a will substitute among long-married couples (ever since it became permissible to alter a marital property regime during the marriage in 1965) attests to the changing attitudes of French couples. Opinion surveys done in France revealed that respondents in general favored improving the

---

154. French Civil Code, art. 1094–2.
155. Michel Dagot, "Le conjoint survivant, héritier resérvataire?" D. 1974. Chr. 39,40.

position of the surviving spouse but also showed continuing attachment to the traditional idea that property should be preserved for children.[156] In this respect, American attitudes as expressed in the 1978 Bar Foundation survey are quite different; most parents appear content to leave the matter of providing for children entirely to the discretion of the surviving spouse, at least if there are no children from prior marriages in the picture.

West Germany

The idea that a surviving spouse should share in the other's property can be implemented by giving the survivor a share in the acquests, as in France, or an indefeasible share of the whole estate, as in most American states. The latter technique was regarded as simpler and therefore preferable by the parliamentary committee that drafted the final version of the 1957 West German Equal Rights Law, which (among other things) reformed marital property law. Therefore, even if West German spouses have lived under the legal regime of *Zugewinngemeinschaft*, the equalization claim used in divorce cases is not employed if one spouse dies intestate. The appraisals and calculations necessary for the determination of the equalization claim were regarded as so cumbersome that they would unnecessarily delay the liquidation of a decedent's estate. So the Code provides that, in intestacy, "the equal sharing in the marital increase is to be achieved by increasing, by one-fourth of the estate, the share of the surviving spouse" irrespective of whether there has been any difference of increase in the particular case.[157] As this works out, a surviving spouse who has been married under the rules of the *Zugewinngemeinschaft* is entitled to one-half of the estate if the decedent is survived by descendants and to either three-fourths or all of the estate in other cases, depending on the relationship of other survivors to the decedent.[158]

In addition to his or her intestate share, the West German law of succession gives the surviving spouse certain other benefits. A surviving spouse who is intestate heir together with parents, descendants of parents, or grandparents is entitled to the wedding gifts and household goods. One who is intestate heir together with descendants of the decedent is entitled to such items if they are necessary for the conduct of an appropriate household.[159]

By increasing the share of the surviving spouse, the 1957 Equality Law diminished the proportion of the estate to which the other intestate successors were previously entitled. The intestate share of children, for example, was

156. Max Henry, "L'intérêt de la famille réduit à l'intérêt des époux," D.1979, Chr. 179, 182.
157. West German Civil Code, §1371 par. 1.
158. West German Civil Code, §1931, 1924, 1925, 1926, 1932.
159. West German Civil Code, §1932.

reduced from three-fourths to one-half the estate under the legal regime. The statute attracted some criticism on this ground.[160] But the 1957 law is a recognition of the fact that in West Germany, as elsewhere in modern industrialized societies, the blood tie has been weakening, as has the significance of inherited wealth. Both tax law and the Civil Code favor joint wills in which each spouse leaves everything to the other for life, with the remainder going to the children upon the death of the surviving spouse.[161]

If the predeceasing spouse has attempted to disinherit the survivor by will, the widow or widower receives the equalization claim as in a divorce case. In addition to the equalization claim, the disinherited spouse is entitled to the reserved share (*Pflichtteil*) of the decedent's estate which was his or hers under the prior law.[162] The *Pflichtteil* of a disinherited spouse is one-half of what would have been due had there been no will. Complex rules apply to cases where a surviving spouse has been partially but not wholly disinherited. Other persons who are given a monetary claim against the heirs in cases of disinheritance are descendants or parents of the decedent who would have taken a share by intestate succession. They, too, are entitled to claim one-half of what they would have received in intestacy.

The Centrality of Modern Marriage

In the inheritance law of all the countries surveyed here, the conjugal relationship has increasingly moved into the foreground. The precise adjustment of the positions of surviving spouse and blood relatives varies greatly, however, from France, where the kinship group still has a strong position, to the American states, where the widow or widower not only enjoys preferential treatment but is everywhere protected to some extent against disinheritance.

The uniform trend toward the sharing of spouses' property on death is not surprising. Under modern circumstances, except among the very well-to-do, wealth transfers to children tend to take place while the parents are alive. In contemporary technological societies, most parents who are able to do so invest in their children's skills and education at a relatively early stage rather than seeking to accumulate an estate for their children's benefit. Once the

160. See the articles by Wolfram Müller-Freienfels, "Family Law and the Law of Succession in Germany," 16 *International and Comparative Law Quarterly* 409, 430 (1967) and "Equality of Husband and Wife in Family Law," 8 *International and Comparative Law Quarterly* 249, 265 (1959).

161. See Gerrit Langenfeld, "Freiheit oder Bindung beim gemeinschaftlichen Testament oder Erbvertrag von Ehegatten?" 1987 *Neue Juristische Wochenschrift* 1577.

162. See generally, Max Rheinstein and Mary Ann Glendon, "Interspousal Relations" in *International Encyclopedia of Comparative Law*, ed. Aleck Chloros, vol. 4 (Tübingen: J. C. B. Mohr, 1980), 109–11.

children have been given a start in life, increasing longevity requires that the parents' efforts then be directed toward providing for their own retirement, old age, and eventual widowhood. So far as the last event is concerned, American testamentary and French marital contract patterns show a definite trend for the spouses to seek to assure a continuing financial base for the survivor. The main obstacles to inheritance by spouses in the past were feelings about blood ties, family land, and inherited wealth. Such feelings were always more characteristic of some sectors of society than others and are now becoming fainter, even where they were once strong. Unlike in the divorce situation, neither public policy nor significant bodies of opinion push strongly for maintaining independence of the spouses' economic interests in the area of succession. The trend appears to be related to the modern predominance of what sociologists call the *joint and conjugal family*, and the common tendency to view an amicable marriage, at least, as a pooling of the economic interests of the spouses. The ease of divorce tends to phase out many of those unions which in earlier times might have furnished occasions for disinheritance.[163] These factors are reflected in current testamentary and *inter vivos* gift behavior as well as in legal changes, all of which reveal an increasing preference for the surviving spouse over children of the marriage and also over other blood relatives of the decedent.

163. At the same time, however, remarriage, the formation of new families, and the increase in *de facto* marriages pose new problems for succession law.

6

Informal Family Relations

Boire, manger, coucher ensemble
Est mariage, ce me semble.
Old French Proverb[1]

In the foregoing chapters, we have surveyed recent developments in marriage formation law, the law of the ongoing family, divorce and its legal consequences, and the law of inheritance. In the shadow of these evolving bodies of law, another set of legal norms has been taking shape as courts and legislatures have responded to a substantial rise in informal family behavior. Cohabitants who are not legally married have children, acquire and mingle their property, separate, and die, just as legal spouses do. They, too, enter contracts with, and are injured by, third parties. They pay taxes, and receive social benefits. In this chapter we examine the new law that has been produced as informal unions have increasingly claimed the attention of the French, West German, English, Swedish, and American legal systems. We will observe how changing social conduct has brought new legal forms into existence, and how it has drained old legal categories of some of their content.

As late as the 1960s, informal cohabitation was not considered a legal subject. When the previous version of this book was written in the 1970s, there was very little law explicitly and openly dealing with the relationships among *de facto* family members except in the Nordic countries. It was as though jurists everywhere had agreed to pretend the phenomenon did not exist. We now know, of course, that cohabitation arrangments of various sorts were becoming increasingly common during that period. We know, too, that there has always been a certain amount of family behavior that was not oriented to legal norms. After all, informal families predate legal families—Adam and Eve did not plight their troth at city hall. And, as *The Tinker's Wedding* reminds us, even when legal regulation of marriage and family life appeared, it did not penetrate all sectors of society to an equal degree. Legal systems have always had to deal with procreation and cohabitation that did not conform to the categories constructed by lawmakers. When the behavior in ques-

---

1. Quoted in Georges Ripert and Jean Boulanger, *Traité de droit civil*, vol. 1 (Paris: Librairie Générale de Droit et de Jurisprudence, 1956), par. 1254.

tion was more common among the poor or among racial and ethnic minority groups, the law generally ignored or condemned it.

In recent years, however, both the extent, and the types, of extralegal family behavior have changed. Not long ago, many marriage-like situations involved partners who were not legally eligible to marry, usually because one or both of them was already married. Indeed, as we saw in chapters 2 and 4, one of the reasons why restrictions on marriage and divorce were relaxed beginning in the 1960s was that strict marriage and divorce laws were believed, under modern conditions, to promote *de facto* unions. Another large proportion of informal unions, especially earlier in the century, was composed of persons who belonged to subcultures of the poor, or to racial and ethnic minorities for whom the legal structures of traditional marriage and divorce were sometimes irrelevant and with whom the framers of such laws were rarely concerned—groups ignoring and ignored by traditional family law. In addition, there have always been some people who have rejected marriage on ideological grounds as an unacceptable infringement of individual liberty, or as incompatible with the dignity of a mutual ethical commitment. A pregnancy or the birth of a child was often the occasion for formalizing a nonmarital union. But unwed mothers on their own rarely felt able to keep and raise what was then known as an "illegitimate" child.

Traditional family law rigorously policed the boundaries of the legitimate family. It carefully regulated the conditions under which children born outside legal marriage would be permitted to acquire rights in relation to their parents, especially the all-important right of inheritance. As for couples who had not entered into formal marriage, the law, for the most part, ignored them, or pretended to ignore them. As Napoleon put it, "Concubines put themselves outside the law, and the law has no interest in them."[2] The French and German Civil Codes dealt extensively with nonmarital children, but maintained a lofty silence with respect to cohabitation. In the common law countries, the situation was more complex. In some places, such as Scotland and a few American states, marriage could still be entered informally in the old way by exchanging consents and living together as husband and wife.[3] But in England and most of the United States, as on the continent, cohabitants were in principle regarded as legal strangers to each other, with no claims at all arising from their relationship.

2. Quoted in Jacqueline Rubellin-Devichi, *Les concubinages: approche socio-juridique*, vol. 1, (Paris: CNRS, 1986), p. 22.

3. For common-law marriage in the United States, see *Clark* 45–62; for "marriage by cohabitation with habit and repute" in Scotland, see J. M. Thomson, *Family Law in Scotland* (London: Butterworths, 1987), 15–18.

A closer look at the traditional law, however, reveals that all systems in one way or another had developed methods to deal with the problems that typically arise whenever persons share a life over a period of time. Indeed, Walter Weyrauch has convincingly demonstrated that common-law marriage in the twentieth century is better understood as a remedial device than as an alternate mode of marriage formation.[4] In his study of the American cases, he pointed out how the scattered geographic positions of the common-law marriage states facilitate inheritance claims by surviving *de facto* spouses from other states who are often able to show that they were "married" by virtue of visits or vacations in a neighboring jurisdiction. Where common-law marriage cannot be used in this way, Weyrauch demonstrated that presumptions, estoppels, and numerous devices of the law of proof are commonly pressed into service to perform the same curative function. The typical response to cohabitation in all traditional legal systems has been, in hardship cases, to pretend it is something else and then to attribute to it the desired legal effects. Thus, if one wants to find "traditional" cohabitation law, one has to look for cases under the headings of betrothal, presumptions of marriage, constructive trusts, implied agreements, partnerships, and so on.

Today, however, both cohabitation and cohabitation law have assumed new forms. The French demographer Louis Roussel, in a comparative survey of population trends in the industrialized countries, noted that until about 1970, demographers did not consider the numbers of unmarried cohabitants or births outside marriage to be statistically significant. By 1985, however, changes in these two areas had been "spectacular" in the countries with which we are here concerned.[5] Just as remarkable as, and presumably related to, increases in the frequency of informal family behavior has been the degree to which it has become socially acceptable. With the ready availability of divorce, hardly anyone now cohabits because he or she is unable to marry. Over the twentieth century, while formal marriage was gaining ground among members of disadvantaged groups who, like Sarah in *The Tinker's Wedding*, saw it as a symbol of social respectability, it was losing favor among the children of the middle classes. Declining marriage rates in all the industrial countries are witness not only to a general postponement of marriage, but also to a certain shift away from formal unions. Experts are no doubt correct in their view that a good deal of youthful cohabitation is more properly analyzed as a form of

---

4. Walter Weyrauch, "Informal and Formal Marriage—An Appraisal of Trends in Family Organization," 28 *University of Chicago Law Review* 88 (1960).

5. Louis Roussel, "Démographie—deux décennies de mutations" (Paper delivered at the Fifth World Congress of the International Society on Family Law, 8–14 July, 1985, Brussels, Belgium).

courtship or trial marriage than as marriage behavior.[6] Nevertheless, for a significant number of couples, cohabitation develops into an alternative, rather than a prelude, to marriage. As for those who once cohabited in order to show their disdain for bourgeois matrimony, what are they to do now that the middle class has unblinkingly adopted cohabitation as a way of avoiding the loss of pensions, alimony, or other benefits terminable on marriage?

The shift from old to new forms of cohabitation has been accompanied by a transition from old cohabitation law, which wavered between expressions of moral disapproval and covert compassionate remedies, to newer, more forthright legal approaches. Increasingly, one sees a casting-off of legal fictions and the direct attribution of economic consequences based on *de facto* dependency, especially in social welfare law. The old techniques still flourish, however, and are increasingly extended to types of cases where relief would formerly have been denied. Yet, in all the systems surveyed here, the distinction between formal and informal marriage has been maintained in principle, while the process of minimizing its practical importance goes forward. As we shall see, the new approaches generally avoid treating cohabitants exactly like legally married spouses, but refrain at the same time from pretending they are complete strangers. Using a variety of techniques, courts and legislatures are increasingly willing to take account of the fact that the lives of the cohabitants have been organized in common for a period of time.

In the account of the new cohabitation law presented here, no attempt is made to deal with all the forms of cohabitation that can give rise to legal questions. The discussion here concentrates primarily on that type of union which has received the most attention from legal systems, namely, marriage-like heterosexual cohabitation. As we review the principal developments of the past several years, we will try to discern the contours of the new legal statuses that are emerging and to measure the effects they have had on the institution of legal marriage, which has long held the center of the stage in family law. We will not enter into the details of the worldwide transformation of the legal status of illegitimate children, but will note where appropriate how a basic change of principle in this area importantly changed the meaning of the legal family.

Unions Libres, **Old and New**

As one might expect in a country where divorce was unavailable for most of the nineteenth century, informal family behavior made its presence felt in the French legal system long before the recent increases in nonmarital cohabita-

6. *Id.*; *König* 52.

tion and births out of wedlock. The Civil Code of 1804 had numerous provisions on paternity and filiation, and many standard civil law treatises even devoted a few paragraphs to "concubinage" or "free unions." Enough of a cluster of legal effects had accrued to the status of unmarried cohabitation to prompt some learned writers to compare it to the Roman *concubinatus*, a kind of inferior marital status.[7] Although the Civil Code did not directly deal with the situation of unmarried cohabitants, the law developed by the courts in cases involving them seems in certain ways to have been fashioned in the image of legal marriage set forth in the Code.

The ways in which the legal effects of cohabitation may imitate those of legal marriage in France can be seen in remedies available to a woman (the plaintiffs in the French cohabitation cases are nearly always female) when the cohabitation terminates. Where the relationship has come to an end because the parties have separated, French courts, since the middle of the nineteenth century, have been available to help resolve their disputes over property. In such cases, the partners to a free union are legally in a position similar to that of couples married under the regime of separation of assets, and the problem is to sort out his property from hers. As in all separate property regimes, the practical difficulties of proving the origin of assets or of establishing the proportion of each person's contributions can often result in an equal division.[8] In some cases, the plaintiff may be able to show that there was a *de facto* partnership (*société de fait*) between the cohabitants. If the plaintiff can make out the elements of such a partnership (an agreement to pool assets and to share profits and losses), the liquidation of the association closely resembles the sharing of acquests that takes place upon termination of the legal marital property regime.[9] Nonpartnership assets are returned to their respective owners, and the jointly acquired property is divided equally. Sometimes, in addition, a cohabitant can recover compensation for services rendered in the business of the other.[10]

There is of course a great difference between being able to count on an equal division of acquests and having to prove that one is entitled to the division of whatever has been accumulated by joint efforts. The legal avenues open to cohabitants in France *can* produce outcomes similar to the legal

---

7. *II Carbonnier* 277.

8. Danielle Huet-Weiller, "La cessation du concubinage," in *Les concubinages: approche socio-juridique*, vol. 2, ed. Jacqueline Rubellin-Devichi (Paris: CNRS, 1986), 107, 111–15.

9. The relevant provision of the French Civil Code is Article 1832, which provides that: "The *société* is a contract in which two or more persons agree to combine assets or efforts with a view toward sharing the benefits or savings that may result. The partners are bound to contribute to losses." Representative cases are collected in *II Carbonnier* 287–88.

10. Huet-Weiller, above, note 8 at 116–19.

community property system, but they also involve pitfalls which are well-illustrated by a 1982 case involving two farmers in a small village in the south of France. Jeanne D. sued her former companion, Gilbert S., to recover her share of the assets of a *société de fait* that she claimed had existed between them while they lived together in the home of Jeanne's elderly aunt.[11] Her story, which was accepted by the trial court, was that she had contributed financially to the acquisition of several parcels of land by Gilbert and had helped him in farming them during the seven years of their association. Gilbert admitted that Jeanne had helped him out in his farming operations, but denied she had made any financial contributions. The Court of Appeal of Montpellier reversed the lower court's decision for Jeanne, holding that the "mode of life that existed between the couple was inconsistent with any intention to associate themselves with a view toward sharing profits and losses derived from common funds." What seemed decisive for the appellate court was that Gilbert's and Jeanne's arrangement had included the right of each one to have sexual relations with other persons. Witnesses from the village had testified that Jeanne D. had freely exercised this option. In a revealing passage, the Court expressed the following opinion:

> [A] free union cannot give rise to definite legal consequences unless the situation of the cohabitants is characterized by a certain degree of stability resembling that of marriage, this stability depending in part, by reason of the monogamous customs which are at present those of the majority of the population, on the condemnation, at least in principle, of sexual relations with others during the period of the relationship. . . . [T]he cohabitation of a man and a woman who agree that each one may have mistresses or lovers as they wish, is nothing but an affair, even if it lasts for a length of time, and it cannot be considered as concubinage having a certain stability.

Having thus explained the etiquette "in principle" of modern sexual relationships, and classified a seven-year collaboration and cohabitation as a mere "affair," the court went on to deal with Jeanne's claim that she had helped to pay for Gilbert's land. Rather than viewing this as a straightforward claim for restitution, the court suggested that if Jeanne had given any money to Gilbert, this was probably only "a means of pursuing a liaison with a man who was perhaps about to leave her because of the numerous affairs" in which she had engaged.

The fate of Jeanne D. not only shows how difficult it may be to get courts to find the elements of a *de facto* partnership in a given case, it also illustrates

11. Montpellier Court of Appeal decision of 8 June 1982, D. 1983. Jur. 607, note by Odile Dhavernas.

the pervasive tendency in family law to devalue nonmarket work by women. Although Jeanne did not pursue an independent cause of action for the work she had done on Gilbert's lands, the court left no doubt about how it would view such a claim: "If D. assisted him in his work as a farmer, this circumstance is sufficiently explained by the fact that they lived under the same roof and that he rendered services to her, notably by occasionally taking her place in caring for her aunt."

Although as the Jeanne D. case shows, the *société de fait* is an uncertain remedy, it has been widely used in France to grant relief to plaintiffs in cohabitation cases. Most importantly, it has been successfully invoked, not only where the cohabitants were engaged in farming or business together, but even where their "partnership" consisted merely in acquiring a home and running a household. In this latter sort of case, the sole asset of the partnership often turns out to be the "marital" home.

Besides having a chance to be granted a share in the couple's acquests, a French cohabitant who has been abandoned by her companion can sometimes obtain compensation which resembles the remedies available to legal spouses in divorce cases. Where the behavior of the partner who terminates the liaison is particularly egregious, he may be ordered to pay damages under the general principle of tort law that anyone who, through his "fault," causes harm to another must make reparation for such harm.[12] In other words, even though it is not legally wrongful to break off a cohabitation relationship, the circumstances under which this happens (or even the circumstances under which the woman was induced to enter the liaison) may give rise to a cause of action. Cases awarding damages to women who were "seduced" by a bad-faith promise of marriage, or who were unceremoniously dropped when they were pregnant, or old, or sick, are analogous to the cause of action which has long existed in French law for reparation of "material or moral prejudice" suffered by a spouse in connection with fault divorce.[13]

When a free union terminates upon the death of one of the partners, French law has never shown any inclination to accord anything resembling inheritance rights to the survivor. But this is consistent with the short shrift traditionally given to a legal spouse, who even today has a relatively weak position in French succession law. As we saw in chapter 5, the needs of the legal widow are considered to be adequately secured by liquidation of the marital property regime, to which the *société de fait* can serve as a rough functional equivalent.

In cases where a person's death has been caused by the wrongful act of a

12. French Civil Code, art. 1382; Huet-Weiller, above, note 8 at 119–21.
13. See above, Chapter 5, text at note 54.

third party, French tort law accords a remedy in principle to anyone who in fact suffers harm as a result. Thus, when wrongful death actions first began to be brought by cohabitants, there seemed to be no legal obstacle to them. In the early 1930s, French courts quite readily granted tort damages to women who had been deprived of their breadwinners, regardless of whether they were legally married. Concentrating on compensation of actual harm, one lower court went so far as to deny damages to the legal widow and grant them to the woman with whom the decedent had been living.[14] Another tribunal awarded damages to two women living with the same man, thus, as a leading treatise put it, "legitimating polygamy and the *union libre* at the same time."[15]

These wrongful death cases eventually produced a famous split within the Court of Cassation. The civil division of the court took the position in 1937 that a cohabitant had no cause of action because she had no "legitimate, legally protected interest," and because the harm to her in any event was too difficult to measure, being based on a relationship which could be broken off at any moment.[16] The criminal division of the Court of Cassation went off in a different direction, developing distinctions between stable and precarious unions, and between nonadulterous and adulterous cohabitation. The criminal division routinely approved damages in cases involving stable unions uncomplicated by adultery.[17] The split in the court was not healed until 1970, when a mixed panel gave its approval to the latter approach.[18]

The 1970 decision, however, proved to be a mere temporary stopping point on the way to a new era. The first indication that a major shift in the treatment of informal family behavior was taking place was the amendment of the Civil Code in 1972 to establish substantial, though not complete, legal equality between legitimate and illegitimate children. Later that year, a wrongful death case involving an adulterous free union came before the criminal division of the Court of Cassation. The plaintiff, a physically handicapped woman, had been deserted long before by a husband whose current whereabouts were unknown. She and her child had been taken in by the decedent, with whom she had lived for thirty-six years and with whom she had had three more children. The Court refused to bar her action, relying on the technicality that the defendant tortfeasor had not met its burden to prove the woman's marriage still

14. Tribunal, Seine, decision of 12 February 1931. D.H. 1931. Jur. 57.

15. Paris Court of Appeal decision of 18 March 1932. D.H. 1932. Jur. 88; Henri Mazeaud, Léon Mazeaud, Jean Mazeaud, *Leçons de droit civil*, vol. 1, tome 1, 4th ed., ed. Michel de Juglart (Paris: Montchrestien, 1967), 51.

16. Court of Cassation decision of 27 July 1937, D.H. 1938. Jur. 5.

17. Mazeaud et al., above, note 15 at 52.

18. Court of Cassation decision of 27 February 1970, D. 1970. Jur. 201.

existed (i.e., that the husband was still alive somewhere).[19] Despite the narrowness of the holding and the exceptionally appealing facts of the case, one commentator described the decision as "astonishing" and "dangerous," and likened it to a previous "lapse" of the Court in which the owner of a horse killed in an accident had been granted damages for emotional suffering.[20]

By 1975, the criminal division was ready to hold that the adulterous character of a liaison need not be a bar to a wrongful death action, even where the adultery was well established.[21] A few days after this decision, the statute making adultery a crime in France was repealed in connection with reform of the divorce law. These developments did not mean, however, that *all* cohabitants would henceforward automatically be awarded damages when one partner was wrongfully killed by a third party. The courts invariably look for evidence of stability and duration before they will hold that legal rights arise from the relationship. The Paris Court of Appeal, for example, found it essential that a married woman cohabitant should have broken off all ties with her husband long ago, and that her arrangement with the decedent had a good chance of enduring.[22] And the Court of Cassation denied relief to both applicants in a case where the decedent had divided his days between two women on the grounds that neither union possessed the requisite character of stability.[23]

Meanwhile, scholarly opinion was changing too. Until the 1970s, the learned writers had been almost uniformly critical of expanding the rights of unmarried cohabitants. While recognizing the necessity of some legal intervention to deal with such matters as sorting out property, they viewed the attribution of legal effects to free unions as undermining the institution of legal marriage.[24] In recent years, however, new voices have begun to be heard, attitudes have become more tolerant, and terminology less pejorative.

In the case of the ongoing informal menage, French courts have not shown much willingness to treat cohabitants as other than legal strangers where private law is concerned. Thus, Civil Code article 220, which provides that spouses are jointly liable for household expenses and for expenses related to their children's upbringing, has been held inapplicable to cohabitants.[25] The legislature, by contrast, has assimilated informal to formal unions in a variety of public law contexts. Social benefit programs geared to children typically

19. Court of Cassation decision of 20 April 1972, J.C.P. 1972. II. 17278.
20. François Chabas, "Le coeur de la Cour de Cassation," D. 1975. Chr. 41.
21. Court of Cassation decision of 19 June 1975, D. 1975, Jur. 679.
22. Decision of 10 November 1976, D. 1987. Jur. 458.
23. Decision of 8 January 1985, J.C.P. 1986. II. 20588.
24. *E.g.*, Ripert and Boulanger, above, note 1 at 452.
25. Court of Cassation decision of 11 January 1984, D.1984. I.R. 275.

treat the marital status of their parents as irrelevant. In numerous statutes relating to leases, certain kinds of pensions, social security, and various types of insurance, cohabitation has been placed on substantially the same footing as legal marriage. Many of these statutes accord the same treatment to all "dependents" or to persons who "live maritally" as they do to persons who are legally connected to one another.[26]

A French development worthy of special note is that cohabitants in France can often gain equal treatment with married persons simply by presenting a document known as a "certificate of marital life." Some 30 percent of all cohabitants are estimated to have these certificates, which can be obtained at any city hall upon application by the cohabitants, supported by the affirmation of two witnesses, that the couple does indeed "live maritally."[27] The certificates have no binding legal effect, but they are accepted by many public agencies and private institutions as evidence of the status of the parties and as entitling them to be treated as "family" members. One might regard this procedure as a sort of marriage by registration—a less formal version of what is happening in the next room of the city hall where the mayor reads the Civil Code to newlyweds—or as a type of customary marriage in the age of bureaucracy.

To sum up, then, in general, the more a particular free union resembles marriage in stability and in the way the partners conduct themselves toward each other and the community at large, the more likely it is to be given effects resembling those of legal marriage. The presence of children in the household seems to play an important role in the courts' assessment of whether legal effects should be accorded. The extent to which the marriage model dominates French cohabitation law is well illustrated by two recent Court of Appeal decisions denying to homosexual cohabitants certain benefits available both to married persons and to cohabitants.[28] In these cases, the courts could find no basis for holding that the terms *living maritally* or *free union*, as used in statutes and regulations, were intended to designate anything other than stable unions presenting the appearance of marriage—which can by definition exist only between a man and a woman. Thus it is easy to understand why some French observers have seen the current situation as one in which the legitimate family prevails when all is said and done: "In appearance, it [the tra-

26. Detailed accounts of these statutes appear in Jacqueline Rubellin-Devichi, "L'attitude du législateur contemporain face au mariage de fait," 1984 *Revue trimestrielle de droit civil* 389, 395–97; "La condition juridique de la famille de fait en France," 1986 J.C.P. I. 3241, pars. 15–21, 33–35. See also, Rubellin-Devichi, ed., above, note 8 at chapters 13 and 15.

27. *Id.*, vol. 1, at 50.

28. Court of Appeal of Rennes decision of 27 November 1985 and Court of Appeal of Paris decision of 11 October 1985, both reported in D. 1986. Jur. 380.

ditional family] has certainly lost ground, but in fact it has imposed the matrimonial model on those who have declined to marry. No longer bothering to disdain its adversaries, it has transformed them in its own image." [29]

On the other hand, it is impossible to ignore the way in which legal recognition of informal family behavior has reflexively affected the legal family. The family law of the Civil Code so fully expressed a certain idea of the legal family that Mazeaud and Mazeaud could write as late as the 1960s that "[t]here is no family in law but the legitimate family. No legal bonds exist between members of the so-called natural family." [30] This position seemed tenable because, although the case law had dealt with certain practical problems of cohabitation, the Civil Code had enclosed the legal family, and only the legal family, in a network of provisions, both symbolic and sanctioned, designed to assure its cohesion, protection and continuation. But the idea of the family enshrined in the Code was shaken to its very foundations by the law of 3 January 1972 establishing substantial equality between legitimate and illegitimate children. Michelle Gobert was one of the first to see that this law represented a complete rethinking of the idea of the protection of the family: "From now on the natural family is no longer neglected by the legislature and the legitimate family is no longer conceived of as a sanctuary. . . . Now that the law takes account of *de facto* relationships, there can no longer be a unitary conception of the family." [31] Her assessment seemed confirmed in 1987 when the legislature, in revising child-custody law, made the new provisions of the Civil Code on parental authority applicable to unmarried as well as married couples. [32]

Though French cohabitation law, new as well as old, often seems to imitate the law of marriage, there is a way in which the free union has made marriage freer, too. Our earlier examination of French marriage law, together with this brief look at the legal treatment of cohabitation, seems to confirm the view of Alain Bénabent:

> The development of the free union in the legal area cannot fail to act as a counterforce on the very structure of marriage. In order that the institution of marriage will not be completely abandoned, it has been necessary to modify it so far as its obligatory ties are concerned. In this way, individual liberty has been aided in its progress against the

29. Christian Scapel, "Que reste-t-il de la 'paix des familles' après la réforme du droit de la filiation?" 1976 J.C.P. 2757.

30. Mazeaud et al., above, note 15 at 39.

31. Michelle Gobert, *La protection de la famille en droit civil* (unpublished monograph) (Paris: Société de législation comparé, 1973).

32. Law No. 87–570 of 22 July 1987 on the exercise of parental authority, *Journal Officiel*, 24 July 1987, 8253(1).

traditional "categories" of marriage by an external action, a sort of flanking and enclosing maneuver, on the institution of marriage.[33]

In this connection, it is interesting that Jean Carbonnier, who so often, as draftsman of French family law reforms and author of essays on legal sociology, counseled that the law must change with the times, recently has become a forceful advocate of maintaining the privileged position of legal marriage. The justification for differentiating between marriage and cohabitation, he wrote in 1985, is grounded in the distinctions between individualistic and collective values, and between evasion of and affirmation of social responsibility.[34] On these matters, according to Carbonnier, the collectivity is entitled to have its say. Another factor that seems to play a role here is the memory of why civil marriage was introduced in France in the first place, and the associated fear that recognition of informal marriage might open the door to recognition of religious marriages. At least this is what Carbonnier seems to be hinting when he writes that legal marriage, along with the other institutions of the Civil Code, is part of the "unwritten constitution of France," where it stands for and serves as a guarantee of the secular character of the modern social order.

The Nonmarital *Lebensgemeinschaft*

In West Germany, to a greater extent than in the other legal systems we examine here, nonmarital cohabitation remains in a twilight zone of non-law. Traditionally in Germany, as elsewhere, there was some use of presumptions and legal fictions to handle problems arising from unmarried cohabitation, but even this sort of case was hard to discover until recently because so few lower court decisions dealing with irregular family situations were published. Furthermore, while whatever negative attitudes French courts and writers of an earlier day manifested toward free unions seemed to arise from the threat such unions were believed to pose to the legitimate family, the traditional German approach was more characterized by disapproval of sexual relations outside marriage as such.[35] Today, these older attitudes have been abandoned, and a substantial body of cohabitation case law has emerged. But the two

33. Alain Bénabent, "La liberté individuelle et le mariage," 1973 *Revue trimestrielle de droit civil* 440, 446.

34. Jean Carbonnier, "Pas de Droits si l'on Refuse le Droit," in *La Famille contre les Pouvoirs*, ed. P. P. Kaltenbach (Paris: Nouvelle Cité, 1985).

35. See Rainer Frank, "The Status of Cohabitation in the Legal Systems of West Germany and Other West European Countries," 33 *American Journal of Comparative Law* 185, 186 (1985). Frank discusses a number of decisions of the West German Supreme Court (the Bundesgerichtshof), in which sexual intercourse outside marriage is branded as immoral. *E.g.*, "Because the law of morality prescribes marriage and the family as the obligatory mode of living it

principles that dominate the new legal approach—protection of the institution of marriage and respect for the presumed intention of cohabitants to avoid legal consequences—combine to prevent informal unions from acquiring a large number of legal effects.

The basic framework within which West German courts and legislatures have had to deal with recent increases in informal family behavior was established by the 1949 Constitution which, as we have often had occasion to note, places marriage and the family under the special protection of the state. The prevailing opinion among courts and commentators is that this provision of Article 6 of the Basic Law accords legal marriage a privileged position in relation to other forms of cohabitation, but scholarly views vary on the question of whether the "family" in Article 6 includes *de facto* families.[36] The principle of protecting marriage is tempered somewhat by two other constitutional provisions: the requirement of Article 6(5) that "Illegitimate children shall be provided by legislation with the same opportunities for their physical and spiritual development and their place in society as are enjoyed by legitimate children," and the command of Article 2 that each individual must have "the right to the free development of his personality insofar as he does not violate the rights of others or offend against the constitutional order or the moral code."

Toward the end of the 1960s, West German legal attitudes toward informal family behavior began to be less severe. In 1969, adultery was decriminalized, and a major statute was passed to improve the position of children born outside marriage. The *Bundesgerichtshof*, which as late as 1968 had said, "Sexual intercourse between unmarried persons in and of itself must be considered a violation of the law of morality,"[37] began to show a little more tolerance toward cohabitation. The basic approach of the West German courts to the legal disputes of unmarried cohabitants, however, is to treat them as though they had deliberately chosen to have a relationship without legal consequences.[38] This approach inevitably works to the detriment of the more economically dependent partner.

---

follows that sexual intercourse should only come to pass within the bonds of wedlock. An act to the contrary constitutes transgression of an elementary norm of sexual propriety." Bundesgerichtshof decision of 17 February 1954, reported in 1954 *Neue Juristische Wochenschrift* 766, 767.

36. *Pro*, K. H. Friauf, "Verfassungsgarantie und sozialer Wandel—das Beispiel von Ehe und Familie," 1986 *Neue Juristische Wochenschrift* 2595; *contra*, Dieter Giesen, "Ehe und Familie in der Ordnung des Grundgesetzes," 1982 *Juristenzeitung* 817.

37. Bundesgerichtshof decision of 26 February 1968, 1968 *Neue Juristische Wochenschrift* 932, 935.

38. *E.g.*, Bundesgerichtshof decision of 3 October 1983, 1983 *Zeitschrift für das gesamte Familienrecht* 1213.

Under West German law, as under French law, cohabitants are permitted to prove that they had entered into an association to acquire property with a view toward equal sharing of their profits. The *BGB-Gesellschaft* (Civil Code partnership) is quite similar to the French *société de fait*.[39] Both legal devices can be resorted to by any two or more individuals, and both may result in a division of partnership assets that can resemble the liquidation of a community property regime. A German Civil Code partnership, unlike the French *société*, need not be for an economic purpose, but in practice West German courts in cohabitation cases require that some economic venture be involved before they will give relief on partnership principles. They also seem to be stricter than their French counterparts about proof of the elements of a partnership. Although there are also instances where West German courts have applied the partnership rules by analogy, they seem to be less ready than French courts to do so in order to reach an equitable result.[40] They do not, for example, attribute any legal significance to what they consider to be the ordinary contributions made by persons living together: performance of housework, care of a sick partner, or money spent on running the household.[41] When they do find that a partnership existed between the cohabitants, it tends to be by virtue of "extraordinary" contributions to the acquisition of particular valuable assets, rather than day-in, day-out financial and other contributions to the aggregate of property acquired during cohabitation. This approach makes it quite difficult for homemakers ever to prevail. In one of the few cases where a plaintiff-cohabitant was successful, the couple had built two three-family houses together on certain land, title to which was in the woman's name. When the couple parted, the man was allowed to recover his substantial contributions in cash and labor on a partnership theory.[42] In another similar case, a man was permitted to recover half the assets of a hotel-restaurant business, title to which was in the name of the female cohabitant. The Court of Appeal in that case found sufficient evidence of a tacit partnership agreement in "the length of the cohabitation and in the extensive work activities

39. The relevant civil code section is §705 which provides that "partners, through the partnership agreement, are reciprocally bound to promote the attainment of a common purpose in the manner specified in the agreement, and in particular to make the agreed contributions."
40. This is the conclusion of a detailed comparative study by Helen Marty-Schmid, *La situation patrimoniale des concubins à la fin de l'union libre. Étude des droits suisse, français, et allemand* (Geneva: Droz, 1986), 402–8. The leading case analogizing from partnership law is Bundesgerichtshof decision of 3 March 1980, reported in 1980 *Zeitschrift für das gesamte Familienrecht* 664.
41. Wilfried Schlüter with D. W. Belling, "Die nichteheliche Lebensgemeinschaft und ihre vermögensrechtliche Abwicklung," 1986 *Zeitschrift für das gesamte Familienrecht* 405, 406.
42. Bundesgerichtshof decision of 24 June 1985, reported in 1985 *Zeitschrift für das gesamte Familienrecht* 1232.

undertaken by the man, which far surpass those of an ordinary employee or even those of a spouse employed in a family enterprise. . . ." [43]

Where there have not been major contributions in money or what the court considers to be money's worth, a cohabitant in West Germany has little prospect of obtaining some kind of financial reckoning upon dissolution of the union. Theories of unjust enrichment, restitution, and implied contract, though theoretically available for this purpose, are rarely applied. Instead, the courts tend to let the loss lie where it falls, discouraging any accounting or adjustment of property relationships when an informal union breaks up. [44] In the past, disputes between ex-cohabitants were occasionally handled under the rather elaborate provisions of the Civil Code concerning betrothal (*Verlöbnis*). [45] The fiction of, or analogy to, a betrothal can permit a partner in a free union to recover certain expenditures or even damages suffered when the engagement is wrongfully broken off. [46] But this entire body of law has an outdated character and is often inappropriate to cohabitaion cases because of its assumption that the parties had at one time agreed to marry. There seem to be no signs of a large-scale resort to this remedy at present.

When a cohabitation terminates with the death of one of the partners, the survivor is no better off than when it ends *inter vivos*. He or she has, of course, no right of inheritance. Nor does West German law accord the surviving cohabitant a right to sue a third party who has wrongfully caused the other's death. This results from the fact that the West German Civil Code, unlike the French, does not in principle permit everyone who is actually harmed by a death to sue for damages. The plaintiff must be someone who had a legal right to be supported by the decedent. [47] In spite of this rather severe overall approach, however, one can detect a little softening of judicial attitudes in recent years toward a cohabitant who has lost her provider through death. The word *family* in the code provision permitting a court to order temporary support to dependent family members from a decedent's estate, [48]

---

43. Oberlandesgericht-Hamm decision of 31 October 1979, reported in 1980 *Neue Juristische Wochenschrift* 1530.

44. See, for example, Oberlandesgericht-Munich decision of 15 November 1979, reported in 1980 *Zeitschrift für das gesamte Familienrecht* 239; Oberlandesgericht-Frankfurt decision of 23 December 1980, reported in 1981 *Zeitschrift für das gesamte Familienrecht* 253; and Oberlandesgericht-Frankfurt decision of 23 October 1981, reported in 1982 *Zeitschrift für das gesamte Familienrecht* 265.

45. West German Civil Code, §§1297–1302.

46. Siegfried de Witt and J.-F. Huffman, *Nichteheliche Lebensgemeinschaft*, 2d ed. (Munich: Beck, 1986), 184–86.

47. West German Civil Code, §844(2).

48. West German Civil Code, §1969.

for example, has been interpreted by one court to include a *de facto* spouse.[49] There has also been a marked reduction in the hostility formerly shown by German courts to testamentary dispositions in favor of a long-time companion of the decedent. In a major reversal of approach, the *Bundesgerichtshof* held in 1970 that these so-called "mistress wills" were not necessarily invalid.[50] Where the testator is unmarried, a will leaving property to his companion will ordinarily be given full effect, and even in the case of a married testator, such a will may be upheld if the testator has adequately provided for his legal heirs. The older view of these arrangements has given way to the notion that a testator may even have had a "moral duty" to provide for a long-time domestic partner.[51]

In other areas of law, informal marriage may be taken into consideration in a negative way in determining whether to deny or cut off maintenance after divorce,[52] or whether an applicant for various forms of public assistance is really in need.[53] This is consistent with the policy of ensuring that married couples are not legally disadvantaged in relation to cohabitants. In West Germany, as elsewhere, a "partner" is often treated like a spouse in various public law areas.

West Germany is the principal example, among the countries studied here, of that legal attitude toward cohabitation which purports to defer to the presumed choice of the cohabitants to remain outside the law. This approach, which has vigorous proponents elsewhere,[54] does have certain advantages. The partners in informal unions know precisely where they stand, legally speaking. Their freedom is respected, including the right to make enforceable contracts governing the economic aspects of their relationship.[55] But such agreements in practice are rare, and this kind of freedom means that, over

49. Oberlandesgericht-Dusseldorf decision of 14 December 1982, reported in 1983 *Zeitschrift für das gesamte Familienrecht* 274.

50. Bundesgerichtshof decision of 31 March 1970, noted in 1970 *Neue Juristische Wochenschrift* 1273.

51. Frank, above, note 35 at 204–5. The leading case is Bundesgerichtshof decision of 10 November 1982, reported in 1983 *Zeitschrift für das gesamte Familienrecht* 53.

52. See de Witt and Huffman, above, note 46 at 80–89; Horst Luthin, "Zur 'objektiven Unzumutbarkeit' einer Leistung von nachehelichem Unterhalt in der Rechtsprechung des Bundesgerichtshofs," 1986 *Zeitschrift für das gesamte Familienrecht* 1166.

53. *E.g.*, Bundessozialhilfegesetz §122 (Federal Social Assistance Law), which provides that persons living in a marriage-like association (*eheähnliche Gemeinschaft*) should not be treated more favorably than legally married spouses.

54. *E.g.*, Ruth Deech, "The Case Against Legal Recognition of Cohabitation," 29 *International and Comparative Law Quarterly* 480 (1980).

55. Bundesverfassungsgericht decision of 24 January 1962, reported in 1962 *Neue Juristische Wochenschrift* 437 (partners to an informal marriage can validly enter into a contract of employment with each other).

time, marriage-like relationships are left to develop in the state of nature, where the weak and dependent are at the mercy of the strong and self-sufficient.

We must emphasize, however, that one important aspect of nonmarital family behavior is not left outside the law in the system just described. In recent years, West Germany, like other countries, has not hesitated to impose financial responsibilities on parents when cohabitation (or a sexual relationship outside marriage) produces children. The legal position of children born outside marriage has greatly improved since the time of the Civil Code of 1896, which stated flatly, "An illegitimate child and its father are not deemed to be related." [56] But the process was a slow one. Despite the command of the 1949 constitution that legislation should furnish illegitimate children with the same opportunities as are enjoyed by legitimate ones, the Civil Code provisions were not amended to conform to the Basic Law until 1969.[57] From that time forward, however, West German public and private law has shown great solicitude for the rights of nonmarital children.

So far as unmarried cohabitants are concerned, it is hard to say whether the relative hesitance of West German courts to intervene in their affairs is due mainly to respect for the cohabitants' free choice of a way of life, or whether it masks a lingering punitiveness. In either case, it is clear that the price of freedom may be high for the socially weaker party, who in most cases will be the woman.

England: A Cautious Accommodation

In England, as in France and West Germany, informal family behavior has increasingly made its presence felt in the legal system. Here, too, a new legal era seems to have been inaugurated when the legal status of illegitimate children was reconsidered. Only thirty years ago, when the Morton Commission issued its report on marriage and divorce, it would have been hard to imagine legal changes of the type that began to take place in the 1960s. The Commission's position on legitimation of children born outside legal marriage was crystal clear:

> So long as marriage is held to be the voluntary union for life of one man with one woman, that conception is wholly incompatible with the provision that one or the other of the parties can, during the subsistence of the marriage, beget by some other person children who may later be legitimated. . . . Any departure from that concep-

56. West German Civil Code, former §1589 II.
57. Nichtehelichengesetz of 19 August 1969, BGBl. I. 1243.

tion can only be made by ignoring the essential moral principle that a man cannot, during the subsistence of his marriage, beget lawful children by another woman. It is unthinkable that the state should lend its sanction to such a step, for it could not fail to result in a blurring of moral values in the public mind. A powerful deterrent to illicit relationships would be removed, with disastrous results for the status of marriage as at present understood.[58]

It was not long, however, before the unthinkable became the law. In 1969, the Family Law Reform Act gave children born outside of legal marriage the same rights to inherit from their parents as were possessed by legitimate children. Most remaining inequalities were eliminated by the Family Law Reform Act of 1987, which expunged the term "illegitimate" from the law relating to children.

So far as the legal position of unmarried cohabitants is concerned, matters had progressed by the 1980s to the point where Cretney could write that the principle that marriage is an essential prerequisite to the creation of a legally recognized family unit is "now subject to many exceptions."[59] Let us consider the extent to which this is the case, first, where the cohabitation is terminated during the lifetimes of the cohabitants, and second, where one cohabitant dies.

So far as property disputes upon dissolution are concerned, the English cohabitation cases resemble nothing so much as the older English and American divorce cases where courts had to sort out the affairs of spouses under the regime of separate property, unmodified by judicial discretion. Indeed, the leading marital property cases, *Pettitt* and *Gissing*, provide the starting points for analysis of cohabitants' rights. One observes the courts engaging in the same laborious process of using whatever device comes to hand in order to avoid inequities.[60] And one discovers, as before, the occasional case where no fiction can quite be made to fit, and the court denies relief, expressing great regret that a long-time companion who raised children, performed domestic labor, and contributed to household expenses receives no share in the property acquired by her partner in his own name.[61]

As the Court of Appeal stated in 1986, the property rights of unmarried

58. *Report of the Royal Commission on Marriage and Divorce*, (London: Her Majesty's Stationery Office, 1956), par. 1180.

59. *Cretney* 4.

60. The cases, replete with constructive trusts, implied contracts, and equitable estoppels, are discussed in detail in *Cretney* 660–69.

61. E.g., *Burns v. Burns*, [1984] 1 All E.R. 244, 255 (Court of Appeal): "But the unfairness of that [non-recovery by a woman who had been a housewife and mother for 19 years] is not a matter which the courts can control. It is a matter for Parliament."

cohabitants must be determined on that "familiar ground which slopes down from the twin peaks of *Pettitt* v. *Pettitt* and *Gissing* v. *Gissing*." [62] As in the case of married persons, this means that in most cases "the fundamental, and invariably the most difficult, question is to decide whether there was the necessary common intention, being something which [in the absence of express agreement] can only be inferred from the conduct of the parties, almost always from the expenditures incurred by them respectively." [63] In *Grant v. Edwards*, the Court of Appeal employed a constructive trust to give a woman who had contributed from her earnings to household expenses, in addition to keeping house and raising children, a share in property acquired by her cohabitant in his own name. The Court stated that the woman could not reasonably have been expected to make such substantial contributions except "on the faith of the common intention between her and the defendant that she was to have some sort of proprietary interest in the house." [64] (It did not, incidentally, seem to the Court to be relevant that the plaintiff was a married woman.) It was sufficient, for purposes of establishing the constructive trust, to show a common intention and the plaintiff's detrimental reliance on that intention.

As in cases involving married persons, common intention cannot be proved by evidence of homemaking, child-raising, and the like. [65] It seems to be crucial for the plaintiff to demonstrate that her indirect contributions to the acquisition of property were "substantial," exceeding a mere sharing of day-to-day expenses, or the ordinary cooperation that married persons and, it seems, cohabitants are presumed to render gratuitously to each other. [66] If recovery is allowed, the contributions of the parties are also important in determining the extent of their interests, for there is no presumption of equal sharing. [67]

It is important to note that this body of decisional law does not accord a special status to cohabitation. It merely applies general principles of property

62. *Grant v. Edwards*, [1986] (Court of Appeal), reported in *The New Law Journal*, 9 May 1986, 439. See also *Cretney* 668–69 and above, Chapter 3, text at note 122.

63. *Grant v. Edwards*, above, n. 62.

64. *Id.*

65. The cases are criticized on this ground in John Eekelaar, "A Woman's Place—A Conflict between Law and Social Values," *The Conveyancer and Property Lawyer*, March–April 1987, 93–102.

66. In *Burns v. Burns*, [1984] 1 All E.R. 244, the plaintiff's position (raising children in a two-earner household) was very similar to that of the plaintiff in *Grant v. Edwards* except that her contributions from earnings were used for "consumer durables" and other household items, while Ms. Grant was found to have made very substantial indirect contributions to the repayment of mortgages by virtue of her having paid part of the household expenses. The cases are hard to distinguish. Indeed, the trial judge in *Grant* dismissed the claim on the authority of *Burns*.

67. *Cretney* 669.

law. But since the relationship of the parties is relevant in determining questions of intent, the tendency in the cases is to find an intent to share assets more easily where the cohabitation has been what the court considers marriage-like. Unlike the French courts, which often consider that a *de facto* partnership encompasses all property acquired in pursuit of the aims of the cohabitants' association, English courts, like West German ones, tend to follow an asset-by-asset approach. In England, however, successful petitions tend to result in the sharing of the marital home, whereas West German courts tend to reserve the partnership remedy for joint business ventures.[68]

The most striking developments in English cohabitation law involve the legal consequences of the death of one of the partners. Since 1975, England (alone among the countries whose law we examine here) has permitted a dependent cohabitant to share in a deceased partner's estate even though he or she is not mentioned in the decedent's will.[69] Although a cohabitant cannot be an intestate heir, the Inheritance (Provision for Family and Dependents) Act of 1975, as we have seen, greatly expanded the class of persons who are entitled to claim maintenance from a decedent's estate. This class now includes such informal family members as anyone who was "treated as a child" of the decedent's family and anyone who was "being maintained" by the decedent immediately prior to his death.[70] Within the latter class of claimants, Parliament seems to have had in view primarily women in long-term *de facto* dependency relationships. At the time, the solicitor general, defending the provision against the criticism that it rewarded immorality, emphasized that it was meant to deal with practical problems:

> Many of us who have practiced in this area have come across tragic cases of a common-law wife who has devoted years to the deceased and, perhaps, helped him to build up a business and who then finds that she is deprived of any benefit or redress because she cannot produce a marriage certificate.[71]

Unlike a surviving spouse who can, as we have seen, receive a substantial share of a decedent's estate under the English family provision legislation, a person claiming as a dependent can only be granted "reasonable maintenance." But once the court allows a dependent's claim, it can, if necessary,

---

68. *E.g.*, Bundesgerichtshof decision of 12 July 1982, reported in 1982 *Zeitschrift für das gesamte Familienrecht* 1065.

69. The temporary maintenance available to a cohabitant under West German Civil Code §1969 is limited to a thirty-day period.

70. Inheritance (Provision for Family and Dependents) Act 1975, s.1(3).

71. Quoted in Sebastian Poulter, "The Death of a Lover—I," 126 *New Law Journal* 417, 418 (1976).

reduce testamentary gifts to members of the "legal" family in order to pay it.

Testamentary gifts to cohabitants are valid in principle, but like any other bequests, they are vulnerable under the family provision legislation if relatives or other dependants of the deceased have not been adequately provided for. So far as wrongful death actions are concerned, prior to 1982 a cohabitant whose partner was killed in an accident was not entitled to sue, because cohabitants were not among the group of dependents authorized by the Fatal Accidents Act to bring such actions. The Act was amended in that year, however, to include dependents who had been living as husband or wife with the decedent for at least two years immediately prior to the death.[72]

Even without specific parliamentary direction, English courts often have been solicitous of surviving cohabitants. In expanding the interpretation of the phrase "members of the original tenant's family" in the Rent Acts to permit a woman to succeed to the rent-controlled lease of the man with whom she had lived for forty years, one judge stated, "The social stigma that once attached to [nonmarital unions] has almost, if not entirely, disappeared."[73] The mode of living of the couple was an important factor in the case, the court observing that the union, to be familial, must have an "appropriate degree of permanence and stability."[74] The limits to the elasticity of the category were shown three years later in a Rent Act case involving a couple with separate bank accounts and separate names, where the woman was held not to have been a member of the deceased tenant's "family," even though she had lived with him for five years.[75]

This common-sense method of working out legal responses to cohabitation, situation-by-situation, carries over into public law. A cohabitant may be denied social assistance because of the support he or she receives from a partner, while unmarried couples with children are deemed to be a "family" for purposes of receiving benefits under the Family Income Supplements Act.[76] In both situations, nonmarital relationships are assimilated to marital ones as the law attempts to pierce the legal forms and address the actual economic relationships. Finally, it should be mentioned that the Domestic Violence and Matrimonial Proceedings Act of 1976 permits the courts to exclude a violent

72. Fatal Accidents Act 1976, s.1(3)(b), as amended by the Administration of Justice Act 1982.

73. *Dyson Holdings v. Fox*, [1976] Q.B. 503, 512 (Bridge, J.).

74. *Id.* at 513.

75. *Helby v. Rafferty* [1978] 3 All E.R. 1016. In 1985, the Appeal Court unanimously ruled that a same-sex cohabitant could not be a member of the tenant's family within the meaning of the Housing Act 1980, *Harrogate Borough Council v. Simpson* [1985] 16 Fam. 359.

76. See A. A. S. Zuckerman, "Formality and the Family—Reform and the Status Quo," 96 *Law Quarterly Review* 248, 272 (1980); Family Income Supplements Act 1970, s.1(1).

person from the home by injunction, regardless of the marital status of the parties or ownership rights in the dwelling.[77]

Little by little, the courts and Parliament have brought into being a considerable body of law which deals in a differentiated manner with a series of recurring problems that arise whenever persons in a relationship become significantly interdependent. The presence of children, the duration of the relationship, the detriment suffered by homemakers, and the degree to which the life of the partners conformed with the court's idea of marriage are all factors which have played an important role in the cases.[78] Thus the body of law we have encountered here (like that we saw in France) has a certain "marital" cast. It does not, however, transform informal marriage into a status, so much as it responds in a pragmatic, nuanced way to the recurring problems that cohabitation generates.

Sweden: Where All Roads Lead?

It is the convergence and consummation of three distinct trends, each one present to some degree in the other systems discussed here, that renders informal marriage in Sweden (and, to a lesser extent, the other Nordic countries) of special interest. These three trends are the emergence of informal marriage as a substantial social institution, its development as a legal institution, and the elimination from legal marriage of many of the features that previously distinguished it from informal marriage.

Informal family behavior is markedly more widespread in Sweden than in England, France, West Germany, or the United States. Roughly 20 percent of all couples in Sweden are unmarried, and virtually all Swedish marriages are said to be preceded by a period of cohabitation.[79] Legal marriage rates there dropped dramatically beginning in the late 1960s, and by 1986 nearly half (48.4 percent) of all children born in Sweden had unwed mothers, most of whom were living with the child's father.[80] These modern developments have occurred against a cultural background where the social practice of cohabitation was not uncommon among country folk, who often deferred marriage

77. Domestic Violence and Matrimonial Proceedings Act 1976, s.1; *Davis v. Johnson* [1978] 2 W.L.R. 553 (H.L.).

78. See M. D. A. Freeman and Christina M. Lyon, "Towards a Justification of Rights of Cohabitees," *New Law Journal*, 6 March 1980, 228.

79. *Report of the Commission on Marital Property Reform*, Bilaga 6, SOU 1981, 85; Louis Roussel, "Les concubinages: le point de vue des sociologues," in Rubellin-Devichi, ed., vol. 1, above, note 8 at 102. See generally, Jan Trost, *Unmarried Cohabitation* (Västerås: International Library, 1979).

80. I am grateful to Professor Anders Agell of the Uppsala University Law Faculty for supplying me with the 1986 figure.

until a child was conceived, and among working-class people in the cities. By the turn of the century, formal marriage and its attendant religious aspects had been subjected to critique by liberal intellectuals, especially in feminist and socialist circles.[81] These quite different strains flowed together and helped to fuel the social transformations that took place in late twentieth-century Sweden, where cohabitation has taken its place beside legal marriage as an accepted and socially approved form of behavior.

In Sweden, the legal reaction to changing customs has been to increase the legal effects of cohabitation and, to a great extent, to merge the legal treatment of the problems to which both marriage and cohabitation give rise. The main lines of the current approach were laid down in a series of directives which were issued in 1969 by the minister of justice to a governmental commission charged with the task of studying Swedish family law and recommending revisions. While stating that legal marriage should continue to have a "central position" in family law, the minister advised that future legislation should be so drafted as not to impose "unnecessary hardships or inconveniences on those who have children and build families without marrying."[82] As for legal marriage, it "should be a form of voluntary cohabitation between independent persons."[83] The object of the new family law should be to solve practical problems which occur in the course of "the cohabitation of a man and a woman with family functions," and "not to give a privileged status to one form of cohabitation over others."[84] The law should "as far as possible be neutral as regards different forms of cohabitation and different moral ideas."[85]

The year 1969 also saw important improvements in the legal position of children born outside legal marriage, an area where Sweden had long been in the vanguard. In public law, many differences between marriage and other forms of cohabitation had already been erased, their elimination spurred, as Jacob Sundberg has written, "by the disappearance of a positive interest in marriage as an institution as well as [by] the building of the social welfare

81. Jacob Sundberg, "Marriage or No Marriage: The Directives for the Revision of Swedish Family Law," 20 *International and Comparative Law Quarterly* 223, 230 (1971); *Rheinstein* 137. The possibility of concluding a valid informal marriage was not foreclosed in Sweden until 1915. Anders Agell, "The Swedish Legislation on Marriage and Cohabitation: A Journey without a Destination," 1980 *Scandinavian Studies in Law* 1, 20.

82. Jacob Sundberg, "Recent Changes in Swedish Family Law: Experiment Repeated," 23 *American Journal of Comparative Law* 34, 48 (1975).

83. Sundberg, above, note 81 at 233.

84. Note, "Family Law—Sweden," 22 *International and Comparative Law Quarterly* 182 (1973); and Note, "Current Legal Developments, Sweden," 19 *International and Comparative Law Quarterly* 164 (1970).

85. *Id.*

state."[86] High taxation, pension schemes, workmen's compensation, and the varied largesse of the welfare state had contributed to the decline in importance of inheritance and marital property. In order to discourage "tax divorces," the tax treatment of married and unmarried persons had been largely equalized. A surviving cohabitant for purposes of some pensions and insurance schemes was treated as a spouse, provided the cohabitants had had a child together or had previously been married to each other. Adultery had ceased to be a crime in Sweden in 1937.

Additional distinctions between formal and informal marriage were eliminated in 1973, in keeping with the 1969 guidelines. Carrying out a directive that said, "[L]egislation should not under any circumstances force a person to continue to live under a marriage from which he wishe[s] to free himself,"[87] the Riksdag made unilateral divorce on demand a reality.[88] In addition, it authorized the courts, upon dissolution of a stable union, to apply rules similar to those governing disposition of the matrimonial home upon divorce, awarding possession of a rented flat to the partner who "needed it the most," normally the custodian of the children.[89] Custody of a child born to unmarried parents ordinarily belongs to the mother, but if the parents wish to have joint custody, they need only apply for it through a simple, nonjudicial procedure. Voluntary mediation services were made available to cohabitants on the same basis as to divorcing spouses. Since 1975, a surviving cohabitant has been entitled to bring a wrongful death action.[90]

Further changes have been implemented pursuant to a policy of protecting the weaker party on dissolution of cohabitation.[91] A new law, effective in 1988,[92] provides that, upon separation of a couple that has lived in a marriage-like relationship, their permanent dwelling and household goods, if owned by one party but acquired for their joint use, shall be divided equally along the pattern established for the property of married couples. An exception is pro-

86. Jacob Sundberg, "Nordic Laws," in *Das Erbrecht von Familienangehörigen in postivrechtlicher und rechtspolitischer Sicht*, ed. Ernst von Caemmerer et al., (Frankfurt: Metzner, 1971), 31, 40.

87. Sundberg, above, note 81 at 233–34.

88. See above, Chapter 4, text at note 160.

89. Sundberg, above, n. 82.

90. Agell, above, note 81 at 28–31.

91. This approach was recommended by the Commission on Marital Property Reform, above, n. 79: "[T]he Commission finds that there is no need for legislation which treats cohabitation as an alternative to marriage. What is needed is to find solutions to practical problems and, in particular, to protect the weaker party at the dissolution of cohabitation."

92. Cohabitees (Joint Homes) Act of 1987, SFS 1987: 232 and 814. The following description of the statute is based on Åke Malmstrom and Anders Agell, *Family and Inheritance Law in Sweden* (Uppsala: 1987) (unpublished monograph).

vided for cases where this would be unreasonable in view of the length of cohabitation or other circumstances. As in the case of married couples, the right to *occupy* the home may be allocated to the partner with the greater need, if this is reasonable under all the circumstances of the case. This right of occupancy applies regardless of title to the dwelling. The cohabitant to whom the home is thus allocated (normally the custodian of the children) is, however, required to compensate the other if the value of the occupancy exceeds what otherwise would have been his or her share of the couple's belongings. Similar provisions govern the allocation of a rented dwelling. Where the cohabitation terminates by death, the survivor is likewise entitled to apply for division of property acquired for joint use.

This new statute, unless excluded by a written contract between the cohabitants, applies to all couples living under "marriage-like conditions," and its provisions were made applicable by subsequent legislation to persons who live together "in a homosexual relationship." [93] The resemblance to a regime of marital property is heightened by the fact that the couple's home (if acquired during cohabitation) cannot be sold without the consent of the cohabitee who is not the record owner. When one considers how few couples in the Swedish high-tax society acquire substantial assets apart from the marital home, the similarity to the property situation of married persons is strong indeed.

Legal marriage in Sweden, then, seems to be stripped to the minimal initial and terminal formalities, alimony in exceptional cases, inheritance rights, and the widely imitated Swedish marital property regime of deferred community. For couples with significant assets, inheritance law and the system of universal community property still represent real practical differences between marriage and cohabitation. Steep taxes on income and net worth together with a comprehensive welfare system, however, reduce the proportion of the Swedish population for whom family property law is of great importance. [94]

The increasing attribution of legal effects to informal marriage, meanwhile, has given rise to new legal problems. For courts and legislatures, the problem is how to define those unions from which legal consequences will flow. For some cohabitants, it is how to avoid "getting married" unknowingly. With respect to the first problem, tax and social legislation typically equate cohabitation with marriage only where the couple has had a child together or the partners were previously married to each other. For the purposes of the means-tested housing allowance, a couple is treated as married if they live

93. Homosexual Cohabitees Act of 1987, SFS 1987: 813. The passage of Denmark's more far-reaching legislation was reported in *Time*, 18 January 1988, 43.
94. According to Jacob Sundberg, above, note 81 at 224.

together under circumstances resembling marriage. In private law, it seems to be up to the courts to appreciate the nature of each situation. So far as those who wish to avoid legal consequences are concerned, the newest law permits the parties to contract out, but it remains to be seen what limits the policy of protecting weaker parties will impose on individual freedom in this area.

As we have already had occasion to note, informal family behavior is significantly more widespread in Sweden than in the other countries we treat in this chapter, and it is more fully accepted there. It is thus hardly surprising to find that Sweden, more than other countries, has directly addressed the situations of unmarried cohabitants through legislation and deliberately pursued a policy of nondiscrimination toward them—a policy about which other countries have shown more hesitation. Only time will tell whether Sweden, in this area as with divorce, prefigures social and legal changes of a type that will appear in most other Western countries.

Informal Unions, American Style

In contemporary American society, nonmarital cohabitation has increasingly entered into the mores of diverse social groups.[95] Various do-it-yourself handbooks advise couples on how to conduct their unmarried life, and etiquette manuals instruct those who do not cohabit on how to be polite to those who do. As is only to be expected in a litigious society, informal unions have erupted into the American legal system, producing a bewildering variety of court decisions, statutes, and ordinances. Among the American states, examples can be found of nearly all the approaches to cohabitation that we have seen in other countries, plus some that seem to be distinctively American. The spectrum ranges from overtly hostile attitudes to full assimilation via common law marriage.

Traditionally, legal issues generated by marriage-like cohabitation have been handled by devices which facilitate the pretense that an informal marriage is really a legal one. Chief among these devices is the presumption that when a couple has lived together, presenting the outward appearance of marriage, their union was initiated by a legal ceremony.[96] In a significant minority of American states, a couple legally eligible to marry, and holding themselves out as husband and wife, are deemed to be legally married by virtue of the

95. The drawings of W. Hamilton in *The New Yorker* magazine since the mid-1970s are a concise social chronicle of upper-middle class cohabitation.

96. The deployment of such a presumption is easier in the American and English systems than in the continental countries with their rigid documentation systems. In West Germany, however, proof of *"faktische Ehe"* is admissible to cure a formal defect in a legal marriage, H.-F. Thomas, *Formlose Ehen* (Bielefeld: Gieseking, 1973), 95–97.

doctrine of common law marriage.[97] Common law marriage in the past was mainly of importance in situations where one partner died without providing for the other by will. But if a valid common law marriage has taken place, it can be dissolved prior to the death of one of the spouses only by divorce. This doctrine can produce some surprises when a cohabiting couple breaks up. A New York man, for example, who tried to sever informally his relationship with his long-time cohabitant found that he needed to go to court to do so, because the couple had spent a few nights in the common law marriage states of Georgia and South Carolina while on a motor trip to Disney World.[98]

Modern legal approaches to cohabitation in the United States tend, however, to be less sweeping than the traditional ones which, when applied, converted cohabitation into marriage. In most states the approach, as in England, tends to be problem-oriented and tailored to various types of situations. We will proceed here, as we have done with the other countries, to sketch out the basic legal techniques employed when cohabitation ends with separation or death. We will conclude by briefly noting a few other recent developments, including some in the area of constitutional law, with potentially important effects on the relationship between the informal family and the legal family in the United States.

It is unfortunate that the most celebrated American *de facto* divorce case is one whose facts are atypical and whose legal basis has been widely misunderstood. *Marvin* v. *Marvin*[99] involved a cohabitation for somewhat less than seven years between two members of the entertainment industry, one of whom was quite well known. During this period, Michelle Triola Marvin was a full-time companion to the late film actor Lee Marvin. The couple had no children and, for the first two years of their association, Lee was married to another woman. When Lee terminated their relationship, Michelle, with the aid of an enterprising Hollywood divorce lawyer, sought to share in the million or more dollars' worth of property that had been acquired by Lee during the period of their association. There was, at that time, a split in the California intermediate appellate courts on the issue of whether the community property laws of that state could be applied by analogy to produce an equal division of acquests between unmarried cohabitants.

The way the California Supreme Court dealt with the *Marvin* case was quite conventional in most respects. To no one's surprise, the court held that community property law did not apply, and should not be extended by analogy, to unmarried cohabitants. In keeping with the modern trend everywhere,

97. *Clark* 45–62.
98. *Kellard v. Kellard*, 13 *Family Law Reporter* 1490 (N.Y. Sup. Ct. 1987).
99. 557 P.2d 106 (Cal. 1976).

it also held that express contracts between cohabitants were enforceable in principle, unless explicitly founded on consideration of sexual services. Since few couples, married or single, make express agreements about finances, the most important part of the court's decision, from a practical point of view, was its holding that an agreement between a couple could be implied from their conduct during the period they lived together. That is, California courts could examine the history of the relationship of the parties to see whether it demonstrated "an implied contract or implied agreement of partnership or joint venture . . . or some other tacit understanding." [100]

While this holding certainly did open the courtroom doors wide to unmarried litigants, and while it does leave the outcomes of their suits largely up to the discretion of judges and juries, the implied-in-fact contract theory was not revolutionary. Similarly unremarkable is the court's holding that, under certain circumstances, cohabitants can recover in *quantum meruit*, or on the basis of resulting or constructive trusts. Far from approving "palimony," the court's decision mentioned the possibility of postdissolution support between cohabitants in a footnote only to say that it was expressing no opinion one way or another on the subject. [101] In another footnote, the court mentioned that the avenues of relief it had enumerated in its opinion should not be understood to exclude the possibility of other "equitable remedies to protect the expectations of the parties" in appropriate cases. [102]

A potentially troublesome aspect of the *Marvin* decision is the court's dictum that "the parties' intention can only be ascertained by a . . . searching inquiry into the nature of their relationship." [103] Such a "searching inquiry" naturally threatens to (and did in the *Marvin* case) turn the lawsuit into a spectacle involving all the worst aspects of fault divorce (which the California legislature abolished in 1970). The prospect of litigation in which the private lives of the parties can be explored in detail has led already to the settlement out of court of a number of suits by alleged same-sex lovers or clandestine playmates of well-known people. Thus, the implied-in-fact contract theory, as elaborated in *Marvin*, seems to have revived something very like the old heart-balm actions (alienation of affections, breach of promise to marry) which had been abolished in most states largely because they lent themselves to blackmail and other forms of abuse.

In the end, however, none of the theories sanctioned by the *Marvin* decision were of help to Michelle. On remand, the trial court found that there had never been an express or implied contract between the Marvins; that Lee had received no unjust enrichment; and that Michelle had not only suffered no

100. Id. at 122.
102. Id. at 123 n. 25.

101. Id. at 123 n. 26.
103. Id. at 117 n. 11.

detriment but had actually benefited socially and economically from the relationship.[104] Seizing on dicta in a footnote of the Supreme Court's decision, the trial judge did award Michelle $104,000 as an "equitable remedy" to assist in her return to self-sufficiency. But this award of what amounted to rehabilitative alimony was later struck down by an appellate court as having "no basis whatsoever, either in equity or in law." [105]

Not only did the *Marvin* case fail to yield a favorable result for its plaintiff after five years of litigation, its reception within the state of California has been cautious,[106] and courts in other jurisdictions are far from stampeding to follow its lead. The reactions of other state supreme courts to the *Marvin* case have ranged from extreme disapproval in Illinois and Georgia,[107] to acceptance in principle and reticence in practice in a handful of states.[108]

The Illinois and Georgia decisions involved the type of plaintiff who traditionally has been discreetly taken care of in American law through presumptions and estoppels when the union terminates with the death of her provider. Both cases involved the *inter vivos* dissolution of long-term cohabitations during which the women had devoted themselves primarily to homemaking. Ms. Hewitt, in addition to raising children and housekeeping, had helped to send her husband to dental school and had assisted him in his practice. In rejecting the implied-contract theory, the Illinois Supreme Court expressed concern about the impact a contrary decision would have on the institution of marriage, while the Georgia Supreme Court denied relief on the basis of the outmoded illegal consideration doctrine. But not all courts that have declined to follow in the California court's footsteps have done so on such old-fashioned grounds. When the New York Court of Appeals rejected the implied contract theory, it did so mainly for practical reasons, saying: "Finding an implied contract such as was recognized in *Marvin* v. *Marvin* . . . to be conceptually so amorphous as practically to defy equitable enforcement, and inconsistent with the legislative policy enunciated in 1933 when common law marriages were abolished in New York, we decline to follow the *Marvin* lead." [109]

104. *Marvin v. Marvin*, 5 *Family Law Reporter* 3077 (Cal. Super. Ct. 1979).

105. *Marvin v. Marvin*, 176 Cal. Rptr. 555, 559 (Cal. App. 1981).

106. In *Taylor v. Polackwich*, 194 Cal. Rptr. 8, 13 (Cal. App. 1983), the court reversed a trial court's award of a four-year occupancy right in the home owned by the man with whom the plaintiff and her children had lived for seven years, saying "[A]n equitable remedy may not be employed to grant [relief] to one who has no underlying right to relief on any theory."

107. *Hewitt v. Hewitt*, 394 N.E. 2d 1205 (Ill. 1979); *Rehak v. Mathis*, 238 S.E. 2d 81 (Ga. 1977).

108. *E.g.*, *Watts v. Watts*, 13 *Family Law Reporter* 1367 (Wis. 1987); *Beal v. Beal*, 4 *Family Law Reporter* 2462 (Ore. 1978).

109. *Morone v. Morone*, 50 N.Y. 2d 481 (N.Y.C.A. 1980).

Most American courts steer a middle course, dealing with dissolution of informal unions *inter vivos* in much the same manner as they did in the old days when relief typically was sought after one of the cohabitants had died. Instead of presumptions and estoppels (which are hard to use when one party is alive to rebut them), the favored techniques are now drawn from implied contracts, constructive and resulting trusts, the law of gifts, *quantum meruit* for services rendered over and above ordinary domestic services, and implied partnerships.[110] The devices, in other words, are quite similar to those used in England, and the courts' degree of willingness to use them in cases involving long-term cohabitations seems about the same. The greater frequency of co-habitation suits in the United States can probably be attributed in large part to the fact that we, almost alone among modern legal systems, do not have a loser-pays rule for civil litigation.

The most radical American developments in this area seem, unlike *Marvin*, to have escaped notice. In three American jurisdictions, without fanfare, the courts have done precisely what the California Supreme Court refused to do in *Marvin*: they have established by judicial fiat the same rules for property distribution upon termination of an informal union as their legislatures have prescribed for dissolution of marriage. In Kansas, Mississippi, and Washington, the courts are proceeding, as they do in divorce cases, to distribute the property of cohabitants in the way that seems to the judge "just and equitable."[111] No doubt courts in these jurisdictions take the informal nature of the relationship into consideration as one factor in deciding what is a fair allocation of property, but the net result is that the courts in these states have decided to let unmarried couples enjoy the same degree of uncertainty about their economic rights as the legislatures in their unfathomable wisdom have granted to married couples. In separate property jurisdictions which take this approach, the wheel has thus come full circle from treating married persons like any other cohabitants to treating cohabitants like legally married couples. Also stepping in where *Marvin* feared to tread are a few isolated decisions

110. Most of the cases are collected in the annual surveys of American family law prepared by Doris Freed, the most recent of which is Doris Freed and Timothy Walker, "Family Law in the Fifty States: An Overview," 20 *Family Law Quarterly* 439, 569–80 (1987). See also, for an informative analysis of the American case law, the national report by Harry Krause to the August 1986 Congress of the International Academy of Comparative Law: "Legal Position: Unmarried Couples," 34 *American Journal of Comparative Law* 533 (1986 Supplement).

111. *Marriage of Lindsey*, 678 P.2d 328 (Wash. 1984) (court should make a "just and equitable" distribution in the light of the parties' relationship and the amount of property acquired); *Eaton v. Johnston*, 10 *Family Law Reporter* 1094 (Kan. App. 1983) (inherent power of courts to do equity extends to dividing cohabitants' property in a "just and equitable" manner); *Pickens v. Pickens* 490 So. 2d 872 (Miss. 1986) (cohabitant entitled to "equitable division" of property acquired by joint efforts including domestic services).

awarding postdissolution support to unmarried cohabitants on the basis of implied agreements, but this sort of case seems likely to remain exceptional.[112]

When a cohabitation ends with the death of one of the partners, the survivor as such has no rights in the decedent's estate. American courts have no such discretionary power to grant allowances to this sort of claimant as their counterparts in England do. Nor are cohabitants included in the class of plaintiffs entitled to bring wrongful death actions under most American statutes. On the other hand, there are no obstacles (other than forced-share legislation and related doctrines) to providing for a cohabitant by will. Furthermore, since a decedent's estate includes only what he owns, the question of who owns what may be raised by a cohabitant at death, along with claims for compensation for services rendered, for enforcement of agreements with the decedent, and so on. The issues and the legal devices to deal with them here are basically similar to those in the dissolution cases.[113]

As in other countries, the status of unmarried cohabitants has been assimilated to that of married persons in a number of public-law contexts. As elsewhere, sometimes this works to their advantage, enabling them to claim benefits extended to couples and families, and sometimes to their disadvantage, if they are thereby rendered ineligible for certain need-based programs. In some California cities, municipal ordinances permit cohabitants, including same-sex couples, to register as "Domestic Partnerships" in order to be eligible for various benefits.[114]

In the area of constitutional law, the United States Supreme Court has altered the legal context in which problems of informal families are treated, most dramatically in a series of decisions beginning in 1968, which held that nearly all laws discriminating against children born outside marriage violated the equal protection clause of the Fourteenth Amendment to the Constitution.[115] In 1972, the Court began to be attentive to the rights of unmarried

112. *Kozlowski v. Kozlowski*, 403 A. 2d 902 (N.J. 1979); see also, *McCullon v. McCullon*, 410 N.Y.S. 2d 226 (Sup. Ct. 1978).

113. The implied partnership theory, for example, was used to effect a division of a cattle-raising business in *In re Estate of Thornton*, 541 P.2d 106 (Wash. 1972).

114. Herma Hill Kay, "An Appraisal of California's No-Fault Divorce Law," 75 *California Law Review* 291, 305 (1987).

115. The landmarks are: *Levy v. Louisiana*, 391 U.S. 68 (1968) (nonmarital children have right to wrongful death action for death of their mother); *Glona v. American Casualty Co.*, 391 U.S. 73 (1968) (mother has wrongful death action for death of her nonmarital child); *Weber v. Aetna Casualty Co.*, 406 U.S. 164 (1972) (workmen's compensation law cannot limit its benefits to dependent marital children); *Gomez v. Perez*, 409 U.S. 535 (1973) (state cannot limit support rights against father to marital children). The only area of private law into which the Supreme Court has hesitated to extend this equalization process is that of intestate succession: *Labine v. Vincent*, 401 U.S. 532 (1971). In the area of public law, however, the distinction between marital

fathers, and to consider the implications of the right of privacy for unmarried persons. It held in *Stanley v. Illinois* that fathers of children born outside legal marriage cannot be presumed to be unsuitable custodians.[116] In the same term, in *Eisenstadt v. Baird*, the Court made it clear that the right of privacy was not merely, as *Griswold v. Connecticut* had seemed to suggest, a right of *marital* privacy:

> If under *Griswold* the distribution of contraceptives to married persons cannot be prohibited, a ban on distribution to unmarried persons would be equally impermissible. It is true that in *Griswold* the right of privacy in question inhered in the marital relationship. Yet the marital couple is not an independent entity with a mind and heart of its own, but an association of two individuals each with a separate intellectual and emotional make-up. If the right of privacy means anything, it is the right of the *individual*, married or single, to be free from unwarranted governmental intrusion into matters so fundamentally affecting a person as the decision whether to bear or beget a child.[117]

A year later, the Court held that the federal food stamp program could not constitutionally restrict eligibility for aid to households consisting of "related" members.[118] Then, the following year, the Court upheld a zoning ordinance that permitted no more than two unrelated persons to occupy a dwelling, perhaps evincing a special tolerance toward unrelated couples, as distinct from communes and other unrelated groups.[119] On the other hand, the Court has held that those who cohabit outside marriage need not be treated in all respects like married people.[120] It remains to be seen whether Supreme Court decisions will further blur the differences between the legal status of being married and that of being unmarried on equal protection grounds. Already, however, a number of state and local laws prohibit discrimination not

---

and nonmarital children has lost almost all significance: *Jiminez v. Weinberger*, 417 U.S. 628 (1974); *Lewis v. Martin*, 397 U.S. 552 (1970); *Cahill v. New Jersey Welfare Rights Organization*, 411 U.S. 619 (1973); *King v. Smith*, 392 U.S. 309 (1968). It remains, however, the fact that unacknowledged nonmarital children must prove dependency on a deceased father in order to be eligible for Social Security Survivor's benefits, *Norton v. Mathews*, 427 U.S. 524 (1976) and *Mathews v. Lucas*, 427 U.S. 495 (1976).

   116. 405 U.S. 645 (1972).
   117. 405 U.S. 439, 453 (1972) (Court's emphasis).
   118. *United States Dept. of Agriculture v. Moreno*, 413 U.S. 528 (1973).
   119. *Village of Belle Terre v. Boraas*, 416 U.S. 1 (1974).
   120. See *California v. Boles*, 443 U.S. 282 (1979) (denial of survivor's social security benefits to surviving cohabitant, the mother of decedent's child, does not violate the Equal Protection Clause).

only on the basis of sex, race, and national origin, but also on the basis of marital status.

In most states, the law on the books has actually changed less than the attitudes of the courts and their readiness to apply familiar techniques to new situations. Most American courts are a good deal less strict about employing legal fictions than are the courts in West Germany. On the other hand, close examination of the American cases reveals that relief is far from automatic. It is most likely to be granted in long-term family-like situations where the plaintiff (usually a woman) has suffered considerable economic detriment through raising children, relinquishing employment, and aiding her partner in his business. It is remarkable how many of these cases involve men and women who once were married to each other and just went on living together for years after their divorce. To deny relief in such a case would be almost unthinkable for modern American judges with a lively sense of their own powers and schooled in disdain for legal formality.

This brief survey of American cohabitation law permits us to see that the various states not only employ most of the approaches to informal family behavior we have encountered elsewhere, but that certain states go to extremes not yet observed in the other countries we have studied. Not even West German courts treat *de facto* spouses with such disapproval as the Supreme Courts of Georgia and Illinois, while not even Sweden converts cohabitation completely into legal marriage as do the common law marriage states. It does not seem likely, however, that the more draconian approaches will find a wide reception in most American states. In Illinois, lower courts have found ways to avoid following the hard line laid down by that state's Supreme Court, and the trend in most other jurisdictions is definitely away from denying relief on moralistic grounds. Nor does common law marriage seem to be on the brink of a revival, for most American jurisdictions have not considered it necessary or desirable to treat informal unions like legal marriages in all respects.

Comparative Observations

The way a particular legal system approaches the various issues generated by informal family behavior seems to be closely related to the place of legal marriage within that system. As we have seen throughout this book, however, the traditionally central position of legal marriage in family law has been extensively eroded everywhere. Indeed, one might almost say that the chief legal significance of formal marriage at present is that it gives rise to certain presumptions from which legal consequences follow. Without the benefit of these presumptions, a child must prove paternity, and cohabitants must convince a court or agency that theirs is the type of relationship to which legal consequences should attach. Since rebutting the presumptions attached to formal marriage, or making out a case for relief in their absence, is often expensive and difficult, the legitimate family retains a privileged status. This is so even in systems (or in areas of the law) where substantially similar treatment for informal and formal family members is available. In the absence of intra-family disputes, however, these matters can be quite simple. Paternity can be acknowledged. Cohabitants can be each others' heirs and donees, and in some places they need merely register their status in order to become entitled to various benefits. So the greatest differences between formal and informal family law appear when family members are at odds with each other.

We have also seen that while a country's legal approach to informal family behavior is importantly affected by the way it views legal marriage, the influence runs in the other direction as well. Legal measures dealing with informal family behavior have themselves been instrumental in reshaping the institution of marriage. In particular, the worldwide transformation of the status of children born out of wedlock has gone far toward depriving marriage of one of its traditionally most important effects: that of distinguishing the family through which rank and wealth could be transmitted. One need not search far for the reasons why this legal function no longer seems so essential as it did in former times. As William Goode has pointed out, in societies where there is no property to inherit and none to protect by making certain that the proper families are united, there is less concern attached to birth outside legal marriage.[121] Thus, as family law extends its reach to the propertyless, many legal refinements developed for the circumstances of the well-to-do are of diminished relevance. Furthermore, as traditional forms of property have declined in importance relative to "new property" derived from individual earnings and entitlements, traditional concepts of legitimacy are less crucial to the maintenance of dominant groups in society than they once were.

Over time, the focus of the law relating to children born outside marriage has shifted, appropriately, from preoccupation with wealth and status to concern for the children themselves. Not only have children of unwed parents been accorded substantially equal rights to support and derived benefits, the establishment of paternity (without which these rights would be meaningless) has everywhere been facilitated, both in law and through technological advances. Legal measures according equal rights to marital and nonmarital children have the most effect, yet are least needed, in countries like Sweden where the majority of children born outside legal marriage start life in two-parent families. In the United States, on the other hand, where births outside marriage are correlated to a high degree with poverty, and where the typical

121. *Goode* 24.

unwed mother is not in a marriage-like situation, the situation of nonmarital children remains a disadvantaged one, despite significant legal reforms.

A related development which is revealing of the diminished significance of legal marriage is a notable increase in official tolerance of, or indifference to, nonmarital sexual relations. Adultery, especially when committed by women, once seemed to be the weak link in a social system that attempted to ensure the transmission of family land within the male line. But with the attenuation of the connection between sexual intercourse and procreation and the decreasing role of inheritance in modern society, laws penalizing private sexual acts between consenting adults have tended to fall into desuetude. Adultery has practically disappeared as a separate ground for divorce, or as the basis for legal action against a third party who disturbs the marital relationship. The idea has surfaced here and there that freedom to engage in sexual relationships of all sorts is an aspect of personal liberty. Where adultery still has legal consequences, its gravamen is perceived as involving the personal relationship of the spouses concerned, rather than a threat to patrilineal succession. Indeed, a distinction seems to be developing between grand and petty adultery, depending on whether the married adulterer was actually cohabiting with his spouse at the time the extramarital relations took place.[122]

The legal history of adultery is part and parcel of the long series of events through which the institution of marriage has been transformed. In patrilineal societies when kinship ties were viewed as more important than the link between husband and wife, and marriages represented alliances between blood lines, a wife's adultery was not so much an affront to her spouse as it was to a set of larger family concerns and social arrangements. A husband's adultery was less serious. Indeed, it might even have useful consequences, since a natural son could always be acknowledged if the legal union failed to produce an heir. But when the spouses themselves began to play a greater role in mate selection, adultery by either husband or wife was more apt to be seen as a personal offense to the other. Modern romantic sensibilities, so sympathetic to the sexual dalliances of men and women trapped in loveless arranged marriages of an earlier time, expected fidelity, and more, from spouses who had chosen each other on the basis of mutual attraction and perceived affinities. But as the idea of marriage as a vehicle for individual self-fulfillment gained

122. E.g. , *Kim v. U.S. Immigration and Naturalization Service*, 514 F. 2nd 179 (D.C. Cir. 1975)(foreign national's cohabitation with a woman while his wife was outside the United States was not "adultery" within the meaning of the Immigration and Naturalization Act). *Cf.*, "Thou has committed/ Fornication: But that was in another country/ And besides, the wench is dead." Christopher Marlowe, *The Famous Tragedy of the Rich Jew of Malta* (circa 1589). See also Paris Court of Appeal decision of 10 November 1976, D. 1978. Jur. 458.

prominence in the twentieth century, consensus about the morality of extra-marital sexual relations weakened; situation ethics and psychotherapy stepped in, and the law retreated in confusion.

So far as the legal treatment of marriage-like cohabitation is concerned, there is considerable variety among legal systems in the way they deal with a range of private law issues, and a certain sameness of approach within the public law context. In public law areas, the law of the informal family is dominated by the interest of modern welfare states in controlling costs and appearing to be even-handed in ministering to the needy. The state, in administering social assistance programs, concentrates on the actual needs and resources of its clients, whom it tends to treat as individuals rather than as family members. On those occasions when it does take family membership into consideration, public law envisions the family as an economic, rather than a legal, entity.

In private law, where judges have played a leading role, the situation is more complex. When a marriage-like cohabitation terminates, the factual circumstances resemble the termination of a legal marriage, and a growing body of decisional law often treats the two situations in roughly similar fashion. As a source of convenient analogies, legal marriage tends to imprint its own image on de facto situations. Thus the legal status of cohabitants is to some degree shaped by the vision of legal marriage that predominates in each country. Within any given system, the law of the informal family embodies the same tension between ideas of separateness and sharing that characterizes modern family law generally, although it does not always resolve the tension in the same way.

This is especially apparent in the dissolution cases. Cohabitants' rights and responsibilities in these situations are largely left to judicial discretion in the countries with which we are concerned here, except in Sweden, where the legislature has recently laid down the main lines of an approach. We have seen that the courts—to varying degrees in the different countries—have been less hesitant than in the past to exercise their discretion in order to effect some kind of financial reckoning when a marriage-like union dissolves. While at first it might seem that the existence of postdivorce spousal support obligations clearly sets marriage apart from cohabitation, the shift in divorce law to a presumption against granting alimony, and the rarity of alimony in practice, deprive this apparent difference of much substance. On the other hand, legal spouses everywhere fare better than cohabitants where property division is concerned. Economic rights derived from marriage continue to play an important role, especially as these have been broadened to include pensions. In general, on property and support questions, we have noted that there is considerable variation among countries, and even among courts within each country, in the degree to which judges will intervene in disputes between cohabitants and in the principles they will apply.

In West Germany, the courts have moved from overt disapproval to a posture of respect for the unmarried couple's choice of an alternative lifestyle. This emphasis on the right of the cohabitants to be free of the restraints of legal marriage, as well as the insistence in West Germany, and by some courts elsewhere, on strict proof of any alleged agreement to share property, generally operates to favor the party who is most self-sufficient and has the greater bargaining power. Courts following this line also tend to presume that domestic services are rendered gratuitously.

The English and American cases, while displaying a certain inconsistency (and in the case of the American decisions, variation from state to state), show more concern overall for a person who has become dependent or suffered detriment over the course of a long relationship, especially if that person has been involved in raising children. Courts in these countries are less willing to say that plaintiffs in such cases should have gone to the trouble of getting a marriage certificate if they wanted the type of protection the law offers to married persons. Though applying legal devices similar to those used by the West German courts, they are more ready to find (or even presume) that the requisite intent and contributions are present, at least in a long-term cohabitation. Like the Swedish legislature's, their approach generally has been pragmatic, addressed to problems arising from the cohabitation of a man and woman with family functions regardless of whether a legal marriage has taken place.

Some American courts have gone further in this direction than Sweden, however, by simply reallocating the property of the cohabitants in the way that seems just under all the circumstances. To some extent, this merely represents an open exercise of discretionary powers exerted by courts elsewhere under the guise of implying contracts and partnerships, or compensating cohabitants for unjust enrichment. But the candid American redistribution of assets encompasses potentially more property, and erases the distinction between the legal position of cohabitants and that of spouses under the standard American discretionary distribution statute. In favor of this approach is the fact that it can avoid the injustices and anomalies that frequently arise from the use of legal fictions as remedial devices. Fictions can acquire a life of their own and be unthinkingly extended to situations where neither current social policies nor the reasonable expectations of the parties would be promoted by a redistribution of assets. By the same token, they can lead to denial of relief in deserving cases where the fiction cannot quite be made to fit. The main problems with the American discretionary approach in cohabitation cases, however, are essentially the same as those in divorce cases: unpredictability and a popular sense of unfairness. The better solution in both situations would be to confine wide-ranging judicial discretion to those situations where it is necessary to assure the economic welfare of children.

The French approach is distinguished by a relatively greater degree of solicitude for the status of legal marriage, which, as we have seen throughout, colors all aspects of French family law. On the one hand, this prevents cohabitation from being totally assimilated to marriage; on the other, it tends to select out for special treatment especially "marriage-like" cohabitations. Just as legal marriage is more extensively regulated in France than elsewhere, free unions there draw to themselves a relatively broad set of legal effects—and a large body of scholarly writing.

In Sweden, where legal marriage has lost many of its distinctive attributes, it may be more accurate to speak of an assimilation of marriage to cohabitation than *vice versa*. Sweden, as we have already had occasion to note, is something of a special case, set apart by the relatively greater proportion of family behavior which takes place outside formal marriage there, by its predominantly legislative approach to cohabitation, by the relatively greater assumption by the state of what were once family responsibilities, and by its explicit policy of nondiscrimination towards cohabitation.

In one area of private law, legal marriage retains its traditionally preferred position in all five countries surveyed here. The law of inheritance remains a bastion of the legitimate family. Even improvements in the status of children born out of wedlock have frequently stopped short of establishing full equality between marital and nonmarital children in the area of succession. As for surviving cohabitants, they are not included among the heirs to a decedent's estate in any of the countries treated here. Their legal position contrasts quite strikingly with the steady improvement we have seen everywhere in the legal treatment of surviving spouses. On the other hand, a variety of legal fictions have long been employed in order to permit surviving long-term cohabitants to share in the property of a decedent and in England, a cohabitant is now entitled to claim maintenance from the estate of a person by whom she was being supported. Furthermore, as John Langbein has shown, inheritance currently plays a decreasing role among twentieth-century methods of family wealth transmission.[123]

The foregoing survey, though revealing a good deal of variety, nevertheless supports a few generalizations about the legal treatment of informal family behavior in the countries surveyed here. Just as we have seen a universal

123. John Langbein, "The Twentieth-Century Revolution in Family Wealth Transmission," 86 *Michigan Law Review* 722 (1988).

trend, with varying degrees of strength, to diminish the legal consequences of marriage, we have observed an increasing body of legal effects being attributed to marriage-like cohabitation. Nevertheless, a distinction between legal marriage and cohabitation is maintained everywhere, with marriage even in Sweden being nominally accorded a central position in family law. Where children are concerned, however, the opposite principle governs. Even where some legal distinctions remain, the idea is firmly in place that a child ought not to suffer legal disadvantages because of the marital status of its parents. Thus, it may be that the legally relevant distinction in the future will be between childless unions and those where children are being or have been raised. The law's intervention in the former may be confined to sorting out property problems, while the latter may enjoy a certain privileged status on account of the public interest in the nurture and socialization of future citizens.

The reflexively interacting developments we have seen in the law of marriage, cohabitation, and status of children are all part of a general movement away from formalism in modern law. The mere fact of ceremonial marriage does not necessarily give rise to a full set of legal effects, nor does the mere fact that there has been no marriage ceremony necessarily preclude legal effects. Increasingly, long-standing cohabitations entail legal consequences, while marriages of short duration do not.[124] In private law, we encounter informal situations similar to those we have seen throughout our study of the personal and property relations of married couples. When cohabitants separate, the law struggles with the same problems of public and private responsibility, separateness and solidarity, autonomy and dependence, that pervade divorce law. When informal family relations are disrupted by death, inheritance law, which at first seems to be a fortress of the legitimate family, appears on closer inspection to be more like a museum. In public law, the interest of modern welfare states in curtailing unnecessary expenditures while relieving man's estate leads them to disregard formal legal categories. In the X-ray vision of the bureaucrat, families are perceived as economic units, or are simply dissolved into their individual component parts.

---

124. For example, section 416(c) of the U.S. Social Security Act defines a widow for social security purposes as a "surviving wife of an [insured] individual, but only if . . . she was married to him for a period of not less than nine months immediately prior to the day on which he dies. . . ."

7

State, Law, and Family

A good part of the struggles of mankind centre round the single task of
finding an expedient accommodation—one, that is, that will bring happiness—between this claim of the individual [to liberty] and the cultural
claims of the group; and one of the problems that touches the futu of hu
manity is whether such an accommodation can be reached by means of some
particular form of civilization or whether this conflict is irreconcilable.

Sigmund Freud, *Civilization and its Discontents*[1]

New Lamps for Old

By the turn of the twentieth century, Western family law systems had come
to share, generally speaking, a common set of assumptions. Domestic relations law was organized around a unitary conception of the family as
marriage-centered and patriarchal. Marriage was treated as an important support institution and a decisive determinant of the social status of spouses and
children. It was supposed in principle to last until the death of a spouse and
was made terminable during the lives of the spouses, if at all, only for serious
cause. Family solidarity and the community of life between spouses were
emphasized over the individual personalities and interests of family members.
Within the family, the standard authority structure and pattern of role allocation decreed that the husband-father should predominate in decision making
and should provide for the material needs of the family. The wife-mother was
to fulfill her role primarily by caring for the household and children. Procreation and child-rearing were assumed to be major purposes of marriage, and
sexual relations within marriage were supposed to be exclusive, at least for
the wife. Marriage, procreation, and divorce were supposed to take place
within legal categories. Illegitimate children had hardly any legal existence
to all.

Underlying all these particular assumptions was the premise that government could and should regulate family formation, organization, and dissolution in the light of widely shared ideas about marriage and family life. At the
same time, it was a legal tenet that the state should refrain from crossing the
threshold of the home of the functioning family, especially where the upbringing of children was concerned. The role of government in providing for basic
human needs was relatively small. In France and Germany, all these charac-

---

1. James Strachey, trans. (New York: Norton, 1961), 43.

teristics taken together constituted the "family of the Civil Code"; in England and the United States, they were the elements of a legal construct of the traditional family whose traits were scattered through court decisions and statutes. The story Western legal systems were telling about family life varied in emphasis and detail from country to country. It was everywhere more in touch with the ideas and behavior of the middle class than the poor or the well-to-do.

In the wake of the legal developments we have examined in the foregoing chapters, not one of these formerly basic assumptions has survived unchanged. Most have been eliminated, and some have been turned on their heads. True, the edifice of traditional family law remained standing until the 1960s, but cracks in its foundations had appeared much earlier. The past twenty years have witnessed the movement from undercurrent to mainstream in family law of individualistic, egalitarian, and secularizing trends that have been gaining power in Western legal systems since the late eighteenth century.

These legal trends captured and formalized several aspects of the social and economic developments that had gradually undermined an assumption that lay at the very heart of nineteenth-century family law—that family and marriage were the essential determinants of an individual's economic security and social standing. For most of human history, marriage and kinship were the basic relationships through which rank and status in society were conferred. Today, however, an individual's wealth, power, and standing are decreasingly determined by family membership and increasingly by his or her own labor force activity or, in a negative way, by his or her dependency relationship with government.[2] Families, of course, continue to exert an extremely important influence on the life prospects of their members. But this influence operates for the most part indirectly, mainly through the psychological and material advantages families are able to give their children in connection with education, which in turn provides access to preferred statuses.[3] As the role of families in determining wealth and status has altered, however, an entire world view has been turned inside out. As a French jurist has put it,

> Instead of the individual "belonging" to the family, it is the family which is coming to be at the service of the individual. The preeminent place of the family among our institutions is retained, but

2. See generally, Mary Ann Glendon, *The New Family and the New Property* (Toronto: Butterworths, 1981).

3. See James Coleman et al., *Equality of Educational Opportunity* (Washington, D.C.: Government Printing Office, 1966); Christopher Jencks et al., *Inequality: A Reassessment of the Effect of Family and Schooling in America* (New York: Basic Books, 1972); and John Brittain, *The Inheritance of Economic Status* (Washington, D.C.: Brookings Institute, 1977).

not for the same reason: no longer is it because the family serves society, but because it is a means for the fullest development of the individual. When it no longer fulfills this role, the bonds diminish or disappear.[4]

Although modern family law, as we have seen, has incorporated this new point of view to a great extent, it remains marriage-centered in many ways. But family law now treats marriage as primarily the concern of the individuals involved. In this respect, the law mirrors the heightened intensity and instability of relationships held together more by emotional than economic ties.[5] Now that children no longer serve to the extent they once did as helpers in the family business or farm, extra earners, or hedges against helpless old age, the parent-child relationship, too, has become intense and unstable in a way that seems to be new. As René König has put it, the modern family is "based . . . on unreinforced and primarily personal relationships, being dependent on the outside world for the satisfaction of most of its needs. And this makes itself more and more felt in the inner order of the family."[6] In the foregoing chapters, we saw how the close, companionate, aspect of contemporary marriage finds legal expression in the improved position of the spouse in gift and succession law, while its fragility is reflected in modern divorce law, where terminability has become almost a matter of right.

What, in this process, has become of the relationship of the state to the family as expressed through law? So far as marriage is concerned, the present period of legal change must be regarded (against the background outlined in chapter 1 of the gradual rise of ecclesiastical and, later, secular regulation) as following a downward curve of dejuridification. From another point of view, however, the retreat of the law from overseeing such matters as who marries whom and how, what rights and duties spouses have toward each other, and how such unions are terminated, is perhaps not so momentous a shift as it may first appear. After all, family law was initially concerned only or mainly with the propertied and later with the middle classes. In the twentieth century, when the law began to take increasing notice of groups it had previously neglected, and they in turn began to take notice of it,[7] the apparent discrepancy between law and mores widened. Many of the legal changes described

4. Alain Bénabent, "La liberté individuelle et le mariage," 1973 *Revue trimestrielle du droit civil* 440, 495.

5. On the modern couple relationship compared to marriage in earlier times, see *Goode* 25, 66; *Stone* 685.

6. *König* 30.

7. See Max Rheinstein, "The Family and the Law," in *International Encyclopedia of Comparative Law*, vol. 4, ed. Aleck Chloros (Tübingen: J. C. B. Mohr, 1974), 12.

in the foregoing chapters can be regarded as adjustments to the needs of new clienteles to whom much of traditional family law was irrelevant because they were without significant property or social position. From this perspective, then, we can see how narrow the application of family law had been until the relatively recent past. Like the tinkers we met in chapter one, most of the travelers through this world have been ignored by the state and its laws made for fine ladies and gentlemen. The Church, too, often excused ordinary folk from strict compliance with its more formalistic rules. But when it didn't, then like Michael and Sarah, sure, they must have excused themselves.

At the same time that family law was beginning to interact with the lives and consciousness of a broader segment of the population, it was also adapting to major changes in the needs and behavior of its traditional clientele. Just as it had to take account long ago of the heightened importance of personal property when land ceased to be the basic form of wealth, family law has had to adjust to the ever-growing significance in today's society of various forms of "new property" derived from employment or dependency relationships with large public and private organizations. As the relative importance of family, work, and government entitlements in assuring economic security shifted, changes took place, too, in ways of thinking about family relationships.

The twentieth century also saw the appearance of new forms of state intervention in family life. Scholarly discussions frequently relate this phenomenon to the family's "loss of functions," calling attention to the fact that many tasks formerly performed by or within families have been taken over by outside agencies. But families have always shared their functions with other social institutions. What is modern is that today these institutions are apt to be distant bureaucratic entities—large school systems, social welfare agencies, and so forth—rather than neighbors, patrons, and the local school or parish. Traditional patterns of marrying and rhythms of living have given way to new ones organized around the schedules and timing of schooling and the world of work.

As the nature of the interdependence between families and outside support systems changes, private law dealing with domestic relations tends to lose ground to or merge with a broad range of public laws and programs affecting the family. This is especially so in the more advanced welfare states. In Sweden, for example, Jacob Sundberg has called attention to the progressive decline of family law as it is integrated with social welfare law:

> Family law as conceived by the Ministry of Justice [private law of the family] was buried by the family law created by the other ministries, the coffin being draped with a flag reading "family policy." When the Swedish Minister of Justice proclaimed the neutrality prin-

ciple, what he really did was to strike colors in surrender. His rivals
in the tax and welfare departments had already shot the traditional
family law conception to pieces.[8]

In the four countries with which we have been primarily concerned, matters
have not reached this point. In England, France, the United States, and West
Germany, it would be more correct to say that public and administrative law
affecting families tends to be of greater significance for poor families, while
traditional family law (support, marital property, inheritance) and tax law
figure more prominently in the lives of middle-class majorities. Nevertheless,
domestic relations law has everywhere taken on a more public and administrative character as it concentrates on what John Eekelaar has denominated
its "adjustive" and "protective" functions, settling disputes about money and
children or responding to problems of abuse and neglect.[9]

   In the process of withdrawing regulation from some areas of family life
while subjecting others to new forms of official intervention, the law has
tended to focus primarily on individuals. Families of course continue to consist of individuals linked together in special ways, and the law frequently
takes these connections into account, more so in the civil law systems, as we
have seen, than in the Nordic and common law countries. But pervasive in all
the recent developments we have surveyed is the tendency for law and social
programs to break the family down into its component parts and to treat
family members as separate and independent. This shift of legal emphasis
from "the" family, or even "families" in all their various forms, to the individual family member seems to have come about more by accident than by
design. The effect, however, is that, without any particular purpose to do so,
modern legal systems in varying degrees have come close to realizing a dream
of the French revolutionaries: that citizens would one day stand in direct relation to the state, without intermediaries.

   Although the tendency to make individuals, rather than family units or
households, the principal subjects of the law affecting families is more pronounced in the Nordic and Anglo-American world than in the continental civil
law countries,[10] its manifestations can be seen everywhere in the Western and
westernized world. As we have seen, the great theme that has dominated

   8. Jacob W. F. Sundberg, "Facteurs et tendances dans l'évolution moderne du droit de la
famille des pays nordiques: Rêves et Réalités," in *Famille, droit et changement social dans les
sociétés contemporaines* (Proceedings of the Eighth Journées d'études juridiques Jean Dabin)
(Brussels: Bruylant, 1978), 60–61.
   9. *Eekelaar* xvii.
   10. See Mary Ann Glendon, *Abortion and Divorce in Western Law* (Cambridge: Harvard
University Press, 1987), 112–42.

marriage-formation law for well over a century has been the progressive liberation of individuals from constraints on their freedom to marry. And, just as individuals have gained the freedom to choose a spouse, they are now also freed, by modern divorce law, to correct that choice. Even more striking than the ease with which people can enter and leave the marriage relationship, is the relaxation of family support ties. Family support is becoming less a matter of right, while individual access to public assistance is becoming more so. The adult family member is increasingly treated as self-sufficient (or potentially so) through his or her own employment and entitled, if unable to work, to be provided by the state with minimum decent subsistence. Though child support everywhere is still recognized as an obligation of both parents, contributions from absent fathers in practice play a decreasing role—relative to public assistance and the mother's earnings—in the support of female-headed families.

With the notable exception of continental family allowances, public-assistance programs are typically geared to individuals and their needs, regardless of family status. The extreme case would seem to be Sweden, where, during the half century when the Social Democratic Party was continuously in power, it was the announced objective of the government to use family law "as one of several tools available when we endeavor to create a society where every adult person assumes responsibility for himself and does not allow himself to be economically dependent on relatives, and where equality between men and women has become a reality."[11] A report prepared by Alva Myrdal for the Swedish Social Democratic Party in 1971 predicted, "Income from one's own job and the modern social insurance system are the two foundation stones upon which the security of the individual will rest in the future."[12] In the four countries that have been the focus of the present study, the transposition of emphasis from families to individuals in laws and programs has taken place more on pragmatic than on ideological grounds. Still, individualistic trends in public and private laws everywhere have been given an additional common thrust as norms of family law are increasingly reviewed for conformity to "higher law" expressed in national constitutions or international conventions.

But it would be a mistake to characterize the new family law as merely having kept up with the times and as having simply substituted new, widely shared ideas about family life for old ones. In fact, the family laws that have emerged over the past two decades in the United States and Western Europe

11. Former Swedish Minister of Justice, Herman Kling, quoted in Sundberg, above, note 8 at 64.
12. Quoted in Zona Sage, "Dissolution of the Family under Swedish Law," 9 *Family Law Quarterly* 375, 379 n. 20 (1975).

are often as much at variance with prevailing social attitudes and practices as were the traditional systems they replaced. Most glaringly, the legal imagery of separateness and independence contrasts everywhere with the way most functioning families operate and with the circumstances of mothers and young children in both intact and broken homes. Yet the law holds self-sufficiency up as an ideal, suggesting that dependency is somehow degrading, and implicitly denying the importance of human intersubjectivity. Other discrepancies are particularly apparent in areas where family law has been influenced by new ideas, not about families, but about law and morality. Such ideas include the problematic notions that courts and legislatures should not attempt to impose "values" (except for equality, individual liberty, and tolerance); and that "values" (except for equality, individual liberty, and tolerance) are a matter of subjective taste or preference. The result is often that other normative legal propositions have tended to be phased out, even when they are quite widely shared. As we have seen, these legal developments have gained more ground in the heterogeneous United States than elsewhere. There, the posture of legal neutrality has been welcomed by judges and legislators, who are otherwise hard put to justify preferring the values of one sector of the population to those of another.[13]

By relinquishing most of its overt attempts to promote any particular set of ideas about family life, modern family law is thus tracking certain well-established trends in modern law. In its pragmatism, its antiformalism, its aspiration towards neutrality with respect to diverse life-styles and opinions, and its bureaucratic character, family law has been swept along by the strong currents that presently predominate in Western legal systems. The new family laws, like the new lamp Aladdin was given in exchange for his old one, harbor a genie in their recesses. Their animating spirit promises liberty, equality and progress without end. But all too often its gifts have had a way of turning to ashes.

Along with the prevailing currents, there are of course countercurrents and undercurrents. We have seen that these are in general stronger in the continental Romano-Germanic world than in the Anglo-American or Nordic systems. In France, especially, and to some extent in West Germany, we have noted a tendency for law reformers to try to maintain widely shared ideals in family law while still accommodating, to a greater or lesser degree, the needs and desires of those who do not share or cannot live up to these ideals. We have also seen more evidence in these countries of the survival of customary

13. On the inappropriateness of American family law models for law reform in smaller, more homogeneous, countries, see Mary Ann Glendon, *Irish Family Law in Comparative Perspective* (Dublin: Trinity College, 1987), 5, 18–23.

and classical ideas of law, and we have seen the occasional use of law-making as an opportunity for social dialogue. In continental law, rights tend to be seen as naturally paired with responsibilities. The individual is more often envisioned in a social context. There also seems to be more recognition in the Romano-Germanic systems that law, along with other social forces, can contribute in its own small but not insignificant way to the construction of the world of meaning within which beliefs, feelings, and attitudes are formed.

The remainder of this chapter first explores more fully some of the implications of the increasing emphasis on the individual that we have observed in family law and then outlines in tentative fashion a new approach to family law reform that may be termed ecological. The chapter concludes with an effort to place the role of law as it affects family life in appropriate perspective.

State and Individual without Intermediaries

A variety of factors, as we have seen, contributed to bringing the state and its agencies into an ever more direct, unmediated relationship with individual men, women, and children. The historic significance of this development is apt to be overlooked unless we remind ourselves of how much once stood between the state and the individual citizen and of how modern both of these concepts are. The "state" as we know it did not emerge until national monarchies began to consolidate their power in the seventeenth century.[14] In the feudal period, the monarchy had been only one of several competing and overlapping centers of power and was by no means always predominant among them. As for "individualism," Tocqueville pointed out that the very word "was unknown to our ancestors, for the good reason that in their days every individual belonged to a group and no one could regard himself as an isolated unit."[15] The centralized modern state and the free, self-determining individual were both made possible by the destruction or decay of the old society of groups. They were, in a sense, born together.

To the French revolutionaries, the old feudal statuses, the Church, the guilds, and even some aspects of family organization were seen both as oppressive to individuals and as threats to the nation-state. In imitation of the program of the Reformation to eliminate institutional intermediaries between man and God, the revolutionary leaders aimed at suppression of the *corps intermédiaires* of the old regime under the slogan "There are no rights except

14. An outstanding treatment of this subject is still Bertrand de Jouvenel, *Sovereignty: An Inquiry into the Political Good*, trans. J. F. Huntington (Chicago: University of Chicago Press, 1957).

15. Alexis de Tocqueville, *The Old Regime and the French Revolution*, trans. Stuart Gilbert (New York: Doubleday Anchor, 1955), 96.

those of individuals and the State." [16] The implication for family law was that it should become an instrument of liberation: "The happiness of man is systematically promoted and protected, above all against the group, and the indissoluble and sacred character of bonds and hierarchy." [17] This part of the French revolutionary program was, however, a conspicuous failure at the time. Ironically, it did not begin to become a reality until the idea had been largely forgotten and mediating structures had become so weak as not to be perceived as menacing. By that time—our own era—the state and other large impersonal organizations had become powerful beyond the imaginations of eighteenth-century thinkers and statesmen.

The founders of new governments in France and the United States were especially hostile to groups of the type that Rousseau had called "partial societies" and Madison, "factions." [18] Strong competing centers of power were not only socially divisive and inimical to national unity, but they posed a threat to the very existence of republican experiments. Concentrating on this and other obstacles to the success of their ambitious projects, the statesmen-architects of new republics not only could not begin to imagine the power central governments would wield in the modern era, they simply took for granted (and indeed counted on) the continuing existence of such groups as families, neighborhoods, parishes, townships, and small-scale associations of various sorts. Not amounting to factions, these constituted the everyday world of their members. They were the very fabric of society. Edmund Burke's was a lonely voice warning that these groupings, too, would in the long run be jeopardized by social forces that were breaking down all connections among individuals. He gave an early and often-quoted formulation to an idea that would engage the attention of certain (mainly French) social theorists in the nineteenth century when it became plain to them that mediating groups could no longer be taken for granted:

> To be attached to the subdivision, to love the little platoon we belong to in society, is the first principle (the germ as it were) of public affections. It is the first link in the series by which we proceed towards a love to our country and to mankind. [19]

Perhaps because France was the country where mediating groups were not merely crumbling with the advance of modernity but had been the targets of

16. Marcel Waline, *L'Individualisme et le droit* (Paris: Domat Montchrestien, 1945), 323.

17. E. du Pontavice, quoted in Alain Bénabent, above, note 4 at 494.

18. Jean-Jacques Rousseau, "The Social Contract," in *The Social Contract and Discourses*, trans. G. D. H. Cole (New York: Dutton, 1973), 247–48; *The Federalist*, nos. 10 and 51.

19. Edmund Burke, *Reflections on the Revolution in France* (New York: Doubleday Anchor, 1973), 59.

vigorous attack, two great nineteenth-century French writers were quick to reckon the potential costs of losing Burke's "little platoons." Tocqueville saw that some of the costs would be political, in terms of the very freedoms that the republican experiments aimed to promote. Groups that the French and American founders had regarded as impediments to the consolidation of national power, could, Tocqueville perceived, also operate as useful checks when governments became excessively strong and centralized.

Small local political communities, in particular, were regarded by Tocqueville as essential to a vital democracy. He believed that the chances for achievement of a free democratic polity in France had been seriously hurt by the deliberate virtual elimination of local and participatory government. With the destruction of local and regional centers of power as well as the decline of the guilds and churches, nothing was left to obstruct the consolidation of the central government. But, by the same token, nothing remained to shore up society or hold its parts together.[20] Tocqueville's travels in the United States led him to believe that local governments like those he saw operating in New England would preserve the United States from the evils of over-centralization that afflicted France.

> Local institutions are to liberty what primary schools are to science; they put it within the people's reach; they teach people to appreciate its peaceful enjoyment and accustom them to make use of it. Without local institutions a nation may give itself a free government, but it has not got the spirit of liberty. Passing passions, momentary interest, or chance circumstances may give it the external shape of independence, but the despotic tendencies which have been driven into the interior of the body social will sooner or later break out on the surface.[21]

A number of important ideas about mediating structures emerge from Tocqueville's writings. In the paragraph just quoted, he envisions participatory

---

20. *Cf.* the following observation by Czeslaw Milosz: "The importance of the movement in Poland, of Solidarity, is that it is not just a Polish phenomenon. It exemplifies a basic issue of the twentieth century. Namely, resistance to the withering away of society and its domination by the state. In the Poland of Solidarity, owing to some historical forces, there was a kind of resurgence, or renaissance, of the society against the state.

"Quite contrary to the predictions of Marx, this is the basic issue of the twentieth century. Instead of the withering away of the state, the state, like a [cancer], has eaten up all the substance of society. Destroying society, as a matter of fact. As a worker's movement, Solidarity resisted this. Whether various societies that have been conquered by the state will awaken in the future, I don't know." "An Interview with Czeslaw Milosz," *The New York Review of Books*, 27 February, 1986, 34.

21. Alexis de Tocqueville, *Democracy in America*, vol. 1, trans. George Lawrence (New York: Doubleday Anchor, 1969) 63.

organizations as schools for citizenship where the widest possible range of persons may become familiar with "those formalities without which freedom can advance only through revolutions"; where they may develop "a taste for order," and accumulate "clear, practical ideas about the nature of [their] duties and the extent of [their] rights." [22] In the vein of Burke, who believed the *feeling* of citizenship had to be rooted in attachment to a smaller group, Tocqueville questioned whether the *practice* of citizenship could survive without experience in a theatre smaller than the national polity.

From this proposition, Tocqueville moved to a consideration of what happens to individuals in societies where the skills of governing are lost among most of the population. In a famous passage which expressed all his fears for France, but which turned out to be prescient for other twentieth-century states in varying degrees, he amplifies the Rousseauan distinction between citizens and subjects:

> There are countries in Europe where the inhabitant feels like some sort of farm laborer indifferent to the fate of the place where he dwells. The greatest changes may take place in his country without his concurrence; he does not even know precisely what has happened; he is in doubt; he has heard tell by chance of what goes on. Worse still, the condition of his village, the policing of his road, and the repair of his church and parsonage do not concern him; he thinks that all those things have nothing to do with him at all, but belong to a powerful stranger called the government. For his part, he enjoys what he has as tenant, without feeling of ownership or any thought of improvement. . . . Furthermore, this man who has so completely sacrificed his freedom of will does not like obedience more than the next man. He submits, it is true, to the caprice of a clerk, but as soon as force is withdrawn, he will vaunt his triumph over the law as over a conquered foe. Thus he oscillates the whole time between servility and license.
>
> When nations reach that point, either they must modify both laws and mores or they will perish, for the fount of public virtues has run dry; there are subjects still, but no citizens. [23]

Tocqueville repeatedly drew attention to the connections among individualism, preoccupation with material comfort, and susceptibility to despotism. [24]

22. *Id.* at 70.
23. *Id.* at 93–94.
24. These themes have been elaborated with elegance and power in the work of Christopher Lasch, especially with respect to the political implications of American individualism. See, in particular, *Haven in a Heartless World* (New York: Basic Books, 1977), and *The Culture of Narcissism* (New York: Warner, 1979).

> For in a community in which the ties of family, of caste, of class,
> and craft fraternities no longer exist, people are far too much dis-
> posed to think exclusively of their own interests, to become self-
> seekers practicing a narrow individualism and caring nothing for the
> public good. Far from trying to counteract such tendencies, despo-
> tism encourages them, depriving the governed of any sense of soli-
> darity and interdependence; of good-neighborly feelings and a desire
> to further the welfare of the community at large. It immures them,
> so to speak, each in his private life and, taking advantage of the
> tendency they already have to keep apart, it estranges them still
> more. Their feelings toward each other were already growing cold;
> despotism freezes them.[25]

For Tocqueville, then, the simultaneous rise of the free, self-determining
individual and the centralized nation-state were historical achievements which
represented dangers as well as advances for human freedom. The elimination
or mere decay of institutional subsystems standing between individuals and
the state represented a loss of countervailing power, contributed to atrophy of
the skills of governing, and imperiled a certain strength of character and independence of mind that he believed could be developed only within families
and local communities. Paradoxically, then, some types of social organizations that under feudal conditions had often operated as sources of oppression
began to seem capable of counteracting both official power and individual
selfishness in large commercial republics. A reassessment of the role of modern forms of intermediate associations seemed in order—one that would take
due account of the beneficial functions they could perform under new social
conditions.

In France, scholarly interest in the social functions of mediating structures
continued to develop as the structures themselves lost ground in the nineteenth
century. It was almost as though the revolutionaries, by sloganizing the issue
and "naming" their existence as a problem, had made it possible for the heirs
of the revolution to see the decline of such groups as posing another kind of
problem. But in countries where mediating groups as such had attracted less
attention, their social functions were barely recognized, except obliquely by
such writers as Otto Gierke, Charles Horton Cooley, and G. H. Mead. Marx
and Maine, of course, had been quick to see the increasing separateness of
the individual as the old society of groups dissolved. And though Maine welcomed the process as one of liberation, Marx saw more deeply into the price
the free, self-determining individual would have to pay in isolation and alienation. But the Marxist legal tradition, at least until recently, showed little
interest in preserving groups that could pose obstacles to the formation of

---

25. Tocqueville, above, note 15 at xiii.

socialist states and that might carry forward harmful survivals from the bourgeois and feudal past.

For whatever reason, it was the French who made the subject their own. Emile Durkheim took up the problem where Tocqueville had left it, adding the insight that the weakening of intermediate associations could not only impede effective citizenship but might also have harmful implications for the development of the human personality. In the conclusion to his famous study of suicide, Durkheim called attention to what he believed were the human costs of the dis-integration of modern society—the loss of connections not only to other people, but to the past and the future; in short, a profound loss of meaning.[26] Like Tocqueville, Durkheim feared that the unmediated relationship of state and individual boded ill for social and political life:

> A society composed of an infinite number of unorganized individuals, that a hypertrophied State is forced to oppress and constrain, constitutes a veritable sociological monstrosity. . . . Where the State is the only environment in which men can live communal lives, they inevitably lose contact, become detached, and consequently society disintegrates. . . . The absence of all corporative institutions creates, then . . . a void whose importance it is difficult to exaggerate. It is a whole system of organs necessary in the normal functioning of the common life which is wanting.[27]

Unlike Tocqueville, however, Durkheim doubted that local communities, religious groups, or families could provide much support for the individual in the modern world. A half century after his great predecessor had completed his work, it seemed to Durkheim that "the bonds attaching us [to communities] become daily more fragile and more slack"[28] and that communal religions had already lost most of their authority and effectiveness.[29] In his view, not even families could be expected to play much of a role in alleviating individual isolation or promoting social cohesion. In 1897, when popular sentimentality about family life was perhaps at its high point, Durkheim wrote a darkly pessimistic assessment of the state of the family. He noted the discontinuities that were coming to characterize family relationships:

> Changes have actually occurred in the constitution of the family which no longer allow it to have the same preservative influence as formerly. While it once kept most of its members within its orbit

26. Emile Durkheim, *Suicide*, trans. John Spaulding and George Simpson (New York: Free Press, 1966), 297–392.

27. Emile Durkheim, *The Division of Labor in Society*, trans. George Simpson (New York: Free Press, 1964), 28–29.

28. *Id.* at 27.

29. Durkheim, above, note 26 at 374–75.

from birth to death and formed a compact mass, indivisible and endowed with a quality of permanence, its duration is now brief. It is barely formed when it begins to disperse. As soon as the children's first growth is over, they very often leave to complete their education away from home; moreover, it is almost the rule that as soon as they are adult they establish themselves away from their parents and the hearth is deserted. For most of the time, at present, the family may be said to be reduced to the married couple alone. . . .

Consequently, since it plays a smaller role in life, it no longer suffices as an object for life. Not, certainly, that we care less for our children; but they are entwined less closely and continuously with our existence and so this existence needs some other basis for being. Since we have to live without them, we also have to attach our thoughts and acts to other objects.[30]

This periodic dispersion of family members made it impossible to maintain a sense of belonging over generations. Durkheim noted the declining importance of the traditional symbols of family continuity—the family name with its associated memories, the ancestral home and land with their history commanding the attachment of all in the blood line. Once a group with an abstract and impersonal unity, the family was becoming "just a number of individuals united by bonds of mutual affection."[31] The process seemed to Durkheim to be an irreversible one.

Once, when each local environment was more or less closed to others by usages, traditions, the scarcity of communications, each generation remained perforce in its place of origin or at least could not move far from it. But as these barriers vanish, as these small environments are levelled and blended with one another, the individuals inevitably disperse in accordance with their ambitions and to further their interests into the wider space now open to them. No scheme can therefore offset this inevitable swarming of the bees and restore the indivisibility which was once the family's strength.[32]

Nothing that has happened since Durkheim penned these passages suggests that he was mistaken. If anything, the process he described seems to have intensified. Yet Durkheim had no more wish than Tocqueville did to bring back the institutions of the *ancien régime*. Instead, he reposed his hopes in what seemed to him, at the dawn of the twentieth century, to be the most promising source of social cohesion—occupational associations, or "corporations," by which he meant not labor unions or business organizations as

30. *Id*. at 377.   31. *Id*.
32. *Id*. at 378.

such but all groups of individuals who cooperate in the same profession, trade, or occupation.[33]

Unfortunately for this theory, occupational life, like political life, was itself already becoming dominated by large organizations. Corporations and other impersonal associations could sometimes serve to countervail public power, if not co-opting or co-opted by it, but they could hardly supply what was lost as the society of groups became a society of individuals. How disappointed Durkheim would have been to read the following letter sent by a French worker to the correspondence section of *Le Nouvel Observateur* in 1976:

> Bernadette and I do not want to have children. . . . She works at the Post-Telephone-Telegraph Service and I am a delivery man. We live in a studio apartment in a nearby suburb.
>
> Although the majority of people we run into do not understand us, we do not plan to pass the rest of our life like this; that is, with each of us carrying out every day a monotonous task, which is repetitive, without initiative, without responsibility, without real social meaning, and, furthermore, on the physical level, exhausting and numbing.
>
> If we had had one or two children, we would have had to put them in a nursery, then in day care, then in school, which means spending even more time in transportation, and seeing one's children "on the fly" in the evening, with even more work to do around the house. Our salaries do not permit either one of us to stop working. I think that children brought up under present-day conditions will be even more unhappy and disoriented than we are. . . . A real family is a family where a common task is carried out every day with the sole aim of making those who survive us happier than we are.

The situation described by the letter-writer is far from atypical in contemporary societies. For Bernadette and her husband, considerations of cost and proximity to transportation or their places of employment probably determined their decision to live in a drab, cheerless subdivision on the outskirts of Paris. Increasingly, in the countries with which we have here been concerned, the neighborhoods where people live and the groups to which they belong are not communities "combining all or most of the things necessary for the good life, but associations formed on the basis of highly specialized similarities of private pursuit and fortune."[34] Once it was widely believed that

33. Id. at 378–84; Durkheim, above, note 27 at 1–38. *Cf.* Hegel's theory of "corporations" in *Philosophy of Right*, trans. T.M. Knox (Oxford: Oxford University Press, 1942), pars. 250–56.

34. Wilson Carey McWilliams, "Democracy and the Citizen: Community, Dignity, and the Crisis of Contemporary Politics in America," in *How Democratic is the Constitution?*, ed. Rob-

the family could serve as a kind of haven, to which one could retreat from the psychic assaults of urban life and the disappointments of the world of work.[35] But such a refuge, if it ever existed, could hardly remain untouched by the forces that were transforming the world around it. Indeed exaggerated expectations of what personal relationships could provide by way of compensating for deprivations elsewhere, may themselves have contributed to rendering family intimacy and solidarity ever harder to achieve.

Family Ecology

Although the legal system has shifted its focus from families to individuals, society still relies on families to play a crucial role in caring for the young, the aged, the sick, the severely disabled, and the needy. Even in advanced welfare states, families at all income levels are a major resource for government, sharing the burdens of dependency with public agencies in various ways and to greater or lesser degrees. Historically, most social welfare programs were developed on the premise that individuals should receive public assistance only when their families (understood to include a wide circle of relatives) were unable to care for them. That assumption gradually shifted. Public welfare programs have assumed more responsibility for assuring a minimum standard of living to all members of society, especially when it appears that a citizen's needs are the result of social and economic forces beyond his or her control. In some areas of life, the idea of primary public responsibility is nearly unquestioned, as, for example, with the formal education of children. In others, the idea of displacing private responsibility is quite controversial, as in the case of child support after divorce. But even with the proliferation of various kinds of public assistance, services, and institutional care, families are still the major means through which societies deal with dependency. Families in all their many forms thus perform important services not only for their members but also for the state.

The ability of families to carry out the tasks for which society relies on them, however, has been dramatically altered by changes in family structure, in the labor force participation of women, and in the nature of dependency itself. The modern two-earner family with children, and the single-parent family in particular, must rely more on outside support systems for dealing with their dependent members than the homemaker-breadwinner household, which has now become atypical. And while the pool of available caretakers within the family has been shrinking, the composition of the group in need of

---

ert A. Goldwin and William A. Schambra (Washington, D. C.: American Enterprise Institute, 1980), 79, 99.

35. Christopher Lasch, *Haven in a Heartless World* (New York: Basic Books, 1977).

care has altered to include far fewer children and far more disabled and elderly people than it did at the turn of the century. In this historically novel situation, no complete substitute has been devised for the voluntary provision of care, services, and income by family members—nor does one appear to be on the horizon. Family support will in all likelihood remain an indispensable mechanism through which society as a whole deals with the dependency of the young, the disabled, and the frail elderly. Increasingly, however, families need help in performing their tasks, and since the family members who perform these tasks are still predominantly women, the problem of family assistance is inextricably intertwined with several other difficult issues relating to population policy, gender equality, and labor policy.

All the countries whose law we have examined here are struggling with the tensions involved in trying simultaneously to maintain a productive labor force, to establish decent conditions for child-raising, to achieve a suitable rate of population growth, and to assure equal treatment for men and women. All are engaged in trying to work out an understanding of sexual equality that takes account of women's roles in procreation and child raising without perpetuating their subordination. In spite of the fact that the notion of equality (variously understood) has been one of the most powerful transforming influences in modern family law, the principal unresolved problems for family law and policy remain those relating to the situation of women who are raising children, performing the bulk of other homemaking and caretaking roles, and working at jobs where their pay, status, and security are inferior to those of most male workers.

A variety of programs have been devised to assist women in performing their various roles. Some countries have been quite generous in providing assistance for maternity, child care, and family allowances. But no one is sure what law and government can or should do with respect to the deeper problems which render the roles of mother and caretaker so risky. There is much vague talk about "strengthening" the family, but so far little reason to think we know whether and how this might be accomplished, or what role, if any, law might have to play. Some favor more public aid to families; others claim that governmental assistance is apt to have harmful and debilitating effects. But debates framed in terms of a choice between intervention and nonintervention are as simplistic and unhelpful as those which try to distinguish sharply between individual and social interests.[36] These false dichotomies tend to obscure the facts that modern governments cannot avoid influencing

36. For critiques, see Martha Minow, "Beyond State Intervention in the Family: For Baby Jane Doe," 18 *University of Michigan Journal of Law Reform* 933, 1010 (1985), and Bruce C. Hafen, "The Constitutional Status of Marriage, Kinship, and Sexual Privacy—Balancing the Individual and Social Interests," 81 *Michigan Law Review* 463, 470–71 (1983).

families, directly and indirectly, in countless ways and that individuals benefit, not only from having "rights," but also from being surrounded by certain kinds of social arrangements.

Another way of thinking about strengthening families would be to take a more ecological approach—to ask whether governments might be able to assist families and their members indirectly by attending to the health of surrounding small-scale communities. There is at present in legal discourse little recognition that family members may need nurturing environments as much as they need rights, or that families themselves may need surrounding communities in order to function at their best. By systematically—though for the most part unintentionally—ignoring the "little platoons" from which families and individuals have always drawn emotional and material sustenance, modern legal systems probably contribute to some extent to their atrophy. By pursuing other social aims in such areas as welfare, urban renewal, and industrial policy without considering the impact on families, neighborhoods, churches, and other associations, governments have often eroded the conditions in which such associations flourish. This legal inattention to matters of vital concern to many ordinary folk may be attributable in part to the special preoccupations of the technocrats who predominate in modern governments, political parties, corporations, the mass media, and other large-scale organizations that operate at considerable remove from the life of the average citizen.[37] For members of this "new class," strong ties to persons and places, religious beliefs, or attachment to tradition are frequently relatively unimportant or even counter-productive.[38] Geographically mobile, and deriving prestige, power, and satisfaction from their work, those who wield the most influence in modern societies are often "very free in adopting measures that undermine the geographical stability and delicate communities on which others depend for practical and emotional support."[39]

Claude Lévi-Strauss is the latest in the line of French social theorists to try to draw attention to the political importance of the endangered personal environments represented by local communities, families, religious and occupational organizations, and other voluntary associations. He made a point, on the occasion of being invited to speak before the French National Assembly's special commission on liberties, of insisting that meaningful freedom cannot be achieved in a society of isolated individuals:

37. Robert E. Rodes, Jr., "Greatness Thrust Upon Them: Class Biases in American Law," 1983 *American Journal of Jurisprudence* 1.

38. Wilson Carey McWilliams, "American Pluralism: The Old Order Passeth," in *The Americans, 1976*, ed. Irving Kristol and Paul Weaver (Lexington: D. C. Heath, 1976), 293, 315.

39. Rodes, above, note 37 at 6.

Notwithstanding Rousseau, who wanted to abolish any partial society in the state, a certain restoration of partial societies offers a final chance of providing ailing freedoms with a little health and vigor. Unhappily, it is not up to the legislator to bring Western societies back up the slope down which they have been slipping for several centuries—too often, in history, following our own [French] example. The legislator can at least be attentive to the reversal of this trend, signs of which are discernible here and there; he can encourage it in its unforeseeable manifestations, however incongruous and even shocking they may sometimes seem. In any case, the legislator should do nothing that might nip such reversal in the bud or, once it asserts itself, prevent it from following its course.[40]

Beyond such general prescriptions, however, no one seems to have any specific proposals for the reinvigoration of mediating structures. Perhaps this is because, as Lévi-Strauss obliquely hints, partial societies (like all other human institutions) have a dark side that would have to be faced.

Nevertheless, there is a slender but growing stream of challenges to the prevailing modes of legal and political discourse that take into account only individuals, the market, and the state. Notable among these is a monograph by Peter Berger and Richard Neuhaus advocating not only that governments should view the protection of neighborhoods, churches, families, and other voluntary associations as an important social aim, but that such organizations should be used in preference to governmental agencies wherever possible to carry out social purposes.[41] But to articulate such a proposal is to expose a whole range of new problems and pitfalls. How could such a policy be put into operation when legal theory barely possesses the concepts or the vocabulary to deal with groups as such? The political and technical difficulties would be formidable, and the subject has attracted little attention from mainstream jurists who are often heavily preoccupied with individual rights, with attacking or aggrandizing the state, or with tending the machinery of bureaucracy.

Furthermore, it is doubtful whether policymakers in liberal democracies (even if they could be convinced that mediating structures merit attention) would accept Lévi-Strauss' startling advice to encourage counter-tendencies to what he views as social decline "however incongruous or shocking they

40. Claude Lévi-Strauss, "Reflections on Liberty," in *The View from Afar* (New York: Basic Books, 1985), 288.

41. Peter L. Berger and Richard J. Neuhaus, *To Empower People: The Role of Mediating Structures in Public Policy* (Washington, D.C.: American Enterprise Institute, 1977). See also the essays by Wilson Carey McWilliams: "On Equality as the Moral Foundation for Community" in *The Moral Foundations of the American Republic*, ed. R. Horwitz (Charlottesville, Va.: Univ. of Virginia Press, 1977), 212; McWilliams, above, note 34 at 100–101.

may sometimes seem." It is much more likely that any legislative efforts on behalf of groups would be carried on with close attention to such matters as how the group's internal functioning comports with widely shared values (or, in the case of associations larger than families, the values to which the political regime is committed).[42] Everyone knows that families and tight-knit communities can be hotbeds of inequality and constraints. The weak, dependent, and different can be abused and neglected, as well as protected, within families. And families or individuals can be ostracized or isolated, as well as supported, by local communities and voluntary associations. A family or a group, can, under certain conditions, become a terrifying tangle of pathology.

Why then, did Lévi-Strauss make his suggestion to the French National Assembly in such a radical form? Was the anthropologist implying that preservation of meaningful liberty in a society may require citizens with particular sorts of virtues—such as self-restraint, cooperativeness, and generosity—that can be developed only within relatively small groups? And that the groups within which such virtues are fostered should not be expected to be themselves models of democracy and freedom? Or was he merely reminding us of how difficult it is to rise above our own cultural prejudices?

Certainly it is often the case that the central values of mediating groups are unpopular or that the members of such groups are religiously or ethnically different from the majority.[43] Obviously, there are very delicate balances to be struck, and one must assume that any major change in the law's approach to intermediate associations would generate new problems that are presently

42. Richard Stewart, for example, writing mainly of associations more remote from everyday life than the mediating groups with which we are here concerned, has described the problem as how to make "institutional subsystems" not only more independent but more responsive to their constituents, without undermining "the integrity of the general political and economic order and the allegiance of subsystems to society-wide values and goals." Richard B. Stewart, "Reconstitutive Law," 45 *Maryland Law Review* 86, 100–101 (1986). Stewart's vision of an institutional framework that would simultaneously serve "the republican and communitarian values nurtured within organizations" and the "societal values of diversity and aspiration that transcend particular organizations . . ." (Book Review, 101 *Harvard Law Review* 371, 387 (1987)) is an appealing one, resting on the idea that participation in a group's deliberative process "can have a constitutive function, transforming the preferences and values of individual members and nurturing sentiments of solidarity." (*Id.* at 381.) But if participation, responsiveness to members, and deliberation are to be assured by governmental regulation or supervision, what wisdom and art will be required to promote and maintain these processes without destroying the group! The history of labor law in the United States illustrates both the difficulties and the possible advantages of the attempt.

43. The Swedish no-spanking law illustrates the tension between promoting widely shared values and protecting mediating structures. Corporal punishment may seem shocking to the majority in the light of generally accepted ideas about child-rearing, but it may be a type of discipline that is integral to the family structures of foreign guest workers in Swedish cities.

unforeseeable. There seems to be no course of action that is simple or free of hazards, but the risks of continuing along the path of increasing individual isolation in the immensely powerful public and private bureaucracies of the present day seem greater than those of trying to promote, or at least to refrain from harming, relatively frail intermediate groups.[44]

What Difference Does Law Make?

At this point It seems prudent to note that reflection on the history of family law indicates that one should be cautious about expecting too much from family law and family policy. We have had numerous occasions in the present study to notice the limited power of law, on its own, to advance or retard broad social changes in the area of family life. Upon examination, the developments that have taken place in family law over the past twenty-five years, striking as they are, have often turned out to be less remarkable than pre-existing and ongoing shifts in ideas about family life or patterns of family behavior. The law reforms that began in the 1960s did not destroy the traditional family. What they mainly did was to consolidate and, sometimes, increase the power of several movements that were already going forward.

But just as we must guard against having exaggerated expectations of what law can accomplish on its own, we must also take care not to fall into the opposite error of unduly minimizing its potential to influence social trends. A country's law, like its art, religion, economy, and history, both affects and is affected by the culture in which it arises, and though the effects of law are modest, they are not always trivial. Diffuse and ambiguous social phenomena can be given form, shape, and a decisive direction by law. Many of the legal trends described in the foregoing chapters are tributaries to the formation of cultural schemes of meaning that determine to a great extent how we experience, remember, imagine, or project the basic events and relationships of our lives. This is what renders illusory and somewhat dangerous the notion that family law can be completely neutral. In a way that is no less real for being

44. The enormously complex problem of the instrumentation of designs to foster mediating structures while still protecting individuals is beyond the scope of this book. So far, nearly all the scholarly work along these lines has been concerned with local government or business and labor organizations. With respect to these types of associations, the legal sociologist Gunther Teubner has postulated what he calls a "regulatory trilemma": the likelihood that legal regulation that does not respect the internal regulatory and reproductive processes of social subsystems will either (1) be irrelevant, or (2) have a destructive effect on the area of social life involved, or (3) itself disintegrate under pressures from the political or social sectors. "Juridification: Concepts, Aspects, Limits, Solutions," in *Juridification of Social Spheres: A Comparative Analysis in the Areas of Labor, Corporate, Antitrust and Social Welfare Law*, ed. Gunther Teubner (Berlin: Walter de Gruyter, 1987), 21, 27.

unquantifiable, laws permitting unilateral divorce on demand, for example, must have a certain influence on the way people think and feel about personal commitments.[45]

The question for policymakers is how much weight, if any, to give to this sort of factor in the law-making process. It seems likely that when the law is in harmony with other social forces, it will synergistically produce a greater effect in combination with them than it could on its own. But when the messages communicated through law run counter to those prevailing elsewhere in the culture, the effect of law on ideas and behavior must be small. This line of reasoning leads to the suspicion that, in the countries with which we have here been concerned, law and government may have been more influential in contributing unintentionally to those dis-integrating trends identified by Durkheim and others than when they have deliberately set out to try to "strengthen" families. We have pointed to the possibility that governmental action might be able to indirectly lend support to individuals and families by attending to the conditions within which families and other mediating structures might prosper. But like the analogous problems of protecting the air and water, this would require both the political will to act and a certain sense of the long-run which is notably lacking in modern society. And, as in the case of natural ecological systems, the possibility exists that the task is beyond the capacity of law to affect for the better.

Up to this point we have expressed concern about the law's occasional power to adversely affect family life and doubts about its ability to have more than a weak effect in supporting or strengthening families. It seems likely that other social forces will be more influential than law in determining whether the most pessimistic intimations of Tocqueville and Durkheim will be borne out. If in fact our societies are producing too many individuals who are capable neither of effective participation in civic life nor of sustaining personal relationships, it is probably beyond the power of law to reverse the process. But it is far from clear that we are in such a dismal situation. The tale currently being told by the law about marriage and family life is probably more starkly individualistic than the ideas and practices that prevail in the countries examined here. It is true that individuals have been emancipated in fact, law, and imagination from group and family ties to a historically unprecedented degree, but it is also the case that most men and women still spend most of their lives in emotionally and economically interdependent family units. Furthermore, family historians and sociologists have documented the remarkable

45. Louis Roussel, Jacques Commaille, Jean Kellerhals, and Jean-François Perrin, "Vue d'ensemble," in *Commaille*, 233–37.

capacity of the family to endure throughout history—its ability to assume new forms, weather great historical changes, and to adapt to new conditions—all without help from law.

However frail and faltering they may currently seem to be, families remain, for most of us, the only theater in which we can realize our full capacity for good or evil, joy or suffering. By attaching us to beings and feelings that are perishable, families expose us to conflict, pain, and loss. They give rise to tension between love and duty, reason and passion, immediate and long range objectives, egoism and altruism. But relationships between husbands and wives, parents and children, can also provide frameworks for resolving such tensions. Even though, after the loosening of legal and economic ties that we have traced in this book, the principal bonds which remain to unite the family may be the ties of human affection, we can perhaps—if we are hopeful—recognize in those fragile connections analogies for the Love that invites a response from all men and women of good will. A note sounded by a player on one instrument may draw forth a corresponding note from another; a child, hearing an accordion outside the window, may begin to sing and dance.

Index